THE CHRISTIAN RELIGION

AMERICAN ACADEMY OF RELIGION

TEXTS AND TRANSLATIONS SERIES

Edited by
James A. Massey

Number 2

THE CHRISTIAN RELIGION
by
G. W. F. Hegel
Edited and Translated by Peter C. Hodgson

GEORG WILHELM FRIEDRICH HEGEL

THE CHRISTIAN RELIGION
LECTURES ON THE PHILOSOPHY OF RELIGION
Part III. The Revelatory, Consummate, Absolute
Religion

Edited and Translated by Peter C. Hodgson
Based on the Edition by Georg Lasson

SCHOLARS PRESS

Distributed by
Scholars Press
PO Box 5207
Missoula, Montana 59806

THE CHRISTIAN RELIGION
LECTURES ON THE PHILOSOPHY OF RELIGION
Part III. The Revelatory, Consummate, Absolute Religion

G. W. F. Hegel
Edited and Translated by Peter C. Hodgson

Library of Congress Cataloging in Publication Data

Hegel, Georg Wilhelm Friedrich, 1770-1831.
  The Christian religion.

  (Texts and translations series - American Academy of
Religion ; no. 2 ISSN 0147-8931)
  Translation of Vorlesungen über die Philosophie der
Religion. III. Teil, Die vollendete oder offenbare, die
absolute Religion.
  1. Religion—Philosophy. I. Hodgson, Peter Crafts,
1934-   II. Lasson, Georg, 1862-1932. III. Title.
IV. Series: American Academy of Religion. Texts and
translations series - American Academy of Religion ; no. 2.
B2939.E5H62   201   79-424
ISBN 0-89130-276-X

Printed in the United States of America
1   2   3   4   5   6
Edwards Brothers, Inc.
Ann Arbor, Michigan 48104

TABLE OF CONTENTS

This translation of Hegel's lectures on the Christian religion originated in the Nineteenth Century Theology Group of the American Academy of Religion. An Advisory Committee of that Group is responsible for the selection of projects and the editing of manuscripts. The Advisory Committee consists of:

Francis S. Fiorenza (Villanova)
Robert P. Scharlemann (University of Iowa)
Peter C. Hodgson (Vanderbilt)
Jack Verheyden (Claremont School of Theology)
Claude Welch (Graduate Theological Union)

The editor wishes to express his thanks to the Advisory Committee for making Hodgson's translation available to the Texts and Translations series.

James A. Massey

1. The Four Lecture Series: Sources and Structure

Hegel lectured on the Philosophy of Religion four times in Berlin, in the summer semesters of 1821, 1824, 1827, and 1831—the last occurring only shortly before his death on 14 November 1831. As was the case with his other Berlin lecture cycles—on the History of Philosophy, the Philosophy of History, and Aesthetics—Hegel did not prepare these materials for publication, and the lectures were brought out posthumously by an alliance of friends and disciples, based primarily on student lecture notes or transcripts (*Nachschriften*), and, to the extent they were utilized, on Hegel's own lecture manuscripts. The texts for all these works represent editorial compilations, not the words of the philosopher written directly for publication.

a. The 1821 Lectures

Hegel's own manuscript for his 1821 lectures on the Philosophy of Religion survives to this day in the Staatsbibliothek of the Prussian ministry of culture, formerly the Royal Library of Berlin. It is a quarto-size lecture notebook bound in leather, consisting of 104 sheets (208 pages). Hegel wrote on the inner half of each sheet, front and back, leaving wide margins on the outer half of each side. On many pages the outer margins are almost completely filled with additional notes, some of which are keyed to the main text by means of reference marks. The manuscript is very difficult to decipher because the writing is small and crowded, many words are abbreviated, sentences are often incomplete (utilizing a peculiar shorthand), and the ink has frequently bled through from the opposite side. Following an Introduction of 18 pages, the manuscript was divided into three main parts: the Concept of Religion (38 pages), Determinate or Finite Religion (84 pages), and the Revelatory, Consummate, or Absolute Religion (64 pages). The only student transcript of the 1821 lectures, utilized by the editors of the second edition of the *Werke*, was that of Leopold von Henning, which has been lost.

Although Hegel had touched on the subject of religion in many of his previous writings--notably the early essays of the 1790's, the *Phenomenology of Spirit* of 1807, and the *Encyclopedia of the Philosophical Sciences* of 1817--he had never done so in systematic, sustained fashion, and he had no previous plan to follow, with the exception of the Third Part, for which both the *Phenomenology* and the *Encyclopedia* offered a brief model. This was really a "first sketch," prepared lecture by lecture between 30 April and 25 August 1821. Thus it is not surprising that, when Hegel repeated the lectures on subsequent occasions, the structure and to some extent the contents of the material were revised considerably, especially for the Introduction and the First Part. It is likely that Hegel laid the original manuscript aside when he lectured on the Concept of Religion in 1824, but it is evident from the texts that he made use of it as the basis for his discussion of the Revelatory Religion in 1824 (though not in 1827). Thus the marginal notes for the Third Part would most likely have been added when he prepared the materials for presentation in 1824, although a few may represent immediate additions to the text.[1]

Following a brief introduction in which the concept and chief characteristics of the Revelatory Religion

are considered, the Third Part of the 1821 MS. is divided
into three main sections, which correspond precisely to
the structure established in the Concept of Religion and
applied analytically to each of the Determinate Religions: A. Abstract Concept, B. Concrete Representation,
and C. Community, Cultus.[2] The Abstract Concept takes up
the ontological proof of the existence of God, based on
general philosophical considerations, while Concrete
Representation sets forth the concept of God in terms of
the specific *Vorstellungen* of the Christian Religion:
the concept of God in and for itself (the immanent Trinity), the concept in diremption or differentiation (creation and preservation of the world), and the concept in
the history of redemption or reconciliation (the creation of human being, sin and evil, the incarnation of
Christ). The section on Community and Cultus is likewise divided into three parts: the standpoint of the
community in general (the spiritual presence of the risen
Christ), the existence of the community (its specific institutional and cultic forms), and the passing away of
the community.

b. The 1824 Lectures

When Hegel lectured on the Philosophy of Religion in
1824, Gustav von Griesheim made a detailed transcript, as
he did of Hegel's other lecture series as well. Two fair
copies were prepared, one of which was used by Hegel to
lecture in 1827, to which he added his own notes and
additions. This copy has been lost, but the other (without Hegel's additions) survives in the Prussian State
Library. Two other transcripts, by Michelet and Foerster
(used in the second edition of the *Werke*) have been lost,
but transcripts by Kehler, Hotho, Pastenacci, and Deiter
are still extant (Lasson used the first three as well as
Griesheim). The Kehler transcript covers only the Introduction and the beginning of the Concept of Religion,

while the Hotho notes contain a paraphrase rather than an
exact transcript. Pastenacci parallels Griesheim closely,
but the surviving copies of it and of Deiter are in poor
condition and can be used only with difficulty. Obviously the key text for the 1824 lectures is the Griesheim transcript, which not only is clear and complete but
also received the imprimatur of the philosopher himself.[3]

Although Hegel used the 1821 MS. as the basis for
the 1824 lectures, some significant *structural* and *sub-
stantive* changes occur in the Third Part, but the basic
order of the text remains unchanged. The contents of the
Abstract Concept are moved to the Introduction, and the
old tripartite division inherited from the treatment of
the Determinate Religions is replaced by three "elements"
or "moments" constitutive of the Development of the Idea
of God. The first element is the Idea of God in and for
itself (the immanent Trinity); the second element encompasses the themes of *both* differentiation-estrangement
and incarnation-reconciliation (the second and third
parts of Concrete Representation in 1821); while the
third element replaces the final section of the 1821 MS.,
Community and Cultus. Hegel has here arrived at the mature division of his lectures on the Revelatory or Absolute Religion, and the trinitarian underpinning is now
clear: the first element represents the figure of the
"Father," the second element that of the "Son," and the
third that of the "Spirit." (It remained only for the
1831 lectures to add the specific designation of the
three "Kingdoms.") Although a trinitarian structure also
underlay the pattern inherited from the Concept of Religion, Hegel came to realize that the pattern of the Concept analysis did not work well when it was applied to
the Revelatory Religion. The ontological proof taken up
in the Abstract Concept is not part of the specifically
Christian understanding of God but rather belongs among
its presuppositions. The subordinate parts of Concrete
Representation correspond to only two of the three ele-

ments of the Idea of God (the "Father" and the "Son"),
while the third main division of the 1821 MS., Community
and Cultus, actually belongs among the "concrete representations" of Christian faith, corresponding to the
third element in the Idea of God (the "Spirit").[4]

In treating the third element in 1824, Hegel dropped
the transitional section concerned with the spiritual
presence of Christ, replacing it with a section on the
origin of the community, concerned largely to show that
the confirmation of the faith that Jesus was the Christ
is based not on miraculous proofs but rather on the witness of the Spirit. The ambiguous concluding section of
the 1821 MS. on the "passing away" of the community was
replaced entirely by another conclusion, which describes
how the faith of the community is "realized" in secular
culture.

c. *The 1827 Lectures*

The 1827 lectures, as we have indicated, were based
on the Griesheim transcript of the 1824 lectures, and
thus the structure of these two sots of lectures is quite
similar. Transcripts by Meyer and Droysen, used by the
original editors, have been lost, but Lasson had access
to the fair copy of an anonymous transcript, whose text
corresponded to an astonishing degree with parallel sections of the second edition of the *Werke*. He also made
use of a transcript by Erdmann, whose text agreed closely
with the other sources. The thorough agreement among all
the transcripts for the 1827 lectures means that the text
for these lectures is secure, although brief passages may
have been omitted by both the *Werke* and Lasson (most
likely doublets to the 1821 MS.). The transcripts used
by Lasson have also been lost, but recently two new and
anonymous transcripts for 1827 have been discovered--one
by Heinz Kimmerle in Berlin, the other by Karl-Heinz
Ilting in Warsaw. The Kimmerle transcript provides a

good check on the structure of the 1827 lectures, but its
contents are sparse in comparison with the text in the
Werke and Lasson. The Ilting transcript will be utilized
by him for a new edition of the lectures.[5]

While the Third Part of the 1827 lectures duplicates
the three elements in the Development of the Idea of God
worked out in 1824, some significant changes occur in the
Introduction. The discussion of the ontological proof is
removed from the Revelatory Religion entirely to the Concept of Religion, and the section on "characteristics" of
the Christian Religion found in both 1821 and 1824 drops
out, being replaced by a lengthy discussion of the "positivity" of this religion--its primary "characteristic"
as a "revealed" religion. This is followed by another
new section concerned with the "transition" to the Revelatory Religion, which provides Hegel with the occasion to
summarize the developmental thesis elaborated in the
Second Part on Determinate Religion, where he treats the
religions of nature (primitive religion, Buddhism, Hinduism, Persian and Egyptian religion) and the religions of
spiritual individuality (Jewish, Greek, and Roman). Although Lasson states that the "positivity" section appears at the very beginning of the 1827 lectures, the
transcript newly discovered by Kimmerle indicates that it
was preceded by a brief definition of the concept of the
Revelatory Religion, paralleling the 1821 and 1824 lectures.[6]

d. The 1831 Lectures

Karl Hegel, the philosopher's son, prepared a transcript of the 1831 lectures, used by the original editors,
but unfortunately it, together with other transcripts of
this last series of lectures, have been lost. It is possible to recover something of its content by locating
those passages in the *Werke* for which no parallels exist
in the 1821 MS. or the extant transcripts for 1824 and

1827. However, some of these additional passages may derive from miscellaneous papers and notes of Hegel rather
than from the 1831 lectures, and it is not possible to
reconstruct the structure of the latter with any confidence. It does seem likely, nonetheless, that the division of the Absolute Religion into three "Kingdoms" of
the "Father," "Son," and "Spirit," which in the *Werke* replaces the three "elements," derives from the 1831 lectures. Hints of this usage occur already in the earlier
lecture series but not the formal division.[7]

2. *Editions of the Text*

   a. *The Werke (1832, 1840)*

     Philipp Marheineke, one of Hegel's most prominent
theological colleagues and at the time Rector of the University of Berlin, prepared an edition of Hegel's *Lectures on the Philosophy of Religion* that appeared only a
year after the philosopher's death, in 1832.[8] Working in
considerable haste, Marheineke did not utilize the 1821
MS. at all, but relied instead on the fair copy of the
Griesheim transcript with Hegel's additions, the Meyer
transcript of 1827, which Hegel himself had checked, and
Karl Hegel's transcript of the 1831 lectures. He omitted
a lot of material from these transcripts, working them
into a makeshift order that basically followed the 1827
and 1831 lectures, and seeking whenever possible to avoid
doublets. He did not distinguish sources but collated
everything into an editorially constructed text. Despite
these shortcomings, the original edition of 1832 is considered to be a "classic" work of sorts. Not only is it
the form in which Hegel's *Religionsphilosophie* was received by Strauss, Baur, Feuerbach, Marx, and others, but
also the relative simplicity of its editorial procedure,
which derived the structure from the latest lecture

series and did not attempt to correlate the 1821 MS. with
this structure, makes the first edition preferable in
some respects to the second, despite the greater wealth
of materials found in the latter.[9]

The second edition of 1840 also bore Marheineke's
name, but the detailed work was in fact done by Bruno
Bauer, a right-wing Hegelian who shortly after completing
this edition underwent a radical shift to a left-wing,
atheistic posture. Now for the first time Hegel's own
manuscript of 1821 was utilized, together with Henning's
transcript of these lectures and a number of additional
transcripts for each of the other three lecture series.
These supplementary materials were simply added to the
structure originally established by Marheineke, which
meant that the order of the 1821 MS. had to be disrupted
when incorporated into a structure determined by the
later lectures. Bauer worked quite freely with the materials for 1821, interweaving exact phrases or sentences
from Hegel's own manuscript with free variations deriving
most likely from Henning's transcript. The variations
from the manuscript are at some points so radical as to
be explicable in no other fashion. The result is a peculiar mixture of what Hegel intended to say in 1821
(based on his own manuscript) and what he may in fact
have said according to Henning. But since the Henning
transcript has been lost and no others are available for
the first lecture series, it is impossible to verify the
accuracy either of Henning's note-taking or of Bauer's
incorporation of his transcript. Lasson suspected Bauer
of deliberate falsifications of Hegel's meaning at
points, probably because of the editor's antitheological
stance, but there is no firm textual evidence to support
this. The second edition in fact highlights both radical
and orthodox statements of Hegel, and Bauer probably completed his editorial work before his atheistic turn, even
though he subsequently justified the latter in part by
an appeal to the second edition of Hegel's *Religions-*

philosophie. The defects of this edition are rather
attributable to the fact that it was a patchwork of
sources, none of which were distinguished or identified;
the original order established by Marheineke was only con-
fused by the incorporation of the 1821 MS.; the procedure
for editing the 1821 materials was dubious; and some
valuable passages from 1824, 1827, and 1831 were dropped
in a further attempt to eliminate doublets.[10]

The second edition of the *Werke* was brought out in
English by E. B. Speirs and J. Burdon Sanderson in 1895.[11]
The translation is usable but it does not provide a
felicitous or precise rendering of Hegel in English.
Technical terminology is handled with a disconcerting
looseness, and in latter portions especially the translation has a rather stilted, awkward quality. The work was
begun by Miss Sanderson--a more skillful translator than
the Rev. Speirs--but she died after completing only the
first half, containing the Concept of Religion and the
Religion of Nature. This is a further reason for offering a separate edition of the Revelatory Religion at this
time.

b. *The Lasson Edition (1925-1929)*

The attempt by Georg Lasson to produce a critical
edition of the *Lectures on the Philosophy of Religion*
represents a notable advance beyond the second edition of
the *Werke*. Lasson followed two basic principles: (1) to
distinguish and identify the sources; (2) to use Hegel's
own manuscript as the organizing basis for the edition,
correlating the transcripts for the later lecture series
with it section by section. He attempted to provide an
exact transcription of the 1821 MS., working the marginal
additions into the text as smoothly as possible (foot-
noting only those fragments that would not fit the context or flow of argument), and, when necessary, completing
Hegel's shorthand sentence structure grammatically and

semantically by means of bracketed editorial insertions,
with the objective of producing an intelligible, readable
text. With one possible exception, there is no evidence
of a deliberate "Christianization" of the text by Lasson,
as charged by Ernst Bloch and other critics.[12] He did
his work honestly and industriously.

Nonetheless, Lasson did not succeed in producing a
truly critical edition. In part, the materials simply
resisted his editorial conception. The structural variations between lecture series for the Introduction to the
lectures as a whole and for the Concept of Religion were
so great as to make it virtually impossible to correlate
these materials section by section without disrupting the
order of one or more of the manuscripts. In an attempt
to circumvent this difficulty, Lasson created a structure
of his own for the Concept of Religion that only worsened
matters.[13] Less serious problems confronted Lasson in
the second main division of the lectures, Determinate Religion; but it was only in the third division, the Revelatory or Absolute Religion, that his editorial conception
worked properly, because here, despite the structural
differences that still persisted between the 1821 MS. and
the subsequent lectures, the actual *order* in which topics
were taken up did not vary significantly from 1821 to
1831. For this reason in the Third Part the lectures can
in fact be correlated under common section headings without doing violence either to the original manuscript or
to the subsequent transcripts, and this is by far the
most *useful* editorial procedure when it can be accomplished. Lasson did make some erroneous judgments in arranging the text of the Revelatory Religion, but these
can be rectified, as the present edition demonstrates.

Apart from the question of arrangement, Lasson's editorial procedures in determining the actual reading of
the texts left much to be desired.[14] Here again, however,
the problems are more severe for the Concept of Religion
than for the Revelatory Religion. By the time he arrived

at the last division of the lectures, his method of editing the 1824 transcripts had much improved, and he followed the most reliable of these transcripts, that of
Griesheim, closely, although he still allowed himself to
make minor stylistic alterations, to smooth out transitional passages, and to omit a few passages containing
doublets. Serious questions have not been raised about
his edition of the 1827 transcripts, although some doublets have most likely been omitted here as well. His
reading of the text of the 1821 MS. was quite accurate
considering its philological difficulties, but he erred
in not identifying the frequent passages from the margins
that he worked into the text. His location of some of
these passages has been subject to question, as has been
the adequacy of some of his bracketed editorial insertions. A few minor errors occurred in his reproducing
the text of the *Werke* for passages not paralleled by the
extant transcripts. Finally, despite his intention to
distinguish all of the lecture sources, he succeeded in
doing so clearly only with regard to the 1821 MS., which
is set off by a distinctive typeface and quotation marks
at the beginning and end of each section. Materials from
the 1824 and 1827 transcripts and from the *Werke* are run
together in a continuous text and can be identified only
with difficulty by using an awkward apparatus printed at
the back of each volume.

c. The Present Edition

Despite these questions about both arrangement and
text, Lasson's edition of the Third Part of the Philosophy of Religion--the Revelatory or Absolute Religion--is
usable as the basis for an English translation, and most
of the serious problems arising from his editing can be
corrected.[15] The same cannot be said about the first two
parts of the lectures because here the problems created
by Lasson's handling of the sources are too severe to be

overcome. For new translations of the Concept of Religion and Determinate Religion we shall have to await the
new critical edition of the *Religionsphilosophie* to be
prepared by the Hegel-Archiv at the Ruhr-Universität in
Bochum.

Regarding the preparation of the present edition,
the following particulars should be noted.

(1) By means of a system of superscripts, this edition clearly identifies the several manuscript sources:
Hegel's own manuscript of 1821 (^{m} . . . ^{m}), the lecture
transcripts by students of 1824 (^{a} . . . ^{a}) and 1827
(^{b} . . . ^{b}), and passages from the second edition of the
Werke (^{w} . . . ^{w}) most likely based on the lectures of
1831.

(2) Each of these sources is given in its original
order, with only a few minor and duly noted exceptions.
Since Lasson transposed the order of the 1824 and 1827
lectures rather freely, this has required some changes in
the structure of his work and in his selection of section
headings (notably in the Introduction and in Chapters II
and V). In each chapter section, the ordinary procedure
is to begin with the 1821 MS., followed by the 1824 and
1827 transcripts in that order, concluding with passages
from the *Werke* as appropriate (the remaining passages
from the *Werke* that do not *clearly* derive from the 1831
lectures but rather from other manuscript sources are
placed in the notes). Occasionally the internal logic or
development of a section justifies a variation in this
pattern. Although the primary objective has been to correlate parallel sections under a series of headings that
clearly reflect the progression of Hegel's thought, it
should be possible to read each of the lecture sources
separately if desired, thus gaining a sense of how
Hegel's thinking changed and matured during the Berlin
period.[16]

(3) A microfilm of Hegel's own manuscript of 1821
has been studied by the editor and two German student

assistants. This has enabled us to locate all the passages originally found in the margins but included by
Lasson in the main text without notation: these passages
are now identified by another system of superscripts
(+ . . . +). We found a few places where we believe
Lasson mislocated the marginal addition in relation to
the text, and we have corrected the paragraph order here
and there. Some of Lasson's bracketed editorial insertions have been modified, and I have added quite a few of
my own.

(4) Lasson omitted a few brief passages and transitional sentences from the Griesheim transcript. These
have been furnished by Jaeschke and are included in the
translation at the appropriate points.

(5) All passages from the *Werke* have been checked
against the original and two or three transcriptional
errors corrected.

(6) In so far as possible the translation has been
checked against parallel or nearly parallel passages in
Speirs-Sanderson and sometimes their renderings have
proved helpful.

(7) Marginal fragments in the 1821 MS. that could
not be worked smoothly into the text were relegated by
Lasson to the notes. All these have been translated, although often the meaning is obscure, awkward, or fragmentary, and the translation is correspondingly rough.

(8) Notes containing marginal additions, variant
readings of the sources, and passages from the *Werke* are
provided by Lasson, while most other notes are by the
present editor, including all those that discuss the
structure of the text and its meaning. With this simple
division, it seems unnecessary to designate the source of
each note.

(9) Because this Introduction has had to concern itself solely with textual and translational matters, an
Appendix at the end of the work provides a theological
commentary on the text.

Despite these efforts, the present translation cannot claim to represent a truly critical edition of the text, since the translator has had to rely basically on Lasson's *reading* of the manuscript sources and has not been able to check in detail the actual wording of the text against the extant original manuscripts. (Such would require an expert in philology and old German handscript.) I have intended mainly to provide a study edition that will serve in the interim until the new critical edition of the *Religionsphilosophie* is published, at which time it would be appropriate to issue a second edition of this translation based on the newly edited texts.

d. *Future Editions*

Karl-Heinz Ilting of Saarbrücken is completing work on a new edition of the 1821 MS. and the 1824 transcripts (utilizing copies of Griesheim, Pastenacci, Hotho, and Deiter). His plan is to publish the manuscript in one volume and the transcripts in two additional volumes, keeping each of the lecture series entirely separate. Recently he found a new and previously unknown transcript of the 1827 lectures in Warsaw, which will permit him eventually to prepare a new edition of the 1827 text. However, since this and the sparse manuscript discovered by Kimmerle are the only transcripts of these lectures now in existence, he will have to rely heavily on the printed versions of the *Werke* and Lasson, especially since he does not have access to the transcripts used by these earlier editions. Ilting's editions of the 1821 MS. and the 1824 transcripts are not available to me since an agreement was reached earlier between Ilting and Darrel E. Christensen according to which Christensen would prepare English translations of the texts, possibly to be published simultaneously in dual-language editions. However, it is not certain when or even whether the translation part of this project will materialize.

Ilting's editions will be of great benefit to Hegel specialists, but the volumes will be so numerous and expensive as to lie beyond the reach of most students (he produced four massive volumes of Hegel's *Vorlesungen über Rechtsphilosophie* using the same editorial principles). The publication of each of the lecture series in separate sequences, while very likely unavoidable for the Concept of Religion and possibly Determinate Religion, will lose the study advantages afforded by correlating parallel sections under a single arrangement of headings, as is feasible with the Revelatory Religion. Thus even if Christensen's translation project comes to fruition, a place will exist for both editorial conceptions in the English-speaking world.

Under sponsorship of the Deutsche Forschungsgemeinschaft a new "Kritische Gesamtausgabe" of Hegel's works will appear over the course of the next quarter-century, edited by the Rheinisch-Westfälische Akademie der Wissenschaften at the Hegel-Archiv in Bochum--undoubtedly the definitive critical edition of Hegel's works. The edition will appear as *Gesammelte Werke*, published by Felix Meiner Verlag, Hamburg. The work is proceeding chronologically and is presently in the Jena period of Hegel's writings. A volume of lecture manuscripts from the Berlin period will be issued in the next few years, including the 1821 manuscript of the *Religionsphilosophie*, but the lecture transcripts will not appear for another fifteen to twenty years.

3. *Title, Translation, Acknowledgements*

a. *Which Title?*

In his own lecture manuscript Hegel titled the Third Part "Die vollendete Religion oder offenbare." Griesheim calls it simply "Die offenbare Religion," while the

Pastennacci transcript for 1824 gives a string of titles:
"Die offenbare Religion. Die vollendete Religion oder
die geoffenbarte Religion, christliche Religion." The
anonymous transcript for 1827 used by Lasson repeats "Die
offenbare Religion," while Erdmann offers as a title the
words used by Hegel in the opening sentences of the 1827
lectures: "Die vollendete Religion, die Religion, die
für sich ist, oder die Religion, die sich selbst objektiv
ist."[17]

   The evidence seems to indicate that Hegel's preferred
title was "Die offenbare Religion," followed by "Die
vollendete Religion." *Offenbar* is a difficult term to
render into English; my proposal in this context is to
translate it as "revelatory," with the stress on the *process* of making "open" or "manifest," in order to distinguish it from *geoffenbart*, which refers to something that
has been "revealed" in historical, "positive" fashion.
Hegel clearly intended a distinction as well as a relation between these terms (see pp. 16-17). In the *Phenomenology* he described Christianity as "Die offenbare Religion," whereas in the *Encyclopedia* he titled it "Die
geoffenbarte Religion"; thus the *Lectures* indicate a reversion to the earlier (and more suggestive) title.
Vollendet also resists felicitous translation: "consummate" is preferable to "final," "perfect," or "complete,"
because it gathers up all these meanings.

   Notably, none of the extant manuscripts use the title
"Die absolute Religion," although this phrase occurs in
the text of the lectures along with all the others. It
was the *Werke* of 1832 that introduced the title "The Absolute Religion," and it is conceivable but unlikely that
Hegel used it himself when he lectured for the last time
in 1831. Although this is the title by which the Third
Part of the Philosophy of Religion has become familiar
(Lasson perpetuated the tradition), it is probably the
least suitable of any of the titles. For Hegel there cannot
be an absolute religion in the same sense as an absolute

philosophy because the *forms* of religious representation are destined to be "sublated" in philosophical concepts, by means of which absolute knowledge of the Absolute is attained. But what philosophy gains in the knowledge of truth it loses by way of its "partiality," and thus the community of faith must live on in a continuous process of the worldly actualization of reconciliation (pp. 296-297). Christianity is the most "absolute" *of the religions* because in it *"what* God is, and the fact that he is known *as* he is," is made utterly open or manifest (*offenbar*) (p. 11). In other words, its "absoluteness" follows from its "revelatory" character, not vice versa.

To adjudicate the question of title, I have decided to use the *historical* name for this religion, "The Christian Religion" (an expression also employed in the text itself), while indicating that Part III of the *Lectures on the Philosophy of Religion* is variously described as "The Revelatory, Consummate, Absolute Religion."

b. Translation of Terms

In order to preserve Hegel's terminology and to render it as consistently and precisely as follows, I have followed two basic principles. First, with certain unavoidable exceptions, any English term renders one and only one German term. For example, "Idea" always translates *Idee*, never *Vorstellung*. However, it appears to be impossible to avoid using "know" to translate both *kennen* and *wissen* and sometimes even *erkennen*; or "thought" for both *Denken* and *Gedachte*; moreover "perception" is employed for both *Anschauung* and the few occurrences of *Wahrnehmung* because "intuition" often does not seem to provide a natural rendering of *Anschauung* in this text. Second, as few English terms as possible are used for each German word, although it has not been possible to insist on a one-to-one equivalence in every case because German terminology sometimes requires different English

renderings in different contexts. For example, *Vorstellung* is normally translated "representation" but is sometimes given as "imagination" or even "image." By referring to the Glossary readers will be able to tell in most
cases what the German original is for the words listed
there. (To economize space, the Glossary is indexed only
on German words, so one will have to hunt around a bit
until the listings have become familiar.)

I have avoided the use of capitals except for *Geist*
("Spirit") and *Idee* ("Idea"). *Geist* is the ultimate
Hegelian category, descriptive of that process of consciousness which encompasses finitude and sublates it,
yet is itself intrinsically infinite. God is Spirit but
so also is human being in the modality of finitude and
differentiation. It is a term, moreover, that has both
religious (representative) and philosophical (conceptual)
connotations. Hegel can pass back and forth between
these several referents of *Geist* or intend them simultaneously, and it finally proves arbitrary to attempt to
capitalize Spirit in some instances but not in others.[18]
Idee for Hegel carries Platonic overtones, referring to
the "realm" of purely logical relations and meanings, the
"self-thinking Idea," the "logical Idea," which tran-
scends nature and finite Spirit as the "universal principle" of both, yet which is actualized by means of its embodiment in nature and finite Spirit, and which finds its
telos in absolute Spirit.[19] Since in English philosophy
"idea" with a small "i" has traditionally meant what Hegel
would call *Vorstellung*, I have avoided the use of "idea"
entirely and employ "Idea" to translate *Idee*.

The happiest choice for *Aufhebung* appears to be "sublation," which could well become the standard English
term for this peculiarly Hegelian concept when the double
meaning of "annulment" *and* "preservation" or "elevation"
is intended. *Bestimmung* always poses translation problems
and I have been looser in its rendering than several of
my readers would have preferred, offering a notable ex-

ception to the principle of using as few English terms as possible for each German word. I have dealt with the *geschichtlich-historisch* problem by using "historic" and "historical"--not a very happy solution but probably the best available without deploying circumlocutions. Hegel uses the latter term only infrequently, and while the distinction between the two terms is significant for him, he does not follow it consistently. The difference between *offenbar* and *geoffenbart* has been discussed in the preceding section. For the translation and meaning of *natürlich* and *Natürlichkeit*, see n. 23, p. 164; for *Reflexion*, n. 73, p. 305.

   Verstand is rendered as "understanding" because this has become the accepted translation of this Kantian concept that Hegel adopted and modified; I have misgivings about the translation because the natural meaning of "understanding" in English is rather different from *Verstand* as a *terminus technicus* in German idealism. It would be appropriate to add a qualifier such as "abstract" or "analytic" before "understanding," but this is too cumbersome as a routine translation policy. *Verstand* supplies the abstract categoreal forms by which *Vorstellung* ("representation") produces synthetic images based on sense perception. *Verstand* apprehends objects in terms of their distinct, separate, contradictory attributes and is unable to grasp the identity that underlies the different aspects in which things show themselves. Thus representation remains a finite, undialectical mode of thought, properly applied only to sense-based experience. When the attempt is made to render non-empirical, non-ostensive realities such as God representatively, thought readily falls into contradiction and illusion. *Vernunft* ("reason"), by contrast, is intrinsically infinite and dialectical, constitutive of the very structure of actuality itself, the "soul of the world," its moving vital principle, unifying apparent contradictions in higher syntheses. As such it is the instrument of *Begriff* (the "concept" or conceptual thought).[20]

Finally, a word about *Mensch*. My original intention
had been to produce a non-sexist translation, but it soon
became apparent that this would require a massive re-
structuring of both syntax and semantics, and the result
finally would not be Hegel. It is easy enough to render
Mensch as "human being" rather than as "man," but what
does one do with the almost inevitable use of masculine
singular pronouns, or with the figures "Father" and "Son"
as symbols of the trinitarian relations (even if they are
mere *Vorstellungen*!)? Certainly Hegel's philosophy is by
no means intrinsically sexist--indeed he had a profound
vision of human liberation and of the eventual elimination of all forms of oppression, including that of women
by men (see p. 235)--but he was conditioned by the dominant masculinity of his culture, which pervaded the form
of his thinking but not, I contend, its essential content.
Surely this is a problem that must now be faced with reference to almost every major figure in the Western tradition.

c. Acknowledgements

When I naively set to work on this project several
years ago, I never imagined the complications and com-
plexities it would engender, nor did I anticipate how interesting, indeed utterly absorbing, it could become
(H. S. Harris warns of Hegel's Puck-like capacity to
cause sober persons to lose their senses!). I am indebted to an unusually large circle of fellow-workers who
helped to make the project both more complex and more interesting.

Richard Crouter, Carleton College, first alerted me
to the problems with the Lasson edition and while on
leave in Marburg put me in touch with the current work of
the Hegel-Archiv, in addition to providing wise counsel
on several matters. The thorough study of the manuscripts

and previous editions by Walter Jaeschke, a member of the editorial staff at the Hegel-Archiv in Bochum, has proved absolutely indispensable to my work, and he has offered expert assistance on many details by correspondence. H. S. Harris, Glendon College of York University, undertook an evaluation of the translation for the American Academy of Religion, providing an extraordinarily detailed and helpful set of suggestions for improvement. Francis Fiorenza, Villanova University, Chairperson of the Nineteenth Century Theology Group, worked out arrangements for publication in the Texts and Translations Series of the AAR, while James Massey, University of Louisville, Editor of the Series, brought these to fruition. The fine dissertation on Hegel's Christology by James Yerkes, Earlham School of Religion, was an inspiration to my work. Kem Luther, Eastern Mennonite College, generously loaned his microfilm copy of the 1821 MS., while Manfred Zumpe and Anke Mollenkott, exchange students from Göttingen in Vanderbilt Divinity School, did the arduous work of checking the marginal additions. Professors Crouter, Yerkes, and Luther, as well as Mark Taylor, Williams College, each read portions of the translation and provided me with valuable editorial counsel.

Two graduate students at Vanderbilt University have helped at different stages: Robert Orr prepared a rough draft of the translation, while Paul Lakeland, S.J., carefully proofread the final copy. The Vanderbilt University Research Council provided indispensable support for the project with generous grants over a three-year period. Mary G. Floyd skillfully typed both a draft edition, sent out to my informal network of consultants, and the camera-ready copy, while Aline Patte offered helpful assistance with last-minute details.

NOTES FOR EDITOR'S INTRODUCTION

1. Walter Jaeschke, *Der Aufbau und die bisherigen Editionen von Hegels Vorlesungen über die Philosophie der Religion* (Unpublished M.A. Thesis, Free University of Berlin, 1970), pp. 38-39, 94-95. See also the "Feststellung des Textes" of Georg Lasson's edition of the *Vorlesungen über die Philosophie der Religion* (Leipzig: Verlag von Felix Meiner, 1925-1929, r.p. Hamburg 1966), I/1:312-321; II/2:234-239.

2. See the Comparative Analysis of the Structure of the Text following this Introduction; also Jaeschke, *Aufbau*, pp. 28, 31, 36-37, 84-85.

3. Jaeschke, *Aufbau*, pp. 4-7.

4. Jaeschke, *Aufbau*, pp. 29-31, 36-37. See below, n. 2, p. 99, and n. 20, p. 102.

5. Jaeschke, *Aufbau*, pp. 4-5, and correspondence dated 23 Oct. and 6 Dec. 1977.

6. Jaeschke, *Aufbau*, pp. 32-34, and correspondence; Lasson, II/2:238. Our discussion of the "transition" section in the Appendix will provide an occasion to offer an overview of the structure of the *Lectures on the Philosophy of Religion* as a whole.

7. Lasson, I/1:320; II/2:238-239.

8. As Volumes 11-12 of *Werke: Vollständige Ausgabe durch einen Verein von Freunden des Verewigten* (Berlin: Duncker and Humblot, 1832[1], 1840[2]). The 2nd ed. of the *Werke* was reprinted in the *Jubiläumsausgabe* edited by Hermann Glockner (Stuttgart: Fr. Frommanns Verlag, 1927-1930), and in the edition edited by E. Moldenhauer and K. M. Michel (Frankfurt: Suhrkamp Verlag, 1969).

9. Jaeschke, *Aufbau*, pp. 59, 68-70, 92; Lasson, I/1:318-319. See also Reinhard Heede, "Hegels Religionsphilosophie als Aufgabe und Problem der Forschung," *Hegel-Bilanz: Zur Aktualität und Inaktualität der Philosophie Hegels*, ed. R. Heede and J. Ritter (Frankfurt: Vittorio Klostermann, 1973), p. 46.

10. Jaeschke, *Aufbau*, pp. 54-58, 65-70, 93; Lasson, I/1:319; II/2:238; Heede, *Hegel-Bilanz*, pp. 47-48, 51-52.

11. *Lectures on the Philosophy of Religion, Together with a Work on the Proofs of the Existence of God* (3 vols.; London: Kegan Paul, Trench Trübner & Co., 1895; r.p. Routledge & Kegan Paul and Humanities Press, 1962 et seq.).

12. Bloch makes the charge in the preface to the reprint of the 2nd edition of the *Werke* by Suhrkamp Verlag in 1969. The one exception is Lasson's handling of the concluding section of the 1821 MS., "Passing Away of the Community" (see below, n. 87, p. 307). On

the issues involved here, see Jaeschke, *Aufbau*, pp. 42-43, 84-85; and Heede, *Hegel-Bilanz*, pp. 49-50.

13. Jaeschke, *Aufbau*, pp. 71-83, 89. Cf. Emanuel Hirsch's three critical reviews of the Lasson edition in *Theologische Literaturzeitung*, 50 (1925): 421-423; 53 (1928): 376-379; and 55 (1930): 425-427. Also Heede, *Hegel-Bilanz*, pp. 55-56.

14. For what follows, see Jaeschke, *Aufbau*, pp. 50-52, 58, 94.

15. Jaeschke concurs with this judgment and supports the present project: correspondence dated 23 Oct. 1977, 6 Dec. 1977, 29 April 1978. So do the other persons with whom I have consulted, except for Darrel E. Christensen, who believes that the only viable method for editing the lectures is to publish each lecture series seriatim in a separate volume, as K.-H. Ilting plans to do.

16. For these first two editorial tasks, an Appendix to Jaeschke's *Aufbau* has proved indispensable. The Appendix divides the text of the Absolute Religion into 388 distinguishable units and correlates the 2nd ed. of the *Werke* and Lasson unit by unit, providing the manuscript source for each unit (and in the case of the 1821 MS. and the Griesheim transcript, the manuscript pagination for each unit). Moreover, Jaeschke himself has carefully checked a draft copy of this translation and regards as accurate its designation of sources and arrangement of texts.

17. Lasson, II/2:234-237.

18. See Emil L. Fackenheim, *The Religious Dimension in Hegel's Thought* (Bloomington: Indiana University Press, 1967), pp. 18-22, 44-58.

19. On the relation between the logical Idea, nature, and finite Spirit, see Fackenheim, *Religious Dimension*, pp. 75-112. See also Hans-Georg Gadamer, "The Idea of Hegel's Logic," in *Hegel's Dialectic: Five Hermeneutical Studies*, trans. P. Christopher Smith (New Haven: Yale University Press, 1976), pp. 75-99.

20. On these definitions, see the *Encyclopedia of the Philosophical Sciences*, trans. W. Wallace & A. V. Miller (2nd ed.; 3 vols.; Oxford: Oxford University Press, 1970-1975), §§ 6, 24-25, 44-45, 80-82, 451-464; *Werke*, 11:138-150, 153; James Yerkes, *The Christology of Hegel* (AAR Dissertation Series 23; Missoula: Scholars Press, 1978), pp. 89-90, 91-93; and Malcolm Clark, *Logic and System: A Study of the Transition from "Vorstellung" to Thought in the Philosophy of Hegel* (The Hague: Martinus Nijhoff, 1971), pp. 55-67.

xxx

COMPARATIVE ANALYSIS OF THE STRUCTURE OF THE TEXT

---

*For the 1821 MS. and the 1824 and 1827 Transcripts, the page references are to the pagination of this edition and indicate the first page on which each new section of the manuscript or transcripts begins.

GLOSSARY

This glossary contains a selection of frequently used and/
or technical terms, especially those posing problems in
translation.

German	English
absolut, Absolute	absolute, the absolute
allgemein; Allgemeine	universal, general; the universal
Anderssein	other-being
Anschauung	perception, intuition
an sich	in itself, implicit, intrinsic
Ansich; Ansichsein; Anundfürsichsein	in-itself; being-in-itself; being-in-and-for-itself
aufheben; Aufhebung	annul, sublate, annulment, sublation (when the double meaning of "annulment *and* preservation or elevation" is clearly intended, the translation uses "sublate," from Lat. *sublatio*, which contains the same double meaning)
auflösen	resolve
Begierde	desire, appetite
beglaubigen; Beglaubigung	confirm; confirmation, corroboration
begreifen	conceive, comprehend
Begriff	concept, conception
bei sich	present to itself
bestimmen; Bestimmung	determine, define, characterize; determination, definition, character(-istic, -ization), condition, quality
bestimmt; Bestimmtheit	determinate, definite; determinateness, determinacy

Betrachtung	consideration, contemplation, observation
bewähren	verify
Bewusstsein	consciousness
bildlich	figurative
denken; Denken	think; thinking, thought
einzeln	single, individual, isolated
Element	element, moment (cf. "Moment")
Empfindung	feeling, experience, sensation, sentiment
Entäusserung	divestment
Entfremdung	estrangement, alienation
Entzweiung	disunion, estrangement, rupture
erheben	elevate, raise
erkennen; Erkenntnis	cognize, recognize, know; cognition, knowledge
Erscheinung	appearance
fassen, auffassen, erfassen	comprehend, grasp
für sich	for itself, explicit
Fürsich; Fürsichsein	for-itself; being-for-itself
Gedachte, Gedanke	thought
Gefühl	feeling
Gegensatz	antithesis, opposition
gegenständlich; Gegenstand	objective; object
Gegenwart	presence, present
Geist	Spirit
geistig; Geistige; Geistigkeit	spiritual; the spiritual; spirituality
Genuss	communion, partaking, enjoyment
geoffenbart	revealed (cf. "offenbar")
Geschichte	history, story
geschichtlich	historic
Historie	history (with "Historie" in brackets following)

historisch	historical (refers to the objectifying historiographical approach to the factual data of history, construes "Geschichte" as mere "Historie")
Idee	Idea
in sich	within itself (to be distinguished from "an sich")
jenseits; Jenseits	above and beyond, otherworldly; the other world
kennen	know
Kultus	cultus
Manifestation	manifestation (cf. "Erscheinung")
Mensch; Menschheit	man, human being; humanity
mittelbar	mediated
Moment	moment, element (cf. "Element")
Moralität	morality (cf. "Sittlichkeit")
natürlich; Natürliche	natural; the natural
Natürlichkeit	natural state, natural life, naturalness, existence according to nature
offenbar	revelatory, open, manifest (cf. "geoffenbart")
Offenbaren; Offenbarung	revealedness; revelation
Positive	the positive, positivity
realisieren; Realität	realize; reality (cf. "verwirklichen," "Wirklichkeit")
Recht	justice
Reflexion	reflection
Sache	matter, thing
scheinen; Schein	shine, seem, appear; show
schliessen	reason, argue, conclude
Schmerz	anguish, sorrow
Seiende(s)	existent reality, entity
sein; Sein	be, exist; being
setzen	posit
sinnlich	sensible, sentient

sittlich; Sittlichkeit	ethical; ethics, ethical realm, ethical life (cf. "Moralität")
teilen; Teilung	divide; division, separation
trennen; Trennung	separate; separation
Unglück	misery, unhappiness
unmittelbar	immediate, unmediated
unterscheiden; Unterscheidung	distinguish, differentiate; distinction, differentiation
Unterschied	difference
urteilen; Urteil	judge, divide; judgment, (primal) division
vermitteln; Vermittlung	mediate; mediation
vernünftig	rational
Vernunft	reason
Verschiedenheit	difference, diversity
versöhnen; Versöhnung	reconcile; reconciliation
Verstand	understanding
verwirklichen; Verwirklichung	actualize; actualization (cf. "realisieren")
vollendet	consummate, accomplished
vorhanden	existing, existent, present, available
vorstellen; vorstellend	represent, imagine; figurative, representative, imaginative
Vorstellung	representation, image, imagination
wahr; wahrhaft; Wahrheit	true; truthful; truth
Wesen	essence
Widerspruch	contradiction
Willkür	caprice, arbitrariness
wirklich; Wirklichkeit	actual; actuality
wissen; Wissen	know; knowledge, knowing
Wissenschaft	science, scientific knowledge
Zufälligkeit	contingency
Zweck	end, goal, purpose
Zweckmässigkeit	expediency

KEY TO SIGNS

^{m} . . . ^{m} = Hegel's Original Manuscript of 1821.

$^+$ . . . $^+$ = Passages from the Margins of the 1821 Manuscript.

^{a} . . . ^{a} = Lecture Transcripts of 1824 (by Hegel's Students).

^{b} . . . ^{b} = Lecture Transcripts of 1827 (by Hegel's Students).

^{w} . . . ^{w} = *Werke: Vollständige Ausgabe durch einen Verein von Freunden des Verewigten*, Vols. 11-12, 2nd ed., ed. Philipp Marheineke and Bruno Bauer (Berlin: Verlag von Duncker und Humblot, 1840).

Lasson = *Vorlesungen über die Philosophie der Religion*, ed. Georg Lasson (2 Vols., 4 Parts; Leipzig: Verlag von Felix Meiner, 1925-1929; r.p. Hamburg, 1966). Text of *Die absolute Religion* contained in Vol. II/2, pp. 3-232.

1 2 3 etc. = Editorial notes. Marginal additions and variant readings in the 1821 MS., as well as footnoted passages from the *Werke*, are provided by Lasson. Most other notes are by the present editor. Notes are at the ends of each of the chapters.

[. . .] = Editorial insertions into the text by Lasson and the translator.

Italics = Words italicized in the Lasson text are reproduced in italics, except for proper names. In addition, the translator has added italics at some points to help bring out the meaning. It is impossible to know which words Hegel actually emphasized when lecturing. The *Werke* contains many more italicized words than the present edition.

Numbers in Brackets = Pagination of the Lasson edition.

Biblical   = "Cf." preceding a biblical reference indi-
Texts   cates that the quotation is not exact.
              Paraphrased biblical texts do not have quo-
              tation marks and the reference is preceded
              by "cf." Translations generally follow the
              Revised Standard Version except where Hegel's
              citations differ from the biblical text.

CHAPTER I

INTRODUCTION: DEFINITION OF THE REVELATORY RELIGION[1]

Section 1. The Concept of the Revelatory Religion

[3] [m]This religion [was] earlier defined[2] as the one
in which the *concept* of religion has become an object to
itself; [it is] the totality in which the concept of reli-
gion--[which] in its determinations developed in various
ways--is *posited*, has existence for others and so becomes
an object of consciousness.[m]

[b][3]The first stage was the Concept of Religion in
general; the second, religion in its particularity or Determinate Religion, the last of these being the Religion
of Expediency.[4] The third is the Consummate Religion, the
religion that exists for itself, is an object to itself.
This is always the course in scientific knowledge:
first the concept; then the particularity of the concept--
reality, objectivity; and finally the stage in which the
original concept is an object to itself, exists for itself, becomes objective to itself, is related to itself.
This is the course of philosophy. First the concept of
conceptual knowledge--the concept that *we* have. But at
the end science grasps its own concept so that the concept
exists for itself.

So also the sphere into which we are now entering is
the concept of religion that exists for itself, i.e., the

1

Revelatory Religion. Religion is for the first time made
open and manifest when the concept of religion exists for
itself, i.e., when religion or its concept has become objective to itself--not in limited, finite objectivity but
such that it exists objectively in accordance with its
concept.[b]   [a]This is the Consummate Religion, the religion
that is the being of Spirit for itself.[5]

[4] This can be defined more precisely as follows.
Religion, in accord with its general concept, is the
consciousness of God, consciousness of absolute essence.
Consciousness, however, is a differentiating, a division
in itself. So we have two elements: consciousness and
absolute essence.

God is himself self-consciousness, differentiating
itself in itself. Since God, as this differentiating of
itself in itself, is consciousness, so is he, as consciousness, such that he gives himself as object for what
we call the side of consciousness. With the consciousness of God we arrive at one side, which we have called
religion.[6]

In the consciousness of God, therefore, two sides
are to be found: the one is God, the other is that upon
which consciousness as such rests.[a]   [b]These two are first
of all separated under finite conditions, empirical consciousness on the one hand, and essence in the abstract
sense on the other. They exist alongside each other under finite conditions and to this extent are both finite,
since we always have two elements in consciousness, which
are related to each other in finite, external ways. Thus
consciousness knows absolute essence only as something
finite, not as the truth.

But when religion comprehends itself, the other element in it emerges. The consciousness of God means that
the finite consciousness has this God, who is its essence,
as an object, knows him as its essence, and thus objectifies itself. Thus the content and object of religion
is this whole--*consciousness relating itself to its es-*

sence, knowing itself as it knows its essence and knowing its essence as its own.[b] [a]This is the content that has now made itself an object. It is the whole that is an object to itself; the reality of religion has identified itself with its concept. In other words, religion has become objective to itself.[a]

[b]This means: *Spirit* is the object of religion, and the object of the latter--essence knowing itself--is Spirit. Here for the first time Spirit is as such the object, the content of religion, and Spirit exists only for Spirit. Since it is content or object, and since as Spirit it is self-knowing and self-distinguishing, [5] it gives itself as the other side of subjective consciousness, which appears as finite. It is the religion that is completed by itself.

This is the abstract determination of this Idea or the sphere where religion is in fact Idea. This is because an Idea in the philosophical sense is the concept that has an object, has existence, reality, objectivity, is no longer merely inner and subjective but objectifies itself, whose objectivity, however, is at the same time a return to itself, or--to the extent that we speak of the concept as a goal--is the completed, accomplished goal, which precisely as such is objective.[b]

[m]Religion, defined generally as the consciousness of God--God the absolute object, but as consciousness and subjectivity, [as] the true object--is the whole. That God whom we designate as a mere object *over against* consciousness is an abstraction. God [is] this whole; hence he is the universal, the absolute universal, he is power, the substance of all that exists, the truth--but as consciousness, as infinite form, infinite subjectivity, i.e., as *Spirit*.[7] In this fashion the concept of religion [is] objective to itself, [for it exists] in its object. It is not the case that religion as subjectivity makes re-

ligious feeling its object, [for] religious feeling, which itself is subjectivity, is rather the annulment of religion. Rather, the *concept* of religion *as* a real object is the content of religious consciousness, but precisely therein it is also subjective--the *Spirit indwelling* the subjective religious self-consciousness, God manifesting himself in it. This manifestation [of God] occurs in spiritual self-consciousness, and this [is an] infinite form of his reality--i.e., his reality [considered] as [one] side. God himself is one in all, or as said earlier, infinite form and unity, universality.[m]

[14] [a][8] The consciousness of God or the self-consciousness of God as the return of consciousness into itself is precisely what we have called spirituality in general.[9] This is Spirit, not to exist immediately but rather vis-à-vis itself. Spirit is *for* Spirit so that the two are distinguishable; they are defined vis-à-vis each other--the one as universal, the other as particular; the one as inner, the other as outer; the one as infinite Spirit, the other as finite Spirit. Such is this distinction as it is found in religion; at the same time, however, there occurs the sublation of this distinction, the self-consciousness of freedom, a spiritual quality, which on the whole existed in the preceding formative stages of religion *for us*, but which now is the object of religion. The individual self-consciousness finds therein the consciousness of its essence; therefore, it is free, and precisely this freedom is spirituality--and this, we say, is religion, i.e., Spirit now exists objectively. The Spirit previously given us stands on neither the finite nor the universal side. Only the relation of Spirit *to* Spirit is religion. Religion has thus become objective because the object of finite consciousness is known as Spirit, and it is known thus only in so far as the universal (this one substance, which is absolute essence, truth) is also the absolute power in which everything is posited as organic,

exists as negated, but which power exists not only as substance but also as subject. The freedom of self-consciousness is the content of religion, [15] and this content is itself the object of the Christian[10] Religion,
i.e., Spirit is its own object. The nature of spirituality consists in the fact that this absolute essence distinguishes itself as absolute power and likewise as subject, and imparts itself to that which is distinguished
from it while remaining undivided, so that the other is
also the whole--this and the return to itself constituting the totality of spirituality. Absolute Spirit is
thus the object, Spirit is identical with Spirit. This
is the concept of religion, and this concept is the absolute Idea that has existed for us in the religions.

In this religion, religion has become objective to
itself; the object or content by means of which religion
fulfills what is objective to it is its *own* determination,
namely, that Spirit exists only *for* Spirit. Universal
and individual Spirit, infinite and finite Spirit, are
inseparable: their absolute identity is religion, which
has precisely this content. Since we have expressed it
this way above all, one can say that the whole, the absolute, *is* religion. One can say this in contrast to the
definition of religion as an activity involving the
praise of God, for here one knows and acknowledges God
only as an object standing over and above us, indeed, as
an object that must remain over and above us. Theology
would then chiefly involve recognizing God only as something objective, which must remain absolutely separated
from subjective consciousness--thought of, indeed, as an
external object like the sun or the sky, so that God is
an object of consciousness in the sense of retaining the
character of something other and external. In contrast
to this, one can designate the concept of the Absolute
Religion as follows: the content of its activity is not
this external object but rather religion itself, i.e.,
the unity of the image that we call God with the subject.

The extent to which this is also the character of our own time we have still to consider.

The great advance of our age is that of recognizing subjectivity as an absolute moment; this is its essential character. But it depends on how one defines it. One can view the present age as being concerned [16] with religion, religiousness, or piety, assuming, however, that little depends on the object of religion. Men have various religions; it matters little which one if only they are pious. Nothing depends on whether one believes this or that dogma. One cannot know God as an object, cannot recognize him, and it is assumed that the only thing that counts is one's subjective attitude. This standpoint may be recognized in what we have set forth; it is the standpoint of the age, and at the same time a very important advance, constituting a permanently valid moment. It consists in the fact that the consciousness of the subject is to be recognized as an absolute moment. The same content is on both sides, and this implicit identity of both sides is religion.

The following remarks may be made about this great advance. In the abstract determination of *consciousness*, religion is so constituted that its content flees into the distance and, at least apparently, remains far away. Consciousness is aware of its object as something independent, like a determinate thing over against me, e.g., a mountain, sun, sky. Religion may have whatever content it likes; secured from the standpoint of consciousness, its content stands over and above it, and even when the specification of supernatural revelation is added, its content again remains absolutely given and external to us. By means of such a representation, the divine content is merely given, inaccessible to reason; we are to be related to it only passively in faith, but still in a subjective condition. That passive relation is not the only demand; rather it issues in the subjectivity of sentiment and feeling, the result of which is the sentiment of di-

vine worship. The devout person submerges himself with
his heart, devotion, and will in his object; thus at the
pinnacle of devotion he has annulled the separation that
marks the standpoint of consciousness. This separation
has another form: the finite subject is placed opposite
the object as absolute Spirit, or exists from the point
of view of the consciousness or feeling of the individual.
Therefore, as already noted, the standpoint of consciousness leads also to a subjectivity, to a non-alien condition, to a [17] submersion of Spirit in the depths, to an
elevation into the distance, which is no distance at all
but rather absolute nearness, presence. To be sure, this
devotion or intensity, defined for itself, can also be
considered as a separation. The Spirit, the grace of
God, dwells in men, one says, thinking of it thereby as
something so alien that one must put up with it--an alien
thing working in us, to which we are passively related.

Against this separation the objection is raised that
it is a question of religion as such, a question, that is,
of a subjective consciousness having the intention of doing God's will, and that therefore religion as such is
the absolute. It is in religion or the subject, accordingly, that the inseparability of subjectivity and of the
other or objectivity exists. But the validating of this
objectivity is the important thing; or to put it otherwise, the subject is absolutely essential for the whole
sphere of religious relations. With this, the standpoint
of *self-consciousness* enters in, and this standpoint elevates the subject to the rank of an essential characteristic. It is in harmony with the freedom of Spirit that
it has re-established its freedom and that there can be
no standpoint for it at which Spirit would not be present
to itself. This is the important definition of the concept of Absolute Religion--a definition according to
which religion is only that which is objective to itself,
in fact *is* the objective. But this is only the concept
of religion; this concept is one thing, the consciousness

of this concept is something else. Hence in the Absolute
Religion there can be the *concept* of this in-itself, but
at the same time the *consciousness* of something else; in
other words, it too can be unfree.

In the third place, however, the consciousness of
this concept is identical with what the concept is in itself. This is the aspect that has emerged and come to
consciousness in the determination that it is with religion that we have to do. The concept, taken only in itself, is itself still one-sided; likewise, it appears in
a one-sided form in which subjectivity is one-sided and
has only the determination of one out of two, is only infinite form, only pure self-consciousness, pure knowledge
of itself. It is intrinsically without content because
religion is grasped only in its being-in-itself; it is
not the religion that is objective to itself, but religion that does not yet exist in its real, self-determin-
ing, [18] content-giving form. What has no objectivity
has no content.[11]

But even in so far as religion is without content,
it must still have a content. For truth always has the
right to exist, although, to be sure, in either a true or
a stunted form. Thus there must be a content; in the
present case the content has a contingent, finite, empirical character because it is not determined by subjectivity itself; and we find, therefore, a similarity with the
Roman age. The period of the Roman Emperors has many
similarities with our own. Just because the subject [as
we conceive it in our time] is abstract, it is finite.
This is the highest pinnacle that we have reached, [to
wit] that the subject as the empirical accident thrown up
by nature *is* this pinnacle. Freedom, therefore, is only
of this kind: it has to have a fortuitous content; it
lets a [world] beyond subsist, a [goal of] yearning; it
denies the differentiating activity of consciousness
(what we call the standpoint of consciousness) and spirituality in general, repudiating thereby the essential

moment of Spirit and so falling into spiritless subjectivity; it is that which is richest in Spirit, but after
the reversal into abstraction, the poorest in Spirit. We
have said that religion itself is the content, the object. Here this means that, since it is itself the content, religion is what is above and beyond, the object;
as religion, it is only the one side, while the content
stands on the side of finite subjectivity.

The Absolute Religion, on the other hand, has the
concrete character of subjectivity or of infinite form,
which is equivalent to substance. We may call it knowledge, recognition, pure intelligence--this subjectivity,
this infinite form, this infinite elasticity of substance,
dirempting itself within itself, making itself an object
for itself. The content [19] is, therefore, an organic
content, because it is the infinite, substantial subjectivity, which makes itself both object and content. In
this content, however, the finite subject is distinguished once again from the infinite object. God regarded as Spirit, when he remains over and above, when he
does not exist as the living Spirit of his community, is
himself characterized in a merely one-sided way as object.

This is the first definition of the concept: it is the
concept of the Idea, the absolute Idea. The reality is
now the Spirit that exists *for* Spirit, that has made itself an object.[a]

[5] ^{w12} We have now arrived at the realized concept
of religion, the Consummate Religion, in which it is the
concept itself that is its own object. We have defined
religion as being in the stricter sense the self-consciousness of God. [6] Self-consciousness in its character as consciousness has an object, and it is conscious
of itself in this object; this object is also consciousness, but it is consciousness as object, and is consequently finite consciousness, a consciousness that is
distinct from God, from the absolute. Determinateness

and consequently finitude are present in this form of
consciousness. God is self-consciousness; he knows himself in a consciousness that is distinct from him, that
is implicitly the consciousness of God, but is also this
explicitly since it knows its identity with God, an identity that is mediated, however, by the negation of finitude. It is this concept that constitutes the content of
religion. We define God when we say that he distinguishes himself from himself and is an object for himself
but that in this distinction he is purely identical with
himself, is in fact Spirit. This concept is now realized;
consciousness knows this content and knows that it is absolutely interwoven with this content; in the concept
this is the process of God, it is itself a moment. Finite consciousness knows God only to the extent that God
knows himself in it; thus God is Spirit, indeed the
Spirit of his community, i.e., of those who worship him.
This is the Consummate Religion, the concept become objective to itself. Here it is manifest what God is: he
is no longer a being above and beyond this world, an unknown, for he has made known to man what he is, and this
not merely in an external history but in consciousness.
We have here, accordingly, the religion of the manifestation of God, since God knows himself in finite Spirit.
God is absolutely open or manifest: this is here the
essential condition. The transition was our having seen
that the knowledge of God as free Spirit is still tinged,
so far as its substance is concerned, with finitude and
immediacy. This finitude had further to be discarded by
the labor of Spirit; it is nothingness, and we have seen
how this nothingness has been made manifest to consciousness. The unhappiness, the anguish of the world was the
condition, the preparation on the subjective side for the
consciousness of free Spirit as absolutely free and consequently infinite[13] Spirit.[w]

Section 2. Characteristics of the Revelatory Religion[14]

[32] *m*[15] The Christian Religion is the religion of
revelation. What God is, [+]and the fact that he is known
as he is,[+] not merely in historical or some similar
fashion as in the other religions, is made manifest in
it. Open manifestation is its character and content,
namely, the revelation, manifestation, being [of God] for
consciousness, [+][indeed, the revelation] for consciousness that it is itself Spirit, i.e., [that it *is*] consciousness and *for* consciousness.[+] God is manifest only
as one who particularizes himself and becomes objective,
initially in the mode of finitude, which is his own; [+]he
is not, however, [*something*] manifest, not some palpable
thing.[+] Already in Greek and Roman religion, this mode
of finitude [exists] for others, but [this is] only an
abstract finitude, [+]which [remains] finite and [is] not
at the same time infinite.[+] God has created the world,
has revealed himself, etc. [This] beginning [is re-
garded] as something *accomplished*, i.e., as a single act,
once for all, not to be repeated. [God's] eternal decree [is represented] as [a singular act] of will and
therefore as arbitrary [and untrue], but on the contrary,
this is his eternal nature. The nature of Spirit itself
is to manifest itself, make itself objective; this is its
activity and vitality, its sole act and infinitely its
act.[16] Here one finds, [33] above all, separation and
finitization, defined therefore as a divine moment itself
(as [the name] Creator[17] already [suggests]), because
this objectification is infinite form--a manifestation
simultaneously taken back into the infinite.[18] The universal [comes] *into* the finite but not *as* something finite; [it is] glorified in the form of Spirit--in the
other religions [as well] ([the Religion of] Beauty,
Indian religion). [But in those religions,] God is still
something other than what he reveals himself to be. [+]A
necessity [hovers] over the gods.[+] God is the inner

and the unknown; he is not as he appears to consciousness. But precisely here [in the Christian Religion it
is maintained]: (α) that he appears, reveals [himself],
in his *own* determination; (β) [that] precisely this appearance in itself [is] the universal, not in a fixed,
finite determinate [34] form; rather this appearance--
the transfigured divine world--is received as it is.
(His being is his act, his revealedness itself.)[19]

[20][The Christian Religion is, in the second place,]
the religion of *truth*. If by "truth of the Christian Religion" [we mean] that it is historically accurate,
[then this] is not what [is intended] here; rather, truth
is its *content*, for it has and knows the truth, it knows
God *as he is*. A Christian Religion that did not know
God, [or in which] God [were] not revealed, would be no
Christian Religion at all. Its content [is] the truth
itself in and for itself; it consists only in the being
of truth for consciousness; [+]likewise [it knows] God
only as Spirit. (Hitherto revealed, [now] truth in and
for itself. -- Feeling -- opposite of the truth.)[+] This
content, however, is Spirit; it is the concept, which is
absolute reality. Existence, appearance, outward [move-
ment], objectivity are in accord with the concept; they
are only the empty form of other-being. The concept
[is] the entire content of reality. Spirit is itself the
process of giving itself this show [*Schein*] and sublating
it, of positing it as sublated; both together are revelation since this show is the appearing [*Scheinen*] of God,
an infinite appearing yet not beyond appearing.

[21][The Christian Religion is, thirdly,] the religion of *reconciliation*--of the world with God. God, it is
said, has reconciled the world with himself. The fall of
the world from God means that it has fixated itself as
finite consciousness, as the consciousness of idols; [it
means that it holds fast to] the universal not as such
but rather in external ways or [in regard to] finite purposes. To desist from this separation is to turn back--

this is the perceived return of reality, the absorption
of the finite in the eternal, the unity of divine and
human nature, [the] state of being-in-itself and the process of eternally positing this unity. [+]In this perception of the truth, [self-consciousness has] absolute certainty of itself. This certainty seals all subjectivity
within itself, and the latter finds *itself* in Spirit and
its [35] truth.[+] [This is,] accordingly, the religion of
freedom--the speculative, objectively universal, absolute
passage to being-in-and-for-itself; [+][as] a speculative
concept, it [is] itself already [present] in the concept
of religion itself.[+] *m*

   a[22] The next point of definition is that this religion is the *Revelatory Religion*. God reveals himself.
As we have seen, revealedness means the overturning of
infinite subjectivity, the judgment of infinite form,
determining it to be for an other; this self-manifesta-
tion belongs to the essence of Spirit itself. A Spirit
that is not open or manifest is no Spirit. It is said
that God has created the world; this is spoken of as an
event that once happened and will not happen again, and
as being of such a character that it either may be or may
not be. On this view, God could have revealed himself or
not, and revelation would be of an indifferent, capricious, or contingent character, not belonging to the concept of God. But God's essence as Spirit is to be for an
other, to reveal himself; he does not create the world
once and for all, but rather is the eternal Creator, the
one who reveals himself eternally. He is this *actus*:
this is his concept, his determination.
   This religion is, therefore, the Revelatory Religion: it is Spirit *for* Spirit. It is the religion of
Spirit and not a secret or mystery. It is not closed
but open and determinate; it means to be for an other,
which is only momentarily an other. God posits the other
and then sublates it in his eternal movement. Spirit is

precisely this, to appear to itself.

What is it that God reveals? The infinite form that we have called absolute subjectivity. This entails the determining or positing of distinction, the positing of content. What God thus reveals is that he is the manifestation, that he constitutes this distinction within himself. His being or nature is eternally to make this distinction, to take it back into himself, and thereby to be present to himself. What is revealed is that he exists for an other. This is the definition of revealedness.

Hence this is the religion of *truth* and *freedom*. For truth means to be related to something in objectivity without its being alien or strange. Freedom expresses the same thing that truth is, with an element of negation. [36] Spirit is for Spirit, and it is what it is for Spirit. It is its own presupposition; we begin with Spirit. It is identical with itself, the eternal perception of itself; at the same time, it is comprehended thus only as a result, an end. It is already that which presupposes itself and is likewise the result; it exists only as end and as precisely this self-distinction. The truth is this adequacy of being, this object- and subject-being. That Spirit is itself the object makes it the reality, the concept, the Idea--and this is the truth.

Likewise, this is the religion of freedom. Like truth, freedom, abstractly conceived, is the relation to something objective without its being alien; the only difference is that in the case of freedom the negation of the difference, of otherness, is brought into greater prominence. This appears in the form of *reconciliation*. At the outset, the distinctions stand over against each other: God, who confronts a world estranged from him; the world, which is estranged from its essence. Reconciliation is the negation of this separation and division; it means that each recognizes itself in the other,

finds itself and its essence. Reconciliation, consequently, is freedom and is not something quiescent; rather
it is activity, the movement that makes the estrangement
disappear. All of these qualities--reconciliation, truth,
freedom--describe a universal process, and thus cannot be
expressed in a simple proposition except onesidedly. A
determinate form is to be found in the fact that, as we
said earlier, in any religion the representation of the
unity of the divine and the human comes to the fore.
This unity requires, however, more precise definition.
God has become man; this is, accordingly, a revelation.
This unity, however, is only the in-itself, but as such
it is the movement that eternally brings itself forth.
This bringing-forth means liberation and reconciliation,
which is only possible through the in-itself. *Substance*
identical with itself is this unity, which as such is the
foundation; but as *subjectivity* it is that which brings
forth. We may view this as the concept of this religion.

The result of the whole of philosophy is that only
this is the Idea of absolute truth. In its pure form it
is the logical result, but it is likewise the result of
viewing the concrete world. The truth consists in this:
that nature, life, Spirit are thoroughly organic, that
everything [37] which exists for itself, everything
which is distinguished, is itself only the mirror image
of this Idea, such that the Idea presents itself in it as
something isolated, as a process in it, and thus it manifests this unity in itself.

[23]The general relation [of the Christian Religion]
to the preceding religions has been expounded from the
beginning [of these Lectures] and follows from what has
been said. The religion of nature is religion from the
standpoint of *consciousness* alone. In the Absolute Religion, this standpoint is also found, but it exists
within it only as a transitory moment. In nature religion, God is an other, represented in a natural form,
such as sun, air, mountain, or river. The latter are de-

fined as something other, or to put it otherwise, religion appears only in the form of consciousness. The
second form was spiritual religion, the religion of
Spirit that remains finitely determined; in this respect
it is the religion of *self-consciousness*, namely of absolute power, of necessity. The One, the power, is something defective because it is only abstract power; in
regard to its content, it is not absolute subjectivity.
The One, which is absolute power and only in the abstract sense wisdom, is not yet Spirit because it is only
abstract necessity, abstract presence-to-itself. The abstraction constitutes its finitude, and it is the particular powers and gods, defined according to their spiritual
content, that first constitute a totality. The third
form, to which we are now proceeding, is the religion of
the *freedom* of self-consciousness, or of the consciousness that exists within itself and likewise is the objectivity of Spirit for itself. This objectivity of
Spirit for itself is the determination of consciousness,
and freedom is the determination of self-consciousness.[a]

Section 3. *The Positivity and Spirituality of the Revelatory Religion*[24]

[19] [b]The Consummate Religion has as its object what
it actually itself is, namely, the consciousness of essence; thereby, it is objectified. It exists as and only
as its--or our--original concept. This Absolute Religion
is the Revelatory [*offenbar*] Religion, the religion having itself as its content and fulfillment. But it is
also called the *Revealed* [*geoffenbart*] Religion--meaning
thereby, on the one hand, that it is revealed by God,
that God has revealed himself in it; and on the other hand,
that it is a *positive* religion in the sense that it has
come to humanity from without, has been given to it. In
view of the peculiar meaning that attaches to the notion

of the positive, it is interesting to see what positivity
is.

The Absolute Religion is, of course, a positive religion in the sense that everything that exists for consciousness is objective to consciousness. *Everything
must come to us in external fashion.* The sensible is
for this reason something positive. Above all, there is
nothing so positive as what we have before us in immediate perception. Everything spiritual comes to us in
this fashion, whether it be the spiritual in general or
the spiritual in finite or historic form. This mode of
external spirituality, and Spirit expressing itself outwardly, are likewise positive. The ethical realm, the
laws of freedom, represent a higher, purer spirituality;
[20] the ethical by nature has nothing externally spiritual about it; it is not external and contingent but belongs to the nature of pure Spirit itself. But even the
ethical has the character of coming to us externally,
chiefly in the form of education, instruction, doctrine:
it is simply given to us as something having validity.
Laws--e.g., civil laws, laws of the state--are likewise
something positive: they come to us and exist for us as
valid; it is not the case that we can leave them behind
or pass them by, but rather that they, in their externality, have an essential, subjectively binding power even
for us subjectively. When we grasp or recognize the law,
when we find it rational that crime should be punished,
this is not because law is positive but rather because it
has an essential character for us. It is not simply
valid for us externally or because it exists; rather it
is also valid for us internally, it is rationally valid
as something essential, because it also is itself internal and rational. Positivity detracts not at all from
its character as rational and therefore as something that
is our own. The laws of freedom always have a positive
side, a side marked by reality, externality, contingency
in their appearance. Laws must be determinate. Already

in the character and quality of punishment externality
enters in, even more so in the quantity of punishment.
Positivity cannot be omitted from punishment; it is
wholly necessary--this final determination of immediacy.
This immediacy is something positive, i.e., not at all
rational in and for itself. For example, in the case of
punishment round numbers determine the amount of the
fine; it is not possible to determine by reason what the
absolutely just penalty is. Whatever is *by nature* positive is also irrational. It must be determinate, and is
defined in such a way that it contains nothing[25] rational in it.

This aspect is also a necessary part of the Revelatory Religion. Since in it historic, externally appearing elements are found, there also occur in it positive
and contingent events, which may take one form or another. Because of the externality and appearance that
are posited along with revelation, the positive is always present. However, we must distinguish between the
positive as such, the abstract positive, and [the positive in the form of] rational law. The law of freedom is
not valid simply because it exists but rather because it
is the determination of our rationality itself. When we
are conscious of it in this way, then it is not something
that is merely positive or externally [21] valid. Religion also appears as positive in all that comprises its
doctrines. But it should not remain in this form; it
should not be the subject of mere representation or of
bare remembrance.

The second aspect of positivity is connected with the
confirmation of religion, namely, that what is external
should attest to the truth of a religion, and should be
regarded as the foundation of its truth. At one time
confirmation took the form of the positive as such--
namely, *miracles*, which are supposed to confirm the fact
that this individual has given specific doctrines.

Miracles are alterations in the sensible world that are
capable of being perceived, and this perception itself is
sensible because it consists in a sensible alteration.
In regard to this form of positivity, it has already been
remarked that it certainly can bring about a kind of confirmation for the sensible person. But that is only the
beginning of confirmation, an unspiritual confirmation,
by which precisely what is spiritual cannot be confirmed.
The spiritual as such cannot be directly confirmed by the
unspiritual, the sensible. The chief thing in this aspect of miracles is that they are in this fashion actually put aside. For on the one hand the *understanding*[26] can attempt to explain miracles naturally, or it
can bring many plausible arguments to bear upon them; but
this means to confine one's attention to the external,
event-like character of miracles and to direct one's arguments to this aspect. The main point of view of *reason*[26]
in respect to miracles, on the other hand, is that what
is spiritual cannot be externally confirmed. For the
spiritual is higher than the external; it can be confirmed only within and through itself; it is verified
only in and through itself. This is what can be called
the witness of the Spirit.

This has found expression in the history of religion.
Moses performs miracles before Pharaoh, the Egyptian magi-
cians imitate him, which is to say that no great value is
placed on miracles. The principal point, however, is
that Christ reviles the Pharisees, who demanded such signs
of him, saying: After my resurrection many will come,
doing miracles in my name--and I have never known them
[cf. Matt. 7:22-23]. Here Christ himself rejects [22]
miracles as a true criterion of truth. This is the essential point, and we must hold fast to the principle that
confirmation by miracles, as well as the attack on miracles, belong to a lower sphere that concerns us not at
all.

The witness of the Spirit is the true witness. This

witness may take many forms. It can be whatever accords
with Spirit in an indeterminate, general way, whatever
awakens a deeper harmony or is brought forth from within.
In history, all that is noble, lofty, and divine speaks
to us internally; to it our Spirit bears witness. This
witness may remain nothing more than this general harmony, this inner agreement, this empathy and sympathy.
But beyond this, the witness of the Spirit may also be
connected with insight and thought. In so far as this
insight is not sensible in character, it belongs directly to thought; it appears in the form of reasons,
distinctions, etc., in the form of mental activity, ex-
ercised along with and according to the specific forms of
thought, the categories. This thinking may appear in
more or less mature forms; it may serve as the presupposition of one's heart or of one's spiritual life in
general--the presupposition of universal principles,
which are acknowledged to be valid and which direct the
life of a man, serving as his maxims. These need not be
conscious maxims, but they are the means by which the
character of a man is formed, the universal that has obtained a firm foothold in his Spirit. This is a permanent
element in his Spirit and governs him. On such firm
foundations, on such presuppositions, on such ethical
principles, the powers of reasoning and defining are able
to begin. In this respect the levels of development and
ways of life of men vary considerably, just as their
needs do. However, the highest need of the human Spirit
is to be able to think in such a way that the witness of
the Spirit exists not merely in the harmonious mode of
sympathy, nor in such a way as to provide firm foundations on which views may be established and firm presuppositions from which conclusions can be drawn and deduc-
tions made. The witness of Spirit in its highest form is
that of philosophy, according to which the concept develops the truth purely as such from itself without presuppositions; in and through this development, which it

recognizes, it perceives the necessity of truth.

Faith and thought have often been opposed in such fashion [23] that it is said: one can have an awareness of God, of the truths of religion, in no other way than that of thought. Hence some are convinced that proofs for the existence of God are the only means of knowing the truth. However, the witness of the Spirit can occur in manifold and various ways; it is not to be expected that for all of humanity the truth is made manifest in a philosophical way. The needs of human beings are different in accord with their education and their free spiritual development; among these differences, in accord with the stage of development, is that standpoint we call trust or belief on the basis of *authority*. Miracles have their place here, but it is interesting to note that miracles have been reduced to a minimum--namely, to those of which the Bible speaks.

In general, however, there is still something positive in these various forms of the witness of the Spirit. That sympathy of which we have spoken earlier--the feeling with which one cries out, "Yes, that is the truth"-- is so immediate and secure a form of certainty that it is indeed something positive, having precisely the immediacy characteristic of the positive. One ought to bear in mind, however, that only human beings have religion. Religion has its seat and soil in the activity of thinking. The heart and feeling, which directly experience the truth of religion, are not the heart and feeling of an animal but of a thinking human being; they are a thinking heart and a thinking feeling, and whatever of religion is found in this heart and feeling is a thought of this heart and feeling. Likewise, in any process of reasoning, which (as we have remarked earlier) has a firm foundation and presupposition, the foundation is something positive, posited, given. Ratiocination has a foundation that it has not itself investigated, that has not been brought into conceptual clarity. Surely, however, in so far as we

begin to draw conclusions, to reason, to give grounds, to
advance to the categories of thought, we do this always
by means of thinking.

Since the doctrines of the Christian Religion are
set forth in the Bible, they are thus given in a positive
fashion; and if they are subjectively appropriated, if
the Spirit gives witness to them, this happens in an entirely immediate fashion, [24] the innermost being of a
person, his Spirit, his thought, his reason being
touched by them and assenting to them. Thus for the
Christian the Bible is the basis, the fundamental basis,
which has this effect on him, which strikes a chord within him, and gives firmness to his convictions. Beyond
this, however, a man, because he is able to think, does
not remain in the immediacy of assent and testimony, but
moves beyond them into the realm of thoughts, meditations,
reflections. These thoughts and reflections result in a
developed religion; in its most highly developed form it
is *theology* or scientific religion, whose content, as the
witness of the Spirit, is also known in scientific fashion.

But perhaps the opposing thesis will be advanced by
the theologians who say that one ought merely to hold to
the Bible. In one respect, this is an entirely valid
principle. For there are in fact many people who are
very religious and hold merely to the Bible, do nothing
else than read the Bible, quote passages from it, and
lead thereby a very pious, religious life. But theologians they are not; such a practice has nothing of a
scientific, theological character.[27] As soon, however,
as religion is no longer merely the reading and repetition of passages, as soon as what is called explanation
or interpretation begins, as soon as an attempt is made
by inference and exegesis to find out the *meaning* of the
words in the Bible, then one enters into the process of
reasoning, reflection, thinking; and the question then
becomes how one exercises this process of thinking, and

whether one's thinking is correct or not. It helps not
at all to say that one's thoughts are based on the Bible.
As soon as these thoughts are no longer merely the words
of the Bible, there is given to their content a form,
more specifically, a logical form. Or certain presuppositions are made by this content, and with these one enters into the process of interpretation. These presuppositions are the permanent element in interpretation; one
brings along certain notions [*Vorstellungen*], which
guide the interpretation.

The interpretation of the Bible exhibits its content,
however, in the form of a particular age; the first interpretations in the early period of the church were
wholly different from contemporary ones. Among the presuppositions that one brings to the Bible today belong,
e.g., the notions [25] that man by nature is good or
that God cannot be known. Imagine how someone with these
prejudices in mind must distort the Bible! People bring
these prejudices to the Bible, although the meaning of
the Christian Religion is precisely to know God: it is
the religion in which God has revealed himself, has said
what he is. Thus here again the positive may appear in
another form: people bring along certain propositions
concerning how man has the feeling of being created thus
and so. Thus it becomes a question whether this content,
these notions and propositions, are true; and this is no
longer the Bible, these are rather the words that Spirit
comprehends internally. If Spirit gives expression to
them, then this is already a form given by Spirit, the
form of thinking. The form that one gives to this content is to be investigated. Here again the positive
enters in, having the meaning presupposed, for example,
by the formal logic of syllogism, namely, finite relations of thought. In terms of ordinary syllogistic relations, only the finite can be grasped and known, only the
intelligible. This way of thinking is not adequate to a
divine content; the latter will be ruined by it. The-

ology, in so far as it is not a mere rehearsal of the
Bible but goes beyond the words of the Bible and concerns
itself with what exists internally for feeling, utilizes
forms of thinking, engages in thinking. If it uses these
forms haphazardly, merely as presuppositions and prejudices, its thinking becomes contingent and arbitrary.
However, the investigation of these forms of thought falls
to philosophy alone. Theology, when it turns against philosophy, either is unaware of the fact that it uses such
forms, that it thinks, and that it is a question of proceeding in accord with thought, or it fosters a deception;
it reserves for itself the right to think as it chooses,
knowing, however, that this arbitrary knowledge damages
our knowledge of the true nature of Spirit. This contingent, favored way of thinking represents the positive
element that is found here. Only the concept *for itself*
liberates itself truly and thoroughly from the positive.
In philosophy and in religion, freedom in its highest
form consists in the process of thinking itself and as
such.

Doctrine itself, its content, also takes on the form
of the positive, as noted above; it is valid, it is
firmly established, it simply exists and is acknowledged
by everyone. Everything rational, the whole of law, [26]
has this form. However, only its *form* is positive; its
content must be that of Spirit. The Bible has this form
of positivity, yet according to one of its own sayings,
"the letter kills, but the Spirit gives life" [2 Cor. 3:6].
The question, then, is what kind of Spirit is brought into
connection with the letter, which Spirit gives life to the
positive? We must know that we bring with us a concrete
Spirit, a thinking, reflecting, feeling Spirit; we must
be conscious of this Spirit, which is at work, comprehending the content. This comprehension is not a passive ac-
ceptance, but since it is Spirit that comprehends, it is
at the same time its activity. Only in the mechanical
sphere does one of the sides remain passive in the process

of reception. Spirit, therefore, plays a role in the
positive realm; it has its images and concepts, its essence is logical, its activity is one of thinking--an activity that Spirit must recognize.

Thought in this form can now pass into one or another of the categories of finitude. It is, however,
Spirit that begins in this fashion from the positive but
itself exists essentially alongside it. It is the true,
just, and holy Spirit that comprehends the divine and
knows its content to be divine. This is the witness of
the Spirit, which, as we have shown above, may be more or
less developed. In regard to positivity, the main point
is that Spirit should conduct itself in a thinking fashion and its activity be found in the categories or determinations of thought; here Spirit is purely active, per-
ceptive, rational. Most people are unaware of the fact
that Spirit is also active in the midst of receptivity.
Many theologians, because they work exegetically and (so
they believe) in a passively receptive way, do not know
that they are thereby active and reflective. If thinking
is merely contingent, it abandons itself to the categories
of finite content, of finitude, of finite thinking, and is
incapable of comprehending the divine content; it is not
the divine but the finite Spirit that moves in such categories. As a result of such a finite comprehension of the
divine or of what exists in and for itself, as a result of
this finite thinking of the absolute content, the fundamental doctrines of Christianity have for the most part
disappeared from dogmatics. Not alone, but still pre-
eminently, it is now philosophy that is essentially orthodox; [27] the propositions that have always been valid,
the basic truths of Christianity, are maintained and preserved by it.

Since we are now going to consider this religion, we
shall not set to work in *historical* fashion, which would
entail starting with external matters, but rather we
shall proceed *conceptually*.[28] That form of activity that

begins with externals appears to be capable of comprehension only on one side, while on the other it remains
merely activity. Here we connect activity essentially
as such with the consciousness of thinking related to itself, related to the course of the categories of thought
--a thinking that has tested and acknowledged itself, that
knows how it thinks and which are the finite and which the
true categories of thought. For purposes of education or
instruction, it is appropriate that we should start from
the side of positivity; but in so far as we now proceed
scientifically, we put this aside.[b]

Section 4. Transition to the Revelatory Religion[29]

[6] [b]This is the point at which to survey our previous course and to discuss the relation of this course to
the final stage of religion; here for the first time we
are able to comprehend the course as a whole and its meaning. We refer back to what has already been said. Religion is Spirit as consciousness of its essence. On the
one hand, there is a Spirit that is the Spirit of differentiation; the other Spirit is Spirit as essence, as
true, non-finite Spirit. This separation, diremption,
distinction, which resides in the concept of Spirit, is
what we have called the elevation of Spirit from finite
to [7] infinite. Just as Spirit defines itself as finite,
it defines itself vis-à-vis Spirit as infinite. This elevation appears metaphysically in the proofs for the existence of God. Finite Spirit makes infinite Spirit its
object, knows it as its own essence. If we allow ourselves to speak this way, the word "finite" becomes an
indefinite, abstract word, in turn making the word "infinite" also indefinite; Spirit, then, though it must be
something infinitely definite, is shown to be only inde-
finite--indeed, not only indefinite but also onesided.
One must be clear about these logical definitions of

"finite" and "infinite." When we say "infinite Spirit,"
the word "infinite" itself is understood in a onesided way
because it has the finite over against it. In order not
to be onesided, Spirit must encompass finitude within itself, and finitude in general means nothing other than a
process of self-distinguishing. Consciousness is precisely the mode of finitude of Spirit: here is distinction. One thing is on one side, another on the other
side; something has its limit or end in something else.
Finitude is this distinguishing, which in Spirit takes the
form of consciousness. Spirit must have consciousness,
distinction, otherwise it is not Spirit; accordingly, this
is the moment of finitude in it. It must have this character of finitude within itself--that may seem blasphe-
mous. But if it did not have it within itself, and if it
confronted finitude from another side, then its infinitude would be a bad infinitude. When one views the character of finitude as something contradictory to God, then
one takes the finite as something fixed, autonomous--not
as something transitional, but rather as something essentially autonomous, which remains an absolute limitation. The finite is not, however, the absolute. Neither
are finite things absolute, nor is the absolute the logical or conceptual definition of finitude; rather the definition of the latter is precisely not to be true in itself. If God only had the finite over against himself,
then he himself would be finite and limited. Finitude
must be posited in God himself, not as something insurmountable, absolute, autonomous, but above all as this
process of distinguishing that we have in Spirit and in
consciousness--a distinguishing which, because it is a
transitory [8] moment and because finitude is no truth,
is also to be eternally sublated. Infinite Spirit is
posited in a onesided abstraction when we say that the
finite elevates itself to the infinite. The finite is
here taken just as indefinitely as infinitude. There is
something missing here; this abstraction of the infinite

is to be sublated, and just as much the abstraction of
the finite, in which we initially perceive abstract infinitude. The contemplation of finitude is what gives us
development, further determination.

We began with the *concept of religion*.[30] Religion
is Spirit related to itself and thus to its essence, to
true Spirit, with which it is reconciled, finding itself
in it. Because this concept of religion is *only* a concept, it is finite; it is not yet the Idea, the realization, the actualization of the concept. It is the truth
in itself, not yet *for itself*; but the essence of Spirit
is to be for itself what it is in itself or what its concept is. Since, therefore, finitude is so defined that
this being-in-itself is only Spirit in its concept or religion in its concept, any advance appears to entail the
sublation of the onesidedness, deficiency, and abstraction of the concept, whether it be conceived as finitude
or as abstract infinitude. Our advance had, accordingly,
the signification of annulling this definition, this abstraction. The second step is this: whatever is conceptual to begin with--i.e., merely conceptual or subjective in the sense that it has the content only in it-
self--is at the same time the first or immediate. Whatever exists only in itself, according to its concept, is
in its existence at first only immediate, and immediacy,
accordingly, is the finitude that is first beheld by us.

This course we have taken. First we considered the
concept of Spirit or of religion. But this being-in-
itself or the concept merely as such is nothing other
than the immediate modality of the concept, immediate
being, and this we found in *the natural*.[31] The natural
is what immediate being is; finitude is immediate being.
Spirit in its immediate being is empirical consciousness,
immediate self-consciousness, which views itself as essence, knows itself as the power of nature. This immediate Spirit is indeed fulfilled, determinate in itself,
concrete, but it is only empirically concrete. For the

content [9] by which it is filled is the content of desires, instincts, passions; and this first fulfillment is
the fulfillment of Spirit's merely natural state. This
constitutes the finitude of Spirit, its natural, empirical self-consciousness. Spirit is fulfilled, but empirically, not yet by its concept; to accomplish the latter
it must become *for* itself what it is *in* itself, it must
arrive at its concept. This progression is logical: it
lies in the nature of determination thus to determine itself further--this is logical necessity.

The further form of this finitude we have also seen.
This finitude, which is unmediated being, can also be defined as the singular being of immediate, finite Spirit
with itself, or as Spirit that has not yet arrived at the
separation by which this natural state and desire are distinguished from itself, and therefore does not yet exist
within itself, has not yet attained the determination of
freedom. In order to be free, Spirit must remove the immediate, natural, empirical, withdrawing from it. The
next step, therefore, is the distinction, the withdrawal
into itself of Spirit from its submersion in the natural.
We have seen various forms of this.[32] The outstanding
example is the religion of India--this being-in-itself,
Brahma, pure self-consciousness, this separation by means
of which the being-within-itself of pure self-consciousness is posited in abstraction from everything concrete
and natural and from all desire and imagery. But this
separation is at the same time abstract: this way of
thinking is on the one hand merely empty, on the other
hand an immediate self-consciousness that has not yet
distinguished itself from itself, has no object, and is
nothing other than subjective, abstract knowledge. From
this recognition emerges a first form of unity or reconciliation, namely, that this interiority is filled by externality, that it shows itself no longer as an abstraction but as something concrete, that it takes this externality into itself, showing itself above all as power.

This is the unrefined condition wherein the internal has
only the meaning of something external that remains wholly
in a state of nature.

The second stage was the beginning of a *spiritual religion*,[33] namely, a religion of entry-into-self, a religion of the freedom of Spirit, for which the natural
(which was the previous fulfillment) is not an autonomous
content, constituting a fulfillment in unmediated [10]
fashion, but rather is merely the appearance of something
interior, which is ethical in character and has rational
interiority as its determination. This interiority is so
concrete within itself, therefore, that concreteness belongs to it; it constitutes its own determinateness or
nature; it is the ethical. The natural indeed is part of
its manifestation, its appearance; but this concrete interiority, the ethical, is not yet posited as subjectivity within itself. Thus this finitude succeeds in distinguishing the ethical into particular moral powers; it
is only a collection of these powers with a particular
content--an encompassing totality, to be sure, and therefore complete, but it is not subjectivity.

The other mode of finitude is that the appearance
still has a sensible form; Spirit exists as a sensible
thing. One can make light of the fact that its particularity has not been taken up into absolute harmony or
unity. In this second sphere of entry-into-self we have
observed, in contrast to the Religion of Beauty,[34] that
the Religion of Sublimity[35] is fulfilled in spirituality
such that these particularities, these moral powers, are
brought together in a purpose by means of which the One
Spirit is defined as existing within itself, as wise.
Here, therefore, we have Spirit in its freedom, at once
concrete and determinate in itself; this means that it
exists as the Wise One. This Spirit first merits for us
the name of God. Spirit thus has an end within itself,
it is determinate within itself. But the content of its
subjectivity, its infinite determination, its inner con-

tent known as purpose, is still abstract.

The third stage[36] is the one at which purposes or
ends obtain a comprehensive, universal content, but first
of all in the world in external fashion. Wisdom is an
end, but in the form of abstraction. This end develops,
hence its mode is one of externality. [Here we find] a
purpose in the world, a unity, but still an abstract
unity, which even in this reality is only abstract because it has the form of domination. Ends, therefore,
take the form of subjectivity possessing comprehensive
reality, but in such fashion that the subject, while comprehensive, is only finite.

The transition [to the Revelatory Religion] consists
of Spirit entering into itself; it is the concept that
has only itself as an end--this self-existent mode whose
end is only itself, is God himself. [11] The Idea has
only itself as an end; and now this concept is purified
in order to have a more comprehensive end, yet an end
taken back into subjectivity. Spirit now has as its end
or purpose its concept, its concrete essence itself; its
end is eternally realized, objectified, and free--indeed
is freedom itself because this end is its own nature.
Thereby finitude is sublated. This progression has the
more exact character of containing that which determines
itself within itself, the determinateness of Spirit. It
is comprised by the Spirit that shows itself as posited
within itself. Spirit is precisely that which determines
itself infinitely. The series of forms that we have
passed through is, to be sure, a series of stages following one upon the other; but these forms are encompassed
in the infinite, absolute form, in absolute subjectivity,
and the Spirit so defined as absolute subjectivity *is*
Spirit.

We have seen on the one hand a stripping off of
these determinations, these modes of finitude and of
finite forms; but on the other hand Spirit, which is the
concept itself, so determines itself that the concept

must first move through these forms in order to be Spirit.
Only when this content has moved through these forms is
it Spirit. Spirit is essence--but only in so far as it
goes out from itself and turns back to itself, only in so
far as it is that which turns back and is present to itself, that which posits itself from itself as present to
itself. This positing produces the distinctive determinations of its activity, and these distinctive determinations are the forms through which Spirit has to move.

We have said that Spirit is immediate. This is a
mode of finitude. All the same, it is Spirit, the concept, that determines itself. The first of its determinate forms is that of self-diremption and of immediate
existence according to this form of finitude. The concept determines itself, posits itself as immediate; that
concept for which Spirit so determines itself, posits itself as immediate, we ourselves still are. The last form,
however, is that this concept, this subjectivity for
which Spirit exists, is not to remain something external
to Spirit, but rather is itself to be absolute and infinite subjectivity, infinite form. The infinite form is
the circuit of this determining process; the concept is
Spirit only because it [12] has achieved determinacy
through this circuit, has moved through it. In this
fashion it first becomes concrete. This means on the one
hand a stripping off of the modes of finitude, on the
other hand a self-diremption and a return to self from
diremption; only so is it posited as Spirit. At first
Spirit is only a presupposition; that it exists as Spirit
and is comprehended as Spirit is nothing immediate and
cannot happen in immediate fashion. It is Spirit only as
that which dirempts itself and turns back to itself by
moving through this circuit. What we have moved through
in our reflections is the becoming, the bringing forth of
Spirit by itself, and as such, eternally bringing itself
forth, is it Spirit. This course is, therefore, the comprehension or grasping of Spirit. It is the concept that

determines itself and takes these determinations back into itself, the concept. The absolute objectification of
Spirit consists precisely in the fact that the concept
determines itself and is fulfilled by its self-conception.
The circuit of these forms is the process of self-positing by the concept. These forms, gathered together in a
unity, are the concept. The result is the concept that
posits itself, has itself as its content. This, then, is
the absolute Idea. The Idea is the unity of concept and
reality, of concept and objectivity. Truth consists in
the adequacy of objectivity to the concept, but what is
adequate to the concept is only the concept itself in so
far as it has itself as its object. The content as Idea
is the truth.

Freedom is one aspect of the Idea: the concept, because it is present to itself conceptually, is free. The
Idea is the truth, but precisely so is it freedom. The
Idea is the truth, and the truth is absolute Spirit.
This is the true definition of Spirit. The concept that
has determined itself, has made itself its own object,
has posited finitude in itself, has fulfilled its finitude with itself, and precisely thereby has sublated its
finitude--that is Spirit.

[13] The task of philosophy is to cognize what God,
the absolute truth, is. The customary, usual procedure
is, apart from proofs for the existence of God, to assert
this and that about God and to define him by means of
predicates. His attributes tell us what he is, render
him determinate. We are accustomed to say of God that
he is the Creator of the world, all-just, all-knowing,
all-wise.

But this is not the true way of cognizing what the
truth, what God, is; it is the way of *representation*, of
understanding.[37] It is also necessary, of course, to define the concept by predicates, but this is a reflected,
incomplete way of thinking, not thinking by means of the
concept, thinking the concept of God, the Idea. Predi-

cates signify particular determinations; attributes are
particular determinations distinguished from one another.
If one thinks of these differences determinately, they
fall into contradiction with each other, and this contradiction cannot be resolved. One tries to resolve it
solely through abstraction by allowing the attributes to
temper each other mutually or by abstracting from their
particularity. The outcome is that in this fashion God,
because he is thus defined by predicates, is not grasped
as living. This is another way of making our earlier
point, that the contradictions are not resolved, or at
best only abstractly so. The vitality of God or of Spirit
is nothing other than to determine himself (which also
can appear as a predicate), to posit himself in finitude,
distinction, contradiction, but at the same time eternally
to sublate this contradiction. This is the life, the
deed, the activity of God; he is absolute activity, actuality, and his activity is eternally to reconcile the
contradiction: this is he himself. Definition by predicates is in this respect incomplete, for they are only
particular determinations whose contradiction is not resolved. They represent God as though he himself were not
the resolution of these contradictions, as though he himself were not the one who resolves them. It would appear,
then, that it is only our human particularity that [14]
comprehends specific, distinguishable aspects in him, and
that these characteristics are much rather merely our own.
But the particularity belongs not merely to our reflection; rather it is the nature of God, of Spirit, it is
his concept itself. Just so, however, he is the one who
resolves the contradiction--not by abstraction but in
concrete fashion. This is, then, the living God. The
vitality of God signifies that the particularities in him
and their resolution are not merely an external aspect
and are not grasped merely from our side.[b]

Section 5. *Division of the Subject*[38]

[28] [b]Since we have now indicated the place of the
preceding in relation to the Idea of God itself--namely,
that it is the concept itself that constitutes these dis- .
tinctions, thereby attaining to itself, becoming for the
first time Idea--we are thus able to view the Idea in its
development and completion. Turning first to the *division of the subject*, we find the following distinctions,
based on God as the absolute Idea:

(1) First, God is the absolute Idea for us in the
mode of *thought* or *thinking*. This content, in so far as
it exists for thought, for the ground of thinking, can
and must also be grasped in the mode of representation.
Since the eternal Idea exists for the thinking of the
whole of humanity, which transpires outside the philosophical realm and transposes itself into the form of [ordi-
nary] thinking, this thinking must also take the form of
representation. The Idea of God is first to be considered as it exists for thinking or in itself. This is *the
eternal Idea of God for itself*, what God is for himself,
i.e., the eternal Idea based on thinking in general.

(2) Second, God is the Idea, not for us in the mode
of thinking, but rather for finite, external, empirical
Spirit, for sensible perception, *for representation*. The
mode of existence that he gives himself for the sake of
representation is, in the first instance, nature; and
therefore one of the ways God exists for representation
is that finite, empirical Spirit should recognize God in
nature. The other way, however, is that he should exist
as finite Spirit for finite Spirit. Thus, finite, concrete Spirit is itself necessarily involved in the process by which God exists for it, is revealed to it. To
be more precise, God as such cannot actually exist for
Spirit as finite; rather, the basis of his being for
finite Spirit lies in the fact that the latter does not
hold fast to its finitude as something existent, but

rather is just this, its own reconciliation with God. As
finite [29] Spirit it is placed in a condition of separation, fall from God, existence outside of God; since it
is still related to God in this existence outside of him,
the contradictory character of its estrangement and separation from God is made evident. The concrete Spirit,
defined finitely as finite, exists therefore in contradiction to its object or content, and here above all the
need is found to sublate this contradiction and separation, which appears in finite Spirit as such--the need,
in other words, for reconciliation. This need supplies
the starting point, and the next step in the advance is
that God exists *for* finite Spirit: the latter arrives at
the knowledge and certainty of the divine content, which
is represented imaginatively to it--to the imagining
Spirit, Spirit in finite, empirical form. This can only
happen in so far as Spirit indeed appears to it, but in
external fashion, and in so far as it brings to consciousness in external fashion what God is.

(3) Thus we have God, first, in the sphere of thinking in general; secondly, we have him in the form of representation. Thirdly, God is present, one may say, for
feeling or *experience*, for subjectivity and in the subjectivity of Spirit, in the innermost being of subjective
Spirit. Here reconciliation or the sublation of that
separation has been made actual; here *God as Spirit exists in his community*--the community that has been liberated from that antithesis or opposition. Consciousness
and certainty now have their freedom in God.

These are the three ways by which the subject is related to God, the three modes of the existence of God for
subjective Spirit. Since it is *we* who made this distinction, we have arrived at it more or less empirically; the
distinction has been received by us empirically. We know
from our Spirit that first of all we are able to think
without this opposition or estrangement in us, that
secondly we are finite Spirit, Spirit in its estrangement

and separation, and that thirdly we are Spirit in the
state of feeling or subjectivity, of return to itself, of
reconciliation, of innermost feeling. Of these three,
the first is the ground of universality; the second, of
particularity; the third, of individuality.[39] These three
grounds are a presupposition that we have taken up as our
definition. They are not to be viewed, however, as
several different grounds existing externally [30] or as
externally existing modes vis-à-vis God; rather it is the
Idea itself that constitutes this distinction.[40] The
absolute, eternal Idea is:

(1) First, in and for itself, God in his eternity
before the creation of the world and outside the world.

(2) Secondly, God creates the world and posits the
separation. He creates both nature and finite Spirit.
What is created or exists as other-being divides of itself
into two sides--physical nature and finite Spirit. What
is thus created is at first an other, posited outside of
God. But God's essential character is to reconcile to
himself the alien, the particular, that which is posited
in separation from him, and to restore what has fallen,
just as the Idea has dirempted itself, fallen away from
itself, and brings itself back to its true condition.
This is the way, the process of reconciliation.

(3) In the third place, through this process of
reconciliation, Spirit has reconciled with itself what it
differentiated from itself in its act of diremption and
judgment, and thus it becomes the Holy Spirit, the Spirit
present in its community.

These are not external distinctions, which *we* have
made merely in accord with what we are; rather they are
the activity, the developed vitality, of absolute Spirit
itself. Its eternal life entails a development and a return of this development into itself; this vitality in
development, this actualization of the concept, we have
now to consider.[b]

_w41
We have, speaking generally, to consider the Idea
as divine self-revelation, and this revelation is to be
taken in the sense indicated by the three determinations
just mentioned.

According to the first of these, God exists in pure
form for finite Spirit only as thinking. This is the
theoretical consciousness in which the thinking subject
exists in a condition of absolute composure and is not
yet posited in this relation itself, not yet posited in
the process, but exists in the absolutely unmoved calm
of thinking Spirit. Here God exists for thought, and
this is so in the simple conclusion that he brings himself into harmony with himself, is immediately present
to himself, by means of his differentiation--which, however, here exists only in the form of pure ideality and
has not yet reached the form of externality. This is the
first condition, which [31] exists only for the thinking
subject, which is occupied with the pure content only.
This is *the Kingdom of the Father*.

The second determination is *the Kingdom of the Son*,
in which God exists, in a general way, for representation
in the element of image. This is the moment of separation or particularization. From this second standpoint,
what in the first stage represented God's other, without,
however, being defined as such, now receives the character or determination of the other. Considered from the
first standpoint, God as the Son is not differentiated
from the Father, but is expressed merely in the mode of
feeling. In the second element, however, the Son is
characterized as the other, and thus we pass out of the
pure ideality of thinking into the realm of representation. If, according to the first determination, God
begets his only Son, here he brings forth nature. Here
the other is nature, and the differentiation comes into
its own. What is thus differentiated is nature, the
world in general, and the Spirit that is related to it,
the natural Spirit. Here what we have earlier designated

the subject comes into play as itself the content; man is involved in this content. Since man is here related to nature and is himself natural, he has the character of subject only within the sphere of religion, and consequently we have here to consider nature and man from the point of view of religion. The Son comes into the world, and this is the beginning of faith. When we speak of the coming of the Son into the world we are already using the language of faith.[42] . . . Thus what God is appears to [finite Spirit] in an empirical form. Since, however, the divine comes into view and exists for Spirit in history, the latter no longer has the character of external history; it becomes divine history, the history of the manifestation of God himself.

This constitutes the transition to *the Kingdom of the Spirit*, which contains the awareness that man is implicitly reconciled with God and that this reconciliation exists for man. The process of reconciliation itself is contained in the cultus.[w]

NOTES FOR CHAPTER I

1. The arrangement of sections in this chapter, as well as the section headings, have been changed from the Lasson edition in order to conform more precisely to the order of the introductory materials in Hegel's manuscript of 1821 and the student transcripts of the lectures for 1824 and 1827. A perfect arrangement is impossible because Hegel varied the order in each of the three years. For details see the Editor's Introduction.

2. *Werke*, 11:83-84 (ET 1:83-85); Lasson, I/1:74-76.

3. From here to the next manuscript section, Lasson interweaves passages from the 1824 and 1827 transcripts in a fashion uncharacteristic of the remainder of the work, except in one other instance (pp. 194-196).

4. See the Appendix, Commentary on Chap. I.4.

5. The Hotho notes of the 1824 lectures add the following: "Since the absolute is posited as self-knowing Spirit and since re-

ligious consciousness has this Spirit as its object, religion has become objective in relation to itself."

6. The Hotho notes add the following: "In religious consciousness the finite subject has its essence as its own object. The
finite subject is itself a moment of the infinite; the unity of the
two was the concept of religion."

7. +Infinite form: (α) content, object, Spirit -- (β) which
exists as in the self-consciousness as object, as truth.+

8. This section from the 1824 lectures is located by Lasson in
Section 2 of his chapter division.

9. *w*The universal power is the substance which--since in itself
it is quite as much subject as substance--now posits its being-in-
itself and in consequence distinguishes itself from itself, communi-
cates itself to knowledge, to finite Spirit; but in so doing, because it is a moment in its own development, it remains present to
itself, and in the dividing of itself returns undivided to itself.*w*
(12:194; ET 2:330. From the Hotho notes of the 1824 lectures.)

10. Lasson reads *geistig* ("spiritual") rather than *christlich*.
The correction is provided by Walter Jaeschke from the Griesheim
transcript.

11. This sentence is from the Hotho notes of the 1824 lectures.
The following passage in the *Werke*, 12:196-197 (ET 2:333-334), is
also from Hotho: *w*It is the right of truth that knowledge should
have in religion its absolute content. Here, however, the content is
not true but only stunted. . . .
    Religion is the knowledge that Spirit has of itself as Spirit;
when it takes the form of pure knowledge it does not know itself as
Spirit and is consequently not substantial but subjective knowledge.
The fact, however, that it is nothing more than this, and is therefore limited knowledge, is not apparent to subjectivity in its own
form, i.e., the form of knowledge; rather it is its immediate po-
tentiality which it finds, first of all, within itself, and consequently in the knowledge of itself as the absolute infinite and in
the feeling of its finitude and likewise of infinitude as a being-in-
itself beyond and above it, in contrast to its being-for-itself--a
feeling of longing after something above and beyond it that is unexplained.*w*

12. 12:191-192 (ET 2:327-328). This introductory paragraph of
the *Werke* is placed in a footnote by Lasson, but since its source is
most likely the 1831 lectures we have located it in the text.

13. Lasson erroneously reads *menschlich* ("human") rather than
unendlich. He also adds a final sentence which is not contiguous
with this paragraph, which is partially duplicated elsewhere in the
text, and which we have omitted.

14. Lasson places this section at the beginning of his Chapter II
calling it "The Revelation of God." However, in both the 1821 MS.

and the 1824 lectures it follows immediately after the materials contained in Section 1 of Chapter I and is obviously part of the Introduction, setting forth "Characteristics" (*Bestimmungen*) of the
Revelatory Religion.

15. The MS. adds as a heading: "The Character of Revelation"
(*Bestimmung, was Offenbarung ist* --).

16. [+]History of Spirit, Greek [*gr.*, possibly "grand"] and free
-- abolition of finitude -- objective, absolute freedom.
    Christian Religion wholly speculative -- can be grasped only as
speculative [in] content. -- Most sublime and only true Idea of
philosophy in the form of faith. Tertullian.
    Concept of religion -- side of reality developed.
    Witness of the Spirit --
    from the concept -- begun with the goal
    subject as infinite.
    Man -- side of consciousness -- God as reflected in Spirit --
in Spirit vis-à-vis [God] -- finite Spirits.
    (α) Content. When the time [was] fulfilled, the soil prepared,
    finitude had to [be] abolished from the side of finite
    Spirit -- on its side, the finite side; thus [it] becomes
    capable of the absolute consciousness that God reveals or
    manifests himself. Revelation means infinite form, [which
    is] revealed by God. Of course -- because God can only re-
    veal himself, it is only God who makes himself manifest, not
    an external force or understanding that could disclose him.
    (β) Object of self-consciousness. -- Exactly this likeness --
    process -- once finitude [is] forgotten, this antithesis --
    subject as free, thereby present to itself -- in Spirit, in
    its essence -- is free -- represented in Christ as this
    other -- knowledge of this determination, this subjectivity,
    is another matter. -- This knowledge is the modern asser-
    tion that religion concerns the unique, the subjective, not
    the content.
    (γ) Wholly speculative.
    Two things: (α) nature, (β) consciousness.
      Nature is not these two but only one of them, manifesting
      itself in Spirit, which is these two itself. Nature
      manifests itself.
    Two sorts of forms: (α) predicates and (β) actions, deeds.[+]

17. *Schöpfer* comes from the verb *schöpfen*, meaning literally to
draw or scoop out.

18. [+]Precisely the divinity of Spirit without antithesis (not
merely as nature or common, sensible consciousness) -- the eternal
positing sublated in the antithesis -- religiously as Spirit, as comparable to itself -- this manifest only to Spirit -- objectively as
Spirit, object in religion, at the same time as nothing other.[+]

19. [+]Certainty -- objective to itself. Truth -- concept and
reality. Spirit in Spirit: only thus Spirit.[+]

20. [+](β) infinite content.[+]

21. $^+$(γ) both together: reconciliation.$^+$

22. Lasson erroneously attributes this section to the 1827 rather than to the 1824 lecture transcripts. The correction is provided by Jaeschke.

23. Cf. Sec. 4 below.

24. We come now to the two sections that comprise the bulk of the Introduction in the 1827 lectures, following the brief remarks on the concept of the Consummate or Revelatory Religion from 1827 (above, pp. 1-3). Although Lasson notes in his appendix (II/2:238) that the "Positivity" section precedes the "Transition" section in the manuscripts, he reverses the order in his printed text because he believes it is more logical for the discussion of the transition to the Christian Religion to come at the beginning of the introductory chapter. However, it is clear upon closer inspection that the "Positivity" section in 1827 replaces the discussion of the "Characteristics" of this religion in 1821 and 1824, since "positivity" is a fundamental characteristic of Christianity as the Revealed Religion. Since the order of the 1827 lectures was determined by the order of 1824 (in 1827 Hegel used the Griesheim transcript as the basis of his lectures), it is understandable that he should first take up the matter of positivity, then turn to the question of transition, greatly expanding brief remarks at the end of the Introduction in the Griesheim transcript (above, p. 15). Thus we have restored these two sections to their proper order.

25. The Lasson edition omits "nothing" (*nichts*) (cf. *Werke*, 12: 200).

26. On the distinction between "understanding" (*Verstand*) and "reason" (*Vernunft*), see the Editor's Introduction, p. xxv.

27. ^{w}Götze, the Lutheran zealot, had a celebrated collection of Bibles; the Devil, too, quotes the Bible, but that by no means makes the theologian.^{w} (12:204; ET 2:342.)

28. This distinction is important. In what follows, Hegel offers a speculative transfiguration of Christian faith, not an historical (*historisch*) description of it. It is already being viewed and interpreted from the standpoint of the absolute philosophy. The same is true of the *Philosophy of Religion* as a whole, which accounts for its tendency to downplay historical data, which are introduced primarily as illustrative of the various conceptual determinations of religion. Hegel by no means intends to deny the positive, historic character of religion, and of the Christian Religion especially; but since his intention is to proceed *scientifically* in this work, as he says in the last sentence of the paragraph, and since scientific knowledge entails the speculative grasp of what is true, real, rational, and spiritual, merely historical details are de-emphasized.

29. This section includes Lasson's Section 1, "Logical Transition to the Absolute Religion," and the first two paragraphs of his Section 2, "Infinite and Finite Spiritual Subjectivity." The latter

section title does not correspond to any of the manuscript divisions, and we have dropped it entirely. The transition in question is not, strictly speaking, "logical." Rather it is historical in the sense of describing the process by which finite Spirit "rises" to the absolute, a process that constitutes the history of religion. The section could also be titled "Survey of Previous Developments," and that is in fact the heading used by the anonymous 1827 transcript recently discovered by Kimmerle. Both *Rückblick* ("survey") and *Übergang* ("transition") occur in the text itself. See the commentary on this section in the Appendix, especially the schema illustrating the systematic structure of the Philosophy of Religion (p. 318).

30. Part I of the *Philosophy of Religion*. Here Hegel begins a compact and somewhat obscure summary of the preceding two parts of his *Lectures*.

31. The "Religion of Nature" comprises the first of the two main divisions of Part II of the *Lectures*, "Determinate Religion." The religion of natural immediacy, or magic, represents the first and most primitive form of nature religion.

32. Hegel here turns to the second and third forms of the Religion of Nature, namely, the oriental religions of substance (Hinduism, Buddhism) and the religions of transition to free subjectivity (Persian and Egyptian religion).

33. The "Religion of Spiritual Individuality" comprises the second main division of Part II. In this paragraph Hegel summarizes the first of these religions, namely Greek religion.

34. Greek religion.

35. Jewish religion. In the 1027 lectures, the Religion of Sublimity is treated second among the religions of spiritual individuality, whereas in the other lecture series it appears first, followed by the Religion of Beauty.

36. The Religion of Expediency, or Roman religion. Literally, the religion of "conformity to an end" (*Zweck-mässigkeit*).

37. See the Editor's Introduction, p. xxv.

38. In the 1821 and 1824 lectures, the "division" is set forth not as part of the introductory materials but in relation to the development of the Idea of God (Chap. II.2). Hence Chaps. I.5 and II.2 parallel each other.

39. The distinction between universality, particularity, and individuality is based on Hegel's doctrine of the triple syllogism in Part I of the *Encyclopedia of the Philosophical Sciences* (abbreviated *Enc.* in subsequent citations), trans. W. Wallace & A. V. Miller (2nd ed.; 3 vols.; Oxford: Oxford University Press, 1970-1975), §§ 183-187. The logical Idea represents the principle of universality; Nature, the principle of particularity; and finite Spirit, the principle of individuality. Each of these in turn

mediates between the other two; together, they constitute the structure of Hegel's entire philosophical system.

40. In other words, although we first arrive at a knowledge of this distinction empirically or externally, it has its basis in the immanent trinitarian life of God. Epistemologically, we move from the economic to the immanent Trinity, but ontologically the immanent Trinity is the ground of the economic Trinity. (See Chap. II, n. 32.)

41. 12:221-223 (ET 3:4-6). Lasson places this section of the *Werke* in a footnote, questioning its originality because of its reference to the "three Kingdoms," which are nowhere explicitly described as such in the extant manuscripts, and because a segment from another context in the 1827 transcripts has been inserted into the text in the third paragraph below (Lasson, II/2:239). However, there are later references to the "Reich des Vaters" in one of the unquestioned passages from the *Werke* (p. 213), and to the "Reich des Geistes" in both the 1821 manuscript and the 1824 lectures (see n. 19, p. 299). Jaeschke judges this section of the *Werke* to be derived from the 1831 lectures, and thus we are including it in the text.

42. The *Werke* here interpolates a segment from the 1827 transcripts, which the present edition gives in its original position on pp. 35-36.

CHAPTER II

THE CONCEPT OF GOD[1]

Section 1.   The Abstract Concept of God

[37][m][2] [We have] already [developed the] concept [of
the Consummate Religion] through [our consideration of]
religion [as such]. Metaphysically, [it has] this form:
God is Spirit, God has reality. ([This] representation of
God [is] subjective. [The] transition [entails the]
elimination of subjectivity.) [God] exists in virtue of
his concept; [this is developed more fully by the] proofs
for the existence of God.[3]

   [38] Previously [we had the] transition from finite
being to infinite universality, i.e., from immediate being to being in its truth, [or from being to] concept;
now [we have the transition] from concept to being.[4]
[The] concept [is the] presupposition.[5]

   [We have seen] the definition of God as the *absolute Idea*--i.e., as *Spirit*. However, [three things may
be said about] Spirit as the absolute Idea: (α) [It ex-
ists] only as the pure, universal, infinite end. [+]The
end is the concept itself;[+] [+]for this reason the end
[is] so highly regarded.[+] [It is] the unity of concept
and reality, such that the concept in itself is the
totality, and likewise the reality. (β) This reality,
however, as previously shown, is revelation--the manifes-

tation existing for itself. Finite self-consciousness,
or what is called human nature, [stands] over against
this concept. Since we call the absolute concept the
divine nature, the Idea of Spirit is to be the unity of
divine and human nature.

[Here] humanity has arrived at this perception.

But the divine nature itself is only this, to be
absolute Spirit; hence precisely the unity of divine and
human nature is itself absolute Spirit.

(γ) However, the truth cannot be expressed in such
a proposition. The two are also different, the absolute
concept and the Idea as the absolute unity of its reality.
Spirit, therefore, is the living process by which the *implicit* unity of divine and human nature becomes *explicit*,
is brought forth. What exists *in itself* must likewise be
brought forth (goal, cultus); it will be brought forth by
and drawn into the Idea itself. Nothing is brought forth
that does not exist in itself.

[39] [6]The *abstract* determination of this Idea is the
unity of the concept and of being, and it is this abstract determination that metaphysics has in mind with
the so-called *ontological* proof of the existence of God;
it is concerned to show the unity of concept and being in
a formal way.

In making the transition in the preceding so-called
proofs from a finite being to an infinite power, necessary in and for itself, acting in accord with its ends,
[metaphysics] does not proceed by way of representation,
does not place representation at the basis of the process.
It proceeds from being, and it is concerned only with the
determination of this being; it proceeds from finite (and
therewith subjective) objectivity, and passes over to the
universality of truth. The concept is the same, for the
concept of contingent being is [the concept of] necessity,
of expediency. The concept itself is the relation of
truth and substantiality.[7]

Here, therefore, [occurs] the transition from the

concept itself to objectivity. This unity is itself presupposed [+]in and for itself[+] in the concept of God.
God is only this; there is no other concept of him. At
the point of entry into religion, this unity must be
demonstrated, it must be present. The concept is this
subjectivity or process realizing itself within itself,
giving itself objectivity; it is the goal, which is found
only in the form of otherness.

[40] Being: this abstract quality is so impoverished that it just is not worth the trouble to speak of
it; this immediate Idea is only the entirely empty moment
of the unity of the concept with itself. However, being
is very much in opposition to the concept or to representation, to fixed subjectivity. [+]That is, the antithesis is sharp because precisely at the depths at which
Spirit exists, the totality of the subject belongs within
itself; it is substantial objectivity, and therewith infinite antithesis. [The] concept appears not to need being, just as [the] soul appears not to need the body.
The appearance of the antithesis is a sign, the activity
of subjectivity existing for itself.[+] That this subjectivity is a nullity is a matter of interest for reason.
On the present level of discussion, which concerns the
concept of God, the antithesis now becomes this highest
antithesis between representation or subjectivity on the
one hand, and objectivity or being on the other. Previously, the antithesis was only between finite and infinite being, so that being was the common factor, and
the antithesis was subordinated to this generality. The
interest of reason and [the] importance of the antithesis
are first present in the totality of the two sides.

[+]The importance [concerns] how the antithesis between thinking and being [is] to be resolved. It gets
established by the experience that, because subjectivity
[as] *one* side [has] this antithesis only in subjective
fashion, [the] concept [comes] off badly: we have concept[s] in the head, hence [they have] no reality. But

only as opposed to what? Here [we encounter] real subjectivity: the empirical subject [is] the whole, from
which the concept as one of its abstract modes is separated and made into a mere "only." Man *is*: there is no
question about that. He has concepts and thoughts, but
these [are] only a few of the many things that he has;
and in contrast to his concrete nature, they are one-
sided.

In the proofs for the existence of God that we are
about to consider, this disparagement of the concept proceeds from the same comparison, which presupposes God as
content, as the most perfect being, in comparison with
which the mere *concept* of God is imperfect. Why does
God exist? Anselm answers: because God is perfect,
i.e., the unity of concept and reality. [But] why [is
the] concept of God *only* a concept? [This is the] modern question and [the] [41] answer [runs as follows]:
because man is a concrete identity, the unity of concept
and being. [From this the] conclusion [is drawn] that we
must therefore hold on to this "only." [But] on the contrary, [we must] give up the "only." [This] perfection
is unsatisfying because it [exists] not in perception
but rather in thought.[+ 8]

The metaphysical proof takes this course: [The
first step is] the concept of God, which in itself is a
possible concept. [God is] the most real essence, merely
positive, i.e., abstractly positive. [The second step is
the proposition that] being exists, [that it has] reality.
Hence, [thirdly, God too falls] under this reality.

Against this proof Kant [objected] that one could
not "unpack" being from the concept,[9] for being is something other [than] the concept. Being is not a reality,
it is not a definition or a predicate; it adds nothing to
the content of an object, therefore [is] nothing real.
To be sure, [being is a] mere [determination of] form.
[With] Anselm, the proof [runs] simply as follows: God
should be what is most perfect; if God were merely an

image, then he would not be the most perfect; for we regard
as perfect that which is not merely an image but also
achieves being. [This is] quite correct. Perfection is
presupposed; generally speaking, truth is identical with
image or concept, but also the opposite determination
comes to the fore, namely, being.[10] [This also is] quite
correct. [The] presupposition, "perfection is this unity
[of concept and being]," is present in our imagination,
[in the imagination] of all men, [and] it lies at the
basis of all philosophy. If it is permitted to make presuppositions, then surely this one can be made. [It]
contains every human signification *ut actu*, not like the
laughable logical proposition, A = A, what is, is. +The
latter cannot be denied, but in good company, i.e., within the guild, [it may be smiled at].+ Against this, the
understanding now says: concept and being are different.
Quite so: thus separated, [42] they are finite, untrue,
and it is precisely the concern of reason and of ordinary, rational human sense not to remain with the finite
and untrue, nor to take them as something absolute.[11]
+Thinking is generally objective within itself.+ Concept without objectivity is only an empty image or
opinion; being without a universal concept [disintegrates
into] externality and appearance.

　　Metaphysics has subjected the simple thoughts of
Anselm to the formality of argument, and thereby has appropriated their true meaning and content. The concept
of God [as] the most real--this content [is] the abstract
affirmation. God [is] not a concept, [however, in the
sense] that [he] might be one of several concepts, others
of which are equally as good. God is not *a* concept but
the concept: this [is] the absolute reality and ideality.
God [is] all-real, therefore the reality of being; i.e.,
being is contained in his concept. [This is] correct;
[as said] earlier, being [is] this immediate identity,
therefore a moment of the concept. However, the concept
as subjectivity [is] differentiated from being, and its

concern is precisely to annul this distinction;[12] in
other words, subjectivity is to be removed from the concept, being [is to be] exhibited in the concept [+]as a
reality, i.e., [in the] form of attributes, predicates,
as in the images of man, reason, etc. On the whole, the
concept as such is what exists, the subject of being as
its predicate.[+] We have thereby shown that the concept
[in our sense] is not what is ordinarily meant by "concept," i.e., something opposed to objective reality, something that is *not supposed* to have being in it. The concept negates its character of existing subjectively; this
character is negated, or rather, [43] the concept itself
is this dialectic [of negation and being negated]. This
condition or turn constitutes the true transition. It is
a question, then, of the negation of the subjectivity of
the concept in itself; and this is not accomplished--not
even in the case of Anselm, where at least it is appealed
to as a presupposition or absolute foundation--in such a
way that perfection or [the] truth should only be this
unity of the concept and reality.

Therefore Anselm's thought [is] wholly correct--
generally [he] radiated a healthy human understanding--
even if he [only] succeeded in isolating the representations as such. However, at the same time God himself
is precisely this unity for Anselm. This unity of subject and being is subjective, hence for him it is sense-
less to dwell on such determinations. However, this
formal process sets forth the concept of "possibility"
and others like it, such that these concepts and this
possibility are intended to remain, while the interest of
reason is precisely to sublate them.[13] *m*

[a]The *concrete* concept of this sphere is that
Spirit is *for* [44] Spirit and that it is itself Spirit
only in this way. The two sides into which Spirit differentiates itself are both Spirit, together they are the
totality, and this constitutes the reality of Spirit.

With the metaphysical concept, however, we have before us the purely *abstract* concept in its determinations or moments, without these being the totality, and without their having the just indicated concrete content. Therefore what constitutes the metaphysical concept is that the content is the pure concept; accordingly, we are expected to speak of the "mere" concept, which however is real through itself.

The pure concept is concretely the concept existing for itself, i.e., Spirit is concrete because it distinguishes itself in itself, stands over against itself as Spirit. The determination is here only the pure concept, which is self-realized, in itself real; and this perception or determination we only call reality, or what is defined as having being and existence vis-à-vis the concept; it is the abstraction of a reality. But this concept also has a content, and this content is God, but God as generally represented, the God of representation, not as Spirit developed within itself; and we shall see that this content is the concept pure and simple. In appearance, however, we have the concept of God, which is self-realized; we shall see, however, that the final thing upon which it depends is the general relation of the concept to reality, to being.

It appears that mostly we have to speak of specific concepts of God, not of the concept generally. We shall see, however, that this content "God" dissolves or submerges itself, and that it has the content of the unity of the pure concept and reality.

The metaphysical concept is the concept of God and his unity with reality. In the form of the proof of the being or existence of God, it is a question of a proof that represents this transition or mediation, namely, that being follows from the concept of God. This is called the ontological proof.

It is to be noted that with the other proofs we proceeded from finite being as representing something im-

mediate and inferred from its existence the existence of
the infinite, or true being, which appeared for us in the
form of infinitude, necessity, absolute power, which at
the same time is wisdom, positing its own ends.[14] Here,
on the contrary, we have proceeded from the [45] concept
and arrived at being. Both ways are necessary, and it is
necessary to point out their unity, to proceed from one
as well as the other, for the identity of the two is the
truth. Both the concept on the one hand and being, the
world, the finite, on the other are onesided qualities,
and only in the Idea is their truth to be found; i.e.,
both exist as posited. Neither of the two should have
the character of remaining only a beginning or origin,
but rather each should present itself as passing over into the other; i.e., each must be posited. Both present
themselves as moments, and this must be pointed out.
This transition has two opposite meanings. Each is portrayed as a moment, i.e., it passes over from immediacy
into the other, such that it is posited--reduced to
otherness as something posited or brought forth from an
other. In this transition each is in the first instance
reduced to something transient and untrue; but on the
other hand it also has the significance of bringing forth
an other, of positing the other, and the other is what
then proceeds from it. Hence one of these two sides
represents movement, but so, too, does the other.

    Now we shall consider the transition from concept to
being. We start with the concept, above all the concept
of God. From this content or concept, the transition
into being must be demonstrated. This is the first task;
but secondly one must immediately say that the notion of
"being" is wholly impoverished: it is abstract equality
with itself, a relation of identity to itself, the annulment of difference; it is affirmation, indeed, but in its
final abstraction, a wholly indeterminate immediacy. If
nothing more were in the concept, then this final abstraction at least would indeed have to be furnished it. But

the concept itself is defined only as infinitude; or,
concretely signified, it is the unity of the universal
and the particular, the universality that particularizes
itself and so returns into itself. Thus this negation of
the negative, this relation to itself, is being, taken
abstractly. This identity with itself, this determination, is at once essentially contained in the concept.

It must be said further that the transition from the
concept to being is of the greatest importance and holds
the deepest interest [46] for reason. To grasp the relation of the concept to being is also of special interest
to our time. We must now give an account of the more
proximate reason why this transition is of such interest.
The appearance of this opposition or antithesis between
concept and being is a sign that subjectivity has attained
its being-for-itself, has become a totality. The special character of the Revelatory Religion is the form by
which substance is Spirit.[15] The reason why this antithesis appears so difficult and unending is that what we
have called the side of subjective Spirit--this reality,
finite Spirit in itself--has arrived at the comprehension
of infinitude. Only when the subject is the totality and
has attained this freedom in itself, is it being. At this
point it is the case that being is indifferent to the subject, that the latter exists for itself and being stands
over against it as an indifferent other. This is the more
proximate reason why the antithesis can appear as infinite; at the same time, therefore, the impulse to resolve
this antithesis is found in the life-process. Likewise, in
its totality lies the demand to sublate this opposition of
the other, but the sublation has become infinitely difficult because the antithesis is so endless, and the other,
as something over against and above and beyond, is so entirely free.

The grandeur of the standpoint of the modern world
is this deepening of the subject within itself, whereby
the finite knows itself as infinite and is burdened by
the antithesis that it is driven to resolve.[16] The

question now is how it is to be resolved. The antithesis is this: I am a subject who is free, a person for
myself; therefore I also release the other to be free,
who stands over against me and remains an other. The
ancients did not arrive at this antithesis, at this estrangement, which only Spirit can bear. Only the highest
power can arrive at this antithesis, and to be Spirit is
to comprehend oneself infinitely in antithesis.

[47] Our present standpoint implies that we have on
the one side the *concept* of God and on the other, opposed
to it, the *being* of this concept. Accordingly, what is
demanded is the mediation of the two, so that the concept itself will determine upon being, or being will be
conceived from the concept, and so that the other, the
antithesis, will proceed from the concept. The way this
happens, as well as its form of understanding, are briefly
to be expounded.

The form taken by this mediation is that of the ontological proof of the existence of God, which proceeds
from the concept. But what is the concept of God?[17]
[48] In the ontological proof the concept of God is defined as the most real. It is to be grasped only affirmatively and is determinate within itself, but its
content should have no limitation. It is the whole of
reality and is only reality, without limits; thereby
actually only a dead abstraction remains, as we have
earlier remarked. This concept is possible and is seen
in the form of the understanding. The second point is
that being is a reality, non-being a negation, a lack,
utterly antithetical. Being is reality; among the
realities of God, therefore, being is also found.

The next point concerns what Kant has brought forward
against this proof and what generally is taken for granted
as an annihilation of it. Kant says that being cannot be
"unpacked" from the concept of God, for being is something other than the concept. The two are distinguished
and opposed to each other; therefore the concept cannot

contain being; the latter stands opposed to it. Moreover,
says Kant, being is not in any sense reality. All reality is attributed to God, but in the concept of God being
is not contained; it is not a determination of content or
a predicate. Whether I imagine a hundred dollars or actually possess them makes no difference conceptually; the
content is one and the same whether I have them or not.
Kant takes the content as that which constitutes the concept, and distinguishes form from content. The content
is what is contained in the concept. One can say this,
to be sure, if one understands by concept the determination of content, distinguishing from it the form, which
contains thought on the one side and being on the other.
But content belongs to the side of the concept, and to
the other side remains only the definition of being. In
brief, [49] it amounts to saying that the concept is not
being and that the two are distinguished. We can know
and apprehend nothing of God; we can, to be sure, form
concepts of God, but it is not thereby established that
these concepts also exist. This, then, is what the
Kantian destruction of the proof reduces to. We know
quite well, of course, that one can build castles in the
air, which have no existence in reality. This has, indeed, a rather popular appeal, and therefore Kant has
succeeded, according to the consensus, in producing a
refutation of the proof.[18]

    Anselm of Canterbury, a thoroughly learned philo-
sophical theologian of the twelfth century, set forth the
proof as follows: God is the most perfect being, the
quintessence of all reality. Now if God is a mere image,
a subjective representation, then he is not the most perfect, for we regard as perfect only that which is not
merely imagined but also has being. This is entirely
correct--a presupposition that lies at the basis of all
humanity and has formed the foundation of the whole of
philosophy. Everyone holds it within himself, namely,
that everything only imagined is imperfect, and that only

what also has reality is perfect. Now God is most perfect; therefore he must, just as he is the concept, also
be real and existent. People are also aware in their
imagination that image and concept are different, and
likewise that what is merely imagined is imperfect, but
that God is perfection.

Kant does not demonstrate the difference between
concept and being; it is merely accepted in popular fashion. Its truth is granted, yet the healthy human understanding forms images only of imperfect things.

On the Anselmian proof and on the form given it in
the ontological proof, the following more precise observations may be made. The form of the proof is that God
is the quintessence of all reality and consequently also
enjoys being. This is entirely correct. Being is so
poor a quality that it adheres immediately to the concept. The other point is that being and concept are
also in fact different. Being and thinking, reality and
ideality, are different from and opposed to each other.
The true difference is also antithetical, and the task
therefore is to annul this antithesis. The [50] unity of
both qualities is to be exhibited in such a way that it
results from the negation of the antithesis.

"In the concept being is contained." This reality
when it is unlimited gives us only empty words and mere
abstractions. In the first place, the determination of
being as affirmative and as contained in the concept is
to be exhibited; this, then, is the unity of concept and
being. Secondly, however, they are also different from
each other; thus their unity is the negative unity of the
two, and the task is now that of annulling the distinction. The distinction must come to speech and the unity
be established and exhibited in accord with this distinction, such that the distinction itself is the movement,
the concept, determining itself to being.

To exhibit this is the task of logic. The concept
is the movement by which it determines itself to being,

the dialectic by which it determines itself in opposition
to itself. This logical dimension is a further development, which surely is not given in the ontological proof,
this being one of its deficiencies.

We want now above all to consider the form of the
Anselmian proof and then to compare with it the view of
the present time.

The form of Anselm's thought has already been observed, namely, that the concept of God, as implied by its
content, has reality presupposed within it because God is
the most perfect being. In this regard, the following is
to be noted: I have said the essential thing is the transition from concept into reality, namely, that the concept posits itself objectively. So actually it makes no
difference whether it is precisely the *concept* of God
that realizes itself, or whether it appears that this connection, this necessity, can refer only to God. The point
is just that the concept objectifies itself for itself.

God, therefore, is the most perfect being. The only
exception is when he is posited in the imagination without reality; and when measured against what is most perfect, the mere concept of God appears to be deficient.
The concept of perfection is the measure, and God as a
mere concept or thought is inadequate to this measure.
Perfection, however, is only an indeterminate notion.
What is it, then, to be perfect? One thinks of something
specific by it; we see this specificity [51] directly in
something that is the opposite of that to which it is here
applied. That is, imperfection is only the *thought* of
God, and hence perfection is the unity of thought or concept with reality. This unity is therefore here presupposed. Since God is posited as the most perfect, he has
here no further definition; he exists only as such, and
this is his determinateness. From the unity of concept
and reality it is evident that it is actually only a question of this unity, which is the definition of perfection
and simultaneously of God himself. In fact, this is also the

definition of the Idea in general, but here it is only
the abstract Idea, and the unity surely belongs still
more to the definition of God.

In regard to the Anselmian way, the presupposition
is in fact that of the unity of concept and reality.
This explains why the proof cannot afford satisfaction
for reason, since the presupposition is precisely what
is at issue. But it is a further insight that the concept is what determines itself in itself, objectifies
itself, realizes itself; and this insight has first
emerged from the nature of the concept, which was not yet
available to Anselm, nor was it yet able to exist even in
later times--the insight concerning the extent to which
the concept itself annuls its onesidedness.

The other way--and this is one of the most important
points--is the one we compare with the view of our own
time, and has been formulated especially by Kant. According to it, man thinks, perceives, wills, and his willing exists *alongside* his thinking; he *also* thinks, *also*
conceives; he is a sentient, concrete being, and *also* a
rational one. The concept of God--the Idea, the infinite,
the unmoved--is *only* a concept, which we have created; we
dare not forget that it is only a concept and that it is
only in our heads. One may ask, Why is it *only* a concept? The concept is something that is imperfect, since
thinking is only one quality or activity among others in
human beings. This means that we measure the concept by
the reality that we have before us, in concrete human
beings. To be sure, man is not merely a thinking being;
he is also sentient and can indeed have sensible objects
in his thinking. This is in fact merely the subjective
aspect of the concept. We find [52] it to be imperfect
because of the standard applied to it, since this standard is the concrete man. One could say that the concept
is *only* a concept and designate the sensible--what a person can grasp with his hands--as reality; in so far as it
exists in feeling, whatever one sees, feels, or senses is

reality. One could assert, and many indeed do, that
nothing other than what we sense is to be acknowledged as
actuality. However, the situation could not be so bad
that men would ascribe actuality only to the sensible and
not to the spiritual. It is still the concrete, total
subjectivity of man that hovers as the standard, measured
by which the conceptualizing activity is *only* conceptual.

When we now compare the two ways of thinking, that
of Anselm and that of the modern world, they have in common the fact that they both make presuppositions. Anselm
presupposes perfection, which in itself is still indeterminate, while the modern view presupposes concrete man
in a general sense. Compared with perfection on the one
hand and empirical concretion on the other, the concept
appears to be somewhat onesided and unsatisfying. In
Anselm's thought, perfection is in fact defined as meaning the unity of concept and reality. Also in the case
of Descartes and Spinoza, God is the first reality, the
absolute unity of thought and sensible being (*cogito,
ergo sum*), the absolute substance—likewise with Leibniz.
What we thus have on one side is a presupposition, which
in fact is something concrete, namely, the unity of subject and object; and, as compared with this, the concept
appears imperfect and deficient. Now the modern view insists that we must continue to hold that the concept is
only a concept, which does not correspond to the concrete.
Anselm, on the contrary, says we must give up wanting to
let the subjective concept stand as something firm and
independent; rather we must depart from its onesidedness.
Both views share the fact that they have presuppositions;
the difference is that the concrete lies at the basis of
the modern world, while in the metaphysical, Anselmian
view, on the contrary, the basis is formed by absolute
thought, the absolute Idea, which is the unity of concept and reality. The old view is superior in so far as
it takes the concrete to refer not to empirical human
beings and empirical actuality but rather to thoughts; it

is also [53] superior because it does not hold fast to
the imperfect. In the modern view the conflict between
the concrete, which generally is valid for it, and the
"mere concept" remains unresolved. The subjective concept exists, is valid, must be maintained as subjective,
and is what is real; therefore one must remain with it,
and beyond it one may not go.

Thus the older view has by far the advantage because it lays its foundation on the Idea. Yet in one of
its characteristics the modern comprehension is broader,
since it posits the concrete as the unity of concept and
reality, while by contrast the older view remains with an
abstract form of perfection. For even when Spinoza said
that substance is the unity of concept and being, he
merely asserted it and did not prove it. However, thinking in fact has that unity immediately before it.[a]

Section 2. The Development of the Idea of God[19]

[m][20] Determinateness in the form of reality--being's
mode of existing in the Idea--is the determinateness of
the concept itself. [+]Reality is the actuality of the
concept, developing from it, posited through it.[+] This
[has already been] indicated; here, in the Spirit, [it
becomes the truth]. God is Spirit: [this is realized]
in the concept of revelation, of manifestation. Precisely this reality is his determinateness;[21] it is the
concept that absolute Spirit itself is. What Spirit or
its concept is can be explicated only through its realization, [its] totality, because its concept is precisely
to be the Idea.[22]

[54] Ordinarily the matter is represented differently: the process of conceptualizing and its determination [come first], followed by an appropriate realization.
So [it] indeed [appeared] in earlier times: e.g., [the]
power of the Lord [is the] reality of the One, [and all

remaining] reality [is] external being, determined by
this Lord as the power of this reality. [This is] here
the case because the determination of the concept is abstract; external being therefore differs [from it, and]
the determination of the Lord occurs only *in* the concept.
Hence the Greek gods [are subordinated to] external
necessity [and exist in] the shape of isolated elements
and powers. But if the concept [is] now [grasped as]
Idea, [i.e., the] identity of concept and reality, this
means precisely that reality itself constitutes the determinateness of the concept, and the concept in its determinateness is not to be explicated other than through
this realization itself.

Reflection[23] behaves differently than this. It interprets determinacy as such in the form of a predicate,
something at rest, not as the activity of realization;
and it construes its development in the mode of a simple,
abstract determination. Hence various predicates result
for it, and the same basic determination, if it is one,
is applied to various sides; but these various sides are
themselves grasped empirically, i.e., externally, to be
the nature of the object.

Thus there appear diverse predicates[24] of God as he
exists in the determinacy of Spirit: omnipotence, righteousness, goodness, wisdom, providence, omniscience,
etc.--and then, subsequent to these predicates and outside of them, as it were, the *history of God*, the activity of God and his work: creation of the world, his
Son, the Trinity, love for humanity, redemption. In this
fashion the manifestation [of God] is separated from this
determination [of predicates].

+If the difference [is] now removed from such attributes in themselves and likewise from their relation
to the simple subject, it then emerges in another fashion.+

Since there are [such] attributes, [they are] different from each other, although [predicated] of infinite

being *sensu eminentiori, excellenti.* [55] But [they] are
determinate and therefore finite; and it is said that
they express only our relations to God, not his nature,
which remains unknown and unexplained since there is no
way of explicating or making it available other than
through these predicates. This deficiency [in definition
by predicates is] correct. But [it is] equally correct
that this method of predication [can be] employed in a
popularly correct manner. General reflections, although
within themselves a rather indeterminate mode of representation, +bring a grand meaning before the soul [and
permit] its further development [to be experienced] even
without the sense of being exclusive and finite, as indeed we accept and utilize figurative, symbolic representations and poetic images often enough. It is another matter when they are taken as exclusively opposed
to other attributes in their specific reflective meaning. Then [emerges] the contradiction; [they are] subjective, hence exist only in relation to us, to subjective representation. We are the ones who also negate
them. However, this [is merely] external reflection, external dialectic. But [it is] not [a question of] externals; rather, *determinacy* [is the] predicate. God is
precisely the Idea that determines itself and raises its
determination to infinitude--the Idea that is only infinite self-determination. +

When determinacy is taken in the fashion indicated,
it results in contradiction. But the imagination over-
looks this, elevates itself above limitation, and holds
before its eyes the universal content. However, as already remarked, the abstract predicates contain their
meaning in movement, and this reality is the true finitization of the predicates,[25] in which their absolute form
(wisdom, purpose in and for itself, which maintains itself in reality, [in] the show of an other) is contained,
and whatever can appear as diverse aspects of this content consists only of moments of this movement itself.

The determination or (expressed in a more external
fashion) the formation of God is therefore his Idea, and
the latter is [his] movement; [his] attributes concern
and proceed from the modality of his distinction.

[56] God is:[26]

(α) In the first instance, *the concept of God*, the
concept as determinateness, i.e., as element; the [pro-
cess of] thinking himself, God in his *eternity*, the Idea
in and for itself, God [as] *triune*.

(β) To be the concept entails a determination of
subjectivity by the absolute Idea for our benefit and
likewise within itself. The concept [is] this *diremption*
or *differentiation*, producing the form of immediacy, [so
that it appears] as independent. [The] concept [must],
precisely in its mediation, reflect itself back into
identity with itself, whereupon the differentiation first
attains the character of an immediate world or nature.
God is the creator of nature and its wise preserver;
[this is] the appearance of God in nature.[27]

(γ) [Thereby,] objectivity [comprises itself] as
finite Spirit. This immediacy or finitude, [that is to
say,] is finite Spirit, the appearance of God in finite
Spirit as a whole, *the history of redemption* and *reconciliation*--the eternal, divine history itself. The subjective side of this history, as [it transpires] in
finite Spirit, [in] the individual, takes the form of the
cultus.

[+]Since *we* are familiar with this determination of
the concept in advance, we shall say that [it exists] in
three elements or moments [in itself]. However, "in itself" [means] either that these distinctions make the
transition into one another in terms of the concept itself, [or] it can and must at least be our reflection by
means of which the first [determination] is the general
concept, the concept in the element of universality.[+]

These [are] the three spheres in which the divine
Idea is to be considered; it is wholly present in each of

them, although differentiated according to the determination of the moment.^{m}

[64] a^{28} We proceed here to *concrete representation*,
to the *development* and more proximate *determination of
the Idea* [of God].^{29} We have defined the metaphysical
concept as the concept that realizes itself, is itself
real; the whole of finitude subsists in it. God is the
absolute Idea; hence this reality is suitable to the concept. What we have called reality is, more precisely
understood, not the natural being of nature religion, the
sky, the sun; this too is thought. This reality in the
metaphysical sense is reality in general, or being. It
constitutes the determinacy of God. On the other hand,
determinacy is not constituted by a predicate or a
plurality of predicates. Predicates are qualities such
as truth, spirituality, ethical power; they are not, to
be sure, natural and immediate, but they are set up by
reflection--given a content, which by means of reflection
has borne the form of universality, of relation to self.
Thus this determinate content has become just as unmove-
able and firm in itself as the natural [65] content is
initially. We say of the natural that it exists, its
predicates are just as identical with themselves as is
the case with immediacy. They do not correspond to the
reality of the concept; rather this reality is closer to
the first point, namely, that the concept in itself is
real, wholly concrete, free, activity present to itself--
in a word, Spirit. The subjective side, the concept, is
itself the Idea; the other side, the reality, is likewise
the whole, Spirit, posited simultaneously in distinction.
Reality is the reality of the Idea itself, so that both
sides are the Idea, the free Idea, present to itself;
thus Spirit knows itself, is present to itself. It is
real, places itself vis-à-vis itself as an other Spirit,
and is then the unity of the two.

The more precise explication of this Idea is that

universal Spirit, as the whole that it is, posits itself
in its three determinations, develops itself, realizes
itself, and that it is first complete only at the end,
which at the same time is its presupposition. It exists
in its first determination as the whole, presupposes itself, and exists likewise only at the end.

Thus Spirit is to be viewed in the three forms, the
three elements, in which it posits itself. These are:
first, eternal being, in and with itself, the form of
universality; second, the form of appearance, of *particularization*, of being for an other; third, the form of return from appearance into self, or absolute *individuality*.[30] It is in these three forms that the divine Idea
explicates itself. Spirit is the divine history, the
process of self-differentiation, of diremption and return
into self; it is therefore to be viewed as the divine
history in each of its three forms.

These three forms are also defined with a view to
subjective consciousness. The first form is defined as
the element of *thought*. God exists in pure thought, as
he is in and for himself, as he is manifest but not yet
come to appearance, God in his eternal essence, present
to himself, yet manifest. The second form is that he
exists in the element of *representation*, in the element
of particularization. Here consciousness is engrossed,
existing in relation to the other in an object, and this
is the appearance. The third element is that of *subjectivity* as such. This subjectivity is partly the immediacy of disposition, thought, imagination, sensation, but
partly also the subjectivity that represents the concept,
thinking [66] reason, a free Spirit, which is free within
itself only through its return into self.

In regard to *place* and *space*, the three forms may be
explained as though they take place in different locales,
so to speak. Thus the first is *outside the world*, space-
less, beyond finitude--God as he is in and for himself.
The second form is the *world*, the divine history as real

--God in complete existence. The third is the *inner place*, the community, first of all in the world, but also the community in so far as it simultaneously raises itself to heaven, already having heaven on earth within itself, full of grace--the church in which God is active and present.

One can also distinguish and define the three elements in regard to *time*. The first element is thus God outside of time as the eternal Idea in the element of the pure thought of *eternity*. But inasmuch as eternity is set over against time, time explicates itself in and for itself and lays itself out in terms of past, present, and future. Thus the second element is the divine history. Its appearance is in the *past*; it exists, has being, but a being that is reduced to a mere show. As appearance it is immediate being, which is simultaneously negated; this is the past. The divine history thus exists as past, as properly historic. The third element is the *present*. But in the first instance this is only the limited present, not [yet] the eternal present, but rather the present that distinguishes past and future from itself and exists in the element of feeling, of immediate subjectivity, the spiritual Now in this individual. At the same time, however, the present has also to be the third element; in this way the community raises itself to heaven too. Hence this is also a present that raises itself, essentially reconciled, perfected through the negation of its immediacy to universality--a perfection, however, that does not yet exist and so is to be grasped as future, a Now of the present that has perfection before it. But since the community is still posited temporally, perfection is distinguished from this Now and is posited as future.

These are the three universal elements in which we have to consider the divine history.

It should be noted that I have not made the distinction, employed earlier, between *concept*, *form*, and

cultus;[31] in further [67] treatment the practices of the
cultus will be shown to enter into play. In general,
however, it can be remarked that the element or determinant in which we exist is Spirit; Spirit is what manifests itself, is utterly for itself. In the form that
it is comprehended, it is never found alone but always
with the determination to be open, to be for an other,
its own other, i.e., for the side that is finite Spirit.
And cultic life is the relation of finite Spirit to the
absolute. Accordingly, we find the aspect of cultic life
in each of these elements immediately before us. We have
therefore to distinguish between how the Idea exists for
the *concept* in the various elements, and how it comes to
representative expression. Religion is universal and exists not only for educated, conceptual thought, for philosophical consciousness, but also the truth of the Idea of
God is revealed for the representative consciousness and
has the necessary determination of existing for representation in general.[a]

Section 3. The Idea of God In and For Itself:
The Trinity[32]

[56] [m][33] God is Spirit in the element of thought--
that which rightly is called the eternal God, God as such.
For here the show of finitude, God's divestment and his
appearance in an autonomous reality, has not[34] [yet]
transpired.
      [57] God is Spirit--that which we call the *triune*
God, [a] purely speculative content, i.e., [the] *mystery*
of God. God is Spirit, absolute activity, *actus purus,*
i.e., subjectivity, infinite personality, infinite distinction of himself from himself, [+]divinity standing
over against itself and objective to itself,[+] [as the
terms] "Son" and "generation" [suggest]. However, this
process of distinguishing is contained within the eternal

concept, i.e., [within] universality as absolute subjectivity. Thus it is posited in its infinite differentiation, not [so as] to arrive at obscurity, i.e., mere
being-for-itself, opaqueness, impenetrability, finitude;
rather it remains in immediate unity with itself simultaneously with its distinction. Accordingly, in its differentiation within itself, the entire divine concept,
Son and God, +this absolute unity-in-distinction, is
identical with itself: [this is] *eternal love.*+

Spirit, love, perception of oneself in another:
this immediate identity [is] expressed therefore in the
form of feeling. This [is the] perception itself, but
this perception, this identity, exists only within the
infinite difference (mere sensation [would be] animal
love and accordingly only diversity); however, truth exists only in differentiation,[35] [as] reflection into self,
subjectivity. True differentiation posits the distinction: hence [only] its unity [is] Spirit.

+[We find the] perception of this unity [in the]
poet, for example, who sings of his love, [who] not only
loves but makes his love an object [of contemplation]--
this [is] Spirit.+

God is One, in the first instance the universal.

God is love and remains One, [existing] more as
unity, as immediate identity, than as negative reflection
into self.[36]

God is Spirit, the One as infinite subjectivity, the
One in the infinite subjectivity of distinction.

[We shall add a few] *remarks.*[37]

+(α) [This Idea of God is] the absolute content for
the concept. Speculative science [has] recognized and
demonstrated that [58] this Idea [is] the truth, the whole
truth, the sole truth. [It is] demonstrated [and] posited
by rational mediation. Every determination, every content [is] annulled for it. Faith, so-called, [has] accepted [the Idea] immediately, holds it to be true, and
witnesses to the divine Spirit with its Spirit.+

[Either] the speculative determination of thought
must be allowed to have this character, or [it must suf-
fice] for faith to accept the given, naive, fortuitous
forms of imagination, [such as] "Son," "generation."
That is to say, when the *understanding*[38] applies [itself]
to these speculative representations, introducing its
form, they are immediately inverted, and if it has the
desire, there is no need for it to cease pointing out
contradictions. There are [surely] contradictions; but
likewise they are resolved. The understanding has the
right to exhibit contradictions through the distinction
and reflection of the same in itself; but God, the pure
Spirit, is precisely what eternally sublates this contradiction. Spirit has not waited for the understanding,
which wants to remove the contradiction and those determinations that contain the contradiction. It is precisely
what removes them itself, but likewise what posits these
determinations and distinguishes them through diremption.
To this the understanding opposes an abstract universality
and unity. But this is only another mode of contradiction, which the understanding does not recognize, and
which therefore it does not resolve--it is a permanent
separation, since all universality [stands] on one side
for itself [and there is] no activity or unity in which
the distinctions are annulled and objectively preserved.
[It is only] an abstract universality, at which [one] arrives by negation; negation is its proper determination,
its genesis.

[39]At the very beginning we were reminded that, in the
various simpler, undeveloped religions, reminiscences and
traces of Ideas and characteristics emerged, which only
in subsequent development became the major feature. Thus
we find in the various religions, in one form or another,
the expression of a triad,[40] e.g., in [59] Indian religion. But it is another question whether such a characteristic is the first, absolute determination, which lies
at the basis of everything, or whether it is only one

form that emerges among others, as, e.g., Brahma is the
one, but not the sole object of the cult. [+]Likewise,
just as [the Idea is] contaminated by the understanding's
[notion of] number, so it is with sensible images. [In
the] Trimurti, Siva[41] [is] alteration, and every moment
is fashioned wildly and multifariously, not as the eternal Idea elevated into thoughts, not as thought. Sensible representation [remains] abstract; [it has indeed the
moments] in common, but not the third [moment] as Spirit.
[The second moment, the] Son, the incarnation, [appears
and] expends [itself] in a multiplicity [of figures].
Brahma [is] abstraction, not love.[+]

In the Religions of Beauty and of Expediency, this
[threefold] form can surely appear, at least; the limit-
ing measure that reverts to itself is not encountered in
this multiplicity and particularization. However, the
form is not without traces of this unity. Aristotle,
when he spoke of the Pythagorean numbers, the triad,
said:[42] We believe that we have called upon the gods
completely when we have addressed them three times.[43] It
is primarily the case, however, with Pythagoras, and after
him Plato, who borrowed from Pythagoras, that the latter
defined the abstract Idea in the *Timaeus* as threefold;
the Neoplatonists and later the Neopythagoreans did the
same thing more specifically and thoroughly.[44] In more
recent times the form of triplicity has again been brought
to mind, chiefly by Kant, [an advance] of great importance.

[+]Where the forms belonging to the determination of
God as Spirit [may be found], so also is the issue,
noted earlier, as to whether they constitute a fundamental determination. Some people have wanted to be-
little the Christian Religion because these characteristics [are] older [than it], and because it [has] derived
them from various places. This historical observation
decides nothing at all with regard to the inner truth;
but [60] the ancients [also did] not know what they

really possessed, namely, that [these determinations] contained the absolute consciousness of truth--rather [they
preferred] others. These [were valued only] as existing
among other determinations.[+]

[+]These forms, [taken] from number, [we must] also
stress in regard to [the] understanding.[+] Two harsh or
rigorous factors [emerge] in this connection. If one
attempts to count the moments of the Idea--three equals
one--this appears to be something entirely ingenuous,
natural, and intelligible. But [the problem] is with the
method of counting introduced here: every quality is
fixed as one, and then to grasp that three times one is
only one appears to be the harshest and, so it is said,
the most irrational demand. However, only the absolute
autonomy of the numerical one hovers before understanding, [signifying] absolute separation and splintering.
But logical reflection shows the numerical one rather to
be dialectical in itself and not something autonomous and
genuine; [+][as such it is merely] a thing of the understanding.[+] One needs only to be reminded of *matter*,
which is the actual numerical one and offers resistance,
but is massive; i.e., it shows the tendency not to be
just one but rather to annul its being-for-self, acknowl-
edging this to be a nullity. Of course although it remains only matter, the most external of externalities, it
does so all the same only as an unachieved goal [*beim
Sollen*]. Gravitational mass, which is just this annulling
of the one, constitutes the underlying determination of
matter, and yet matter is the poorest, most external, unspiritual mode of existence.[45]

[46+]Another form is related to this and is still
harder or more demanding.[+] The higher definition of distinction in the absolute Idea is personhood. [The
moments of the Idea] have been designated as *persons* in
the Godhead, and if the determination of the numerical
one already appears to be invincible to abstract understanding, so much more so is personality. Personhood is

the infinite subjectivity of self-certainty; it is reflection into self through distinction, which in abstract
form [61] is exclusively vis-à-vis others. How this infinitely singular one, which indeed is essentially exclusive, and a plurality of such singular individuals,
[is still] to be grasped only as a one, [appears to be]
the harshest contradiction. In any case, however, precisely the divine Idea, as earlier [noted], is not only
this contradiction but also the resolution of it--a resolution not in the sense that the contradiction does not
exist, but rather ⁺so as to show that the antithesis is
to be understood absolutely. But personhood [is] still
this extreme, which in its abstraction [is] maintained
only as resolved and essentially not isolated.⁺ ⁺De-
termination of form is here infinite form, every moment
as subject.⁺ Personhood [is] freedom, [and] precisely
in its infinite being-for-itself it exists truly in its
concept itself, and is thereby the determination of
identity with itself and of universality. Speculatively
understood, this [is] self-emptying precisely at its
highest level; this eternal movement [is] its concept.⁴⁷

This [is] expressed in love, in Spirit. [We have]
the eternal example in self-consciousness, [but] natural
customs also [offer such examples]. Birth [presupposes
that the] parents are of the same species, [but at the
same time they have] particular characteristics. [So
the] family [is] a natural unity of those who are persons,
and moral unity subsists in love.⁴⁸

Attention [must] still be directed to the source of
manifold representations and modes of definition ⁺in
other configurations and more proximate determinations.⁺
⁺The major determinant [is the] purpose [or] concept that
sustains itself. [For example, the] life-process brings
itself forth, i.e., what is exists only as brought forth.
[Thus] distinction in the process [is] already in and for
itself a show, a game, just as reassurance and enjoyment
[are] only the abstract form of movement in the reciproc-

ity of love. Reassurance [posits the] one; even for this
instant [it is] identity as repetition. [62] This instant
is exclusive; [the] law of heaven [is valid] also in this
instant. [The] law remains firm for itself. Calculations
are a pleasure for children. [Why? The] rule [is] firm
in this [individual] case as well; [therefore they] are
entirely certain in advance that the result will be [ac-
cording to the rules, and that makes them happy]. Thus by
this means the particular [is] posited only as a show.[+]

[+]The more precise determination of the distinction,
which falls out in the manifestation of difference, [is
up to us],[+] to wit, when we say: God in himself according to his concept is the infinite, self-dirempting [+]and
self-returning[+] power; he is this only as infinite, self-
relating negativity, i.e., as absolute reflection into
self--which is already the definition of *Spirit*. Since,
therefore, we intend to speak of God in his first determination according to his concept, and from there to arrive at the other determinations, we speak here already
of the third: the last is the first.

[49]Since [an attempt is made] to avoid this, or since
the imperfection of the concept occasions a speaking
about the first only in accord with its determination, it
is thus the universal;[50] and the activity of creating and
producing is already a principle distinct from abstract
universality, which can appear as the second principle,
as manifestation, self-externalization (Logos, Sophia;
the first [is then] the abyss).[51] At the time of
Christ's life and for several centuries after Christ's
birth, we see philosophical representations emerge for
which the image of such a relationship lies at the basis.
These are in part purely philosophical systems, such as
the philosophy of Philo, an Alexandrian Jew, and in part
the work of the other Alexandrines;[52] but above all they
[63] are mixtures of the Christian Religion with philosophical representations--blended with figurative, allegorical [notions]--mixtures created in large part by

heretics, especially the Gnostics. Thus, for example, in
Philo the ὄν is the first, the inconceivable God, the uncommunicative, unnameable ἀμέθεκτος; likewise with a
number of Neoplatonists. The second is the Logos, especially the νοῦς, the self-revealing, self-emerging God,
the ὅρασις θεοῦ, the σοφία, λόγος, then the archetype of
humanity, this man who is the impress of the heavenly and
eternal revelation of the hidden Godhead, φρόνησις,
Chokma +(Neander, p. 15).+53

Valentinus and the Valentinians +(*ibid.*, p. 94)+
called that unity βύθος, the abyss, αἰών, namely the
τέλειος αἰὼν ἐν ἀοράτοις καὶ ἀκατονομάστοις ὑψώμασι,
the eternal, dwelling in invisible and inexpressible
heights[54]--βύθος, which in and for itself is elevated
above all contact with finite things, from whose super-
abundant essence nothing can be imparted directly and in
and for itself, [and which] is the principle and father
of all existence only through the mediation of Sephiroth,
προαρχή, προπατήρ.[55]

The self-revelation of the hidden God must precede
everything else +(*ibid.*, p. 98).+ Through his self-
reflection (ἐνθύμησις ἑαυτοῦ) he produces the only begotten, who is the eternal become comprehensible,
κατάληρσις τοῦ ἀγεννήτου), the first to be conceived, τὸ
πρῶτον καταληπτόν, and, furthermore, the principle of all
determinate existence, the first self-determination and
limitation of the infinite, inconceivable essence. The
Monogenēs is therefore the actual father and basic principle of all existence, πατὴρ καὶ ἀρχή, the ὄνομα ἀόρα-
τον; the βύθος is in and for itself ἀνονομαστός. The
former is the πρόσωπον τοῦ πατρός.

+The great controversy of the Eastern and Western
Christian Churches was joined over the issue as to whether
the [64] Spirit proceeds from the Father[56] or from the
Father and the Son, since only the Son is manifest in activity and is revelatory, and hence only from him [would]
the Spirit [proceed]. But the Spirit in general does not

have this importance of definition; in so far as the νοῦς,
λόγος, σοφία, etc., is defined, it is as the Demiurge,
the second principle, the revealing one, the Man, or as
the immediate transition thereto.[+]

In brief, the source of many of the so-called
heresies lies purely in the turn of speculation, which in
the transition from the one, the universal, to the process of differentiation, distinguishes this activity from
the former, hypostatizes it, separates it from the universal, which stands[57] over against it as abstract. However, considered more closely, this Logos has already itself the characteristic of return within itself, containing a moment that [+]must be distinguished[+] in order
to comprehend the distinction exactly. The resolution
consists in the fact that *Spirit* is the totality, and the
first moment is grasped as first only because to begin
with it has the determination of the third, which is activity.[m]

[67] [a]*The first element*[58] in which we have to consider the Idea of God is the element of thought, the Idea
in its eternal presence, as it exists for free thought,
for the thought whose basic characteristic is to be untroubled light, identity with itself. This is an element that is not yet burdened by other-being. In this
element, however, a determination is necessary in so far
as *thinking in general* is different from *conceptual
thinking*. The eternal Idea, in and for itself in thought,
is the Idea in its absolute truth. Religion has, therefore, a content, and the content is an object. Religion
is *human* religion, and the human being is thinking consciousness (among other qualities, as ordinarily meant);
therefore the Idea must also exist for the thinking consciousness. Man, however, is not only this but also
finds the truth for the first time in the process of
thinking; the universal object, the essence of the object, exists only for thinking, and since in religion

God is the object, he is such essentially for thinking.
He is object as Spirit is consciousness, [59] and he exists
for thinking because it is God who is the object. For
sensible or reflective consciousness, God cannot exist as
God, i.e., in his eternal truth in and for itself. His
appearance is another matter: it is for sensible consciousness. If God existed *only* for sensation or feeling, human beings would stand no higher than the animals;
to be sure, he exists *also* for feeling, but only in the
form of appearance. [68] Nor does he exist for ration-
alizing consciousness, or for popular thinking in accord
with this or that limited content; God is not such a content. He exists, therefore, essentially for thought.
This we must insist upon if we start from the subjective,
from the human.

But we also arrive at precisely the same point when
we start from God. Spirit exists only as self-revealing,
as distinguishing itself *for Spirit*, for which it exists.
This is the eternal Idea, thinking Spirit, Spirit in the
element of its freedom. In this region God is the *self-
revealing* one because he is Spirit; but he is not yet
the *appearing* one. Thus it is essential that God exists
for Spirit.

It may be remarked, secondly, that Spirit is what
thinks Spirit. In this pure thinking there is no difference that divides them; nothing comes between them.
Thinking is pure unity with itself, where all obscurity
and darkness disappears. This thinking can also be called
pure *intuition*, as the simple activity of thinking, such
that between the subject and object nothing is found, and
the subject-object distinction actually does not yet exist. This thinking has no limits, it is universal activity; the content is only universality itself.

In the third place, absolute diremption and differentiation also occur. How does this come about? Thinking
as an *actus* is indeterminate. The most proximate distinction is the one in which the two sides, which we have

seen as two modes of the principle, are separated in accordance with their points of departure. The one side, that of subjective thinking, is the movement of thinking in so far as it proceeds from immediate being and elevates itself therein to the universal and infinite, as we have observed in the first proofs of the existence of God. In so far as it arrives at the universal, its thinking is unlimited; its end is infinitely pure thinking in which all the mist of finitude has disappeared. Here it thinks of God: all particularity has disappeared, and thus religion, thinking upon God, begins. The second side is the one with the other point of departure, which proceeds from the universal, from the result of the first side, a result that also is movement. This movement, which proceeds from the universal, from thinking, from the concept, distinguishes itself in itself and maintains the distinction in itself in such a way that it does not disturb the universality. This is a universality [69] that contains distinction within itself and is in harmony with itself. This is the abstract content of thinking; abstract thinking and its result are what have elevated themselves.

The two sides stand opposed to each other. The first and simpler mode of thinking is also a process, inner mediation; but this process goes on outside of it, extends beyond it. Only in so far as such thinking has raised itself to something higher does religion begin. Thus we have in religion a pure, unmoving, abstract thinking; the concrete element falls, on the other hand, into its object, for this is the thinking that begins from the universal, distinguishes itself, and is in harmony with its distinction. This concrete element is the object for thinking, taking the latter in a general sense. Thinking in general is thus abstract thinking and therefore finite. For the abstract is finite; the concrete is the truth, the infinite object.

The following remarks may be offered on what it is

that concerns this content more closely. We have long
been familiar with this and have therefore only little to
add; we shall mention only a few things, recalling only
what is essential.

God is Spirit; in his abstract character, he is defined as universal Spirit that particularizes itself.
This is the truth, and the religion that has this content
is the true religion. In the Christian Religion this is
called the *Trinity*. Universal Spirit is referred to as
triune in so far as the category of number is applied.
It is the God who differentiates himself within himself,
but in the process remains identical with himself. The
Trinity is called the mystery of God; its content is
mystical, i.e., speculative.^{a}

$_w$^{60} Here God exists only for the thinking person, who
remains silently within himself. The ancients called
this enthusiasm; it is purely theoretical contemplation,
the supreme repose of thinking, but at the same time the
highest activity, manifested in grasping the pure Idea of
God and becoming conscious of this Idea. ^{61}The mystery
of the dogma of what God is, is imparted to human beings;
they believe in it, and have already vouchsafed to them
the highest truth, although they apprehend it only in the
form of representation, without being conscious of the
necessity of this truth, and without comprehending it.
Truth is the disclosure of what Spirit is in and for itself. Man is himself Spirit, and therefore the truth
exists for him. Initially, however, the [70] truth that
comes to him does not yet possess for him the form of
freedom; it is for him merely something given and received, which, however, he can receive only because he is
Spirit. This truth, this Idea, has been called the *dogma
of the Trinity*. God is Spirit, the activity of pure
thinking, the activity that is present to itself. It was
Aristotle chiefly who conceived of God under the abstract
characteristic of activity. Pure activity is knowledge

(in the Scholastic period, *actus purus*), but in order to
be posited as activity, it must be posited in its moments:
to knowledge belongs an other, which is known, and since
it is knowledge that knows it, it is appropriated to it.
This explains why God, who represents being in and for
itself, eternally produces himself in the form of his
Son, distinguishing himself from himself--the absolute
judgment or differentiation [*Urteil*]. What he thus distinguishes from himself does not take on the form of
something other than himself, but rather what is thus
distinguished is immediately only that from which it has
been distinguished. God is Spirit, and no darkness, no
coloring or mixture enters into this pure light. The relation between Father and Son is taken from organic life
and is expressed in imaginative form. This natural relation is only figurative, and, accordingly, never entirely
corresponds to the truth that is sought to be expressed.
We say that God eternally begets his Son, that God distinguishes himself from himself, and thus we begin to say
of God that he does this, and is utterly present to himself in the other whom he has posited (the form of love);
but at the same time we ought to know that God himself is
this entire activity. God is the beginning, he acts
thus; but he is likewise the end, the totality, and it is
as totality that God is Spirit. God as merely the Father
is not yet the truth (thus in the Jewish Religion he is
conceived of without the Son). He is rather both beginning and end; he is his own presupposition, constituting
himself as presupposition (this is simply another form of
differentiation); he is the eternal process. The fact
that this is the truth, and the absolute truth, has
rather the form of something given. But that this should
be consciously *known* as the truth in and for itself is
the work of philosophy and the entire content of philosophy. In it is seen how all that constitutes nature and
Spirit presses forward dialectically to this central
point as its absolute truth.[62] Here we are not concerned

to prove that this dogma, this silent mystery, is the
eternal truth: this is done, as has been said, in the
whole of philosophy.[w]

[a]That to which reason has access is no mystery or
secret; in the Christian Religion, one knows the mystery.
Mysteries exist only for the understanding and for
thought based on sense experience. Here distinctions are
immediate and are applicable to sensible things; this is
the method of externality. But as soon as God is defined
as Spirit, externality is annulled. However, for the
senses there is mystery; externality remains and objects
change, since the sensations of the latter change. The
sun presently exists; it did not once exist, nor will it
exist [71] some day--this is a form of externality in
time. Its being is now, from which its non-being is distinguished. Time is a form of holding-things-apart-from-
each-other; it entails the externality of determinate
things vis-à-vis each other. For the understanding as
well, otherness remains; the understanding, like sense
perception, holds fast to abstract qualities so that each
exists only for itself. The negative is distinguished
from the positive, hence for the understanding it is
something other.

     With the Trinity the unhappy form of counting by
numbers (1, 2, 3) enters into play. Reason is able to
utilize all of the relations of understanding, but they
will be destroyed by it--so also with the Trinity. However, understanding rigidly insists that one make use of
these relations, to which a right has been gained. But
they are misused precisely when one uses them in accord
with understanding, as in the case of the Trinity when
one says, three equals one. Contradictions, accordingly,
and distinctions that go to the point of being antithetical are easily pointed out in such Ideas. Everything
concrete and living contains contradiction within itself;
only the dead understanding is identical with itself.

But the contradiction is also resolved in the Idea, and
the resolution is spiritual unity. The life process is
an example of what cannot be grasped by understanding.
When we say, "God is love," he is present to feeling.
Thus he is person, and the circumstances are such that
the consciousness of one person is had only in the consciousness of the other; the one is only conscious of itself in the other, in absolute divestment: this is spiritual unity in the form of feeling. In the relations of
friendship, the family exists precisely as this identity
of one with an other. It is contrary to the understanding that I, who exist for myself and therefore am self-
consciousness, should have my consciousness in another.
But the resolution or abstract content is, generally
speaking, the relationship that is substantial, universal,
and ethical.

[63]A second comment takes the form of a reflection on
what precedes. We can find traces of the Trinity in other
religions. They are found, for example, in the Trimurti
and in the triad of Plato,[64] while Aristotle says: We
believe that we have called upon the gods completely when
we have addressed them three times. In Plato the one and
the other and their blending together are wholly abstract
in character; in the Trimurti the wildest customs enter
into play, and the third is not the [moment of] return,
but as with Siva, merely alteration, not Spirit.

A further point is that in the Christian Religion
one not only says that God is triune, but also that he
subsists in *three persons*. This is being-for-self pro-
pelled to the farthest extremity--the extremity not only
of oneness or singularity but also of person, of personhood. Here the contradiction appears to be pushed so far
that no resolution, no effacement, of the person is possible. But the latter exists in such a way that God is
only one: the three persons are posited only as different moments. Personhood means that the opposition is
to be taken as absolute, that [72] it is not so gentle;

and precisely for the first time in this extremity it is
sublated. It is the person who maintains himself in love
and friendship and through love gains his subjectivity,
which is his personhood. If in religion one retains
personhood in the abstract sense, then one has three gods,
subjectivity is likewise lost, and the element of divinity is only infinite form or power--or else personhood
remains unresolved, and then one has evil, [65]for the
personhood that does not give itself up in the divine
Idea is evil. In the divine unity personhood is posited
as resolved; only in appearance is the negativity of
personhood distinguished from that whereby it is sublated.

The Trinity has been set forth in the relationship
of Father, Son, and Spirit. This is a childlike relationship, a childlike form. Understanding has no such categories or relations that would be comparable in regard to
their suitability. But it must be recognized that this
expression is merely figurative; Spirit does not enter
into such a relationship. Love would be more suitable,
for Spirit is by all means the truth.

The abstract God, the Father, is the universal--
eternal, encompassing, total universality. We are on the
level of Spirit; the universal here includes everything
within itself. The other, the Son, is infinite particularity and appearance; the third, the Spirit is individuality as such--but all three are Spirit. In the third,
we say, God is the Spirit; but it is also presupposed
that the third is the first. This is essential to maintain and is explained by the nature of the concept [of
Spirit]; it comes to the fore with every goal and every
life process. Life maintains itself; self-maintenance
means passing into difference, into the struggle with
particularity, finding oneself distinguished vis-à-vis
inorganic nature. Life is thus only a result, since it
has produced itself and is a product that in turn produces. This being produced is the life process itself,
i.e., it is its own presupposition; it works through its

process, from which nothing new comes forth: what is
brought forth exists already from the beginning. It is
likewise with the mutual relations of love. In so far as
love exists, so does its expression; all of its activities merely confirm it, whereby it is simultaneously
brought forth and supported. However, what is brought
forth already exists; it is a corroboration whereby
nothing comes forth other than what [73] already exists.
Likewise Spirit presupposes itself, it is what begins.

The differentiation through which the divine life
moves is not external but must rather be defined only as
internal in such a way that the first, the Father, is to
be conceived as the last. This process is nothing so
much as the play of self-preservation and self-confirma-
tion. This definition is important in this respect because it provides the criterion for evaluating many
representations of God and for recognizing the deficiency
contained in them. The latter must be acknowledged, and
the deficiency arises especially from the fact that often
this definition is overlooked.

[66]I have commented that traces and indications of
the Idea of God, which essentially is the Trinity, appeared shortly before and after the time of the origin
of the Christian Religion--representations that the
church termed heretical. These are the Gnostic representations of God's originating out of necessity. Philo,
a Jewish Platonist, defines God as the ὄν--that existent
being who is uncommunicative, unknowable, indivisible,
inconceivable. If the first is defined merely as universal, in terms of existent being or the ον, then this
is surely inconceivable because it is without content;
anything conceivable is concrete and can *be* conceived
only in so far as it is determined as a moment. The de-
fect consists in the fact that the first is not itself
grasped as the whole of totality.

The second determination is that of the Logos,
prov[idence],[67] that which reveals itself, which is the

moving and distinguishing principle, the moment of difference. The representations of this moment are quite
manifold: the Son of God, Sophia, Wisdom, the Archetype
of Humanity, the Primal Man, the eternal, heavenly Revelation, [the principle of] Thought, of Potency. This is
the second, the true distinction, which concerns the
quality of both; but it is only one and the same substance, and hence the difference is merely a superficial
one, even defined as a difference of persons.

    According to another representation, the first is
the βύθος, the Abyss, the Depths, αἰών, the Eternal,
whose dwelling is in the inexpressible heights, who is
raised above all contact, from whom nothing can develop,
the [first] principle, the Father of all existence, the
Propatēr, who is a Father only mediately, *pro archōn*, before the beginning. The revealing of this abyss, of this
hidden God, is defined as self-contemplation, reflection
into self, concrete determination in general. Self-contemplation begets, it is in fact the begetting of the
only-begotten; this is the process of becoming comprehensible on the part of the eternal because it thereby
arrives at its determination. Thus this only-begotten
also signifies the authentic Father, the ground-principle.
The deficiency in this representation is that the first
is not also comprehended as the last in the determination
of totality.

    The content, we have seen, is an object for pure
thinking, for finite, subjective Spirit, which is here
posited in the form of infinitude, of pure intuition or
pure thinking. This relation must be illumined more
closely. First there is the absolute content, the
eternal Idea. This is the object and as such is essential. God is the one who reveals himself, makes himself an object. He is the concrete, the Idea; for pure
thinking he is the object, the simple direction, the concentration of thinking. This object is the absolute
truth for thinking, before which it has utter *reverence*,

very great and true. But it would be meaningless to conceive this merely as a simple definition without analyz-
ing what love is. Love is a distinguishing of two, who
nevertheless are absolutely not distinguished for each
other. The consciousness or feeling of this identity--
to be outside of myself and in the other--this is love.
I have my self-consciousness not in myself but in the
other. I am satisfied and have peace with myself only in
this other--and I *am* only because I have peace with myself; if I did not have it, then I would be a contradiction that falls to pieces. This other, because it likewise exists outside itself, has its self-consciousness
only in me, and both the other and I have only this consciousness of being-outside-ourselves and of our identity;
we have an intuition, feeling, and knowledge of unity.
This is love, and without knowing that love is both a distinguishing and the sublation of the distinction, one
speaks emptily of it.

God is love: he is this distinguishing and the
nullity of the distinction, a play of distinction that is
not serious, the distinction precisely as sublated, i.e.,
the simple, eternal Idea. We behold the fact that the
simple Idea of God subsists in the simple element of
thinking and is the Idea in its universality; this is the
essential determination of the Idea, the determination by
which it has the truth.

We make the following remarks about this Idea, its
content and form.

When God is spoken of in such a way as to explain
what he is, it is customary to make use of attributes:
God is thus and so; he is defined by *predicates*. This is
the method of representation and understanding. Predicates are determinate, particular qualities: justice,
goodness, omnipotence, etc. The Orientals have the feeling that this is not the true way of expressing the
nature of God, so they say that he is πολυώνυμος and does
not allow himself to be exhausted by predicates--for

names are in this sense the same as predicates. [76] The
real deficiency in this way of defining by predicates
consists in the fact that, even when an infinite number
of predicates is employed, they designate only particular
characteristics, of which there are many, and all of
which are bearers of the same subject. Because there are
particular characteristics, and because these particularities are viewed in their determinateness, they fall
into opposition and contradiction, and these contradictions then remain unresolved.

This is further seen when these predicates are taken
as expressing God's relation to the world. The world is
something other than God. Predicates as particular characteristics are not appropriate to the nature of God;
here, then, is the occasion for the other method, which
regards them as relations of God to the world; e.g., the
omnipresence and omniscience of God in the world. Accordingly, the predicates do not comprise the true relation of God to himself, but rather his relation to an
other, the world. So they are limited and thereby come
into contradiction with each other.[71]

We are conscious of the fact that God is not represented as living when so many particular characteristics
are enumerated alongside each other. The same point is
expressed in another way, as stated earlier: the contradictions among the different predicates are not resolved.[72] The resolution of the contradiction is contained in the Idea, which is the self-determination of
God to the act of differentiating himself from himself
and is at the same time the eternal sublation of this
distinction. A distinction left as is would be a contradiction. If the distinction were permanent, then finitude would persist. The two sides confront each other
independently, yet remain in relation; hence an irre-
solvable contradiction emerges. The nature of the Idea is
not to allow the difference to remain but rather precisely
to resolve it. God posits himself in this distinction

and likewise sublates it.

If we assign predicates to God in such a way as to make them particular, then we are immediately at pains to resolve their contradiction. This is an external action, a product of our reflection, and the fact that it is external and falls to us, and is not the content of the divine Idea, means that the contradictions [77] actually cannot be resolved. But the Idea is itself the sublating of the contradiction. Its proper content, its determination, is to posit this distinction and then absolutely to sublate it; this is the vitality of the Idea itself.

[47] [73]The divine concept is the pure concept, without any limitation. The Idea contains the notion that the concept determines itself and thereby posits itself as that which distinguishes itself. This is a moment of the divine Idea itself, and because the thinking, reflecting Spirit has this content before it, the need arises for this transition and progression.

We observed the logical aspect of this transition earlier. It is contained in those so-called proofs by means of which, in the element of thought, the transition ought to be made, in, from, and through the concept, into objectivity and being. That which appears as a subjective exigency and demand is the content; it is a moment of the divine Idea itself. When we say that God has created a world, then this also entails a transition from concept to reality; but the world exists as the essential other of God; it is defined as the negation of God, existing externally, without God, godlessly. In so far as the world is defined as the other, we have the distinction not as a distinction within the concept itself; it is not contained in the concept before us. Now, however, being and objectivity ought to be exhibited *within* the concept as its activity and consequence, as a determination of the concept. Thereby it is indicated that this is the same content and exigency as that found in the form of the proof for the existence of God. In the

absolute Idea, in the element of thinking, God is this
utterly concrete universal, positing himself as an other,
but such that this other is immediately defined to be
himself, and the distinction is only ideal, immediately
sublated, not taking on the form of externality. This
means precisely that the distinction ought to be exhibited within the concept. [48] What this transition
itself concerns we have considered at the appropriate
time. It is the logical element, in which it becomes
clear that the determinacy of the concept is to annul itself, to exist as its own contradiction, to posit what is
distinct from itself. But the concept itself is still
burdened with onesidedness and finitude, as indicated by
the fact that it is something subjective, posited as subjective; the characteristics of the concept and its distinctions are posited only as ideal and not as distinctions in fact. This is the concept that objectifies itself. This is the logical element that is presupposed.

[77] When we say "God," we speak of him merely as
abstract; or if we say, "God the Father," we speak of him
as the universal, only abstractly, in accord with his
finitude. His infinitude means precisely that he sublates this form of abstract universality and immediacy,
and in this way distinction is posited; but he is precisely the one who sublates the distinction. Thereby he
is for the first time true actuality, the truth, infinitude.

This is the speculative Idea, i.e., the rational element, in so far as it is thought, thinking upon what is
rational. For the non-speculative thinking of the understanding, distinction remains as distinction, e.g., the
antithesis of finite and infinite: both are credited
with absoluteness, yet each has a relation to the other
and in this respect they are in unity; in this way contradiction is posited.

The speculative Idea is opposed not merely to sense
experience but also to the understanding; for both,

therefore, it is a secret or mystery. It is a μυστήριον
for sense perception as well as for the understanding.
μυστήριον, in other words, is identical with what is rational; for the Neoplatonists, the expression of it already was known only as speculative philosophy. The nature of God is not a secret in the ordinary sense, least
of all in the Christian Religion. In it God has made
known what he is; there he is manifest. But he is a
secret or mystery for sense perception and imagination,
for the sentient way of regarding things and likewise for
the understanding.

Sense experience in general has as its fundamental
characteristic externality, the being of things outside
of each other. Space and time are externalities, in
which objects exist next to each other and one after another. Thus sense perception is accustomed to have before it various things that are outside each other. It
assumes that distinctions remain explicit and external.
Therefore, what exists in the Idea remains for it a
mystery. For in the region of the Idea, the way in which
things are looked at, the relations ascribed to things,
and the categories employed, are entirely different from
sense experience. The Idea is just this act of distinguishing that simultaneously [78] is no distinction and
does not persist in the distinction. God perceives himself in the distinction, is united with himself in his
other, and thereby is only present to himself, is only
enclosed within himself, and perceives himself in the
other. This is wholly repugnant to sense experience,
since for it one thing is here and another there. Everything is considered to be independent; nothing can de-
pend for its existence on being related to an other. For
sense experience two things cannot be in one and the same
place; they exclude each other. But in the Idea distinctions are not posited exclusively of each other; rather
they are found only in this mutual inclusion of the one
with the other. This is the *truly supersensible*, as

distinguished from the ordinary supersensible of the
understanding, which merely stands above and beyond; for
the latter likewise belongs to the realm of the sensible,
in which things are outside of one another and remain
indifferently within themselves.

Likewise this Idea is beyond the grasp of the understanding and remains a mystery for it. For the understanding holds fast to the categories of thought, regarding them as perennially different and absolutely independent of each other, remaining outside each other
permanently. The positive is not the same as the negative, the cause is not the effect, etc. But for the concept it is equally true that these distinctions are sublated. Precisely because they are distinctions, they remain finite, and the understanding persists in finitude.
Indeed, even in the case of the infinite, infinitude is
on one side and finitude on the other. But the truth of
the matter is that neither the finite nor the infinite
that opposes it has the truth; rather both are merely
transitional. This is a mystery for imagination based on
sense experience and for understanding, and both resist
the rationality of the Idea.

Moreover, the understanding is equally powerless to
grasp anything else whatever, or to grasp the truth of
anything at all. Animal life, for example, also exists
as Idea, as the unity of the concept, as the unity of
soul and body. For the understanding, in contrast,
everything exists for itself. Now to be sure, all things
are different, but it is equally their nature to annul
the difference. Life is simply this perennial process.
What has life exists, and it has instincts and needs;
consequently it has the distinction within itself, and
the latter emerges within it. Thus life itself is a contradiction, and the understanding comprehends such distinctions [79] to mean that the contradiction remains unresolved; when the distinctions are brought into relation
with each other, only the contradiction remains, which is

not to be resolved. This is the case; the contradiction cannot cease when the distinctions are maintained to be perennial in character, just because the fact of this distinction is insisted upon. Life has certain needs and thus is in contradiction, but the satisfaction of the needs annuls the contradiction. I am distinguished from myself in my instincts and needs. But life means to re- solve the contradiction, to satisfy the need, to attain peace, but in such a way that the contradiction emerges once again. The distinction, or contradiction, and its annulment alternate back and forth. They do not occur simultaneously but succeed each other in temporal pro- gression, and accordingly the entire process is finite. When considering instinct and satisfaction explicitly, the understanding is unable to grasp the fact that even in the act of affirmation and self-feeling, the negation of self-feeling, limitation, and lack are simultaneously found. Yet at the same time I as self-feeling infringe upon this lack. This is the determinate representation of μυστήριον; a mystery is called incomprehensible, but what appears as incomprehensible is precisely the con- cept itself, the speculative element or what is thought of as rational. It is precisely by means of thinking that the distinction comes out specifically. The think- ing of the instinct is only the analysis of what the in- stinct is; inasmuch as I think the instinct, I have the affirmation and therein the negation, the self-feeling, the satisfaction and the instinct. To think the instinct means to recognize the distinction that is in it. Now when the understanding comes to this point, it merely says that this is a contradiction; and it remains at this point, it stands by the contradiction in face of the ex- perience that it is life itself which sublates the con- tradiction. When the instinct is analyzed, the contra- diction appears, and then the understanding can say: this is incomprehensible.

The nature of God is likewise incomprehensible; how-

ever, as already indicated, it is only the concept itself,
which contains distinction within itself; and the understanding does not get beyond the fact of the distinction.
So it says: this cannot be comprehended. For the principle of understanding is abstract identity with itself,
not concrete identity, in accord with which these distinctions exist within a single reality.[74] According to
the abstract [80] identity, the one and the other exist
independently, each for itself, yet are at the same time
related to each other. This is what is called incomprehensible. The resolution of the contradiction is the
concept, a resolution the understanding does not attain
because it starts from the presupposition that the two
elements are and remain utterly independent of each other.

One of the circumstances contributing to the assertion that the divine Idea is incomprehensible is that,
because religion is the truth for all persons, the content of the Idea appears in religion in forms accessible
to sense experience or understanding. Hence we have the
expressions Father and Son, a designation taken from a
sentient aspect of life, from a relationship that transpires in life. In religion the truth has been revealed
as to its *content*; but it is another matter that this
content should exist in the *form* of the concept, of thinking, of the concept in speculative form.[75]

A further form of the understanding is the following.
When we say, "God in his eternal universality is the one
who distinguishes himself, determines himself, posits an
other that is his own, and likewise sublates the distinction, thereby remaining present to himself, and is Spirit
only through this process of being brought forth," then
the understanding enters in and counts one, two, three.
Oneness is certainly wholly abstract. But the three ones
are expressed more profoundly when they are defined as
persons. Personhood is what is based upon freedom--the
first, deepest, innermost freedom, but also the most abstract form in which freedom announces its presence in

the subject. "I am a person, I exist for myself"--this
is an utterly unyielding position. When, therefore, this
distinction is so defined, and each individual is taken
as one or indeed as a person, then through this definition of the person what the Idea demands appears to be
made even more invincible, namely, to regard this distinction as that which does not differentiate but remains
absolutely one, the sublating of this distinction. Two
cannot be one; each person is a rigid, unyielding, autonomous being-for-self. Logic shows that the category
of one is a poor category, the wholly abstract unit.
[81] But when we are dealing with personhood, the isolated character of the person, the subject, is surrendered. Ethical life, love, just mean the giving up of
particularity, of particular personhood, and its extension to universality--so, too, with friendship. Inasmuch as I act rightly towards another person, I regard
him as identical with myself. In friendship and love I
give up my abstract personhood and thereby win it ·back as
concrete. The truth of personhood is found precisely in
winning it back through this absorption, this being absorbed into the other. Such forms of understanding show
themselves immediately in experience to be such as to
annul themselves.

　　We are considering the Idea in its universality, as
it is defined in and through pure thinking. This Idea
is the whole of truth and the one truth; therefore everything particular that is to be comprehended as true must
be comprehended according to the form of this Idea. Nature and finite Spirit are products of God; therefore
rationality is found within them. That something is made
by God involves its having within itself the truth, the
divine truth as a whole, i.e., the determinateness of
this Idea. The form of this Idea exists only in God as
Spirit; if the divine Idea is comprehended in the forms
of finitude, then it is not posited as it is in and for
itself; only in Spirit is it so posited. In the finite

forms it exists in a finite way; but the world is something produced by God, and therefore the divine Idea always forms the basis of what generally exists. To know
the truth of something means to know and define it according to the truth, in the form of this Idea in general.

In the earlier religions, particularly in the religion of India, we have anticipations of the triad as
the true category. The idea of threefoldness indeed came
to expression with the recognition that the one cannot
remain as one, that it is what it ought to be not as one
but rather as movement and distinction in general, and as
the relation of these distinctions to each other. However, in these religions the third is not the Spirit, not
true reconciliation, but rather origin and passing away,
or the category of change, which is indeed the unity of
the distinctions, but a very inferior union. The Idea
reaches perfection not in immediate appearance, but for
the first time when the Spirit has entered into the community and, as the immediate, believing [82] Spirit, has
raised itself to the level of thinking. It is of interest to consider these fermentations of an Idea and to
learn to recognize, in the marvellous appearances that
manifest themselves, its foundation.

Among the Pythagoreans and Plato the abstract basis
of this Idea is found, but its determinate characteristics are left entirely in a state of abstraction: partly
in the abstraction of single numbers (one, two, three);
partly (and indeed for Plato) in the more concrete nature
of the one and the other, that which is multiple within
itself, θάτερον, and in the third, which is the unity of
the two. Here the triad is found not in the Indian mode
of fantasy but in mere abstraction. There are categories
of thought that are better than numbers, better than the
category of number, but they are still wholly abstract
categories of thought. They are found, most surprisingly,
in Philo, who carefully studied Pythagorean and Platonic
philosophy, and also among the Alexandrian Jews and in

Syria. Consciousness of this truth, this trinitarian
Idea, arose especially among the heretics, indeed primarily the Gnostics, who however brought this content to
expression in obscure and fantastic images.

An almost countless number of forms can be observed
here. In accord with the major elements, they are as
follows: (1) The Father, the One, the ὄν, which is described as the abyss, the depths, indeed as that which is
empty, the inexpressible, the incomprehensible, which is
beyond all concepts. For in any case what is empty and
indeterminate is incomprehensible; it is the negative of
the concept, and its conceptual character is to be this
negative, since it is only a onesided abstraction, constituting only a moment of the concept. The One for itself is not yet the concept, the truth. (2) Other being,
determinacy, activity determining itself, which according to the broadest designation is λόγος--rationally determinative activity, or precisely the word. The word is
this simple self-expression that neither makes nor becomes a hard and fast distinction, but rather is immediately perceived, and that, because it is so immediate,
is likewise taken up into interiority and returns to its
origin. This second moment is also defined as σοφία,
wisdom, the primal man who is entirely pure, an existent
other as that first [83] universality, a particular and
determinate reality. For this reason it was defined as
the archetype of humanity, Adam Kadmon, the only-begotten.
This is not a fortuitous characteristic but rather an
eternal activity, which does not happen merely at one
time. In God there is only one birth, the act as eternal
activity, a determination that itself essentially belongs
to the universal. The essential point is that this
σοφία, the only-begotten, remains likewise in the bosom
of God; the distinction, therefore, is no distinction.

In such forms the Idea has fermented. The main
point is to know these appearances, no matter how unrefined they are, as rational, to know that they have their

ground in reason, and to know what sort of reason is
present in them. But at the same time one must know how
to distinguish the form of rationality that presently exists and is not yet adequate to the content. This Idea
actually has been placed beyond man, beyond thought and
reason, and indeed has been so placed over against him
that this determinate quality, which alone is the truth
and the whole truth, has been regarded as something
peculiar only to God, remaining permanently above and beyond, and does not reflect itself into the other, which
appears as the world, nature, and man. To this extent,
this fundamental Idea has not been considered as the universal Idea.

This mystery of the Trinity dawned upon Jacob Böhme
in another fashion. His way of imagining and thinking is
rather fantastical and unrefined; he has not yet risen to
the pure forms of thinking. But the ruling and fundamental principle of all the notions that fermented [in
his mind], and of all his struggles [to reach the truth],
was the recognition of the presence of the Trinity in
everything and everywhere; e.g., it must be born in the
hearts of persons. It is the universal foundation of
everything that may indeed be finite from the point of
view of truth, but even its finitude has the truth in it.
Thus Jacob Böhme attempted to represent under this category nature and the heart, the Spirit of humanity.

In more recent times, through the influence of
Kantian philosophy, the triad has again been mentioned as
a type or, as it were, a schema for thought, already in
very specific forms. When this Idea is known as the essential and sole nature of God, then it must not be regarded as something above and beyond this world; rather
it is the goal of cognition to know the truth also in
particular things. [84] If it is thus cognized, then
everything that is true in particular circumstances contains this determinate characteristic. To cognize means
to know something in its determinateness; its nature is

that of determinateness itself, and the nature of determinateness itself is that which is expounded in the Idea.
That this Idea is the truth, generally speaking, and that
all categories of thought are this movement of determinacy, is the [task of] logical exposition.[b]

NOTES FOR CHAPTER II

1. The word "Christian" has beem omitted from Lasson's chapter
title; it is superfluous since the whole of the Third Part of the
Lectures is concerned with the "Christian Religion." Moreover, the
"abstract concept" of God taken up in the first section of the chapter is not specifically Christian. The second section of the chapter provides an overview of the three "moments," "spheres," or
"kingdoms" of the divine Idea, while the Kingdom of the Father in
the strict sense begins only with the third section of the chapter.

2. MS. heading: "a. Abstract Concept. 8/8 21." By this heading, Hegel designates the beginning of the first of the three main
sections of his 1821 lectures (following the introductory materials),
the section treating the "Abstract Concept" of God, i.e., the concept of the identity of concept and being as grasped in the ontological proof of the existence of God. In the 1824 lectures, this
section is taken into the Introduction as its concluding section
(the *Werke* also locates it there, preceding the "Division"), while
in the 1827 lectures, this section is removed entirely from the
Revelatory Religion and is treated in Part I of the *Philosophy of
Religion*, the Concept of Religion (cf. Lasson, I/1:218-225), where
it, together with the other proofs, more properly belongs. (The
Werke removes the 1827 proofs from their proper setting in the Concept of Religion and prints them as an Appendix to the *Vorlesungen
über die Beweise vom Dasein Gottes* [12:535-546].) Lasson calls this
section "The Metaphysical Concept of God" (an unnecessary change
from Hegel's own designation).

3. The MS. adds: "his concept."

4. Here Hegel contrasts the cosmological and ontological proofs
of the existence of God, or (what is the same thing) the phenomenological and speculative approaches to religion.

5. The MS. adds: "[The] concept of this religion [is given]
already with [the general definition of] religion."

6. [+]The purely abstract concept without its concrete determination as Spirit -- but with a content, to be sure -- [is the] God of
representation. Metaphysical concept consists in the self-reduction
of the proof to the point that the concept is real by means of it-

self. Concrete concept is Spirit, Spirit [is] its reality, Spirit
as totality, unity with another Spirit, and only in this way Spirit.
Here: (αα) the concept in general, definition of the concept, its
reality, being. The higher standpoint, pertaining to the modern
world. Proceeding not from existence, but thought beginning from
itself, thence the transition to reality. Concept: infinite negativity the first aspect -- fixation with regard to the midpoint,
free.

   (α) Ostensibly: concept of God and reality of God. With *this*
content, reality is contained in the concept. -- [It is] this content itself that demands it. (β) But the content is common to the
two. Hence there must be a transition as such from concept to
reality. (γ) The content [is] presupposed, but it itself [is] precisely this unity, which [is] not presupposed but proved, i.e.,
[exhibited] in its very determination. -- The transition is to be
exhibited. [The starting point is] not finite, [it does not pro-
ceed] from a being or from something finite.[+]

   In this section of the 1821 MS., several of the marginal additions anticipate passages in the Griesheim transcript, indicating
that Hegel used the original manuscript with emendations as the
basis for his lectures in 1824.

   7. [+]More precisely: (α) here [a matter of] proceeding from
the concept; previously, from existence. The truth of the latter is
the concept, the universal, the universal absolute power subsisting
in and for itself. Here the reverse [is the case]. The two [are]
necessary, hence both exist as posited, i.e., their onesidedness is
sublated; by each the show of immediacy [is] appropriated.[+]

   8. Hegel seems to be saying that because the true concept does
not exclude but rather includes being or existence, it is misleading
or unnecessary to speak of it as "only" a concept. Just as the concept without being is a mere image, so being without the concept is
mere externality (see below). The antithesis between concept and
being must be overcome and their unity demonstrated, this being the
task of the ontological proof. Any notion of perfection that regards God merely as a content or reality and disparages the concept
of God is unsatisfying.

   9. [+]This is done, to be sure, according to the modern point of
view, and precisely this empirical unity of thinking and being is
maintained as the affirmative, authentic reality -- i.e., the empirical human being, the immediate world. (The term translated somewhat colloquially as "unpack" is *herausklauben*.)

   10. [+]As in Anselm the image of perfection, of the most universal,
so here the existence of the concrete.[+]

   11. [+](α) Concept is, as concept, A = A; good, but in this form
[it is] finite, untrue. (β) Not to hold fast to the untrue, the
finite -- generally (γ) not with reference to God. (Finitude always
entails the difference of concept and object.) Perfection the presupposition -- reality.[+]

   12. [+][The] concept [must] abolish its finitude by its own means:

(α) [what is] contained in it, i.e., distinguished from it. When one supposes that one has done away with what is opposed to it, [i.e.] being, precisely then [the concept is] dialectical. (β) For itself, the concept [is] activity, goal, [it actively aims] to objectify itself.[+]

13. [+]Kant says that [being] is not a predicate. Nothing is added to the concept of a hundred dollars if [in addition] they also *exist*. [This is] correct, precisely because and in so far as [being] is already contained in the concept itself. But just the meaning [of Kant's statement] is that [being is] not contained in the concept, at least not in the subjective concept. Such a subjective concept or merely subjective image is what he has in mind, as in the example of the hundred imagined dollars. Here the content as such, i.e., as imagined, [is] distinguished from its being. Nothing is added to the concept by being; therefore [being is] not a predicate, as in the case of ordinary demonstration, when the concept is that which encompasses the predicates, as distinguished from [its] form [of] being. [This is] correct in the finite realm.

But in God the content [is] both concept *and* being; this is the entire content of Anselm's metaphysics; this is the perfection he presupposes. But what right [does he have to] make this presupposition? Here [it] is precisely a question of no longer presupposing that God is the content or the most perfect being, but rather that the unity of concept and being -- which is precisely the most perfect reality -- is the absolute truth. The presupposition, which is to be shown, and indeed the real concept as such, (α) is not God, (β) is not a finite concept, i.e., [one] in which thought and existence are and remain separated.

The distinction made by modern presuppositions: (α) concrete, empirical man -- rational, sensible; (β) *only* a concept, which must remain as such, -- the contradiction with (α) [being] unresolved.[+]

14. A reference to the discussion of "the proofs that proceed from the finite," the so-called cosmological proofs, in the Concept of Religion (Lasson, I/1:210-218).

15. [w]One of the sides in the antithesis is the subject itself, which is the realization of the Idea in its concrete meaning.[w] (12: 212; ET 2:351.)

16. [w]For the infinite has an infinite opposed to it, and thus the infinite itself posits itself as a finite, so that the subject, because of its infinitude, is compelled to annul this opposition, which has immersed itself in its infinitude.[w] (12:212; ET 2:351-352. From the Hotho notes of the 1824 lectures.)

17. At this point Lasson inserts out of context a passage from the 1827 lectures which refers to the ontological proof. However, it should be kept in mind that the 1827 lectures did not treat proofs of the existence of God in the Revelatory Religion but rather in the Concept of Religion. The original context for this passage occurs on p. 89 (n. 73), where we have located it, as may be determined from the order of the 1827 text in the *Werke*, 12:231-232. The correction is provided by Jaeschke.

18. ^{w}And has won great applause for himself.^{w} (12:214; ET 2: 353.)

19. Lasson's heading for this section is "The Development of the Idea and the Trinity." For reasons that will become apparent shortly, we have placed the discussion of the Trinity in a separate section.

20. MS. heading: "b. Concrete Representation -- or rather determination, i.e., development of the Idea. Interweaves itself with the cultus."
This heading designates the start of the second major section of the 1821 MS., entitled "Concrete Representation." This section contains three "spheres" or "moments" (see below, p. 63): (a) the concept of God in and for itself (or God as triune); (b) the concept in diremption or differentiation; (c) the concept in the history of redemption or reconciliation. In these three spheres Hegel sets forth the concrete representations, images, or beliefs of the Christian Religion.
However, when he lectured from this MS. in 1824, he modified this method of division and added to the section heading the words "--or rather determination, i.e., development of the Idea [of God] . . . ." The divine Idea "develops" in terms of its being in and for itself (the immanent Trinity), its self-differentiation in the otherness of the world and finite Spirit (which reaches its pinnacle in the incarnation, suffering and death of Christ on the cross, which is also the turning point, the beginning of reconciliation), and its self-redintegration through the transformed (inter)subjectivity of the community of faith. Here Hegel attains the mature division of his lectures, which in 1831 he designated as the three Kingdoms of Father, Son, and Spirit. The old categories of "abstract concept," "concrete representation," and "community, cultus," which were inherited from the Concept of Religion and applied to the Determinate Religions, are no longer really appropriate for the Revelatory Religion. The Christian concept of God (as the absolute Idea) is not abstract but concrete, and the life of the community of faith, including its cultus, rather than being treated as a separate section, belongs among the concrete representations of this religion as constitutive of the third moment in the development of the Idea of God. (See below, p. 67.)
The present section provides an overview of the three "spheres," "moments," or "elements" in terms of which the divine Idea "develops." (Cf. Chap. I.5.) The next section takes up the Idea of God in and for itself (the immanent Trinity, the Kingdom of the Father). The moment of self-differentiation-leading-into-reconciliation (the Kingdom of the Son) encompasses sections (b) and (c) of "Concrete Representation" in the 1821 MS., while the moment of self-redintegration (the Kingdom of the Spirit) is coterminous with part "C" of the 1821 MS., "Community, Cultus."

21. $^+$(α) Neither natural being nor essence; (β) manner in which the determinacy of the concept, of thought, first appears as predicate, reflection, thought -- indeed not naturally or immediately -- [but] precisely as again established. -- Mode of immediacy as identity with itself -- only as positive determinations, i.e., it should

only be linked with the subject as positive, not simultaneously be distinguished as opposed to what is defined as subject.[+]

22. The point here is that the Idea already contains within itself the element of reality or objectivity. According to Hegel, the Idea is "essentially concrete, because it is the free concept giving reality and determinacy to itself" (*Enc.*, § 213). It represents the final category in Hegel's logic, since it is "the absolute unity of the concept and objectivity" (*ibid.*).

23. See n. 73, p. 305.

24. [+]No reflection on the fact that the simple subject [becomes] diverse as a result of such diversity.[+]
At the beginning of this sentence Lasson changes *zeigt sich* to *zeigen sich* to make it agree with the plural subject *Prädikate*.

25. The MS. reads *desselben* instead of *derselben*.

26. Hegel here summarizes the three "spheres" or "moments" into which part (b), "Concrete Representation," of the 1821 MS. is divided. See above, n. 20.

27. [+](α) Nature, (β) Son of Man -- but the latter for faith, for that Spirit of God. Community [the] knowledge of divinity.[+]

28. In the Lasson edition, this section from the 1824 lectures follows the next section of the 1821 MS. The rearrangement is made necessary by our introduction of a separate section on the Trinity.

29. See above, n. 20.

30. With the distinction between universality, particularity, and individuality, Hegel alludes to the doctrine of the triple syllogism in the *Encyclopedia* (see above, p. 37, including n. 39).

31. A reference to the categories by means of which the Determinate Religions in Part II of the Philosophy of Religion were treated. These categories were carried over to the Revelatory Religion in the 1821 MS. but dropped in 1824 and thereafter. (See above, n. 20.) Hegel here uses the term *Gestalt* (form) instead of the more commonly employed *Vorstellung* (representation).

32. Lasson does not begin a new section at this point, but it is important to do so in order to indicate the beginning of the first of the three "spheres," "elements," or "moments" that occurs in all of the lecture series. The reference here is to the *immanent* or *preworldly* Trinity, the inner dialectic of self-differentiation and self-redintegration that constitutes the divine life. This inner dialectic is outwardly re-enacted in the *economic* or *worldly* Trinity--God's relation to the world in creation, incarnation, reconciliation, and spiritual community. The economic Trinity is actually coterminous with the three Kingdoms of Father, Son, and Spirit. Hegel normally reserves the term "triune" to refer to the immanent Trinity.

33. MS heading: "a. Absolute Idea of Philosophy." The "a" designates the beginning of the first of the spheres of "Concrete Representation," namely, the concept of God in and for itself. Lasson fails to note this heading in the text, although he does include it in his outline of the 1821 MS. in the appendix, II/2:235.

34. Lasson erroneously omits "not" (*nicht*). The correction is provided by Jaeschke and has been confirmed by checking the microfilm.

35. The word play between *Verschiedenheit* (diversity) and *Unterschiedenheit* (differentiation) is difficult to bring out in translation.

36. +Love [is] knowledge -- [of] himself in love [*Die Liebe Wissen, -- sich in der Liebe*].+

37. +Condition of concepts speculative, wholly peculiar, [like] no other condition -- metaphysics [*Verhalten der Begriffe spekulativ, ganz eigentümlich, kein andres Verhalten -- Metaphysik*].+

38. See Editor's Introduction, p. xxv.

39. +(β) Traces.+

40. *Dreiheit*, as distinguished from the terms for "triune" and "Trinity," *dreieinig* and *Dreieinigkeit*.

41. One of the gods of the Hindu triad (Trimurti), the others being Brahma and Vishnu. Siva represents the principle of destruction, and also the reproductive or restoring power.

42. *De coelo*, 268a, 10.

43. +Abstract quality of thought.+

44. +In philosophy wholly exhausted [*ausgegangen*], in theology no more seriousness.+

45. For Hegel's doctrine of matter, see Enc., §§ 262 ff. The hard, resistant material object because of its mass is also a center of gravitational attraction, which reaches out for the other, thereby annulling its being-for-self, its oneness. (I am indebted to H. S. Harris for help in translating and interpreting this passage.)

46. +(β) Personality, absolute moment, although abstract.+

47. +That this determination [is] essential [we have] already seen -- generally speaking, the highest Idea -- the latter [is] absolute reflection, the totality of the aspects in themselves. -- Representation [at the level of] sensibility: (α) 3 gods -- subjectivity would be lost; (β) evil -- or deeper -- +

48. +In Christianity generally -- triune, Father, Son, and Spirit.+

49. +When one begins abstractly.+

50. +Universal -- Father is presupposition.+

51. +Transition, progression from the universal to the particular. Various determinations so that each does not directly [express] in itself [the] fulness of the whole -- this is correct but [only] as an abstraction.+

52. +In the middle between East and West. Eastern idealism sublimates Western actuality into a thought-world.+

53. August Neander, *Genetische Entwicklung der vornehmsten gnostischen Systeme* (Berlin, 1818).

54. +Not to mention many aeons, universal powers . . .+

55. +*Ibid.*, p. 78: "The Brahma of the Hindus." Brahma is not revelatory but rather remains self-enclosed.+

56. The MS. reads: "from the Son" (*vom Sohne*)--a rare error of Hegel.

57. The MS reads *stehen* instead of *steht*.

58. The words "the first element" appear as a heading in the 1824 transcripts, designating the first of the elements or moments in which the Idea of God is developed, namely, the being of God in and for himself, the immanent Trinity.

59. Lasson omits the remainder of this sentence from the Griesheim transcript (correction provided by Jaeschke).

60. 12:227-229 (ET 3:11-13).

61. Beginning at this point, Lasson places the remainder of this paragraph from the *Werke* in a footnote. However, Jaeschke regards the source as the 1831 lectures, and there seems little reason to question its authenticity. Hence we are including the entire paragraph in the text.

62. Hegel takes up the "entire content" of philosophy in his *Encyclopedia of the Philosophical Sciences*, and in the second and third parts of that work, the Philosophy of Nature and the Philosophy of Spirit, he addresses himself to precisely this theme.

63. The following paragraph from the Griesheim transcript is omitted by Lasson, probably because it parallels materials from the 1821 MS. (above, pp. 69-70), and from the 1827 lectures (below, p. 96). The text has been furnished by Jaeschke from a copy of the Griesheim transcript at the Hegel-Archiv.

64. The MS. reads: *in der Drijas, beim Plato. Drijas* is an unintelligible word--possibly a transliteration of Δρυάς, a Dryad or wood-nymph, but it does not fit the context. More likely Griesheim

misheard Hegel's Swabian tongue, being prepared for another strange
Oriental term after "Trimurti" (the Hindu triad). Thus I am translating the text as though it reads: *in der Trias beim Plato.*

65. Lasson omits the remainder of this sentence from the
Griesheim transcript (correction provided by Jaeschke).

66. The next three paragraphs from the Griesheim transcript
are omitted by Lasson, again because of parallels with the 1821 MS.
(above, pp. 73-74) and the 1827 lectures (below, pp. 96-97).
Part of this passage, however, is reproduced by the *Werke*, 12:244-
245 (ET 3:30-31). Text furnished by Jaeschke.

67. The MS. reads *Vors*, possibly an abbreviation for *Vorsehung*,
"providence."

68. These last three paragraphs help to clarify more fully
Hegel's opposition to feeling as the basic form of the religious relationship. Feeling or sensation (*Empfindung, Gefühl*) are basically
receptive (*empfangen*), dependent, passive, whereas the true relation
to the infinite, in Hegel's view, is active, concrete, participa-
tory. It is a relation of reverence (*Ehrfurcht*), not fear (*Furcht*),
of freedom rather than of dependence. This relation takes place in
the form of thinking--properly understood, the thinking of absolute
Spirit "posited within" finite Spirit, not finite thoughts about the
infinite. It is knowledge of the true object, based on the object's
making itself known.

69. Lasson omits the remainder of this sentence from the
Griesheim transcript.

70. These words mark the beginning of the first of the three
major elements for the 1827 lectures, the Idea of God in and for
itself.

71. This could be taken as an allusion to Schleiermacher's
derivation of the divine attributes in *Die christliche Glaubenslehre*,
namely, as modifications of the feeling of absolute dependence. See
also above, p. 34.

72. [w]Nor is their contradiction truly resolved by the removal
of their determinateness, as when the understanding demands that they
should be taken only *sensu eminentiori.*[w] (12:230; ET 3:14.)

73. The next two paragraphs, which refer to the ontological
proof, are transposed by Lasson to a point earlier in this chapter
(p. 54, n. 17).

74. [w]For the understanding God is *the One*, the essence of essences. This empty identity without difference is the false product
of the understanding and modern theology. But God is *Spirit*, who
gives himself an objective form and knows himself therein. This is
concrete identity, and thus the Idea is also an essential moment.[w]
(12:236; ET 3:21.)

75. On the distinction between content and form as a way of understanding the relation between philosophy and religion, see below, pp. 291-293.

B. THE KINGDOM OF THE SON

CHAPTER III

DIFFERENTIATION AND ESTRANGEMENT[1]

Section 1. Creation and Preservation of the World[2]

[85] [m][3] The *second sphere* for representation is the *creation* and *preservation* of the *world as nature*--a finite world, spiritual and physical nature, the inauguration of an entirely other ground, the world of finitude.[4]

We know from the concept the element of differentiation, and more precisely, the determinate differentiation. One side, as the undivided and indivisible concept, [is] the pure subjectivity that keeps itself in unity. The other side is the difference as such in itself, that is to say, being-outside-of-itself. It is the absolute judgment or primal division [*Urteil*] that grants independence to the side of other-being. [It is] goodness that grants the Idea as a whole to the latter in its estrangement, in so far as it can receive this Idea into itself in its modality as other-being, and can represent it.[5]

[6]The relation of this second sphere to the first may be defined by saying that it involves the same Idea implicitly but in another determinate modification. The absolute act of the first judgment or division [is] *implicitly* the same as the second; [but] imagination holds the two apart as quite different grounds and acts. And in

fact they should be [86] distinguished and held apart; if
it is said that they are *implicitly* the same, then it
must be exactly determined how this is to be understood.
Otherwise a false interpretation may arise (one that is
false in itself and also an incorrect grasp of what has
just now been expounded) to the effect that the eternal
Son of the Father, who himself exists objectively and is
himself objectively existing divinity, is *the same as* the
physical and spiritual world--[as though] the Son is to
be understood *only* in this way.[7]

It has already been suggested, however, and is quite
obvious that only the Idea of God $^+$(θεὸς νοητός)$^+$, as
explained previously in what was termed the first sphere,
is the eternal, true God. Subsequently his higher realization or manifestation in the detailed process of Spirit
will be considered in the third sphere.

If the world, as it is immediately, is taken as existing in and for itself, existing as the sensible and
the temporal, then it would be understood either in that
false sense just alluded to or as entailing in the first
instance two eternal acts of God. God's activity, [how-
ever,] is after all utterly one and the same, and in
truth is not a manifold of various activities, some occurring now, some later on, external to one another, and
so forth.

Thus this differentiating [of worldly entities] as
something independent is only the explicitly negative
moment of other-being, of being-external-to-self, which as
such has no truth but is only a moment--temporally speaking, only an instant, yet itself no instant--and only has
this mode of independence in contrast to finite Spirit in
so far as it is itself in its finitude just this type and
manner of independence. In God himself this is the immediately disappearing moment of appearance.[8]

This moment has the range, breadth, and depth of a
world, including heaven and earth with their infinite organization $^+$internally and externally.$^+$ Now if[9] we say

that other-being is an immediately disappearing moment,
[87] that it is only a flash of lightning that immediately
vanishes, the sound of a word that is perceived and vanishes the instant it is spoken, then the moment is expressed such that the momentariness of time floats before[10] [our minds] with its before and after, in which the
moment *exists* as neither the one nor the other.

However, all temporal determinacy is to be elimi-
nated, whether it be in terms of duration or the now; and
only the thought, the simple thought, of the other is to
be held fast. [We say] "simple" because the "other" is
an abstraction. That this abstraction is extended to the
spatial and temporal world is to say that the latter is
the simple element of the Idea itself and therefore receives the Idea entirely in itself. However, because it
is the element of other-being, it is infinitely sensible
extension. If we ask whether the world or matter
$^+(ὕλη)^+$ is eternal, exists from eternity, or whether on
the contrary it has a beginning in time, this question
belongs to the empty metaphysics of the understanding.
[In the phrase,] "from eternity," the latter term, as an
infinite time that is represented according to simple infinity, is itself a reflected infinity, a reflected determination. As soon as the world enters into representation, time commences, and then also, by reflection, this
reflected infinity or eternity arises; but we must be
aware of the fact that this determination does not apply
to the concept itself.

Another question, or what is in part a further development of the previous question, concerns the fact that
the world, or matter, in so far as it is supposed to be
eternal, is uncreated and immediately for itself. The
separation made by the understanding between form and matter lies at the basis of this question. However, matter
or world, according to their fundamental determination,
are much rather this other, the negative, which is itself
only a moment of posited being, and is the opposite of

something independent. Moreover, even in its existence
the world is only what annuls itself, and hence is a moment in the process. The natural world is relative, is
appearance; that is to say, it is relative and is appearance not only for us, but also in itself. This is its
quality, namely, precisely to pass over, moving itself
forward, so as to take itself back into the final Idea.
[88] The diverse metaphysical positions and diverse definitions concerning the ὕλη of the ancients, as well as
that of the philosophizing Christians, and especially the
Gnostics, have their basis in the determination of the
independence of other-being.

A third [question arises, namely, the question concerning the] Demiurge or the Son, [the question concerning the] Creator of the world, +because the world [is]
incomplete and imperfect.+ But it is not a particular
person, God in general, the universal (therefore the
Father), who [stands] over against the objectivity of the
world, over against other-being.

This other-being as world is such that it is purely
and simply what is created, +does not exist in and for
itself;+ and if a distinction is made between beginning
as *creation* and the *preservation* of what exists, precisely this distinction is made in accord with the representation that such a sensible world in fact exists and is
something that is. It has therefore been held all along
with justification that, since being--that which exists
independently for itself--is not attributed to the world,
preservation and creation are identical, and that preservation is a creation. But can one also say that creation
is a preservation? One could say this in so far as the
moment of other-being is itself a moment of this Idea;
[otherwise] it would be presupposed, as in former times,
that something existent precedes creation.

Now, since other-being [is] defined as the totality
of an appearance, it expresses in itself the Idea, and
this is in general what is meant by the *wisdom* of God in

nature, a definition according to which nature has in advance a concept existing in and for itself, which is not
[nature itself] as the element of other-being.

[+]The wisdom of God [is] a profound concept, which is
lacking in the earlier religious standpoints because it
contains the Idea that is determinate in and for itself.[+]
This wisdom is a universal expression, and it is the concern of philosophical knowledge to recognize this concept
in nature and to grasp nature as a system, as an organization, in which the divine Idea is mirrored.[11] This
Idea [+]is made manifest; its content is itself the manifestation,[+] differentiating itself, revealing itself as
an other and [taking] this other back into itself so that
this return is just as much external as it is internal.
In nature, therefore, these stages lie outside of each
other as a system of adjacent entities, the kingdoms of
nature, the highest of which is the kingdom of the living.

[89] But life, which is the highest exhibition of
the Idea in nature, means precisely to sacrifice itself--
the negativity of the Idea vis-à-vis this its existence--
and to become Spirit. Spirit is this coming forth by
means of nature; that is to say, Spirit finds its opposite in nature, such that through the sublation of this
opposite, Spirit is *for* itself, i.e., is Spirit. Nature,
[however, is] the Idea existing only *in* itself, i.e., the
Idea as immediate or posited in other-being.[m][12]

[90] [a]*The second element*[13] is therefore the element
of *representation*, of *appearance* as such. We can say
that the absolute Idea, determined as an object and existing in and for itself, is complete.[14] Nevertheless,
from the subjective side this is not so; the latter is
not complete either in itself--[for] it is not [yet] con-
crete--nor is it complete as consciousness with respect
to what it has as its object. The subject does not view
itself in the divine Idea. This is the second element;
it is what is lacking in the first condition, and this

must now be spelled out.

In this second element, the subjective aspect in
general comes into play, and along with it, appearance.
The subjective aspect contains in its development the
foundation of religion, of truth. The Christian Religion
begins with the truth and from [91] the truth. This is
God; he is the truth, and from here truth first passes
over to the subject. This second aspect must now be defined more closely.

There are two sides from which this definition must
be grasped. First, from the side of the Idea. From this
side we have said: Spirit exists in the determination of
universality and posits itself in the determination of
particularity, which itself is the eternal Idea: God is
the entire totality. It is the *Son* who is to be realized; he unites the two qualities of being the totality
in itself and of being posited as other. Other-being is
the first determination, while the second is that the in-
itself of the other is also the divine Idea. In the process of the analysis both determinations are to be posited finally as distinct, but as it were only for an instant, since they are not distinct in truth. In its being, in its immediate being, the concept includes the
fact that what is being has negation, is only a moment,
and just so is sublated. Representation holds these two
sides apart--otherwise it would not be real representation, according to which negation, the being-in-itself of
the divine Idea, is also a true moment. Representation
holds these sides apart in time.

The other side is what we have defined as finite
Spirit. Here the latter is pure thinking and has the
truth, eternal truth, in view--its relation to which is
called thinking. This thinking is its result, its end.
Finite Spirit begins from immediacy, raises itself from
the sensible to the infinite, to the element of thinking.
But in fact it is not the result of thinking; rather the
latter exists only through the movement of Spirit and its

elevation. Spirit is intrinsically the process of raising up, a process that is now to be considered.

From the first standpoint the situation is this:
God in his eternal truth exists as a state of affairs and
as a mystery in time; in the course of time the angels,
his children, sing his praises. This situation is described as a state of affairs in time, but it is the
eternal condition of thinking for the object. Later on,
what is referred to as a "fall" occurs, which is the
positing of the second standpoint--on one hand the
"analysis" of the Son, the separation of the two moments
that are contained in him. Jacob Böhme represented this
in terms of the notion that Lucifer, the first-born,
fell, and that another was begotten in his place. That
took place in heaven as it were, in the eternal Idea.
[92] But on the other hand there is subjective consciousness, finite Spirit, such that subjective consciousness
as pure thinking is in itself the process, starting from
immediacy and elevating itself to truth.

Thus we enter into the determinacy of space, of the
finite world and finite Spirit. This may now be expressed more precisely as follows: the positing of these
determinate qualities as a momentarily sustained distinction is an emergence and appearance of God in finitude.
For finitude is in fact the separation of what in itself
is identical but is maintained in separation. However,
from the other side, that of subjective Spirit, finitude
is posited as pure thinking; implicitly, however, it is a
result, and it is to be posited as it is in itself, as
this movement. Or pure thinking has to go into itself;
thereby it first posits itself as finite.

[135] [15]Subjective consciousness is itself a movement into itself, so that it might be *for* itself what it
is *in* itself. In itself it is this process, and the
latter should exist for it. Since what it is in itself
is *for* it, its need for reconciliation is thereby justified. Since it is thus for itself and is first posited

as subject, there arises the need that subjectivity
should exist for it in the divine Idea, that it should
know subjectivity within the Idea. At the outset, the
Idea is not yet posited for the subject because it is not
yet conceived. On the other side is the claim that the
need is satisfied or that God appears for the sake of subjective need in the form of subjectivity, of an immediate,
particular individual. [16]These are the two sides that we
have to consider.[a]

[92] [b]We now consider, therefore, the eternal Idea
in the *second element*,[17] in the form of *consciousness*
and of *representation* in general--a consideration of this
Idea in so far as it emerges out of universality and infinitude into the determinacy of finitude.

The first aspect or form is once again that of the
universality of the Idea as to content, but precisely in
the sense that God is over all. He is everywhere present; the presence of God is just the element of truth
that is in everything. At first, the Idea was found in
the element of thinking; this is the foundation, and we
started with it. Universality must precede everything
else in scientific knowledge; *scientifically*, one must
start with the abstract universal. In fact, however,
from an *existential* point of view it comes later. It is
the in-itself, which none the less subsequently appears,
specifically in knowledge--the in-itself that subsequently comes to consciousness and knowledge. The form
of the Idea comes to appearance as a result, which however is essentially the in-itself, the beginning. Just
as the content of the Idea is that the last shall be
first and the first last, so it is that what appears as
a result is at the same time the presupposition, the in-
itself, the foundation. This Idea is now generally to
be considered as it appears in the second element, the
element of appearance.

This progression may be conceived from two sides.

First of all, we see that the subject for which this
Idea exists is the thinking subject. Even the forms of
representation take [93] nothing away from the nature of
the fundamental form, namely, that the latter has the
form of thinking for man. Generally speaking, the subject exists as a thinking subject, thinking this Idea;
yet the subject is concrete self-consciousness. The
Idea must therefore exist for the subject as concrete
self-consciousness, as an actual subject.

Or one can say that the Idea in this first form is
the absolute truth. Absolute truth exists for thinking.
But the Idea must not only be the truth for the subject;
rather the latter must also attain *certainty* of the
Idea--a certainty that belongs to the subject as such, as
a finite, empirically concrete, sentient subject. The
Idea possesses certainty for the subject only in so far
as it is a perceivable Idea, in so far as it exists for
the subject. If I can say of anything, "it exists,"
then it possesses certainty for me; this is immediate
knowledge, this is certainty. The next step in the process of mediation is to prove that what exists also exists necessarily, that the truth is what is certain for
me; this is the transition into the universal. Having
started with the form of truth, we now proceed to the
fact that the truth obtains the form of certainty, that
it exists for me.

The other side of this progression starts from the
Idea. Eternal being-in-and-for-itself is what unfolds
itself, determines itself, judges or divides itself,
posits itself as its own difference; but the differentiation is at the same time constantly sublated: what exists in and for itself thereby constantly returns into
itself--only in this way is it Spirit. The differentiation is defined in such a way that it immediately disappears and is a relation of God, of the Idea, merely to
himself. This act of differentiation is only a movement,
a play of love with itself, in which no seriousness is

attributed to other-being, to separation and disunion.
The other is defined as the *Son*; in the language of feeling, as *love*; or, in a higher mode of determinacy, as
the *Spirit* that is present to itself and free. Within
the Idea, the determination of the distinction is not yet
complete, since generally speaking it is only an abstract
distinction. We have not yet arrived at the peculiar
quality of the differentiation; here it is only *one* determinate characteristic [among others]. The things differentiated are regarded as the same; they have not yet
arrived at a state of determinacy such that they have a
different determination.

From this side the judgment or primal differentiation of the Idea is to be conceived in such a way that
the Son obtains the determination of the other as such,
that this [94] other exists as a free being for itself,
and that it appears as something actual, as something
that exists outside of and apart from God. Its ideality,
its eternal return into what exists in and for itself, is
posited in the first form of identity, the Idea, in an
immediate and identical fashion. In order that there may
be difference, it is necessary to have the element of
other-being, necessary that other-being should actually
exist for there to be something distinguished. Only the
absolute Idea determines itself and, because of this
self-determination, is both certain of itself and absolutely free within itself. In thus determining itself,
it allows this determinate entity to exist as something
free, as something independent, an independent object.
Freedom exists only for the free; it is only for the free
man that an other is also free. It belongs to the absolute freedom of the Idea that, in its act of determining
and judging-dividing, it releases the other to exist as a
free and independent being. This other, released as an
independent being, is what is generally called *the world*.

The truth of the world is only its *ideality*, which
means that it does not possess true actuality. Its na-

ture is to *be*, but only in an *ideal* sense; it is not something eternal in itself but rather something created,
whose being is only posited. For the world to be means
to have a moment or instant of being, but also to annul
this its separation or estrangement from God. It means
to return to its origin, to enter into the relationship
of Spirit, of love--to *be* this relationship of Spirit, of
love, which is the third moment. The second moment is
the process of the world by which it passes over from
fall and separation into reconciliation.

The creation of the world is the second moment.
The first moment, within the Idea, is only the relationship of the Father to the Son; but the *other* also obtains the determinacy of other-*being*, of an existent
entity. It is in the Son, in the determination of the
difference, that the advance to further distinction occurs, that differentiation comes into its own as true
diversity.

As already noted, Jacob Böhme described this transition to the moment of the Son as follows: the first- and
only-begotten was Lucifer, the light-bearer, brilliance,
clarity, but he imagined himself within himself, i.e.,
he posited himself *for* himself, advanced to being and
thereby fell. [95] But the eternal and only-begotten One
immediately appeared in his place. Regarded from this
standpoint, this other is not the Son but rather the external world, the finite world, which exists outside the
truth--the world of finitude, where the other has the
form of being, and yet by its nature is only the ἕτερον,
the determinate, the differentiated, delimited, and
negative. The finite world represents the side of difference by contrast with the side that remains in unity,
and thus it divides into the natural world and the world
of finite Spirit. Nature enters into relation only with
man, and not on its own account with God, for nature is
not knowledge. God is Spirit; nature knows nothing of
Spirit. It is created by God, but of itself it does not

enter into relationship with him--in the sense that it is
not possessed of knowledge. It stands in relation only
to man, and in this relationship represents what is
called his dependent side. In so far as thinking recognizes the fact that nature is created by God, that understanding and reason are within it, it is known by man as
a thinking being. It is posited in relation to the divine to the extent that its truth is recognized.[b]

[89] [w]18 The discussion of the manifold forms ex-
pressive of the relation of finite Spirit to nature does
not belong to the philosophy of religion. Their scientific treatment forms part of the phenomenology of Spirit
or the doctrine of Spirit. Here this relation has to be
considered in so far as it comes within the sphere of religion, and in such a way as to show that nature is for
man not only the immediate, external world but rather a
world in which man knows God; nature is thus for man a
revelation of God. We have already seen how this relation of Spirit to nature is present in the ethnic religions where we encountered those forms that belong to the
advance of Spirit from immediacy, in which nature is
taken as contingent, to necessity and to a wise and pur-
poseful mode of activity. Thus the consciousness of God
on the part of finite Spirit is mediated by nature. Man
sees God by means of nature; nature is thus far only a
veiling and an untrue configuration.

What is distinguished from God is here really an
other, and has the form of an other or object; it is nature that exists for Spirit and for man. Thereby unity
is to be completed and the consciousness attained that
the end and determinate character of religion is reconciliation. The first step is the abstract consciousness
of God, the fact that man raises himself in nature to
God; this we have seen in the proofs for the existence of
God; here also are found those pious reflections as to
how gloriously God has made everything and how wisely he

has arranged all things. These elevated thoughts go
straight to God and may start from any set of facts.
Piety makes such edifying observations, starts with the
most particular and insignificant things, recognizing
therein something generally higher. Very often mixed in
with these observations is the distorted notion that
what goes on in the world of nature is to be regarded as
something higher than what is found in the human sphere.
This way of looking at things, however, is inappropriate
because it starts from particulars. [90] Another form of
observation can be opposed to it: viz., the cause should
be appropriate to the appearance and should itself contain the element of limitation that belongs to the appearance; we require a particular ground on which this
particular effect is based. The observation of a particular appearance always has this inappropriate aspect. Further, these particular appearances belong to the realm of
the natural. God, however, must be conceived as Spirit,
and that element in which we cognize him must likewise be
spiritual. "God thunders with his thundering voice," it
is said, "and is yet not comprehended" [cf. Job 37:5];
the spiritual person, however, demands something higher
than what is merely natural. If God is to be cognized as
Spirit, he must do something more than thunder.

A higher mode of viewing nature, and the deeper relation in which it is to be placed to God, is rather
found when it is itself conceived as something spiritual,
i.e., as the *natural aspect of man*. It is only when the
subject ceases to be classed as belonging to the immediate being of the natural and is posited as that which
it intrinsically is, namely, as movement, and when it has
gone into itself, that finitude as such is posited, and
indeed as finitude in the process of the relation in
which the exigency for the absolute Idea and its appearance come to exist for it. What comes first here is the
exigency for truth, while the way and means of the appearance of the truth are second.[w]

Section 2.   Man as Finite and Natural Spirit[19]

   a. *Natural Man*

   [95] [m][20] *The third sphere* is therefore objectivity in
the form of *finite Spirit*, the appearance of the Idea in
and to the latter, *redemption* and *reconciliation* as the
divine history itself [+]and at the same time as the sublation of external objectivity in general--and thereby as
the real consummation of Spirit.[+]

   This [is] the moment of divine, developed objectivity, the point at which divinity arrives just as much at
its most extreme mode of being-outside-itself as it finds
its turning point; precisely the highest estrangement and
the pinnacle of divestment constitute the moment of return
itself.

   Since this [is] the history of the divine Idea in
finite Spirit, this history itself directly contains two
sides: on the one hand, it is the history of finite consciousness itself [96] as isolated in immediacy; on the
other hand, [it is] this history as an object for consciousness, i.e., in so far as it is the history of God,
existing in and for itself.[21]

   The necessity of such a history is found, first of
all, in the divine Idea: God as Spirit is this process,
whose moments have themselves the form of complete reality and thereby of finite self-consciousness; hence the
divine Idea actualizes itself in and to finite self-consciousness. The other aspect of the necessity of this
manifestation, however, is that it takes place for self-
consciousness, precisely because it is this history in
finite self-consciousness. God must be for himself as
the whole of his revelation; thus he exists only as revealed. However, this history of his must be an object
for him in *its own* objectivity and truth. This true history of finite Spirit is what now must be grasped.

   In accord with the Idea of its truth, Spirit first

exists in its character as universality (Father), +not
in the element of thinking.+ However, finite Spirit
+means precisely that the moments+ of the concept of
Spirit fall indifferently asunder as differentiated and
distinguished, and that the first form of universality is
posited as first +neither in conception nor in thinking;
abstract universality and immediate being are found+
only as existent and immediate.

22The positive is abstract universality, not yet defined as a totality because of the falling asunder [of
the moments]. Hence the first modality of Spirit, as
finite and natural Spirit, is to exist as *natural man.*23

This determination is to be grasped according to its
concept. Immediately, it is an internally unresolved contradiction. Spirit is Spirit only as unending return into itself, as mediation of itself with itself, a mediation that is likewise sublated. Immediacy, on the other
hand, is the non-mediated, indeed the non-living, far
less the spiritual--it is something dead, as though something could exist without this mediation. Spirit essentially ought not to be and remain natural Spirit.

[97] This is a very important and truthful charac-
terization, and for this reason the one according to
which [finite Spirit] must be represented by religion,
as the knowledge of truth. We must now consider what is
contained in it more closely and in more concrete ways.

The natural man does not exist in the form that he
ought to; he is determined by the singularity of his existence. He is in the first instance the *willing* man,
for the will is the faculty of decision; it is that whereby man is constituted as an individual vis-à-vis others,
that which puts up resistance, establishing separation.
He is not yet the thinking man, who24 determines himself
in thoughtful fashion according to the universal and the
good, i.e., (from the viewpoint of the will) according to
a purpose that exists in and for itself. To think and to
determine oneself according to the universal already en-

tails an abandonment of that immediacy and sheer naturalness that adhere to man in an unmediated state.

Thus the natural man is one who is not liberated
within himself vis-à-vis himself and external nature. He
is the man of *desire* or *appetite*, of rudeness and self-
seeking, of dependence and fear. In his dependence on
nature, he can be either mild or savage.[25] In milder
regions (and this is the most characteristic situation),
where nature gives him the means to satisfy his physical
needs, his natural traits are able to remain mild, benev-
olent, characterized by simple needs and conditions;
geography and travel accounts provide pleasing depictions
of such conditions. However, in part these beneficent
customs [are] simultaneously mixed in with barbaric practices and customs (such as human sacrifice), becoming
completely bestial (in the Friendly Islands [Tonga],
tribal chiefs of superior rank allow themselves to be fed
like animals, lying as it were in the feeding trough).
[There are] fascinating depictions of these customs
[from] the islands and coasts of East Asia. But [it] appears [that] such a condition depends on fortuitous cir-
cumstances--such as climate, isolation [98] from others,
an insular situation--and without such this [condition]
is outwardly impossible; in part, however, it does not
derive at all from empirical possibilities. Besides,
such observations and accounts concern the outer, good-
natured disposition of men toward other persons; they do
not enter into the interior aspect of relationships and
conditions, +and hence they establish a narrow standard
for what man ought to be.+ It is not therefore a question of the condition that has befallen him, or that he
would now like to find himself in such a condition, or
indeed mankind as a whole. To all such views--+the in-
sipid possibilities+ and wishes of a sick philanthropy,
+which proceeds from abstractions, not from concrete
conditions+--actuality already stands opposed, and likewise in essence the concept, the nature of the case, and

this is the definition of naturalness. [+]Necessity appears in the form of external conditions; and the retailers of possibility believe that everything has been done when they have posited the possibility that the external circumstances [are] nothing in and for themselves and could be otherwise. But external circumstances [are] only occasions, shaped in one form or another, of a necessary development, which itself [utilizes] such external conditions.[+] Spirit is not determined or defined according to this state of nature and innocence, which is contrary to its concept. [+]As beneficent as such a condition is, it is not without gruesome aspects, but on the whole it also lacks that general self-consciousness and its consequences and developments that constitute the dignity of Spirit. This natural and more or less [savage] state [already] contains, furthermore, [an element of spiritual culture within itself].[+]

The other aspect to be considered here is precisely the concept of Spirit itself without the character of immediacy, without this antithesis. This general concept of Spirit is that which exists in and for itself, it is the divine Idea itself. Man, because he is Spirit, is implicitly this Idea. Indeed, because on the whole the concept is--above all in man as finite--the vis-à-vis of the objectivity of the divine Idea, this Idea can be and is defined precisely as the in-itself of man, i.e., the latter not as it is found in human form but rather in its inner substance, not [as it] actually exists as finite Spirit [but rather] in its [99] truth, as which it no longer exists immediately, or to which it[26] should first raise itself as Spirit--a truth that is itself only truly brought forth as spiritual.

The following two characteristics are found in man existing immediately: (α) his concept or possibility-- for the concept is his possibility, but as such, only as such; (β) his immediacy, his self-consciousness, not as it ought to be. (His concept [is represented] as [his

original] condition, existence, history, and from this
[follows] the transition to his immediate self-conscious-
ness--the Fall.)

The necessary unification of these two characteristics lies in the essence of Spirit, which exists as initi-
ating Spirit so immediately that it posits [itself] as
immediate object vis-à-vis itself. [One must here] observe the distinction between representation and conception. That which is defined conceptually is transposed
in the soil of representation into the conditions of existence, where it makes a transition from one condition
to another. This procedure [we must] first briefly consider.

We need only briefly to be reminded that the portrayal of the first moment, conceptually speaking, is by
means of the representation that man was originally created in the image of God, that his first condition [was]
that of perfection--indeed a spiritual perfection as well
as a physical situation in which nothing was lacking to
him--[and that therefore this moment of the concept] was
brought forth for itself and this characteristic represented as [externally real]. +(Those empirical, beneficent conditions spoken of earlier, even if they appear
to be touching, are scarcely to be given out as a condition of perfection, any more than the condition of childhood in human life. In the state of childhood, desires,
self-seeking, evil, etc., are already to be found, just
as in those empirical conditions, although neither the
bad nor the good are as pronounced.)+ One can paint this
condition further at will, but then precisely by so doing become entangled in difficulties and empty representations, together with their resolution: e.g., the fact
that women bear children painfully is based on the fem-
inine constitution--but how is this [child-bearing] to be
imagined if it is something that ought not to be? [100]
On the same [human] constitution is based the necessity of
the death of individuals--but how then [is it] to be

imagined that they do not grow older and do not die? More
precisely, there is found here a confusion over time and
the unending sensuous persistence of the bodily state.
[27] [This condition has] been grasped thus far, however, as a condition of the highest spiritual perfection,
of man in unity with nature, hence implicitly as an untroubled intelligence, which does not turn away from itself or into itself by means of reflection, an intelligence that penetrates and permeates persons as their
spiritual center, although not by means of standing over
against them or separating from them. +[This intelligence exists,] therefore, as a pure and highest knowledge,+ comprehending the core of metals, the qualities
of plants, and the innermost character of animals. Because it recognizes and grasps their true relation to the
corresponding aspects of human existence, it relates itself to nature as to a suitable garment that does not
destroy its organization: +nature as a body objectified
and cast off, all the tones, colors, and forms of nature
corresponding to an accent of Spirit. The perception of
this unity (the comprehending of nature) *is* man. To
know the characteristics of nature and what corresponds
to them is the cognition of nature from itself.+ But
this way of thinking is empty when it is considered in a
fundamental perspective, in spite of how much it commends
itself as an ideal of fantasy and supposedly has its
roots in the Idea itself, to the effect, namely, that it
is the original condition and that the actual condition
just as much as the ideal conforms to this Idea.
     But the first, immediate relation [of man's immedi-
ate being with his nature] is thus a relation of feeling,
of instinct, i.e., it is an immediate relation in the
consciousness of [101] intuition, +not one that has returned [to itself] out of the infinite antithesis [of
subject and object in reflective consciousness],+ not
one that has been reconstructed by thinking, or developed by it.[28] +It is easy to speak of feelings and per-

ceptions as manifold because perception and feeling
[are] unmediated and hence [are] as manifold as their objects, but both alike [are] only developed [into a mani-
fold] through reflection. It is of no help that heaven
and earth, humanity and the arts in their beauty are
opened up before the eyes of the body; that, what, and
when any of this is in [the mind of] the subject, is
lacking unless it [is unfolded by] an inwardly cultivated
reflection.[+29]

[The] first condition developed by reflection is
that of feeling, which is one of being concentrated and
non-manifold within oneself. Nature in its extensive
wealth does not have a relation to the subject but is
rather totally dense; it is first of all the process of
thinking that develops the wealth of relations for feeling or perception. Otherwise feeling is concentrated
within itself as the feeling of its singularity; and perception is rather only sensible perception, i.e., external relations to externals. [+]It is its own achieved
internality--and achieved it will be[+]--without interest,
theoretical, i.e., without interest in the internal or
its essence, without interest in developed, determinate
internality. These are the laws of nature, which are not
perceived [+]([it] is of no help to continue viewing
heaven so piously, innocently, and credulously);[+] [they
do] not [consist] in an immediate relation but rather are
the product of thought; they [exist] only through pene-
tration into perception and the annulment of the sensible
relation of unmediated externality.[30]

It is an entirely different matter to comprehend
the Idea of Spirit in general as the center of nature and
as the totality of its identity with it, [+]and to recognize the way this Idea is actualized in self-consciousness and the path it utilizes to achieve this end[+]--this
is entirely different than the fact that [the Idea] is
made known and knows itself not merely [102] in universality but rather in a state of determinacy, indeed in

the immediacy of the latter, as it actually is, precisely in the determinacy of immediate being. [+]We must still observe [how] this exposition has laboriously to work itself out in order to comprehend the Fall, [its own] other-becoming, [this] insurmountable knot.[+]

However, it is something else again[31] when this Idea is brought before the imagination: here it is unavoidable that it should be represented as a condition of primitive humanity brought forth by the hand of God. It is a higher faith, and in essence a true faith, that man is created in the image of God; this is his original determination, his true being-in-itself. It is also true that his condition is one that does not correspond to this Idea; it is an ungodly condition, one that ought not to exist, and furthermore it is man's guilt that he should be alienated from the Idea.

Another form [of the] elaboration of this definition, based on the speculative Idea, is that the nature of man is implicitly divine. This is found among the philosophers, both pagan and Christian, who always had in view the profound Idea lying at the basis of Christianity, and who [sought to] grasp, in more obscure or purer forms, the relation of human and divine nature in a philosophically speculative way, and in pure thoughts. [Here] it may be indicated that the first man, i.e., man as such, is comprehended by them as the only-begotten Son of God, as the moment of the objectification of God in the divine Idea: Adam Kadmon, the Logos, the Primal Man. [+](J. Böhme.) This is consistent.[+] [+]Precisely the Idea of man in his truth [is] therefore the moment of God in his eternal being, the moment of manifestation.[+] [m]

b. *Good and Evil*

[m]That man is good "by nature" is a doctrine of recent times. In the modern sense, his inclinations and natural tendencies [are considered to be good] in the

sense that [he] exists not in accord with his Idea but as
he is empirically, by nature, in accord with his vital
agency and existence ⁺[and] will; [he] is good without
mediation [103] of the negative.⁺ Development, for its
part, is only a positive bringing out of these tendencies, ⁺unhindered within itself and not passing through
negativity,⁺ passing [out of] possibility into actuality
and activity without being mediated by a negative moment,
⁺and nurturing good inclinations and tendencies. On this
representation,⁺ whatever is found in man that ought not
to be [could emerge] only through external contingencies
or an accidental failure to satisfy those natural tendencies; it could only be the absence of a free opportunity for their development. [This is the] barren viewpoint of the pedagogy of our time, which on the one hand
nourishes vanity, indulging in the conceit that it produces, and on the other hand does not perceive or investigate the depths of humanity and attains to no depths
itself but moves in barren circles, satisfied with itself.

[There is no doubt] that cultivation and a truly
serious and good education have the effect of putting
aside natural and self-seeking tendencies, chiefly by
means of intellectual formation and attainment, intellectual milk of rationality and generality, and good,
upright customs. ⁺But [this is] precisely what is not
meant when one says "by nature."⁺ But [it is likewise
clear that] in order to attain to such a condition of an
ethical people, the [original] condition must be glaringly
present, and [that] education is itself the history [of
culture] (but in softer tones) and [its] progression.[32]
⁺[One of the] satisfactions of modern times is [to re-
gard] the human being [as] good by nature and his development only [as a] positive bringing out [of the nature
that is within. We place before our eyes] the ethical
condition of the Greeks: certainly the element of negativity appears to recede and [does] not [emerge] in glar-

ing fashion. But [if it were only the] submersion [of a
people] in this kind of self-satisfaction without negativity, [the fall into evil] would break in from the outside whenever the opportunity presents itself. Overly
indulgent and condescending parents are of the opinion
that nothing further is lacking than good educational institutions.[+]

[33]Although the Idea of man as such [is represented
figuratively] as a paradisical condition, this Idea is
actual only [104] in the form of a natural and existent
condition; thus the connection between the first and the
second is a transition--indeed a transition to something
worse, a becoming other, a fall from the divine Idea,
from the image of God. It has been attributed especially
to representation that the connection is represented as a
transition between two conditions. What belongs to it as
such is only [the supposition] that there are two conditions related to each other, and not [that] nature itself
in its immediacy is a transition [into fallenness]. This
[must be] considered more closely.

The first condition [is an] immediately natural
state of general appetites, desires, and tendencies. But
this natural condition is one of *consciousness*. Already
life is immediate, but only as a process; hence still
more, consciousness. The consciousness of appetite is
not without will; rather [the appetite] is the willing
[of consciousness], its willing in its freedom.

[+]Willing what is natural is, more precisely defined,
evil.[+] [It is] the willing of separation, the positing
of one's singularity against others. [Hence] opposition
[is contained] within it--in an immediate sense, [the
opposition between] one's singularity and universality.
Man [*is*] consciousness and also thinking; [this is his]
universal definition, the good [that is] before him. He
[is human] only as a transition, [distinguishing] good
and evil. Evil, generally speaking, [is to be] in a way
that one ought not to be (with this general term we must

here be satisfied). Both good and evil [stand] before a
person; [he has the] choice between them, and his will is
evil. [Hence evil is] his guilt. This evil is his self-
seeking. [His] goals [relate] only to his singularity in
so far as [it] is opposed to the universal, i.e., in so
far as he is a natural [man]. That he is a natural [man]
is a matter of his will, his doing. No excuse to the effect that man exists by nature, education, and circumstances [can] justify [him] or remove [his] guilt. In
this alone, that [evil] is a matter of his guilt, lies
his freedom. Its positedness [is] recognized by man himself, he has dignity only through [the admission of his]
guilt.

Hence it is the case that the previously designated
immediacy of natural being itself exists only as something posited, as a willing, a transition: this [is the]
accurate way of defining the matter. In a purely abstract and natural condition, man is neither good nor
evil; this means, however, that he is not yet actually
human. +Because he is Spirit,+ immediacy [is] posited
within him +as it truly is. [105] [The] world, nature
in its immediacy, created [things] generally, the immediate, [all exist] as such--[the realm of] appearance,
which in itself, however, as such is only the second
[state].+

More precisely defined, this transition is a consciousness of this kind generally; [it is] the cognition,
+feeling, consciousness of the Idea, of the universal,
[a] determining and comprehending of what pre-exists according to the Idea, [a] universal defined in and for itself.+ Only through cognition, then through knowledge
and consciousness, does man exist; his will is not uncon-
scious, it is not an instinct.

[34]But cognition and volition or consciousness are,
generally speaking, the willing of evil just as much as
of the good.[35] Hence the first will, the first existence, [is] not necessarily evil. But will or cognition

is in any case (and in general, as already mentioned) to be understood as that which contains its turning point within itself. Furthermore, the first will is the natural will, the will[36] of appetite or desire; [hence it is also] cognition, will, precisely the form, the infinite form of cognition, whose content however [is] immediate. [The] content is precisely the natural, having singularity and self-seeking as its goal; this is the first, immediate content, yet [only the first and] formal freedom.

Thus evil, [the] will of self-seeking, exists only through consciousness and cognition, and constitutes the first form of will. One must have the concept of the thing in mind. [One] can say that formal freedom indeed exists, but when one talks like that the content [is] given: [the will] is not [really] free, [and so there is] no guilt. It is not important whether this first, evil will is fixed or transitory, whether it is the impulse or the life of an individual or of a people; [it is] a necessary transitional point, whether momentary or enduring. [+]But the divine principle of turning, of return to self, is equally present in cognition; it strikes the wound and heals it, [because] the principle is Spirit and truth.[+ *m*]

[*a*]In the first place, subjective consciousness is posited as it is. As Spirit on the one side, it takes its beginning from the [106] state of immediacy and raises itself to pure thinking, to the infinite, to the knowledge of God. When one considers this in determinate form, it contains what we know from the Christian Religion. Consciousness should enter into itself, become concrete, become what it is in itself; thus it proceeds from immediacy and elevates itself by means of the sublation of this immediacy into thinking. On this rests the fact that its true nature consists in abandoning its immediacy and considering the latter as a modality in which consciousness ought not to exist. If man exists as

immediate, natural man, he ought to consider himself to
be existing in an inappropriate way. This has been expressed as follows: it is said that man is evil by nature, [37]i.e., he ought not to be as he is immediately,
hence he is as he ought not to be.

In the condition of human immediacy two characteristics are present: the first, what man is implicitly, his
talents and rationality, his being what he is internally
and intrinsically, namely, Spirit as such, the image of
God. The second characteristic is his existence according to nature, the fact that his rationality has not yet
developed. What is lacking here is the fact that man is
reason and Spirit only in an implicit way. There is a
lack because Spirit should not exist *in itself*; it is
Spirit only because it exists *for itself*. Nature is only
implicitly rational; this in-itself constitutes its laws.
Precisely on this account it is only nature. In contrast
to this, man should be Spirit for itself, not merely in
itself; being-in-itself, or existence according to nature,
ought to be sublated.

Two different things are implied in this sublation:
What ought to be sublated? Only the *form* of being-in-
itself or its *absolutely primordial* character? That man
is Spirit in itself is what sustains itself and remains,
just as the goal or end sustains itself in the divine
Idea. One can therefore rightly say, because man is
Spirit in itself, he is *good* "by nature." But this being
good "by nature" is not yet good; for man is not yet what
he ought to be so long as he is the natural man only implicitly or immediately. This immediacy is what man
ought not to be, it is what is to be sublated. Thus this
first characteristic is expressed as follows: man is
evil "by nature."

This is a troublesome expression and can produce
many false impressions. The fact of the matter is that
man is "by nature" what he ought not to be. He ought to
be Spirit, but natural being is not spiritual being. It

may be observed that certain objections are raised
against this view. Children are not evil; also this definition seems not to fit many peoples and individuals.
[107] On the whole, the definition cannot appeal to empirical conditions.

Children are indeed without guilt because they have
no will and are not accountable. It belongs to consciousness to be able to decide, to have a will, to possess insight into the nature of actions. In so far as the will
is posited through the process of growing up, it initially appears as caprice, which is capable of willing
the good as much as evil and by no means wills only evil
according to its nature. Hence the condition of children
is one of innocence, neither good nor evil. A man, however, does not exist as a child, he is not innocent in
this sense; he is responsible for what he does. That the
condition of childhood also includes will is empirically
evident; but the child is not yet a man, for the latter
possesses insight and is a willing person. Man is not
to remain in the state of innocence.

With reference to the statement that the will is
caprice, willing this or that, it should be pointed out
that this caprice is not will at all. It is will only in
so far as it comes to a decision, but in so far as it
wills merely this or that, it is not will. The natural
will is the will of appetite, desire, or inclination,
which wills the immediate but does not yet will something
definite; to do the latter it would have to be rational
will, perceiving that law is rational. What is demanded
of man is that he not exist as natural will, that he not
exist as he is merely by nature. The concept of willing
is something different than this; the natural man has his
existence in this concept implicitly, but as long as he
only exists within it, he is only will implicitly and is
not yet actual will, is not yet existing as Spirit. This
is the situation generally, the special aspects of which
must be left out of consideration. The main point is

that such circumstances as that of the child are not to
be brought into view.

[38]Opposed to the opinion that the will is evil, a
further consideration occurs to us. We speak of volition
when we view the human being concretely, and that which
is concrete and actual cannot be merely something negative. The evil will, however, is thought of merely as
negative volition; this is only an abstraction. People
say: men aren't so bad after all, just look around you.
If we contend on the contrary that the will is evil by
nature, then this is the will considered only negatively.
But in fact, although man is not by nature what he ought
to be, he is still implicitly rational, still implicitly
[108] Spirit. This is the affirmative element in him,
and the fact that he is not by nature what he ought to be
concerns therefore only the *form* of volition. The essential point is that man is intrinsically Spirit. That
which is intrinsic persists. The concept of that which
persists and produces itself is found by giving up what
is abstractly negative, the natural will. Thus we have
in mind this concrete element, to which the abstraction
referred to is opposed. We carry this so far that when
we set up a Devil we have to show that there is something
affirmative in him; his strength of character, energy,
and consistency appear far better and more affirmative
than most of the angels.[39] When we come to the concrete
we at once find that affirmative characteristics must
show themselves in it.

In all of this it is forgotten that, when we speak
of mankind, we think of the latter as men who have been
educated and trained by customs, laws, etc. These are
men who are already ethically and morally educated, men
already reconstructed and brought into a certain state of
reconciliation. However, we can speak of what belongs in
the specific sphere of morality only within a specific
condition; it does not concern the nature of Spirit.

In religion as in the presentation of truth, what is essentially represented is the unfolding of the history of what humanity is. It is a speculative way of viewing things that dominates here; the abstract differences of the concept are presented in successive order. If it is the educated and cultured man who is to be considered, then the transformation and reconstruction must appear in him--the discipline through which he has passed, the transition from natural volition to true volition--and his immediate, natural will must appear to be sublated in this process.

The first characteristic, therefore, is that man in his immediacy is not what he ought to be. The second is that man ought to contemplate himself as he is immediately; the fact of being evil is thereby brought into relation with such contemplation. This is readily taken to mean that it is only in accord with this knowledge that man is posited as evil, implying that this contemplation is a kind of external demand or condition, and that when a person does not consider himself in this way, the other characteristic is removed as well, namely, the fact that he is evil. Since [109] this contemplation is made into a duty, one can readily imagine that only it is the essential thing, and that without it there is no content either.^{a}

[112] ^{b}^{40} The absolute Idea must come to be *for* consciousness, and truth *for* the subject: this expresses the *need* for truth. Likewise, the absolute Idea must come to be *in* consciousness, and truth *in* the subject: this expresses the *mode* and *manner* of truth's manifestation.^{41}

[113] Regarding the first point, the need for truth, it is presupposed that there exists in subjective Spirit a demand to know the absolute truth. This need directly implies that the subject exists in a state of untruth. As Spirit, however, the subject at the same time implicitly surmounts its untruth, and consequently the

latter is something that ought to be overcome. Untruth
more strictly defined means that the subject exists in a
state of estrangement from itself; accordingly, the
exigency for truth expresses itself to the end that this
estrangement of the subject within itself and from the
truth should be annulled, that the subject should be
reconciled, and that this reconciliation can in itself
only be a reconciliation with the truth. This is the
stricter form of the exigency. Its determinate meaning
is that estrangement, generally speaking, is in the subject, that the subject is evil, that it is inherently
estranged and contradictory (this is not, however, a contradiction that simply falls apart but rather one that
simultaneously holds itself together). The subject is
thereby estranged for the first time, is within itself
contradiction.

We are thus required to recall to mind and to define
the nature or character of man--how it is to be regarded,
how man himself regards it, what he is to know of himself.
self. Here we come at once upon mutually opposed characteristics. The first is that *man is by nature good*;
his universal, substantial essence is good; he is not
estranged within himself, rather his essence or concept
is that by nature he represents what is harmonious and at
peace with itself. Opposed to this is the second characteristic: *man is by nature evil*. These are the antitheses that exist at the outset for us, for external consideration. However, it must be added that this is not
merely a consideration that we engage in; rather man has
this knowledge of *himself*, how he is constituted, what
his essential characteristic is.

Man is by nature good: this is the more or less predominant emphasis of our time. In the treatment [of this
theme] by the [Christian] community, we may observe how
religious intuition and religious relationships form and
determine themselves in it. If only this one proposition
is valid, that man by nature is good and is not estranged,

then he has no need of reconciliation; and if reconciliation is unnecessary, then the entire process we are here
considering is superfluous.

It is [indeed] essential to say that man is good:
he is implicitly Spirit [114] and rationality, created in
and after the image of God. God is the good, and man as
Spirit is the mirror of God: he, too, is *implicitly* the
good. Precisely on this proposition, and on it alone,
rests the possibility of his reconciliation. However,
the difficulty and ambiguity of the proposition reside
in the definition of "implicitly" [*an sich*]. Man is
"implicitly" good: presumably this is to say everything,
but the "implicitly" designates precisely a one-sidedness
whereby everything indeed is not said. Man is "implicitly" good: this means that he is good only in an
interior, conceptual sense and not in actuality. Man, in
so far as he is Spirit, must be in actuality, i.e., *for*
himself [*für sich*], what he is in truth. To be good "by
nature" means to be good in an unmediated sense; but
Spirit is precisely something that is not natural and unmediated. As Spirit, man steps forth from the state of
nature and passes over into the separation of his concept
and his immediate existence. Physical nature remains in
the condition of implicitness [*Ansich*]; it is "implicitly"
the concept. In it the concept does not arrive at the
state of being-for-itself; in it the separation of an individual thing from its law and substantial essence does
not occur, precisely because such a thing is not free.
The implicitness of nature is represented by the laws of
nature; nature remains true to its laws and does not go
beyond them. It is this that constitutes its substantiality, and hence it is the sphere of necessity. Man,
however, is the one who sets himself in opposition to his
implicit being and his general nature, emerging into a
state of separation. Precisely the fact that he is "implicitly" good contains a deficiency. It is correct to
say that man is good by nature, but this expresses only

one side of the situation. The other side is that man
ought to be *for* himself what he is implicitly or *in* himself. He ought not to remain what he is immediately but
pass beyond his immediacy: this is the concept of Spirit.

The other characteristic emerges directly from what
has just been said. This passing beyond his natural
state, beyond his implicit being, is what first of all
constitutes the disunion or estrangement of man; it is
that which posits the estrangement. It is a stepping
forth from existence according to nature and from immediacy. But this is not to be construed to mean that
only the stepping forth is the beginning of evil; rather
this stepping forth is already contained in the natural
state itself. The in-itself or the implicit constitutes
the immediate; but because the implicit being of man is
Spirit, [115] man in his immediacy is already involved
in stepping forth from immediacy, in falling away from
it, from his being-in-itself. Here lies the basis for
the second proposition: *man is by nature evil*; his implicit being, his natural being, is evil. In his natural being at the same time his deficiency is to be
found. Because he is Spirit, he is distinguished from
his implicit being and he exists in a state of disunion.
One-sidedness is directly involved in this natural condition. When man exists only according to nature [*nur nach
der Natur ist*], he is evil. In an abstract sense, we refer to man "according to his nature" as he exists implicitly, according to his concept; but in the concrete
sense the man who follows his passions and instincts,
who remains within the circle of his desires, and whose
law is that of natural immediacy, is the natural man.
Man in his natural being is likewise a being possessed of
will, and since the content of the will is only instinct
and inclination, he is evil. The form of his willing indicates that he is no longer an animal, but the content
and purposes of his willing are still natural. It is
from this standpoint--indeed the higher standpoint--that

man is evil by nature, and is so just because he is something natural.

The original condition of man, which is superficially represented as the state of innocence, is the state of nature, the animal state. Man is properly speaking culpable; in so far as he is good, he ought not to be so in the sense that a natural thing is good. Rather his guilt and will ought to come into play; it ought to be possible to impute [moral responsibility] to him. Guilt means, in a general sense, the possibility of imputation. The good man is good by and through his will, and hence by means of his guilt. Innocence means to be without a will--indeed, to be without evil, but also at the same time to be without good. Natural things and animals are all good, but this kind of goodness cannot be attributed to man. In so far as man is good, he must be so by means of his will.

What is absolutely required is that man should not persist as a natural being. He is simultaneously possessed of consciousness, to be sure, but as man he can still be essentially natural in so far as the natural constitutes the purpose, content, and determination of his acts of will. We must view this determination more closely: man is man as a subject, and as a natural subject he is a single individual; his will is a singular will and is fulfilled by the content of singularity. This means that the natural man [116] is egoistic or selfish. We demand of the man who is called good, however, that he should at least be guided by general principles and laws. The naturalness of the will is, strictly speaking, the selfishness of the will as distinguished from the universality of willing, and as contrasted with the rationality of the will attuned to the principles of universality.

When we now consider what man is implicitly, the deficiency of his implicit being is simultaneously encountered. However, the fact that man is evil, in so far as his will is natural, does not annul the other side,

the fact that he is implicitly good, which always remains
part of his concept. But man is consciousness and therefore engages in the process of distinguishing; he is an
actual, particular subject, distinguished from his concept. Since, in the first instance, this subject exists
only in a state of distinction and has not yet returned
to unity, to the identity of subjectivity and the concept, to rationality, the actuality that it has is natural actuality, which is selfishness. The condition of
evil directly presupposes a relation between actuality
and the concept: this simply posits the contradiction
intrinsic to implicit being--the contradiction of the
concept and singularity, of good and evil. It is false
to ask whether or not man is good by nature. This is a
false way of posing the question. It is just as superficial to say that he is equally good and evil. Implicitly, according to his concept, he is good; but this
implicit being is one-sided and has the characteristic
that the actual, particular subject is only a natural
will. Both good and evil are posited, but essentially
in contradiction, such that each of the two presupposes
the other. It is not that only one exists; rather they
both exist in this relation and are opposed to each
other.

This is the first fundamental characteristic, the
essential determination of the concept.[b]

c. *The Knowledge of Estrangement and the*
Exigency for Reconciliation[42]

[109] [a]Secondly, however, the relation of contemplation is stated also in such a way as to imply that it is
contemplation or *knowledge* that *makes* men evil. Knowledge itself, then, appears to *be* evil and ought not to
exist; or it is the *source* of evil. In this way of representing the matter we have the connection that exists between the reality of evil and knowledge. This is a point

of essential importance.

The more proximate way of representing this evil is to say that man becomes evil through knowledge, or, as the Bible depicts it, that he has eaten from the tree of knowledge. In this fashion knowledge, intelligence, and theoretical capacity come into a closer relation with the will, and the nature of evil comes closer to being expressed. Here it may be said that it is in fact knowledge that is the source of all evil, for knowledge or consciousness is the act by which separation, negation, judgment, disunion are posited in the process by which being-for-self is more precisely determined. Human nature is not what it ought to be; it is knowledge that discloses this and brings to light the condition of being in which man ought not to be. This imperative is his concept, and the fact that he is not what he ought to be first emerges in the separation, in the comparison with what he is in and for himself. It is knowledge that first posits the antithesis in which evil is found. The animal, the stone, the plant are not evil. Evil first exists within the sphere of estrangement: it is the consciousness of being-for-oneself vis-à-vis an other, but also vis-à-vis an object that is inherently universal in the sense of the concept or rational will. I exist for myself for the first time by means of this separation, and therein lies the evil. To be evil means in an abstract sense to isolate myself. The act of isolation that separates itself from the universal represents the rationality of Spirit, its laws and definitions. But along with this separation emerge for the first time being-for-self and the universal, the spiritual, the lawful, that which ought to be. Thus it is not the case that contemplation has an external [110] relation to evil; rather, contemplation or knowledge is itself what is evil.

This is the antithesis to which man, because he is Spirit, has to advance--to be for himself generally in such a way that he has as his object something confront-

ing him that exists for him--the good, the universal, his
determination. Spirit is free; freedom has within itself
this essential moment of separation. In this separation,
being-for-self is posited and evil has its seat: here is
the source of evil, but also the point at which reconciliation has its ultimate source. It is at once what produces
the disease and the source of health; it is the poison
chalice from which man drinks death and decay and at the
same time the well-spring of reconciliation. For the positing of oneself as evil entails the sublation of evil.[43]

Another characteristic must be added. Man is defined as being for himself in this separation. As consciousness, self-consciousness, infinite self-consciousness, being-for-self is abstractly infinite. That man is
conscious of his freedom, his wholly abstract freedom, is
his infinite presence to himself, which has not come so
fully to consciousness in the earlier religions in which
the antithesis did not proceed to this depth, this absoluteness. Because this has now happened, the dignity of
man is simultaneously posited on a far higher plane.
Thereby, the subject has absolute importance, becomes an
essential object of the interest of God, because he is a
self-consciousness existing for himself. He has pure
certainty of himself within himself. In him exists the
point of infinite subjectivity--abstractly, to be sure,
but it is an abstract being in and for self. This is expressed by saying that man as Spirit is *immortal*, elevated above finitude, dependence, and external conditions,
and that he has the freedom to abstract himself from
everything. This implies that he can escape mortality.
It is in religion that the immortality of the soul is a
factor of major importance because the antithesis involved in religion is infinite.

We call something that can die "mortal," while that
which can reach a state in which death does not enter is
"immortal." When we say "combustible" and "incombus-
tible," combustion is a possibility that impinges on the

object externally. The attribute of being is not such a
possibility but rather an affirmatively defined quality
that [111] a thing already possesses in itself. Hence
the immortality of the soul must not be represented as
though it first emerges into actuality at some later
point; rather it is a present quality. Spirit is eternal, therefore for this reason already present; Spirit in
its freedom does not exist within the sphere of limitation. As thinking and purely cognitive, it has for its
object the universal--this is eternity.[44] The eternity
of Spirit is here brought to consciousness in this cognition, in this very separation, which has reached the infinitude of being-for-self, and which is no longer entangled in what is natural, contingent, and external.
This eternity of Spirit within itself means that in the
first place Spirit is implicit; but the subsequent standpoint implies that Spirit ought not to exist merely for
itself, as natural Spirit, but rather as it is in and for
itself. Spirit should contemplate itself, and thereby
disunion emerges; it should not remain at the standpoint
at which it is not what it is intrinsically, but should
become adequate to its conception, to universal Spirit.
From the standpoint of disunion, its concept is for it
something other, and it itself is a natural will, divided against itself. To this extent, its disunion is
its feeling or consciousness of contradiction; thereby is
established the need for an annulling of the contradiction, an exigency for reconciliation. From this standpoint, the latter assumes a particular form.

    We have said that in this cognition, in this separa-
tion and disunion, the subject takes on determinacy,
grasping itself in the extreme form of abstract being-for-
self, abstract freedom. The soul plunges into its depths,
into its absolute abyss. This soul is the undeveloped,
naked *monad*, the empty soul devoid of content; but since
it is implicitly the concept, the concrete, this emptiness or abstraction stands in a relation of contradiction

to its determinate character, which is to be concrete.
Thus the universal means that in this separation, developed as an infinite antithesis, the abstraction should
be annulled. This abstraction is also in itself a will
and concrete; but the content that the abstract monad
comes upon in itself is the natural will. The soul finds
nothing within itself except desires, selfishness, etc.
This is one of the forms of the antithesis according to
which the ego, or the soul in its depths, [112] and the
real soul, the soul of the natural man, are so distinguished from one another that the real soul does not exist in accord with its concept or point back to it, but
rather finds in itself only the natural will. The sphere
of opposition in which the real side is further developed
is the *world*, and so the unity of the concept has opposed
to it the natural will as a whole, whose principle is
selfishness and the actualization of which appears as
brutality, depravity, etc. The objectivity that the pure
ego has, and that is appropriate to it, is not its natural will and not the world. Rather its appropriate objectivity is only the universal essence, this One, which
has no content in itself and stands opposed to all content, all worldly objects.

The consciousness of this opposition, of this separation of the ego and the natural will, is one of infinite contradiction. The ego exists in an immediate
relation to the natural will and the world, and yet at
the same time is repelled by them. This is infinite
sorrow, the suffering of the world. From this standpoint
a reconciliation can take place, but it is unsatisfactory
and only partial--namely, a neutralization of the ego
within itself in the way that the ego exists for itself
in Stoic philosophy: it knows itself as cognitive, and
its object is what is thought, the universal; the latter
is for it absolutely everything, the true essence, which
alone is valid for it. What is thought belongs to the
subject because it is posited by it. But such a recon-

ciliation is only abstract; everything determinate lies
outside this thought, and the latter is merely formal
identity with itself.

From the absolute standpoint, however, an abstract
reconciliation such as this cannot and ought not take
place. Moreover, the natural will cannot find satisfaction within itself, for neither it nor the state of the
world can satisfy the one who has grasped his infinitude.
The abstract depth of the antithesis demands an infinite
suffering of the soul and along with it a reunification
that is equally complete.[a]

[116] [b]The second point is that the view we have
grasped as essential in the realm of thought should become actual in humanity as a whole--i.e., that man should
realize within himself the infinity of this antithesis between good and evil, and that he, as a natural being,
should *know* himself to be evil in his naturalness. Man
must become conscious of this antithesis within himself,
knowing that he is the one who is evil. It should likewise be added that evil is related at the same time to the
good, that the requirement of the good, [117] of being
good, is at hand, and that man becomes aware of this contradiction, undergoing anguish because of it and the ac-
companying estrangement. We have encountered the form of
this antithesis in all religions. But the antithesis vis-
à-vis the power of nature, vis-à-vis the ethical law, the
ethical will, and ethical life, or vis-à-vis fate--these
are all subordinate antitheses that contain only something
particular. The man who violates a commandment is evil,
but only in this particular case; he stands in opposition
only to this particular commandment. In the Parsee religion,[45] as we have seen, good and evil stand in universal
antithesis to each other. There, however, the antithesis
is *external* to man, and the latter is himself external to
it. This abstract antithesis is not present within him.

It is accordingly required that man should comprehend this abstract antithesis *within* himself. It is not

that he has transgressed merely this or that command, but
rather that he is implicitly evil--evil in toto, purely
and simply evil in his innermost essence. This quality of
evil represents the essential characteristic of his concept: it is this that he must bring to consciousness.[46]
The need for universal reconciliation that resides in man
--and this means divine, absolute reconciliation--follows
from the fact that the antithesis has attained this infinite degree, that this universality of evil encompasses
the innermost essence, that nothing remains outside this
antithesis, that therefore the antithesis is by no means
a particular one. This is the deepest depth. It is with
this depth that we are concerned. Depth means abstrac-
tion--the pure universalization of the antithesis so that
its two sides attain this wholly universal character vis-
à-vis each other.

This antithesis now has, speaking generally, two
forms. On the one hand, it is the antithesis in evil as
such, implying that it is the antithesis itself that is
bad: this is the *antithesis vis-à-vis God*. On the other
hand, it is the *antithesis vis-à-vis the world*, implying a
state of estrangement from the world: this is *misery* or
unhappiness, the estrangement viewed from the other side.

[118] We have first to consider the relation of
estrangement to one of the extremes, namely, to God. Man
is inwardly conscious that in his innermost being he is
a contradiction, and has therefore an infinite *anguish* or
sorrow vis-à-vis himself. Sorrow is present only where
there is opposition to what ought to be, to an affirmative. What is no longer in itself an affirmative also
has no contradiction, no sorrow. Sorrow is precisely the
element of negativity in the affirmative, meaning that
within itself the affirmative is self-contradictory, self-
wounding. This sorrow is one element of evil. Evil
merely for itself is an abstraction; it *exists* only in
opposition to the good, and since it is present in the
unity of the subject, the latter is estranged, and this
estrangement is infinite sorrow. If the consciousness of

the good, the infinite demand of the good, is not likewise present in the subject itself, in its innermost being, then no sorrow is present and evil itself is only an
empty nothingness, for it exists only in this antithesis.

Evil and sorrow can be infinite only when the good
or God is known as *one* God, as a pure, spiritual God. It
is only when the good is this pure unity, only when we
have faith in *one* God, and only in connection with such
a faith, that the negative can and must advance to this
determination of evil and negation can advance to this
universality. The one side of this estrangement becomes
apparent in this fashion, by the elevation of man to the
spiritual unity of God. This sorrow and this consciousness represent the absorption of man into himself, and
likewise into the negative element of estrangement, of
evil. This is an objective, inward absorption into evil;
inward absorption of an affirmative kind is absorption
into the pure unity of God.

At this point it is evident that I as a natural man
do not correspond to what represents the truth, but likewise the truth of the one good remains firmly fixed within me. This lack of correspondence is characterized as
what ought not to be. The problem and demand are infinite. One can say: since I am a natural man, I have,
on the one hand, consciousness of myself, but on the
other hand existence according to nature consists rather
in a lack of consciousness with regard to myself, a lack
of willing. I am a being that acts according to nature;
and to this extent I am innocent, it is often said, [119]
having no consciousness of what I do, being without my
own will, acting without inclination, allowing myself to
be surprised by instinct. But at the point of this antithesis the innocence disappears; for precisely the natural being of man, lacking in consciousness and will, is
what ought not to be. In face of the pure unity and perfect purity that I know as absolute truth, this natural
being is declared to be evil. What has been said implies

that the absence of consciousness and will is to be considered as itself essentially evil. And thus the contradiction remains, turn it how you will. Since this so-
called innocence is defined as evil, my lack of correspondence to my essence and to the absolute remains; and
from one side or the other I know myself always as what
ought not to be.

This expresses the relation to the one extreme, and
the result, the more determinate mode of this sorrow, is
my humiliation, my *remorse* or *contrition*, the fact that I
experience sorrow because I as a natural being do not
correspond to what at the same time I know to be my own
essence in my knowing and willing.

Concerning the relation to the other extreme [the
world], the separation appears as *misery* or *unhappiness*--
the fact that man in the world is not satisfied. His
natural needs have no further right or claim to satisfaction. As natural beings, individuals are related to
each other merely as powers or forces, and to this extent
they are contingent. However, the higher requirements of
man, those having to do with ethics, are requirements and
determinations of freedom. In so far as these requirements, which are implicitly justified in his concept (for
he knows the good, and the good is in him), do not find
satisfaction in existence, in the external world, he is
in a state of misery.

It is misery that drives and presses man back into
himself; and since the fixed demand that the world should
be rational exists in him but does not find fulfillment,
he gives up the world, seeking happiness and satisfaction
in harmony with himself. In order to bring his affirmative side into harmony with his existence, he gives up
the external world, transfers his happiness into himself,
and seeks satisfaction within himself.

[120] We already find these two forms of estrangement in the particular religions. That sorrow or anguish
which comes from universality, from above, we saw in the

Jewish people--in connection with which is retained the
infinite demand for absolute purity in my natural existence, in my empirical willing and knowing. The other
form of estrangement, the being driven back into oneself
by misery or unhappiness, is the standpoint at which the
Roman world arrived--the universal unhappiness of the
world. We saw the formal inwardness that satisfies itself in the world as the dominion of God's purpose, which
was represented, known, and intended as a worldly dominion.

Each of these sides has its one-sidedness. The
first may be described as the feeling of humiliation; the
other represents the abstract elevation of man within
himself--the man who is concentrated within himself--as
in the case of Stoicism and Scepticism. The Stoic or
Sceptic wise man was directed back to himself and was
supposed to be satisfied within himself. Through independence and rigid self-containment, he was supposed to
find happiness and harmony within himself, and to rest
in this abstract, present, self-conscious interiority.

These are the highest, most abstract moments of all;
here the antithesis is at its height, and both sides
represent the antithesis in its most complete universal-
ity--in the universal itself--and in its innermost essence, its greatest depth. Both forms are, however, one-
sided. The first contains that anguish and abstract
humiliation which reflect the highest degree of non-cor-
respondence of the subject to the universal--the estrangement and rupture that are neither completed nor compen-
sated. This is the standpoint of antithesis between the
infinite on the one side and a fixed, abstract finitude
on the other. Here anything reckoned as belonging to me
is simply evil. This abstraction finds its complement in
the other form, namely in the process of thinking within
itself, which implies that I correspond or am adequate to
myself, that I am and can be satisfied with myself. This
second form is, however, just as one-sided, because it

represents only the affirmative side, and indeed the affirmation of myself within myself. The contrition of the
first side is only negative, lacking in self-affirmation;
the second side is now supposed to be this affirmation,
this self-satisfaction. [121] But this satisfaction of
myself within myself is only an abstract satisfaction,
achieved by flight from the world and from actuality--
achieved by an absence of activity. Since this is a
flight from actuality, it is also a flight from *my* ac-
tuality--and indeed not from my external actuality, but
from that of my own volition. The *actuality* of my voli-
tion--I as a specific subject, as realized will--is no
longer mine, but what remains for me is the *immediacy* of
my self-consciousness. To be sure, the latter is completely abstract, but a final bit of depth is contained
in it, and I have preserved myself in it. It is not an
abstraction from the abstract actuality within me or from
my immediate self-consciousness, from the immediacy of my
self-consciousness. On this side, therefore, affirmation
is the predominant factor, but without negating the one-
sidedness of immediate being; while on the other side negation is the one-sided factor. These two moments contain within themselves the exigency for a transition.

The conception of the preceding religions has re-
fined itself into this antithesis; and the fact that the
antithesis has disclosed itself to be, and has taken the
form of, an actually existing necessity, is expressed by
the words, *"When the time had fully come,* God sent forth
his Son" (Gal. 4:4). This means: the exigency for Spirit
is at hand--the Spirit that points the way to reconciliation.[b47]

Section 3. The Representation of the Fall

[m] [We still want] briefly to call attention [to] the
chief elements in [the] figurative representation [of the

Fall]: (α) Adam in Paradise, [in the] [122] Garden of
Eden, ate from the tree of the knowledge of good and evil;
(β) [the] serpent said, "You will be like God" [Gen. 3:5];
⁺(γ) they [Adam and Eve] thereby first became finite and
mortal; and at the same time⁺ (δ) God said, "Behold,
Adam has become like one of us, knowing good and evil"
[Gen. 3:22].[48]

In considering this story, we must first observe its
contradictions--⁺the great contradictions contained [in
it].⁺ It is represented that man [is] forbidden to eat
of the tree of knowledge of good and evil. He trans-
gresses this command, is outwardly tempted by the promise
that by eating he will be like God, foolishly believes it
("Bumblebees and wasps [are] gods--if apple-eating makes
gods!"[49]), and will be punished for it. Hence everything
issues in an entirely finite, commonplace result--it depends on such an external inheritance of evil--entirely
lacking in ideal or speculative character.[50] The first
act of disobedience is something contingent or accidental.
It is no longer a question of the *concept* of sin; rather
it is a *story* that we have before us and of which we are
externally aware.[51] However, what follows consistently
from this result appears[52] equally inconsistent--namely,
that not [*any*] tree but the tree of the knowledge of good
and evil [is represented]. This [is] the major point:
it is not a question of just any tree and ordinary fruit;
[the allusion to] good and evil leads us at once into an
entirely different region. These are absolutely substantial characteristics of Spirit, [surely] not so material
as the eating of an apple.[53]

Thus it is supposedly forbidden to eat of the tree
of the knowledge of good and evil; yet this knowledge is
[123] what constitutes the nature of Spirit--otherwise
[man] is a beast. This knowledge, so the serpent pro-
mises, will make him like God. [This appears to be]
temptation in the form of deceit and pride, and subsequently ⁺(Gen. 3:22)⁺ it is God who says, "Behold, Adam

has become like one of us, knowing good and evil." Here
it is placed on the lips of God himself that precisely
knowledge, [indeed] the specific knowledge of good and
evil (in general, that is), constitutes the divine in
humanity. Just as [the story stands in] contradiction to
the necessity of knowledge, so [too] the latter is opposed by the notion that punishment is incurred by this
knowledge, and that [punishment] takes the form of physical necessity +and mortality.+ [This] likewise appears
to be a contradiction.[54]

It must be generally observed that images and mere
representations cannot portray a deep speculative content in its true and proper form, and therefore essentially not without contradiction. For the speculative
content is precisely the comprehension of the concept of
something—the comprehension of its development and
hence of the inner antitheses it contains and through
which it moves.[55]

Since the original divine Idea has been represented
as a human condition that once existed, it is consistent
for imagination that it should represent the knowledge of
good and evil as a condition that, on the contrary,
should not have occurred, +and from this everything else
follows that appears as inconsistent. Reason does not
allow itself to err as a result of these inconsistencies.+
For in fact we find this first [form of] reflection, according to which the natural is [regarded] as evil, as a
situation that ought not to be, i.e., ought to be annulled—not one, however, that ought not to occur: it
has occurred because man is *consciousness*. (Moreover,
knowledge of good and evil is not for itself evil—another inconsistency.) The latter is the eternal history
of humanity; and the deep insight of this story is that
the eternal history of humanity, to be consciousness, is
contained in it. [124] [We have here the] original,
divine Idea, [man as the] image [of God], [the] emergence
of consciousness and the knowledge of good and evil.

+At the same time [we have] guilt,+ which is something
that both ought not to exist or remain as knowledge, and
also is the means by which man is divine. Knowledge
heals the wound that it itself is.[56]

Man [is] also banished from Paradise; hence he cannot eat of the tree of life (the *Hom* of the Parsees[57])
and live forever. Again, [this is] inconsistent. In one
place [the story has it that the ground shall] bring
forth thorns and thistles [Gen. 3:18] +(this is [the
meaning of] being expelled from Paradise).+ [Thus] finitude [acquires] eternal knowledge--"Because you have done
thus and thus . . . ," [says God, vs. 17; hence the
punishment is] altogether the consequence of knowledge.
Animals are better off, their needs more easily satisfied. In the other place [the expulsion, as remarked
above, is the means to ensure mortality; God says], vs.
22: ". . . lest he put forth his hand +and take also of
the tree of life, and eat, and live forever.+" [Man must
depart from Paradise] merely in order not to eat of this
tree. [But] mortality [is] a necessary consequence of
finitude.[58]

[In this tale the] depth of the Idea [is unmistak-
ably present. It is] speculative, a story concerning
the nature of man himself, [yet it is] never again mentioned in the Old Testament, [neither in the Books of]
Moses [nor in the] Prophets, but only in Sirach 25:24
[with the signification]: the woman is guilty.[59] [It is
a] story that concerns the nature of man himself.

[60]While this representation [of the Fall] was no
longer contained in the Jewish world view or in the [125]
consciousness of its condition, the following insight lay
dormant within it as equally essential: Adam has become
as one of us. This "has become" gives expression to the
special element: not the original, innermost likeness of
God, but the likeness that is to be regained. It is
represented as something that has already come to be, expressing generally this other aspect of knowledge, namely,

that it is in itself the turning point. In [his] translation of the Bible, Johann Meyer[61] interprets this "Adam"
as the new Adam, as Christ, and in fact the latter consists in nothing other than the regained likeness [of
God]. One can refer to this likeness as the promise of
the new Adam. It is expressed figuratively as prophecy
in what God says to the serpent: "I will put enmity between you and the woman, and between your seed and her
seed; he shall bruise your head, and you shall bruise his
heel" [Gen. 3:16]. Since in the serpent the[62] principle
of knowledge is represented as autonomous, existing outside of Adam and indeed [on] the side of evil, it is
wholly consistent that the other side [of knowledge],
that of conversion or reflection, is contained in man in
the form of concrete cognition, and that this other side
will bruise the head of the serpent. This promised, infinite side of knowledge was likewise slumbering in the
Jewish people. [It had been] submerged in the limitation
and particularity of this people; only later did there
[awaken], even though in limited fashion, a compulsion, a
need, a desire to hope chiefly for a worldly and religious
savior--religious, [however,] only in the sense of a
restitution of their form of worship.

[This] entire first point has the closest connection
with the concept of freedom. [It is a] story of human
freedom [and its] collision. Evil [collides] with God's
foreknowledge, goodness, will, etc.; [it] belongs to the
absolute, divine life--which is divine Spirit--that the
divine will [should] unite with human freedom. [Spirit
must] objectify itself [and] in the first instance [re-
mains] unfree [126] finite Spirit, Spirit in itself.
[+]This first [condition, then,] is the wrath of God.[+ *m*]

[*a*][63] In the story of the Fall, sin is described by
saying that man ate of the tree of knowledge, etc. Thereby knowledge issues in estrangement and separation, which
first have good consequences for man, but at the same

time evil ones as well. Figuratively speaking, it is forbidden to eat of the tree, and so evil is represented formally as the transgression of a divine command. Upon this the rise of consciousness is posited; but at the same time it is represented as a standpoint at which consciousness ought not to rest, and which is to be annulled; for one should not remain in the state of the estrangement of consciousness.

The serpent says further that by eating man will become like God, and thereby he laid claim to the pride of man. God, however, says to himself: "Adam has become like one of us" [Gen. 3:22]. The serpent, therefore, has not lied, for God confirms what he has said. Much difficulty has been encountered in the interpretation of this text, and some have gone so far as to explain God's statement as irony. The truer interpretation, however, is that by this "Adam" the second Adam or Christ is to be understood. Knowledge is the principle of spirituality, which however, as noted, is also the principle of the healing of the injury of separation. It is in this principle of knowledge that the principle of divinity is also posited, which through further adjustment must arrive at man's reconciliation and veracity.

It is further represented that man has received natural punishment and natural evil; this is a dubious content, but in any case the labor of Adam is a consequence of knowledge. The animals do not labor; the act of laboring is at the same time the stamp of the higher, spiritual nature of man. It says further that Adam and Eve were driven from Paradise so that they would not also taste of the tree of life. This means that individuals indeed arrive at knowledge, but the individual remains a single person and therefore mortal.[a]

^{b}This accordingly is the manner and method of the
form by which this conceptual determination appears representatively as a story or history [127] and is represented
for consciousness in a perceptible, sensible mode, so
that it is viewed as a happening. Its meaning is that
God has created man in his own image: this is the concept
of man. This concept is now represented as something
that also exists. Man lived in Paradise, and this life
is designated as a state of innocence. It means further
that the tree of the knowledge of good and evil is supposed to have stood in Paradise, and that man disobeyed
God's command by eating of it. On the one hand, it is
formally represented that this eating supposedly was the
transgression of a command. However, the content is the
essential thing, namely, that the sin consisted in having
eaten of the tree of knowledge of good and evil, and
thereby the pretense of the serpent comes about that man
will be like God when he has the knowledge of good and
evil.

It follows from this content that the fruit is an
external image, belonging only to the sensible portrayal.
In terms of content, it means that man has elevated himself to the knowledge of the difference [between good and
evil], and that this knowledge is the source of evil, indeed is evil itself. It is located in the act of knowledge, in the consciousness of being evil. By all means,
the being of evil resides in knowledge, as mentioned
above; knowledge is the source of evil. For knowledge
and consciousness in general mean a judging or dividing,
a self-distinguishing within oneself. Animals have no
consciousness, are unable to make distinctions within
themselves, have in general no free being-for-self vis-à-
vis objectivity. Disunion or estrangement is evil, the
contradiction; it has two aspects--good and evil. In
this disunion only evil is contained, and hence it is itself evil. Therefore it is entirely correct to say that
good and evil reside in consciousness.

The first man is represented as having actually
fallen in this way. Here again we have this sensible
mode of expression. From the point of view of thought,
the expression "the first man" signifies "man as man"--
not any particular, contingent individual, not one among
many, but the absolutely first man, man according to his
concept. Man as such is consciousness; consequently he
enters into this disunion, into the consciousness that in
its further determination is knowledge. However, in so
far as the universal man [128] is represented as the
first, he is also represented as distinguished from other
men. Hence the question arises: If there is only one
man who has done this, how is his deed transmitted to
others? Here the image of the inheritance of sin comes
into play, by which the deficiency residing in the fact
that man as such is perceived figuratively as a first man
is corrected. The one-sidedness implied by the fact that
the disunion belonging to the concept of man as a whole
is represented as the act of a single individual is overcome by this representation of a communicated or inherited
sin. Neither the original representation nor the correction are necessary; rather it is man, it is consciousness,
that falls into this disunion.

However, although evil resides in this disunion or
estrangement, the latter is also the midpoint of the conversion that consciousness contains within itself whereby
the disunion is also sublated. The highest disunion, the
distinction between good and evil (good as such by definition exists only in contrast to evil, and evil only in
contrast to good), is certainly knowledge; and man as man,
as Spirit, eats of the tree of the knowledge of good and
evil. The story reports that an alien creature, the serpent, tempted man by the pretense that, if he knows how
to distinguish good and evil, he will become like God.
In this way the story represents the fact that man's
deed springs from the evil principle. However, the confirmation of the fact that knowledge of good and evil be-

longs to the divinity of man is placed on the lips of God
himself. He says, "Behold, Adam has become like one of
us" [Gen. 3:22]. Thus the serpent's statement was not a
deception. This is customarily overlooked along the
lines of a once-held prejudice to the effect that this is
an irony of God, that God is making a satire. However,
what distinguishes man as man, as Spirit, is precisely
knowledge and disunion.

Labor is then declared to be the punishment for sin.
In general, this is a necessary consequence. The animal
does not labor, or does so only when compelled, not by
nature; it does not eat its bread in the sweat of its
brow or produce its own bread, but rather finds directly
in nature satisfaction for all its needs. Man, too, finds
the material for this in nature, but this [129] material
is, so to speak, the least important element for him; the
infinite provision of the satisfaction of his needs occurs only through labor. Labor done in the sweat of one's
brow, or bodily work, and the labor of the Spirit, which
is the harder of the two, exist in immediate connection
with the knowledge of good and evil. That man must make
himself what he is, that he must produce and eat bread in
the sweat of his brow, belongs to what is most essential
and distinctive about him and is necessarily connected
with the knowledge of good and evil.

The story further depicts figuratively a tree of
life that stood in Paradise; this, too, is expressed in
simple, childlike imagery. The desires of men pursue two
lines: the one is directed toward living in undisturbed
happiness, in harmony with oneself and external nature;
it is the animal that remains in this unity, while man
has to pass beyond it. The other line follows the desire
to live eternally, perchance. And the imagery of the
tree of life is formed in accord with these two desires.
When we consider it more closely, it is seen at once to
be only a childlike image. Man as an individual living
thing, his individual life, his natural life, must die.

But when the story is viewed more closely, this is seen to be the wondrous aspect of it, the self-contradictory aspect. On the one hand, it is said that man in Paradise and without sin would be immortal--in this story, immortality on earth and immortality of the soul are not separated--and he would have been able to live forever. For, if external death were only a consequence of sin, then man in Paradise would be implicitly immortal. On the other hand, however, it is also said that man will become immortal for the first time when he has eaten of the tree of life--but it cannot be assumed as the case that he could have eaten of the tree of life without sin, for this was forbidden him.

The fact of the matter is that man is immortal only through knowledge, for only in the activity of thinking is his soul pure and free rather than mortal and animal-like. Knowing and thinking are the root of his life, of his immortality as a totality within itself. The animal soul is submerged in corporeality, while Spirit is a totality within itself.[b]

NOTES FOR CHAPTER III

1. Lasson's title for this chapter is "Creation, Man, and Sin" --a title that makes the *Philosophy of Religion* sound too much like a textbook of Christian doctrine. However, in this work Hegel presents the contents of Christian faith not directly but only in so far as they have been philosophically transfigured or sublated, a fact that is reflected by the distinctive conceptuality of his treatment. "Differentiation" (*Unterscheidung*) is the characteristic term by which Hegel describes the second moment of the divine life, the divine self-othering in the process of creating a world of nature and finite Spirit and "estrangement" (*Entfremdung*) is the characteristic state into which the created order falls. Differentiation and estrangement represent the first phase of the second major moment or element of the Revelatory Religion; the second phase of this moment occurs when God himself appears as a single individual in the differentiated order he has created ("incarnation") and a reversal in the condition of estrangement begins ("reconciliation")--the subject matter of Chapter IV. These two phases together constitute the "Kingdom of the Son." Anticipations of the reversal already occur with the creation of man as finite Spirit, and

thus the exigency for reconciliation is a theme of the present chapter. These two phases are explicitly suggested by sections (b) and (c) of "Concrete Representation" in the 1821 MS.

2. Lasson calls this section "The Natural World." But the more specific issue is that of God's *relation* to the world--a relation that is brought out by the symbols of "creation" and "preservation."

3. MS. heading: "b." This "b" designates the beginning of the second sphere of "Concrete Representation" in the 1821 MS., the concept in diremption or differentiation.

4. [+]Where? Spatial determination of where the eternal God is. -- Objectivity, development of the same, i.e., adherence to the determinate distinctions.[+]

5. [+]Son, abstract determination of other-being, antithesis of nature and finite Spirit. -- Nature and finite [Spirit], -- its [Spirit's] history in it [the antithesis], its goals and interests shattered in the same.[+]

6. [+]Conjunction of the first and second spheres.[+]

7. Here Hegel establishes an important distinction between the second moment of the divine life *ad intra* (the "eternal Son" of the Father) and the physical and spiritual world. God in the moment of self-differentiation is not simply identical with the world: this would be a crude pantheism, which Hegel consistently avoids. Rather the divine differentiation *ad intra* is the *ground* for the possibility of creating a world of nature and finite Spirit whose destination is *also* to be the otherness of God. The identity of the eternal Son and the world, of the moment of divine self-objectification *ad intra* and *ad extra*, of the immanent and the economic Trinity, is *implicit* (*an sich*) only, not explicit (*für sich*) or presently actual.

8. [+]This instant -- being-for-self.
The objectification of God, as it has been portrayed in the primal Idea, is the truth.[+]

9. The MS. reads *dass, wenn* instead of *wenn*.

10. The MS. reads *so schwebt . . . vor* instead of *dass . . . vorschwebt*.

11. Hegel addresses himself to this task in the second part of the *Encyclopedia*, the Philosophy of Nature.

12. Lasson inserts a passage from the *Werke* after this section of the 1821 MS.; we have relocated it on p. 120 (see n. 18).

13. These words appear as a heading in the 1824 transcript, designating the second of the elements or moments in which the Idea of God is developed, that of differentiation or diremption in the otherness of the world. This second element can also be described in terms of the *representation* of subjective consciousness (as con-

trasted with the purely conceptual thinking of the first element),
which presupposes the *appearance* of God in finitude or the "particularization" of the Idea of God. For the 1824 and 1827 lectures, as
well as for the *Werke*, the second moment includes the creation of
the natural and human world, the "fall" into estrangement, and the
reconciliation accomplished by the incarnation of the Son (Chaps.
III-IV of the present edition).

14. *ᵂ*As objectivity or as intrinsic, the absolute Idea is complete; but the subjective side of the Idea is not yet complete
either in itself as such or with respect to the subjectivity that
[exists] within the divine Idea as [object] for it.*ᵂ* (12:247; ET 3:
34.)

15. This paragraph is located by Lasson in Chap. IV (see n. 10).
However, it occurs here in the Griesheim transcript of the 1824
lectures.

16. This last sentence is omitted by Lasson from the Griesheim
transcript.

17. These words mark the beginning of the second major element
or moment in the 1827 lectures. The division is similar to the 1824
lectures (see n. 13).

18. 12:255-257 (ET 3:43-45). Lasson locates this passage from
the *Werke* immediately after the 1821 MS. (see n. 12), presumably because it continues the discussion of the relation between nature and
finite Spirit in the last two paragraphs of the MS. But the same
matter is discussed in the last paragraph of the 1827 lectures, with
which the passage from the *Werke* is equally well continuous. The
normal editorial procedure of arranging the materials in each section in the sequence *m*, *a*, *b*, *w* should not be disrupted without good
cause.

19. Lasson's heading for this section is "Natural Man," and for
the first subsection, "The Inner Development." Since it is not
clear what the latter words refer to, and since the section heading
applies appropriately to this first subsection, we have transferred
it to the subsection and have adopted a phrase from the 1821 MS. for
the new section heading.
    The use of subsections for Hegel's discussion of man as "finite
and natural Spirit" is problematic, since the same basic theme is
considered in each of the three subsections, but with increasing
specificity and from somewhat different perspectives. Hegel begins,
in the 1821 MS., with a rather general discussion of "natural man,"
i.e., of human existence "according to nature." Because man, as
finite Spirit, is *intrinsically* Spirit, when he exists according to
nature rather than according to Spirit, he is estranged from his own
essential being. (See below, n. 23.) Then Hegel turns in the 1821
MS. to the more specific question as to whether man is good or evil
"by nature" (subsection *b*). The 1824 lectures begin essentially
with this question, although the first two paragraphs of these
transcripts touch on the more general theme of "natural man." The
1827 lectures also begin at this point, as our rearrangement of

Lasson's order makes clear (see below, n. 40). Finally Hegel takes
up, in both the 1824 and 1827 lectures, the role of knowledge in the
occurrence of evil and estrangement (subsection *c*), a knowledge that
also represents the beginning of human awareness of the exigency for
reconciliation. The last three paragraphs of the 1821 MS. also in-
timate this theme, but it remains undeveloped there. These three
themes are related more or less as concentric circles, with the
motif of "natural man" as the most encompassing sphere, underlying
the other two. The question of good and evil then leads to the more
specific issue of knowledge. We have retained the subsectional
divisions to help bring out the development of Hegel's thought and
also to show the differing nuances in the three lecture series.

20. MS. heading: "c. 17/8 21." The "c" designates the beginning of the third sphere of "Concrete Representation" in the 1821
MS., the concept of God in the history of redemption and reconciliation, which continues to the end of Chap. IV in our edition. According to the 1821 MS., the creation of man as finite Spirit and
the fall of the latter into estrangement represent both the pinnacle
of divine self-differentiation and the "turning point," the beginning of the history of reconciliation, which becomes explicit, however, only in the history of Christ. As noted earlier, Hegel modified this method of division in the later lecture series (see n. 20,
p. 102; and n. 1, p. 161. The date on which Hegel began to lecture
on this section was 17 August 1821.

21. The MS. adds: "The latter [is our concern] here, the
former [is the history of] the community."

22. +The consciousness of that which it is.+

23. *Natürlicher Mensch.* In what follows, Hegel has in view not
nature as such but *man* in so far as he exists *according to* nature
(*nach der Natur*, p. 140), or according to the flesh (κατὰ σάρκα),
which, from the biblical standpoint, is already a condition of sin
or evil, by contrast with existence *according to* the Spirit (κατὰ
πνεῦμα). Man as finite Spirit ought to exist according to the
Spirit, and thus for him to exist according to nature intrinsically
contradicts his being as Spirit. Although it is a matter on which
Hegel is often frustratingly ambiguous, it seems fairly clear that
in his view nature as such, the natural world as such--the second
essential moment in the dialectic of the divine Idea--is not intrinsically evil. (See below, pp. 135, 140, 143). Such a position
would lead him away from the biblical doctrine of creation to one of
the pagan theogonies or dualisms. It is only when finite human
Spirit knowingly constitutes its existence, establishes the criteria
for its life, according to the immediacy, particularity, and externality of the physical nature it shares with all created things,
that evil arises.
    The term *Natürlichkeit* poses translation problems and is
variously rendered as "natural state," "natural life," "naturalness,"
"existence according to nature." The adjective *natürlich* is translated as "natural," but when it applies to man it carries the conno-
tation of "existence according to nature."

24. The MS. reads *und* instead of *der*.

25. [+]Immediate man as negative has two aspects: (α) Ingenuous, immediate, innocent. (β) Immediacy for spiritual consciousness in relation to its true determination. Unfree -- feeling of dependence as religious [feeling.][+]

26. The MS. reads *erst* instead of *er*.

27. [+]Three modes of representation may be specified with regard to this primitive condition: (α) Philosophy, on the grounds [of reflection],* maintains that such a primitive [condition] is also the original condition, actually and temporally--not however, in accord with those empirical descriptions, as a condition of merely external well-being, a condition without suffering, of mild, well-meaning customs, and a development of intelligence appropriate to the latter but still more limited; rather it is asserted that he [the original man] is ab[solutely good].
 (β) Man as speculative.
 (γ) Man as naturally good without devolution and restoration.[+]
 *Hegel first wrote: "on speculative grounds." Later he cancelled the word "speculative," but did not substitute another for it.

28. [+](α) Concentrated within itself, feeling, not developed, lacks manifoldness.[+]

29. [+]Reflection [is] differentiating in general.[+]

30. [+](β) Perception -- not the essential and true [nature] of things, but rather sensible [perception.]
 (γ) Only thought.[+]

31. [+]If it is only to be done on that account.[+]

32. [+]A good feature.[+]

33. The MS. adds: "Truth, first moment, without such forms: (α) actual intellectual perfection; (β) generally good by nature."

34. [+](γγ) In consciousness, cognition.[+]

35. [+]Of good or evil is cognition.[+]

36. [+]As first -- [it] is precisely the immediate content of finitude, the first content, the first purpose.[+]

37. Lasson omits the remainder of this sentence from the Griesheim transcript.

38. From here to the end of the "*a*" section Lasson rearranges the Griesheim transcript at several points. According to Jaeschke, the order of the text is more closely followed by the *Werke* (12:262-263; ET 3:50-52).

39. See the citation from the *Werke* below, n. 46.

40. This portion of the 1827 lecture transcripts is located by
Lasson in section *c*, "The Knowledge of Estrangement and the Exigency
for Reconciliation." However, it is clear that the portion we have
relocated is concerned primarily with the question of "Good and
Evil."

41. "Die absolute Idee muss für das Bewusstsein und in demselben, die Wahrheit für das Subjekt und in demselben werden. Das
Erste ist das Bedürfnis der Wahrheit, das Zweite die Art und Weise
ihrer Erscheinung." These sentences could also be translated: "The
absolute Idea must come to be for consciousness and in consciousness:
this is the *need* for truth. Truth must come to be for the subject
and in the subject: this is the *mode* and *manner* of truth's manifestation." One of my consultants prefers this translation, believing
that it reflects the Hegelian distinction between the labor of
Spirit in the history of consciousness and the recollection of the
truth of this labor for and in the subject (the task of the *Phenomenology*). However, I believe my reading of the sentences reflects
more accurately the distinction between the "first point" and the
"second point" made in the paragraphs below and on pp. 147 ff.

42. To Lasson's heading for this section we have added the
words, "of Estrangement."

43. The next three paragraphs of the Griesheim transcript are
concerned with the story of the Fall. We have followed Lasson by
locating them in the next section, pp. 156-157.

44. ^{w}". . . which is not simply duration, in the sense that the
mountains endure, but knowledge.^{w} (12:268; ET 3:57.)

45. The religion of ancient Persia, or Zoroastrianism. Hegel
names it the Religion of the Good or of Light and treats it together with Egyptian religion as the highest of the nature religions,
serving as a transition to the Religion of Spiritual Individuality
(*Werke* 11:406-418; ET 2:70-82; Lasson, I/2:186-199).

46. ^{w}This evil personified in a general way is the Devil. The
latter, as self-willing negativity, is for this reason identical
with himself and must therefore also have the character of affirma-
tion--as in Milton, where the Devil, with his characteristic energy,
is better than many angels.^{w} (12:261; ET 3:49. From the Hotho
notes of the 1824 lectures.)

47. At this point Lasson footnotes a passage from the *Werke*
that is located by the *Werke* itself in another context, namely, the
discussion of the sending of the Son into the world in Chapter V
(p. 241, n. 27). Since the latter context is more appropriate, we
have footnoted the passage there.

48. The MS. adds: "(Profound story -- secondary matter: (α)
God's prohibition against eating [the fruit] -- to be sure, this is
a deviation from the Idea: knowing [good and evil] is what ought not
to be, in the sense that it ought to be sublated.)"

49. "Hummeln und Wespen -- Götter -- wenn das Äpfelfressen Götter tät machen!" Lasson was unsuccessful in tracing the source of this citation; H. S. Harris speculates that it may have been Goethe. Since bumblebees and wasps like to feed on apples, if apple-eating makes gods they are surely good candidates for apotheosis!

50. +So entirely consistent.+

51. +(α) God's prohibition (-- to be sure) -- but: not to eat of a tree, hence formal obedience -- content worthy of it. (β) This individual -- by contrast emerges a guilt, freedom, accountability.+

52. The manuscript reads *ist erscheint* rather than *erscheint*.

53. +But here still more difficult, the inconsistency infinite.+

54. +(ε) Necessary connection [of mortality] with finitude, and indeed not as punishment: "lest he eat also of the tree of life . . ." [cf. Gen. 3:22].+

55. +One of the antitheses is as essential as the other -- for representation, the one [is] the absolute Idea, original t[ruth].+

56. +[We have here] (γ) the determination in which the finitude of Spirit resides: it is not, as is the case [with] the rest of the finite world, an actually existing limitation; rather [the] separation is *consciousness*--its disuniting, its positing, its distinguishing. Hence labor, toil, and mortality [are] consequences or punishment, as it [is] said. On mortality, [cf. Gen. 3:]19: "In the sweat of your face you shall eat bread till you return to the ground, for out of it you were taken; you are dust, and to dust you shall return." The final destination--a higher one only by means of eternal life.+

57. Cf. *Werke* 11:417 (ET 2:81): "Among trees, there is one which is especially marked off--*Hom*, the tree from which flow the waters of immortality." (From Hegel's description of Parseeism.) According to Iranian tradition, a tree of life and regeneration grows on earth, guarded by a serpent or lizard, and has a prototype in heaven. Earthly *haoma*, or "yellow" *hom*, is found in the mountains, having first been planted by Ahura Mazda. Its prototype is in heaven, and it is the heavenly *haoma* or "white" *hom* that gives immortality to those who drink from it. Eliade points out that among ancient religions--Indian, Iranian, Egyptian, Mesopotamian, Israelite --it was common to find a primeval man (or hero) in search of immortality, a tree of life placed in some inaccessible spot, and a serpent or monster guarding the tree. He also points to the ambiguity of the two trees in the Genesis story. Cf. Mircea Eliade, *Patterns in Comparative Religion*, trans. Rosemary Sheed (New York: New American Library, 1974), pp. 287-290.

58. This passage is confusing, and Lasson's bracketed insertions, some of which we have altered, do not help to clarify it. Hegel is concerned to maintain his "fifth point" (n. 54), that mortality is necessarily connected with finitude and is not a punish-

ment. In the story God warns that death will be the penalty for eating from the tree of the knowledge of good and evil, but the serpent
says it cannot be because knowledge will make man "like God" and he
will become eternal. Moreover, the fact that the story contradicts
itself about the expulsion (is man expelled because he has *acquired*
eternal knowledge or in order to *prevent* him from becoming immortal?)
is regarded by Hegel as proof that the whole "punishment" theme is
only mythical. By contradicting itself the myth points away from
itself toward the speculative truth concerning the origin of evil.
(I am indebted to H. S. Harris for help in deciphering this passage; see also the Appendix.)

59. "From a woman sin had its beginning, and because of her we
all die." Hegel erroneously cites Sirach 25:32.

60. The MS. adds: "Always gone forth: the God of Abraham and
Isaac led the people out of Egypt; always their particularity, evil,
stiffneckedness; in brief: wholly prosaic and particular."

61. Johann Friedrich von Meyer (1772-1842), prominent Frankfurt
jurist and government official, also active theologically and philosophically, author of the so-called "Meyer-Bible"; his son Guido was
married to a sister-in-law of Hegel.

62. The manuscript reads *als* rather than *das*.

63. The 1824 lectures treat the story of the Fall only briefly,
in the context of the role of knowledge in the occurrence of evil.
This section has been relocated by Lasson from its original location
in the Griesheim transcript (see above, n. 43).

CHAPTER IV

INCARNATION AND RECONCILIATION[1]

Section 1. The Possibility, Necessity, and Actuality of Incarnation[2]

[130]^m [3] The second [stage of the third sphere] is the elevation of Spirit out of its natural will, out of evil, out of the desires of individuality, out of every type of restriction whatsoever, and therefore also [out of] the restriction of religion, of finite religion. This elevation consists generally in the fact that man comes to consciousness of the universal in and for itself, and indeed is conscious of it as *his* essence. [Thus, man comes to] consciousness of *his* infinity as substantially existing in and for itself. One moment is as essential as the other, absolute objectivity as well as infinite subjectivity. Belonging to self without seeking for self is the infinite form of consciousness, and without self-seeking [this form of consciousness is] precisely universality. God as Spirit, who is infinite subjectivity, infinite determinacy within himself, is both the absolute truth and the absolute goal of the will. That is to say, the particular subject as such acknowledges this goal to be his own goal and yet a goal that is something universal--infinite freedom--and makes [this goal] as such his own even as he is this particular subject.[4]

169

It is this consciousness of the unity of the divine
and human nature that man bears within himself [as] implicitly the divine Idea, bearing it within himself not
only as something additional, but as his own substantial
nature, [+]as his own determination or the unique possibility of such determination: [131] this infinite possibility is his subjectivity.[+] In this consciousness man
knows [+]the divine Idea,[+] the universal, and [knows] himself to be determined for the universal, i.e., elevated
above all locality, nationality, condition, life-situa-
tion, etc. Men [are now] equal; slavery [is] intoler-
able; [man has] worth and absolute validity only in this
regard. His determinate characteristic [lies] in the
spiritual, his goal is an infinite goal; he is absolutely
fulfilled implicitly. [+][It is] not his *merit* to produce
the good, the divine Idea.[+] The only thing that matters
here is that the subject comport himself in such a way
that he may know or intuit that he has the possibility
of an infinite value within himself and that he may actually give himself this value. Such a consciousness
completes religion as the knowledge of God as Spirit, for
it is Spirit, in the process of differentiation [+]and return,[+] that we see in the Idea. This means that the
unity of divine and human nature has significance not
only for the determination of human nature but just as
much for that of the divine. This is because all differentiation, [all] finitude, is a moment, however transi-
tory--a moment precisely of the process of the divine
nature; it develops this process [and shows itself]
thereby to be grounded in the divine nature itself.

This knowledge comprises the highest stage of the
spiritual being of man, i.e., of his religious determination. This is the determinate characteristic of man as
man in general, [and it enters] entirely into the consciousness of his finitude--the ray of eternal light that
shines clearly for him within his finitude.

This knowledge must therefore *come to* him. [+]It comes

to him as humanity in general, i.e., without being conditioned primarily by a particular, localized formation
or education; it comes [to him] as humanity existing immediately[+] according to the mode of religious consciousness in general. This knowledge must [come] to him [in
such a way] that it is actual, empirically universal,
universal for immediate consciousness. This can come
about in no other way than that the unity [of divine and
human nature] should disclose itself in a wholly temporal,
completely common worldly appearance in one particular
man--in that man who is known at the same time as the
divine Idea, [+]not as a teacher,[+] not merely as a higher
being in general, but as the highest [Idea], as the Son
of God.

[132] What is required is this certainty and perception, not a divine teacher, nor a teacher merely of morality, not even a teacher of the Idea, and [likewise]
neither representation nor persuasion, but rather the immediate certainty and presence of divinity. For immediate
certainty of what is present is the infinite form, [the]
way in which the "is," exists for natural consciousness.
All mediation through feelings, images, or reasons is
lacking for this "is," which returns only in philosophical cognition by means of the concept in the element of
universality; hence [philosophy] has something in common
[with immediate certainty]. [+]The "is" of truth as it
exists for immediate consciousness, the infinite form
(the other is the infinite content), the "is" of feeling,
of the heart, affects the content. [The] "is" [is a]
moment or element; form [is] not without content. Not
what is, is true; [the] absolute Idea [exists] *explicitly*
or *for itself* (ontological proof of the existence of God),
[and] solely for the Idea is this "is" the form of truth
--but not as though the "is" gives a content, a particular truth.[+]

This is a point of the greatest importance. [The
Idea exists] (α) *implicitly* or *in itself*, God's objec-

tivity realized--realized in the *whole* of humanity immediately: "from the chalice of the entire realm of
Spirits foams forth to God his own infinitude."[5] (Timur,
millions of souls, roses.) +In [Goethe's] *Divan* [we
read]:

> To produce a tiny flask,
> Which forever holds the scent,
> Slender as [thy] fingertips--
> For this a world is needed,
>
> A world of [life]-impulses,
> Which in the fulness of their striving
> Surmised already the nightingale's loves,
> Its soul-stirring song.+
>
> +Ought such torment to afflict us,
> Since it enhances our desire?
> Has not Timur's dominion
> Consumed myriads of souls?+[6]

[133] +[The Idea exists] (β) *explicitly* or *for itself;* (γ) [in its] *consummate development.*+

[7] +With reference to (β), appearance and existence
[occur] only in the form of *this particular individual.*
[We have] already seen the principle of individuality in
the Greek ideal, and indeed for the perceiving self-consciousness. [Then God reveals himself as] one to the
Jews in their thought but not in their perception; for
this reason [the Jewish conception is] not perfected in
Spirit. To be perfected in Spirit means precisely that
subjectivity should give itself up as infinite: this absolute antithesis is the outermost extremity of spiritual
appearance and negative, infinite return; [i.e., it is]
subjectivity, and precisely this subjectivity [exists as
an] individual for the perceiving consciousness. [This
is] an empirical individual, unlike the Greek ideal of a
stone or metal, [a merely] ideal individuality. The latter lacks precisely the universal infinity that is in and
for [itself]. [It is] not a question merely of a living
being; the universal posited as universal exists only in
the subjectivity of consciousness, [and in fact is] only
this infinite movement in itself in which all determinateness of existence is simultaneously resolved and posited

in the most finite existence. Only in the latter as subjectivity [is there found a] perception of infinite universality, i.e., of thinking that is for itself.

Thus the Idea [exists] directly in the same sort of
nature as that of other men; [it is an] ordinary finite
being and yet simultaneously exists exclusively for itself as an individual [134] wholly different [from other
individuals, just] as every subject exists for itself,
objectively; [hence] other individuals are not already
themselves this divine Idea.

This individual is unique; [there are] not several
[like him]. In one, all [are encompassed]; in several,
[on the other hand,] divinity becomes an abstraction.
[This individual appears] absolutely and exclusively over
against all [and on behalf of] others, in order that they
might be reconstituted.[+]

[133] However, with reference to (γ), the Idea [ex-
ists] only in the form of *this* visible [individual], and
only *one* such an individual [is] precisely infinite unity
and subjectivity. [The Idea exists] in this individual
just as the singular exists as a predicate in a particular judgment--[one, not] several, as in the Indian incarnations. Precisely this prosaic stability of self-consciousness within itself, in this individual, [is] thereby objective; just here [the Idea] first [exists] in and
for itself. [It is] not that a few are chosen--[that is
the] Calvinist view [and] a matter of unhappy fate.
[Likewise, it is] superficial [to posit] several: superficial here means counter to the concept of individual
subjectivity. *Once is always*. Subject must turn itself
to subject--*without choice*. The pledge to make [the in-
dividual] holy has a local, exclusive occasion. In the
eternal Idea [there is] only one Son, one who excludes
other finite beings, [who do] not [exist] in and for themselves [and are not] eternal love.

[134] [+][This is the] consummation of reality in immediate individuality. The most beautiful point of the

Christian Religion is the absolute transfiguration of
finitude, exhibited in such a way that [every person can]
give an account of it and have an awareness [of it].[+] [m]

   [a]We have previously considered the nature of the
exigency for reconciliation. The question that we now
have to answer is this: By what means can this need be
satisfied?[8] What is the reconciling element for it?
Reconciliation can only consist in the fact that for it
the annulment of separation is accomplished; this happens
for it and for the imagination, and what seems itself to
retreat--the infinite and the ego in itself, or pure essence, God, fulfillment--is no real antithesis. This
antithesis is nothing, and the truth, the affirmative,
the absolute is the unity of the finite and the infinite,
the unity of subjectivity in its various characteristics
with objectivity.[9] This is expressed in specific form by
saying that the [135] contradiction is resolved for the
exigency, and the unity of divine and human nature, by
which both natures have set aside their abstraction vis-
à-vis each other, is accomplished. Implicitly these extremes of divine and human nature do not exist; rather
the truth is their identity, the unity of abstract, rigid
being-for-self and its fulfillment, so that concreteness
is the truth and in this respect stands opposed to abstract divinity. Thus even this sharp antithesis has
disappeared, and there remains the determination of divine and human nature as the process of their identity,
which is concrete.[10]
   The subject is in need of this truth, and it must
come to him. Divine and human nature is a difficult,
ponderous expression, and the figurative way of thinking
about it should be forgotten. What is meant here is the
essence of Spirit; in the unity of divine and human nature, everything vanishes that belongs to external par-
ticularization--the finite itself disappears.
   The second question is this: Cannot the subject

bring about this reconciliation from himself alone by his own activity, so that through his devotion and piety he brings his interior state into conformity with the divine Idea, expressing this conformity by his deeds? And further, can this occur not merely for the individual subject but rather for all men, who genuinely want to take up into themselves the divine law, so that heaven would exist on earth and the Spirit would presently live in its community, having reality there? The question is whether or not the subject as subject can bring this about on his own. It is commonly believed that the subject can do this. What we have to notice here, what must be kept carefully [136] in mind, is that we are dealing with the subject in an extreme situation, existing for itself. Subjectivity has the characteristic of a *positing*, in the sense that something owes its existence to me. This positing or activity happens through me, regardless of the content. Such a producing or bringing forth is itself a one-sided determination, and the product is only something posited, existing as such only in abstract freedom. The question, therefore, is whether or not the subject can bring about this reconciliation through its own positing activity.

Such positing must, however, essentially be a *presupposition*, so that precisely what is posited is also something implicit. The unity of subjectivity and objectivity--this divine unity--must be a presupposition for my positing. For only then does the latter have a content; otherwise it remains subjective, formal. In this fashion it first attains a true, substantial content. With the specification of this presupposition it loses its one-sidedness; along with the meaning of such a presupposition it obtains itself, thereby removing and getting rid of this one-sidedness. Fichte and Kant maintain that man can sow and do good only on the presupposition of a moral world order. He does not know whether what he does will prosper and succeed, and he can only

act on the assumption that the good will thrive in and
for itself and is not simply something posited but rather
is by its very nature objective. The presupposition is,
therefore, an essential determination. The harmony of
this contradiction must be so represented that it is a
presupposition for the subject. Since the concept cog-
nizes divine unity, it recognizes that God exists in and
for himself, and that only thereby do the insight, the
activity, the subject have existence; they are nothing
for themselves and exist only by means of the presupposition.

    The truth must therefore appear to the subject as a
presupposition, and the question is how and in what form
the truth might appear in connection with the standpoint
we now occupy. This standpoint is one of infinite an-
guish--of pure depth of soul--and it is for this anguish
that the resolution of the contradiction should take
place. This resolution has, to begin with, necessarily
the form of a presupposition because the subject represents a one-sided extreme. The subject is defined more
precisely as a profound being-within-self, as a flight
from reality, a complete withdrawal from existence and
from fulfillment. Just for this reason, however, the abstraction of the ego is at the same time defined in its
reality as something immediately [137] existing. This
subjective factor, this ego, is therefore itself something presupposed. It has, however, a realistic side as
well, for the Idea is the unity of concept and reality,
and reality is defined according to the definition of the
concept; here it is defined subjectively. The subjective
is this depth that is the ego and its fulfillment, namely,
the world, an other. But what exists as Idea is also actual; thus it has the determinate character of reality.
Empty, naked reality is defined purely and simply as sensible or material. As such it is consciousness--subjec-
tivity and objectivity--and this is as abstract as it determines itself to be. It itself exists in the mode of

sensible being, not yet reflecting this simple, abstract
being-within-self, for the latter is a relation with itself or thinking.

This infinite suffering that is wholly unfulfilled
is without reflection; its sensible content is such therefore as ought not to be, and it still lacks within itself
any extension. In its infinite depth it conducts itself
as sensible consciousness. Since for that very reason
the truth is now supposed to be for it, on the one hand
there is the *presupposition* of--and secondly, because it
is sensible self-consciousness, there thus *appears*--the
unity of divine and human nature, God as the concrete
God. The Idea appears therefore in sensible immediacy,
in sensible presence, for the form of being for others is
the immediate and sensible form.

God appears in sensible presence; he has no other
form than that of the sensible mode of Spirit, which is
that of an *individual human being*--this is the only sensible form of Spirit. Now this is the monstrous reality
whose necessity we have seen. Included with it is the
fact that the divine and human natures are not intrinsically different: *God appears in human form*. The truth
is that there is only one reason, only one Spirit. We
have seen that Spirit does not have a genuine or truthful
existence as finite.[11]

[138] The essential character of the form of appearance is thus explicated. Because it is the appearance *of
God*, it occurs essentially for the community [of faith].
Appearance is a being for an other; this other is the
community.[a]

[b]The deepest need of Spirit is that the antithesis
or opposition within the subject itself should be in-
tensified to its universal, most abstract extreme. This
is the estrangement, the anguish, to which we have referred. That these two [139] sides do not fall completely
apart, but rather constitute a contradiction within the

unity of the subject, demonstrates at the same time that
the subject is an infinite power of unity: it can bear
this contradiction. This is the formal, abstract, yet
infinite energy of unity that it possesses. What satisfies this need is the consciousness of atonement, of the
annulling, negating, and transfiguring of the antithesis,
so that such opposition is not the truth. On the contrary, the truth is much rather the attainment of unity
through the negation of antithesis, the attainment of the
peace and reconciliation that this exigency demands.
Reconciliation is what is demanded by the need of the
subject, and this exigency resides in the subject as an
infinite unity, a self-identity.

The sublation of the antithesis has two sides.
First, the subject must become conscious of the fact that
this antithesis is not intrinsic, but rather that the
truth, the inner nature [of Spirit], implies the sublation of this antithesis. Second, because opposition is
intrinsically and truthfully sublated, the subject as
such, in its being-for-itself, can reach and attain
peace and reconciliation through the sublation of the
antithesis.

That the antithesis is sublated intrinsically or *in
itself* constitutes the condition, the presupposition, the
possibility that the subject should also sublate this
antithesis explicitly or *for itself*. In this respect it
may be said that the subject does not attain reconciliation on its own account, i.e., as a particular subject
and in virtue of its own activity or conduct; reconciliation is not brought about, nor can it be brought about,
by the subject in its way of conducting itself. The subject's activity is only its positing, its doing is only
one side. The other side is what is substantial and
foundational, which on the whole comprises the possi-
bility--namely, that the antithesis at issue does not exist in itself. Put more precisely, antithesis arises
eternally and just as eternally sublates itself, is at

the same time eternal reconciliation. That this is the
truth may be seen in the eternal, divine Idea: God is
the one who as living Spirit distinguishes himself from
himself, posits an other and in this other remains identical with himself, has in this other his identity with
himself. This is the truth.

This truth is what must constitute one side of that
which must come to consciousness in man--namely, the implicitly existing, substantial side. This can be expressed more precisely as follows: the antithesis is altogether incongruous or unsuitable. [140] Antithesis or
evil is the natural condition of human being and willing;
it is the condition of immediacy, which is precisely the
modality of natural life. Along with immediacy finitude
is likewise posited, and this finitude or natural condition is incongruous with the universality of God, which
is the infinite, eternal Idea, absolutely free within itself and present to itself. This incongruity is the
point of departure [of the need for reconciliation]. The
more precise definition, however, does not consist in
saying that this incongruity of the two sides disappears
for consciousness. The incongruity *exists*, it resides
in spirituality. Spirit is the process of self-differ-
entiating, the positing of distinctions. If the latter
are distinguished, then, by the very fact that according
to this moment there are differences between them, they
are not alike: they are differentiated, inappropriate to
one another. *This* incongruity cannot disappear, for
otherwise the judgment of Spirit, its vitality, would disappear, and it would cease to be Spirit. It is much
rather the case that the two sides are not merely incongruous; rather the identity of both persists in spite of
their incongruity. The other-being, the finitude, the
weakness, the frailty of human nature in no way impairs
that unity which forms the substance of reconciliation.
That no harm is done by the element of incongruity has
been seen in the divine Idea. For the Son is other than

the Father, and this other-being is difference--otherwise
it would not be Spirit. But the other is also God and
has the entire fulness of divine nature within itself.
The characteristic of other-being in no way detracts from
the fact that this other is the Son of God and therefore
God. This other-being is that which eternally posits and
eternally sublates itself; the self-positing and sublating of other-being is love or Spirit.

Evil, as representing one side, has been abstractly
defined as *only* the other, the finite, the negative, and
God is posited as goodness and truth on the other side.
But that which is negative and other also contains within
itself affirmation. It must be brought to consciousness
that the principle of affirmation is included within negation, that in affirmation resides the principle of
identity with the other side, just as God as truth is not
only abstract identity with himself but also has in otherness, in negation, in the self-positing of the other, his
own essential determination, which is the distinctive determination of Spirit. This being-in-itself, this implicit unity of divine and human nature, [141] must come
to consciousness in infinite anguish--but only in accord
with being-in-itself, with substantiality, so that the
finitude and weakness of other-being can do no harm to
the substantial unity of the two. Or expressed differently, the substantiality of the unity of divine and human nature comes to consciousness for man in such a way
that man appears to this consciousness as God, and God
appears to it as man. This explains the necessity and
need for such an appearance.

Furthermore, the consciousness of the absolute Idea,
which we have in philosophy in the form of thinking, must
be brought forth not from the standpoint of philosophical
speculation or speculative thinking, but rather in the
form of *certainty*. It is not the case that the necessity
[of the appearance of divine-human unity] is first perceived by means of thinking; rather it must become certain

for men. In other words, this content--the unity of divine and human nature--achieves certainty, obtaining for
humanity the form of immediate, sensible perception and
external existence; it appears as something seen and ex-
perienced in the world. One must have essentially *before*
oneself this form of non-speculative consciousness; it
must essentially be *before* me--i.e., it must become certain for man. Only what exists in an immediate way, in
inner or outer perception, is *certain*. *In order for this
divine-human unity to become certain for man, God had to
appear in the world in the flesh*. The necessity that God
should appear in the world in the flesh is an essential
feature--having been necessarily derived from and demonstrated by the preceding--and only in this way can it attain certainty for man, only so is it the truth in the
form of certainty.

At the same time it should be added that the unity
of divine and human nature must appear in *a single man*.
Man as such [*der Mensch an sich*] is the universal, the
thought of man. Here, however, from this standpoint, it
is a question not of the thought of man but of sensible
certainty; thus it is a *single* man in whom this unity is
perceived--man as a single individual, man in the determinacy of singularity and particularity. Furthermore,
this cannot remain simply the characteristic of singularity *in general*, for singularity in general is again something universal. But singularity from the present standpoint is not something universal; the latter exists in
abstract thinking as such. Here, [142] however, it is a
question of the certainty of perception and feeling. The
substantial unity of which we have spoken is the intrinsic
being of man; hence it is something that lies beyond immediate consciousness, beyond ordinary consciousness and
knowledge. Accordingly it must stand over against subjective consciousness, which comports itself as ordinary
consciousness and is defined as such. Precisely this explains why the unity in question must appear for others

as a single, exclusive man; it does not exist in other
individuals but only in one from whom all others are excluded. Thus the one stands over against the others as
intrinsically human [*das Ansich*]--a single individual who
serves as the ground of certainty.

Thus we have two conditions of this appearance. The
first is that consciousness *is able* to attain this content, which is its reconciliation; it is able to attain
this substantial unity, the consciousness of which is
given. The second condition is the consciousness of the
determinate form of this exclusive individuality.

In the church Christ has been called the *God-man*--
this monstrous construction, which directly contradicts
both the imagination and the understanding. But the
unity of divine and human nature has here been brought
into human consciousness and has become a certainty for
it, implying that other-being or otherness--or, as it is
also expressed, the finitude, weakness, and frailty of
human nature--is in no way incompatible with this unity,
just as in the eternal Idea otherness does not impair the
unity that God is. It is the appearance of a man in
sensible presence; God in sensible presence can have no
other form than that of man. In the sensible and mundane
order, man alone is spiritual; thus if the spiritual is
to exist in sensible form, it must exist in human form.[b]

[137] [w]12 This characteristic, namely, that God becomes man, and consequently that finite Spirit has the
consciousness of God within the finite itself, is the
most difficult moment of religion. According to a common
representation, which we find among the ancients especially, the Spirit or soul has been cast away in this
world, which is foreign in nature to it; this indwelling
of the soul in the body, and this particularization in
the form of individuality, are held to be a degradation
of Spirit. [138] In this lies the characteristic of the
untruth of the purely material dimension, of immediate

existence. Man has spiritual interests and is spiritually active; he can feel that he is hindered in exercising these interests and activities because he experiences himself to be in a condition of physical dependence and must provide his own nourishment, etc. Thus he falls away from his spiritual interests in virtue of being bound to nature. On the other hand, however, the characteristic of immediate existence is at the same time an essential characteristic; it is the final pinnacle of Spirit in its subjectivity.[13] The moment of immediate existence is contained in Spirit itself; it is the determinate character of Spirit to advance to this moment. Natural life is not merely an external necessity; on the contrary, Spirit as subject, in its infinite relatedness to itself, has this character of immediacy in it. Now, to the extent that it is revealed to man what the nature of Spirit is, the nature of God in the entire development of the Idea must become manifest; thus this form [of immediacy] must also be present here, and this is precisely the form of finitude. The divine must appear in the form of immediacy. This immediate presence is only the presence of the spiritual in that spiritual form which is the human form. In no other way is this appearance one that is truthful and genuine--surely not when it is the appearance of God in the burning bush, and the like. God appears as a single person to whose immediacy all sorts of physical necessities are attached. In Indian pantheism a countless number of incarnations occur; there subjectivity, human being, is only an accidental form, and in God it is only a mask that substance adopts and changes in an accidental way. God as Spirit, however, contains in himself the moment of subjectivity and individuality; his appearance, accordingly, can only be a single one, can take place only once.[w]

Section 2.   The Teaching of Christ[14]

[142] [m][15] The next question [is this]:   By what means
does this individual confirm for others that he is the divine Idea?   This question belongs to the transition to the
formation of the community.   [143] "The Spirit will guide
you into all the truth" [Jn. 16:13], says Christ.   The
representation of some sort of spectacular corroboration
--in the form of nature, conversion, success, or in the
form of the Spirit as a divine power, something external
--would much rather issue in a spiritless condition.   And
[it would] be a spiritless plea to say that the existence
of this individual and faith in him could be raised beyond all doubt [in this fashion]. [+][We shall speak]
similarly of miracles later on.[+][16]

[17]His teaching, however, is an aspect of his appearance [that takes the form of a] free relation of spiritual consciousness to spiritual consciousness.   But
since it is a question of the appearance of Spirit in immediate existence and for immediate perception, the divine Idea is portrayed in [the whole of] his life and
destiny, which are integrated by his teaching.   The
teaching taken by itself alone affects only the imagination, only one's inner feeling and disposition; it does
not give this content as a *story* or *history* for immediate
consciousness.

By itself, the teaching can contain primarily only
the universal, the universal ground, since it exists for
subjective representation, [+][for] thoughts.[+] [+]Con-
versely, the universal can exist as such only in inwardness, [only in] thought, not as an external reality;[+]
inwardness is the subjectivity of the Idea.   This universal soil or ground is the element, the world, in which
Spirit must find its home;[18] this is the soil in which
man [has] his worth, his infinitude--an absolute worth in
inwardness, in the Spirit as such--the ground of his elevation into a wholly other and higher sphere.   This uni-

versal ground [+]as a state of affairs[+] is the *heavenly
kingdom*, the kingdom of God--[a] substantial, intelligible world in which all values are cast away that are
sought in earthly, mundane things. [+][This is] not God
alone, the One, but rather [a] *kingdom* of God, the eternal as a home for Spirit, the eternal as the [144] dwelling place of subjectivity.[+] This elevation is brought
before the imagination with infinite energy, summoning
and inciting the interiority of disposition.[19]

Jesus appeared on the scene in the Roman world and
among the Jewish people in particular. This suffering
people [was] stubbornly rooted and submerged [in its tra-
ditions] because of the threat to its worship of God under the domination of the Syrian kings and the Romans.
By contrast, the Romans [were] masters of the world.
Jesus appeared amidst the lost and helpless condition of
the common people and said (Matt. 11:25): "I thank thee,
Father, Lord of heaven and earth, that thou hast hidden
these things from the wise and understanding and revealed
them to babes."

[+][He summons] the Jews, [who should] rid themselves
of the debris [of the past], which has lost its value
[for humanity] and can no longer be of help. [They]
despair at reality, [yet are in] touch with a universal
dimension of human existence, which they could not deny,
but which nonetheless is a completely spiritless universality.[+]

[In the] Sermon on the Mount (Matt. 5:3 ff.), [he
says]: "Blessed are the poor in spirit, for theirs is
the kingdom of heaven. Blessed are those who mourn, for
they shall be comforted. Blessed are the meek, for they
shall inherit the earth. . . . Blessed are the pure in
heart, for they shall see God."[m]

[w][20] Words like these are among the greatest that have
ever been uttered. They are a final means of annulling
all superstition and lack of freedom on the part of hu-

manity. It is of highest importance that, by means of
Luther's translation of the Bible, a folk book has been
placed in the hands of the people, a book in which the
heart, the Spirit, can find itself at home in the highest, infinite fashion; in Catholic countries there is in
this respect a great lack. For Protestant peoples, the
Bible is the means of deliverance from all slavery of
Spirit.[w]

[m]In all of this is found a language of inspiration
that displaces all other human interests, eradicating
them completely--penetrating tones that shake everything
up; and, as Hermes led souls forth from their bodies and
thus out of the temporal sphere, so [+][these words are]
addressed to men [145] who are done with the world and
with whom the world is finished.[+]

[+]Christ speaks further of the Mosaic dispensation of
the law. The entire thrust [of his words] is that this
[type of] service, [this] enslavement, [this] external
activity has no worth. Only *intention* imparts infinite
worth to activity; however, it is not [an] abstract intention but [the] true, inward intention that issues in
a true activity.[+] "Seek first the kingdom of God and his
righteousness, and all these things shall be yours as
well" (Matt. 6:33).

Throughout these exaltations his sadness over the
lost condition of his people and of humanity is conveyed.
In brief, his teaching is a complete abstraction from
what is regarded in the world as great; [+][it is an] elevation to [the] heaven within, access to which is open to
everyone, and before which everything else counts for
nothing.[+]

This substantial element, this universal, divine
heaven--the heaven within--leads in more determinate reflection to moral and other imperatives, which are nothing other than particular prescriptions in specific
circumstances and situations. But even these imperatives

have restricted aspects, and they represent nothing ex-
ceptional for this stage, which is concerned with a
higher, [and indeed] the absolute, truth.

   The most outstanding and at the same time comprehensive teaching of Christ is, as is well known, *love.*
[+][The] moral imperative can be expressed as love: [what
one ought to seek is] not what is legally right but the
well-being of the other; thus [the commandment entails a]
relation to the particularity of the other [and is a mat-
ter] of feeling only.[+] Indeed, [the commandment is,]
"Love your neighbor" [Mk. 12:31]. In the more abstract,
extensive sense of the sphere of human love in general,
the commandment intends love for all men--and thus it becomes a lame abstraction. The man and the men whom one
can love are a few particular individuals. [The] heart
that seeks to embrace the whole of humanity within itself indulges in a vain attempt to spread out its love
until it becomes a mere image, the very opposite of what
love is.

   Love in Christ's sense [is]: (α) Moral love for the
neighbor in [the] particular circumstances in which one
is related to him. (β) The love that expresses the relationship among the apostles, [who are] one in love. [It
is] not [the case that] each [of them has] a [146] particular occupation, interest, or way of life and then in
addition [is] loving. Rather they [are] singled out and
removed [from all others], and love [constitutes] the
very center of their being. [+]Love of enemies is also
contained here.[+] [+][The disciples] are supposed to love
and nothing else; they are released from all else. [They
are] to make only this community and its unity in and for
itself their goal--not the liberation of humanity [as a]
political goal--and [they should] love one another for
that unity's sake. (A man [either] has such an objective
goal, [and] loves for its sake, or he is indifferent, or
he hates [his fellows]. Varying definitions of the end
itself and of the means [to it] are possible; hence

division directly [arises in the community]. In view of
this objectivity [what matters is] holding firm to [com-
munal] ends, and departure [from them is distinctive] for
the subjectivity and particularity of ends.)[21] But love
is the abstract personality [of the community] and the
identity of its ends in *one* consciousness; no possibility
of particularity remains.[+] [The love of Christ is] (γ)
an independent love, which is made the center [of being
and] then immediately becomes the higher, divine love itself; [its] ground is the determinate activity of the
Holy Spirit.

     [The] second aspect of this teaching is a breaking
away in the negative sense from everything established--
[+]precisely this love as such, without an objective goal,
without any goal as such, [represents a breaking away].
At first [Christ directs] himself against the established
order of Judaism (see the Sermon on the Mount). [He does
not] censure the picking of corn on the Sabbath or the
healing of a withered hand, [although he] could have
waited until the next morning. [But all such ordinances
are brought to an end by his proclamation:] "The kingdom
of heaven is at hand" (Matt. 10:7)--[indeed] as an actual
state of affairs.[+] [This proclamation is,] so to speak,
sans-culottism,[22] or in oriental terms, revolutionary.

     "Consider the lilies of the field; they neither sow
nor reap, and your heavenly Father cares for them"[23]--
[as he does for the] birds. "Therefore, do not be anxious for the morrow, saying, 'What shall we eat?' or
'What shall we drink?' or 'What shall we wear?' Such
cares are appropriate to the Gentiles, who seek all these
things" [Matt. 6:31-32]. Even beggars are anxious about
the coming day, for they have their [particular] place
[to secure]. Only thieves and soldiers are capable of
this lack of anxiety; thieves know that tomorrow they
will find [their spoil. He said to the] [147] young man
who came to him: "Give what you have to the poor and
follow me" [cf. Mk. 10:21].

Or [he preaches a breaking away from one's] family.
Matt. 12:46[-50]: "While he was still speaking with the
people, his mother and his brothers stood outside, asking
to speak to him. Someone told him, 'Your mother and your
brothers are standing outside, asking to speak to you.'
But he replied to the man who told him, 'Who is my mother,
and who are my brothers?' And stretching out his hand
toward his disciples, he said, 'Here are my mother and
my brothers! For whoever does the will of my Father in
heaven is my brother, and sister, and mother.'" +Or
Matt. 8:21[-22]: "Another of his disciples said to him,
'Lord, let me first go and bury my father.' But Jesus
said to him, 'Follow me, and leave the dead to bury their
own dead.'"+

+Here [also belongs] the well-known passage:[24] "I
have not come to bring peace on earth, but a sword.[25]
For I have come to set a man against his father, and a
daughter against her mother; . . . and a man's foes will
be those of his own household. He who loves father or
mother more than me is not worthy of me; and he who loves
son or daughter more than me is not worthy of me."+

+[In these utterances there is] no mention of the
state. [To be sure, it is said,] "Render to Caesar" [Mk.
12:17], [but the] consequences [are] not specified.+

In this sense, social groups and bodies will always
arise among a people (among a people, a community, which
with regard to itself also [has] a rational structure in
the world). This contraction [will] take all established
orders back into the simple heart, into simple love, and
appears externally to be only a matter of suffering, of
[self-]giving, of exposing one's neck. +[One finds this]
among [the] Muhammadans especially in Africa.+ But it is
not possible to remain merely with such a retreat, for
the latter represents the fanatic beginning of suffering
and forebearance, whose inner energy is elevated after a
[148] time to an equally fanatic act of violence when it
has gained sufficient strength.

   The third aspect of the teaching of Christ has to
do with the more precise or authentic characteristic of
the kingdom of God, i.e., with the relationship of Christ
himself to God and of humanity to God and Christ. [+]In
this regard, the exaltation of his Spirit [is] evident--
"Woman, your sins are forgiven" [Lk. 7:48]--this enormous
majesty of Spirit, which can make all that has been done
to be undone [and] declare outright that this [has] come
about.[+] His being sent from God [is thereby manifest].
He states very specifically his identity with the Father:
"I and the Father are one" (Jn. 10:30). [+]Then the Jews
took up stones to stone him [cf. 10:31].[+] "All things
have been delivered to me by my Father; and no one knows
the Son except the Father, and no one knows the Father
except the Son and any one to whom the Son chooses to reveal him" [Matt. 11:27]. "The Father loves the Son, and
has given all things into his hand. He who believes in
the Son has eternal life; he who does not believe[26] the
Son shall not see life, but the wrath of God rests on
him" (Jn. 3:35-36).

   Christ refers to himself as the Son of Man--just as
the Arabs [designate themselves] as all being the son of
one race, not this or that individual, but an Arab as
such--[thus Christ as] a man [is] man as such.[27]

   In these and other passages, it cannot be a matter
of exegesis flattening out these expressions [in a manner
such as the following: Jesus was] well-pleasing to God;
all [human beings are] God's children, just as all the
stones and animals are his creation; [Jesus was a] pious
sage. Rather [the words of Christ] confirm the truth of
the Idea of what he has been for his community; they confirm the higher Idea of truth, which appeared in him in
his community.[m]

   [a]The confirmation of the appearance [of God] has two
aspects. The first concerns the content of the appearance, which is the unity of the finite and the infinite,

the fact that God is not an abstraction but a concrete
God. From this standpoint, in so far as it exists for
consciousness, the confirmation is [149] only an inner
matter, a witness of the Spirit. Philosophy must explain
that this is not merely a mute inner witness but also is
present in the element of thinking. This is the one side,
the *imago*-character of human nature: man is the image of
God.

The second aspect [of this confirmation] has been
observed earlier: God, considered in terms of his eternal Idea, has to generate the Son, has to distinguish
himself from himself; he is this process of differentiating, namely, love and Spirit. The suffering of the soul
is the testimony of the Spirit because the latter is the
negativity of the finite and the infinite, subjectivity
and objectivity co-existing in a conflictual process. If
this strife were to disappear, there would be no anguish.
Spirit is the absolute power to endure this anguish, i.e.,
to unite both subjectivity and objectivity and thus to
exist in this unity. In this anguish there is the confirmation of God's appearance. What the other confirmation concerns--namely, that in this man, in this place,
at this time, the appearance came forth--is an entirely
other matter, and it is only to be recognized from the
viewpoint of world history. When the time had come, God
sent his Son; and *that* the time had come is only to be
discerned from history.[28]

The question is now more precisely this: What content must present itself in this appearance? The content can be nothing other than the history of Spirit, the
history that God is, the divine history as that of one
single self-consciousness which has united in itself divine and human nature, the divine nature in this element
of human individuality.

The first component is that of the *individual, immediate man* in all his contingency, in all his temporal
circumstances and conditions. To this extent, this is a

divestment of the divine. It should be noticed here that
this is a reality for the community. This reality is the
unity of the finite and the infinite, but in this sensible mode there is at the same time a divestment of the
Idea, which has to be sublated.

The second component is the *teaching* [of this indi-
vidual]. Of what sort is it? It cannot be what later
became the doctrine of the church or community. Christ's
teaching is not Christian dogmatics, not the doctrine of
the church. Christ [150] did not expound what the church
later produced as its doctrine because his teaching
evokes *feelings* by means of representation. Its content,
which at the highest level is an explication of the nature of God, is precisely intended for the sensible consciousness, and it comes to this consciousness as an intuition. Thus it is unlike a doctrine, which begins with
the assertion of dogmatic propositions. The major content of the teaching of Jesus can only be universal and
abstract, can only contain that which is universal and
abstract.

If something new, a new world, a new religion, a new
concept of God is to be given to the world of representation, then two aspects are involved, the first being the
universal ground, and the second the particular, determinate, and concrete. The world of representation, in
so far as it thinks, thinks only abstractly, thinks only
the universal. It is reserved for the conceptualizing
Spirit to recognize the particular in the universal, and
to see how this particular proceeds out of the concept by
its own power. For the world of representation, the determinate character and the ground of universal thought
are separate. This universal ground may therefore be
employed, by means of doctrine, for the true concept of
God. In brief, this is the *kingdom of God*, which has
been taught by Christ; it is the real divinity, God in
his existence, spiritual actuality, the kingdom of heaven.
This divine reality already contains within itself God

and his kingdom, the community; this is a concrete content, and it is the major content.[a]

[154] [b]29 The appearance of the God-man, as we have
seen, is to be viewed from two perspectives simultaneously: first, as a man in accord with his external circumstances, and this means from a non-religious perspec-
tive--how he appears as an ordinary human being. The
second way is the perspective that occurs in the Spirit
or with the Spirit. Spirit penetrates to the truth [con-
cerning the God-man] because it experiences within itself
this infinite estrangement and anguish; it wills the
truth; it wills to have and ought to have a need for the
truth and a certainty of the truth. This second way
alone represents the religious perspective.

When Christ is viewed in the same light as Socrates,
then he is considered to be an ordinary man, just as the
Muhammadans regard him to be an envoy from God in the
general sense that all great men are envoys or messengers
of God. If one says no more of Christ than that he is a
teacher of humanity, a martyr to the truth, one does not
occupy the religious standpoint. This human side of
Christ, his appearance as a living man, is one side, and
the elements of it can be briefly mentioned.

The first element is that he is *immediately a man*
in all the external contingencies, in all the temporal
relations and conditions, that this entails: he is born
and as a man has the needs of other men, except that he
does not share the corruption, the passions and mere inclinations of others, nor does he engage in particular
worldly interests, in connection with which integrity and
teaching may also find a place. Rather he lives only the
truth, only its proclamation; his activity consists solely
in completing the higher consciousness of humanity.

The second element is that of his *teaching office*.
The question now is this: How can, how must, this teaching be constituted? As already shown it cannot be con-

stituted in a manner similar to the later doctrine of the
church; it must have its own distinctive qualities, [155]
which in the church partly take on another character and
partly are set aside. When the community is established
for the first time, when the kingdom of God has attained
its existence, its actuality, then these teachings take
on added characteristics or fall by the wayside.

Since it is a matter of the consciousness of absolute reconciliation, one finds here a new consciousness
of humanity, a new religion. A new world is thereby constituted, a new actuality, a different world-condition,
because now man's external or natural existence has religion as its substance. This is its polemical side, its
revolutionary attitude toward what is determinate in that
externality which comprises the consciousness and belief
of men.[30] The new religion expresses itself as a new
consciousness, the consciousness of a reconciliation of
humanity with God. This reconciliation, expressed as a
state of affairs, is the kingdom of God, an actuality.
The souls or hearts [of men] are reconciled with God, and
thus it is God who rules in the heart and achieves dominion.   To this extent this is the universal ground.[b]
[w][31]It is disposition or intentionality alone that has
value--not, however, an abstract disposition, nor mere
chance opinion, but rather an absolute disposition that
has its foundation in the kingdom of God. The infinite
worth of interiority thereby first comes into view.[w]

[150][32] [a]This teaching, in so far as it initially remains something universal, has, in this universal as an
abstract universal, the character of negation against
everything that exists at hand. In so far as it affirms
the universal vis-à-vis the latter, it is a revolutionary
doctrine, which partially sets aside all that is established and in part nullifies and overthrows it.[a] [b]This
new religion as yet concentrates itself and does not actually exist as a community, but has its vitality rather

in that energy which constitutes the sole, eternal interest of the man who has to fight and struggle in order
to obtain it because it is not yet associated with world
consciousness and does not exist in harmony with the
state of the world. This kingdom of God, the new religion, thus contains in itself the characteristic of negation vis-à-vis what presently exists.[33] [151] What has
gone before is now altered; the hitherto existing circumstances, the previous condition of religion and the world,
cannot continue as before. It is thus a matter of withdrawing those persons in whom the consciousness of reconciliation should arise from reality as it now exists, of
demanding of them an abstraction from reality. The demand is set forth that one remove oneself from finite
things and elevate oneself to an infinite energy in which
all other bonds have become matters of indifference, for
which all other bonds--indeed, all things hitherto regarded as moral and right--have been set aside.[b] [a]All
earthly, worldly things fall away, are without worth, and
are expressly declared to be so. This is an elevation to
an infinite energy, which is brought before the imagination in such fashion that the universal demands to be
laid hold of for its own sake. We interpret the following sayings in this way. When Christ finds himself among
his disciples and his mother and brothers come to speak
to him, he asks, "Who are my mother and my brothers?
. . .[34]Here are my mother and my brothers! Whoever does
the will of God is my brother, and sister, and mother"
(Mk. 5:31-35). To another he said, "Follow me." But he
said, "Lord, let me first go and bury my father." But
Jesus said to him, "Leave the dead to bury their own dead;
but as for you, go and proclaim the kingdom of God." And
another said, "I will follow you, Lord; but let me first
say farewell to those at my home." But Jesus said to
him, "No one who puts his hand to the plow and looks back
is fit for the kingdom of God" (Lk. 9:59-62).[a] [b]We see
here a polemical attitude directed against ethical rela-

tionships.[b] [a]All those relations that refer to property
disappear. Here belong words of counsel such as the following: "Take no thought for the morrow," or "Give your
goods to the poor." Meanwhile these injunctions cancel
themselves because if the poor were universally to receive such goods, they would become rich, and the same
circumstance would be repeated. Christ says: "Do not be
anxious about tomorrow, for tomorrow will be anxious for
itself" [Matt. 7:34]. Such concerns, however, are proper for man. Yet here family relationships, property,
etc., recede in the face of something that exists in and
for itself, namely, following Christ.[a]

[b]These are all teachings and characteristics that belong to the first appearance of the new religion, when it
constitutes man's sole interest, which he must believe
himself still to be in danger of losing. This is the one
side.

This renunciation, surrender, and setting aside of
all vital interests and moral bonds is an essential characteristic of the concentrated manifestation of the
truth, a characteristic [152] that subsequently, when
truth has attained a secure existence, loses some of its
importance. It is the proclamation of the kingdom of
God. Man must transpose himself into this kingdom in order to enter immediately into its truth. This is expressed with the purest, most colossal boldness, e.g.,
at the beginning of the Sermon on the Mount: "Blessed
are the poor . . . ," etc.

No mention is made of any mediation in connection
with this elevating of the soul whereby it may become an
accomplished fact in man; rather what is expressed is
this immediate being, this immediate self-transposition
into the truth, into the kingdom of God. It is to this
kingdom, to this intellectual, spiritual world, that man
ought to belong. This is proclaimed in the language of
inspiration, in such thoroughly penetrating tones that

they pierce through the soul and draw it out of corporeal
interests. "Seek first the kingdom of God," etc.[b]

[a]This perfect independence is the first, abstract
soil of spirituality. Morality qua morality has its
place here on a subordinate level and is not distinctive:
the imperatives of Christ stem for the most part from the
Old Testament. From another perspective love is once
again regarded as the major commandment--not some im-
potent love for all men in general, but rather the love
of the community for one another. The spiritual nexus of
the community is capable of constituting universality.
Whatever can be regarded as a moral imperative is also
found partly in other religions and partly in the Jewish
Religion.

As mentioned above, that which concerns the distinctive element [in the community's perception of Christ] is
added, as it were, from elsewhere for the representative
consciousness. Wholly concrete examples are to be found
in other spheres. In the Muhammadan doctrine there is
merely the fear of God: God is to be venerated as the
One, and this abstraction simply remains. Therefore this
Muhammadan religion is a formalism, a pure formalism,
which allows nothing to take shape in opposition to it,
and thus it is fanaticism. Or in the French Revolution,
freedom and equality were affirmed such that all spirituality, all laws, all talents, all living relations had
to disappear before this abstraction, and the ordinances
of the state had to come from elsewhere and be forcefully
asserted against this abstraction. For what the abstraction firmly maintains cannot allow [153] the emergence of
something determinate, since the latter is a particularization that is distinct from the abstraction. (I mention all of this so that we may see how far the representative consciousness can go by itself; but what is distinctive must be added in some other way.)

This distinctive element is the characteristic that

here emerges in similarly unique fashion. If, in the universal, the teaching is indeed the basis, then there are
several indications in it that point to its particular
determination; but the main point is that this [distinc-
tive] content is not given through the teaching but
through sensible perception. This content is nothing
other than the life, passion, and death of Christ.[a]

[b]This [distinctive] moment or determinate element
enters into the teaching as follows: because the demand,
"Seek first . . . cast yourself upon the truth," is expressed so directly, it emerges almost as a subjective
expression, and to this extent the person of the teacher
comes into view. Christ speaks not merely as a teacher,
who expounds on the basis of his own subjective insight
and who is aware of his productivity and activity, but
rather as a prophet. He is the one who, just as his demand is immediate, expresses it immediately from God, and
also it is from God that he speaks it. Having this life
of the Spirit in the truth, so that it is simply there
without mediation, expresses itself prophetically in
such a way that it is God who says it. It is a matter of
the absolute, divine truth that exists in and for itself,
and of its expression and intention; and the certifica-
tion of this expression is perceived as God's doing. It
is the consciousness of the real unity and harmony of the
divine will. In the form of this expression, however,
the accent is laid upon the fact that the one who says
this is at the same time essentially human; it is the Son
of Man who speaks thus, in whom this expression, this ac-
tivation of what exists in and for itself, is essentially
the work of God, but not as something suprahuman, which
appears in the form of an external revelation, but rather
as something effected in a man such that the divine presence is essentially identical with this man.
      We still have to consider the fate of this individ-
ual, namely, that he became, humanly speaking, a martyr

to the truth in close connection with the manner of his
appearance, because the founding of the kingdom of God
[154] stands in stark contradiction to the existing state,
which is founded on another aspect or characteristic of
religion.

These are the major elements in the appearance of
this man, in light of a purely human consideration. But
this is only one side, and it is not a religious consideration.$_b$35

Section 3. The Passion and Resurrection of Christ

[155] ^{m} ^{36} With reference to such teachings, we suppose
at the outset that the life of this teacher is in conformity with them; $^{+}$not only this, but also^{+} that his
life is completely devoted to them, that he does not shun
the hazards and the death that he must expect because of
what he has begun among his people. We find it appropriate that he seals his faith by his death--which is not
much [to expect] in any case and is shared [by him] with
a host of others. $^{+}$This first thing [is] of no speculative [significance, and is only what is] abstractly
fitting: that is to say, the content, action, achieve-
ments of this life are defined by that content. [Every-
where we get] an unwavering perception of one and the
same content.$^{+}$

But here life and death have another, quite different relation to the teaching [of Jesus]. Its content is
the kingdom of God--[156] not a universal essence but a
living, spiritual life, a divine community. $^{+}$[The] teaching as such [is only] the universal form of the content,
whereas [the] kingdom of God, as the first, eternal Idea
itself, [is] concrete. The kingdom of God is Spirit determining itself in terms of the universal and passing
over into actuality. This movement, [the] process of
determining, takes place in the life of Jesus. The

eternal Idea is precisely what allows the determination
of subjectivity to appear immediately as something actual, distinguished from mere thoughts. It is what enables it [the determinate subject, Jesus[37]] to become itself (in actualization), and only as actualized is it[37]
the kingdom of God.[+] This kingdom of God is linked with
individuals, who are supposed to attain to the kingdom
through this one individual. The kingdom is the universal Idea represented in imaginative form; it enters into
actuality through this individual, and the history of
Spirit, the concrete content of the kingdom of God, has
portrayed itself in this divine actuality. [+]And since
the kingdom of God is set forth as the teaching of a
divine individual, the divinity of Christ at first is
only implicit. He is the God-man for Spirit only as the
process of Spirit constitutes itself as such. The God-
man has to manifest himself in order that he might represent the progress of the Idea and be [the] manifestation
of its absolute content, its determinate form.[+]

This portrayal--this objectivity of the perception
of the history of Spirit--shows that Spirit in itself
exists as other than itself in the natural will and existence [of man], that it annuls this its other-being,
and that it now exists for itself in all its glory, is-
suing forth to be Spirit through this history. [+]That
this absolute content should be made manifest--as it were
[by] an allegorical or symbolic presentation of the content[+]--is what comprises this perception, the history of
this individual, a process transpiring in the mode of
finitude, the history of Spirit in this peculiar medium,
namely that of external, common human existence.[38] Since
it is the divine Idea that courses through this history,
it exists not as the history merely of a single individual, but rather intrinsically as the history of the actual man who is constituted as the existence of Spirit.

[157] [+]The kingdom of God finds, therefore, its representative (i.e., the mode of its existence) initially

in this existing human being. The life of Christ [is] a
natural, ordinary life; accordingly, his death is a natural negativity, containing within itself an immediate
doubling and opposition--the becoming-other of the divine. This existence is one of a natural, ordinary life,
which shows [itself] to be imprisoned in the conditions
of ordinary human life, [enclosed] within these limits,
within finitude. The highest limit, the supreme finitization, is the death of this first [existence].[+]

The death of Christ has this more exact significance:

[As] the seal of his teaching,[39] [his death] is
grasped in a morally formal way, not as a moment of the
divine Idea. [+]([As an example] of his teaching, of the
love that marked his conduct, [it] belongs in the context of our earlier discussion of fittingness. This is
where his ordinary life as something external and existent belongs.)[+] On one side, he is [a moment of the
divine Idea], so that his death represents the highest
pinnacle of finitude. If the unity of divine and human
nature is to be perceived in an actual individual, then
incarnation as immediate existence in the form of finitude already constitutes this side just as much as immediate existence in the form of divine divestment--[+]a
divestment of itself such that it still exists in this
divestment, but not in the sense of the external world
over against consciousness (this [is] nature in its
goal).[+] It is this immediate existence in which the divine Idea has become subjective. [The] unity [of the
divine and the human] is portrayed therein, likewise the
estrangement, the other-being. However the pinnacle of
finitude is not actual life in its temporal course, but
rather death, the anguish of death; death is the pinnacle
of negation, the most abstract and indeed natural negation, the limit, finitude in its highest extreme.[40] The
temporal and complete existence of the divine Idea in the
present is perceived only in Christ's[41] death. [+]The

highest divestment of the divine Idea--"God has died,
God himself [158] is dead"[42]--is a monstrous, frighten-
ing image, which brings before the imagination the deepest abyss of estrangement.

But this death is at the same time[+] [and] to this
extent[43] the highest love. [It is] precisely love [that
is] this identity of the divine and the human, and the
finitization [of] consciousness is carried to its extreme, to death. Thus here [we find] a perception of the
unity of the divine and the human at its absolute peak,
[+]the highest perception of love. For love [consists] in
giving up one's personality, all that is one's own, etc.
[It is] a self-conscious activity, a giving up [of one-
self] to the highest degree in the other, [manifesting
oneself] precisely in this most extrinsic other-being of
death, which represents the limit of all that lives.
[The] death of Christ [is the] perception of this absolute love itself--a love that does not exist for or on
behalf of others, but rather is precisely *divinity* in
this universal identity with other-being, death. The
monstrous unification of these absolute extremes is love
itself. -- [This is the] speculative way of perceiving
things.[+]

On the basis of this death the assertion is justified that Christ [has been] given up *for us*, [and that
his death] may be represented as a sacrificial death, as
the act of absolute satisfaction. The common objection
to this way of representing [Christ's death is] that each
individual must answer for himself and for his own deeds;
another cannot atone for him, nor can he receive absolu-
tion in this manner. From the standpoint of formal justice this is indeed the case, i.e., from the standpoint
according to which the subject is viewed as an individual
person. Here this standpoint does not apply. In order
to explain this and to get to this point, [we must] consider [it] more closely in the concrete sense.[44] Death
is, in general, both the extreme limit of finitude and at

the same time the [159] sublation of natural finitude, of
immediate existence, the annulling of divestment, the
dissolution of limitation. [Death is] the moment in
which Spirit grasps itself within itself, the moment of
perishing to the natural, of infinite abstraction from
the immediacy of volition and consciousness; [it means]
to be submerged within oneself and to take from this
depth only its determinacy and sheer "is," which has
worth and validity for it. +Its "is," [its] true essence, [is] precisely absolute universality, which appears as love [in] religion as well as in sensation.+
   45Accordingly, this death, this suffering, the anguish of death, is the moment of the reconciliation of
Spirit with itself, with what it contains implicitly.
This negative moment, which pertains only to Spirit as
such, represents its inner conversion and transformation.
+Death is not portrayed here in its concrete significance; at first+ it is represented +and accomplished+
merely as a natural death. In the divine Idea, +this
negation+ can be portrayed in no other way: it is the
external portrayal of the history of Spirit in the natural state. As it actualizes itself, evil in the divine Idea can only have the modality of the natural.
Hence the return [of Spirit to itself] can only occur in
the manner of a natural death.46
   This death, therefore, is one that makes satisfaction for us because it presents the absolute history of
the divine Idea as a history that has taken place in itself and happens eternally. That the single human being
does something, achieves something, attains [a certain]
goal, is grounded in the fact that the matter in itself
is thus related to itself in its concept. Thus my eating an apple means that I destroy its organic self-
identity and assimilate it to myself. That I can do this
entails that the apple in itself (already in advance, before I take hold of it) has in its nature the determination of being something subject to destruction, and at

the same time [160] is something that has in itself a
homogeneity with the digestive process such that I can
make it homogeneous with myself. That the criminal can
be punished by the judge, and that this [punishment] is
the carrying out of the law, its satisfaction, is not
something accomplished by the judge, nor by the criminal
through his suffering the punishment as a particular, external occurrence or consequence. It is [not the case
that] this is an accidental sequence of occurrences,
[which] thus comes accidentally to that conclusion;
rather what has transpired is the nature of the thing
that the law expresses, +the necessity of the concept.+
We have this process before us in a double way--on the
one hand, in thought, in the notion of law and concept;
on the other hand, in the individual case. In the latter,
the process proceeds in such and such a way because this
is the nature of the matter, without which there would be
neither [the] judge nor his action, neither suffering of
punishment by the criminal nor the satisfaction of the
law. The foundation and substance of all this is the nature of the matter.

This applies also in the case of satisfaction for
us, meaning that satisfaction has transpired in and for
itself. It is not an extrinsic sacrifice that is per-
formed, nor a matter of someone else [being] punished so
that punishment might be rendered; +[it is not the] negation of a life or the annulment of other-being+ ([as
in the case of] natural death). Besides, everyone dies on
his own, and everyone must be and achieve on his own, out
of his own subjectivity and obligation, what he ought to
be. For someone to lay hold of the merit of Christ means
that, if one is to accomplish this merit within himself,
this conversion that abandons the natural will and natural interests, and if one is to exist in infinite love,
then this is the matter in and for itself. One's subjective certainty, one's feeling and consciousness, is truth,
is *the* truth: i.e., it is, in and for itself, the true

nature of Spirit, in which Spirit is adequate to its concept.

The ground of redemption is, therefore, this history, +[this] perishing of the natural,+ which is the matter in and for itself. It is not a capricious accident, or merely a particular deed and happening, but rather is true and complete. This verification that it is the truth is the perception given by this history. It is not the history of a single individual; rather it is God who accomplishes it--i.e., [161] it is the perception that this is the universal history existing in and for itself.

[47]We still have to consider the particular characteristic of this death: specifically, it has been defined as the uttermost pinnacle of finitude. In addition to the fact that it is a natural death, it is the death of a criminal, the most degrading death on the *cross*. Taken as something external, life is natural and immediate--immediate for the opinion of another, [who accords it either] honor or shame. +My existence, in the sense of existing in the representation of another, [is] what is accorded value by this representation. I have value and am objective to the extent that I know myself to be valued by others. My value is their representation and comparison of me with whatever they reverence, with what they regard as the in-itself.+ Death [that is] degrading or dishonoring [is the extreme of finitude therefore.] In a natural death, finitude as a natural condition [is] transfigured; but here +civil+ dishonor, [death on] the cross, [is] transfigured. That which is represented as the lowest and which the state uses as an instrument of dishonor is here converted into something of highest value. What has counted as the lowest is now made the highest. We find here the direct expression of a complete revolution against all that is established and regarded as valuable.[48] Since the dishonoring of existence has been elevated to a position of highest honor,

all the bonds of human corporate life are fundamentally
assaulted, shaken, and dissolved. [The] cross corresponds to our gallows. If this symbol of dishonor is
raised up as a banner whose positive content is at the
same time the kingdom of God, then [162] by contrast our
inner loyalties[49] are at root withdrawn from the life of
the state and from civil affairs. The substantial foundation of the latter is removed, and this whole structure
no longer has any actuality. Its inner reality [is now
only] something external--an empty appearance, which must
soon come crashing down. The fact that it is no longer
anything in itself must also become manifest in existence.

+Let us compare what this outward existence disclosed simultaneously, not just immediately at the time
of Christ and of [the origin of] Christianity itself, but
in connections that are in their universal aspect, contemporary.+

For its part, imperial authority degraded everything
esteemed and prized by humanity. Venerable forms of
justice and governance remained; [nonetheless] the well-
being of each individual depended on the caprice of the
emperor, who was subject neither to internal nor to external constraints. +But, besides life, all+ virtue and
worth, the dignity of old age, one's station in life and
race--all these things were thoroughly dishonored. The
slave of the emperor was next to him the highest power,
or had even more power than the emperor himself; the
Senate debased itself in proportion as everything was
debased by the emperor. It was no threat to him; rather
the emperor went his own way vis-à-vis the Senate, and
[the Senators] merely protected their own interests.
Thus, the majesty of world dominion, all virtue and right,
everything sacred in human institutions and affairs, the
majesty of everything that has infinite value--all were
cast upon the dung heap. Likewise the secular regent of
the earth for his part reduced the highest to what is

most +despised+ [and] lowly; +and on the other hand we
see what is despised elevated to the highest, to a standard.+ Accordingly, the secular government, for its part,
overturned the moral disposition [of its citizens] from
top to bottom, and consequently there was nothing left in
the inner [life] to set against the new religion. Everything established, everything ethical, everything commonly viewed as having authority, was destroyed, and
there remained only an entirely bare, external, cold
authority--only death--which was not dreaded by the life
that +had been degraded+ [but still] was inwardly aware
of itself.

50The outcome of this entire course has still to be
considered. It is completed even unto death: the divine
Idea [163] has divested itself unto the bitter anguish of
death and the shame of a criminal; thereby the finitude
of man is glorified unto the highest [by means of] the
highest love. The former is the latter: the deepest
anguish [is the highest love]; and the latter, the highest love, [occurs] in the former. This glorification--
still in the subjective [form] of love and in the extreme of disruption [as] the most violent interiorization
and mere internality--at the same time [gives to] existence its despair. What must still be added is the return contained herein [of the divine Idea to itself] as a
perceptible consummation. With regard to this, I need
only to recall the well-known form of this perception:
51it is the resurrection and ascension. This exaltation
[of Christ], like everything that precedes it, has appeared for immediate consciousness in the mode of actuality. "Thou wilt not abandon thy Righteous One to the
grave, nor let thy Holy One see corruption"52--rather,
this death of death, the overcoming of the grave, [and
of] Sheol, the triumph over the negative, are present to
perception. +[This triumph is] not an abstraction from
or a putting off of human nature, but rather fully pre-
serves it, precisely in death itself and in the highest

love. Spirit is Spirit only as the negation of the negative, which thus contains the negative within itself.
God [is perceived] as reconciled, as love,$^+$ and [like-
wise] this exaltation $^+$of human nature$^+$ to heaven,
where the Son of Man sits at the right hand of the Father,
[where] the identity of divine and human nature and the
glory of the latter appear to the spiritual eye in the
highest possible way.

Therefore, what this life of Christ brings to figurative representation for us--indeed, for the empirical,
general, and immediate consciousness--is^{53} the process of
the nature of Spirit, God in human form. This [process],
in its development, [is] the going-forth of the divine
Idea into the uttermost estrangement, into the contradiction of the anguish of death, which itself is the absolute reversal, the highest love, in itself the negation
of the negative, the absolute reconciliation, the sublation of the antithesis between man and God. The end [of
this process] is presented as a resolution into glory,
[164] the festive assumption of humanity into the divine
Idea. That primal being, God in human form, is real in
this process, which shows the separation of the divine
Idea and its reunion, and for the first time its completion as truth. $^+$This is the whole of history.$^+$

If we now glance back at the three spheres that [we
have] considered,^{54} and at [their] connection, [they may
be summarized as follows]: the first is the eternal God
in his eternal Idea in thinking Spirit (and all Spirit is
thinking); the second is this universal realizing itself
in nature [as] an entirely external existence, a verita-
ble divestment; the third is [the universal realizing it-
self] in an externality that is at the same time absolutely interior, [i.e.,] in finite Spirit, which therefore is at the same time the consummation of externality
in deepest estrangement, in conscious negation, and
thereby the return to the eternal Idea, which has its
initially abstract actualization in self-consciousness

[as an element of] eternal Spirit.

Now this, however, is [only] one side: this return and elevation to the right hand of God is only one side of the consummation of the third sphere.[55] For this third sphere is the Idea in its character as individuality, but in the first instance [it] portrays only a *single* individuality, the divine, universal individuality, individuality as it is in and for itself. One is all; once is always, implicitly, in accord with the concept; it is simple determinateness. But individuality as being-for-self is [+]this act of releasing the differentiated moments to free immediacy and independence;[+] [it is] immediacy, essentially and exclusively. Individuality means precisely that it has at the same time to be empirical individuality.

Individuality, as exclusive, exists for others as immediate and is the return from others into itself. The individuality of the divine Idea, the divine Idea as *one* man, is first completed in [worldly] actuality; at the beginning it has many individuals confronting it and brings these back into the unity of Spirit, into the community, and therein exists as an actual, universal, self-consciousness.[m]

[56] [a]Precisely this suffering and death, this sacrificial death of the individual for all, is the nature of God, the divine history, the utterly absolute, affirmative, universal [165] subjectivity. However, the latter is such as to posit its own negation. In death the moment of negation comes to perception. This moment is an essential moment in the nature of Spirit, and it is this death itself that must appear in this individual. It must not be represented as merely the death of this empirical individual. Heretics have confessed as much. It is much rather the case that *God* has died, that *God himself is dead*. God has died: this is the negation, and this is a moment of the divine nature, of God himself. In this death, accordingly, God is satisfied. God cannot

be satisfied by something else, only by himself. The
satisfaction consists in the fact that the first moment,
that of immediacy, is negated; only then does God attain
peace with himself, only then is spirituality posited.
God is the true God, Spirit, because he is not merely
Father, enclosed within himself, but rather because he is
Son, because he becomes the other and sublates this other.
This negation is perceived as a moment of the divine nature; therein all are reconciled.[a]

[w]57 The eternal Idea itself means that the characteristic of subjectivity as actual, as distinguished from
mere thoughts, is allowed to appear immediately. On the
other hand, it is faith, begotten by the anguish of the
world and resting on the testimony of the Spirit, which
explicates the life of Christ. The teaching and miracles
of Christ are grasped and understood in this witness of
faith. The history of Christ is also related by those
upon whom the Spirit has already been poured out. The
miracles are grasped and related in this Spirit, and the
death of Christ has been truly understood through the
Spirit to mean that in Christ God is revealed together
with the unity of divine and human nature. Thus the
death of Christ is the touchstone, so to speak, by which
faith is verified, since it is here, essentially, that
its understanding of the appearance of Christ is set
forth. This death means principally that Christ was the
God-man, the God who at the same time had human nature,
even unto death. It is the lot of human finitude to die.
Death is the most complete proof of humanity, of absolute finitude;[58] and indeed Christ has died the aggra-
vated death of the evildoer: not merely a natural death,
but rather a death of shame and humiliation on the cross.
In him, humanity was carried to its furthest point.

A special characteristic of this death [166] should
be emphasized first of all, namely, its polemical outward
aspect. Not only is the yielding up of the natural will

brought to perception here; but also all peculiar characteristics, all interests and purposes toward which the
natural will can direct itself, everything that is great
and valued by the world--these are all buried here in
the grave of Spirit. This is the revolutionary element
by means of which the world is given an entirely different form. However, in this yielding up of the natural
will, finitude or other-being is simultaneously transfigured. Apart from its immediate natural state, other-
being has a broader sphere of existence and a wider determination. That it should also exist for others belongs essentially to the existence of the subject. The
subject exists not only for itself but also in its representation by others; it exists, has value, and is objective to the extent that it knows itself to be valued by
others. Its value consists in its representation by
others and rests on a comparison with what they esteem
and what they regard as the in-itself.[w]

[a]Over against God there are finite men; man, the
finite, is posited in death itself as an element of God,
and thus death is what reconciles. Death is love itself; in it absolute love is perceived. The identity
of the divine and the human means that God is present to
himself in the human, in the finite, and this finitude
as seen in death is itself a determination of God.
Through death God has reconciled the world and has reconciled himself eternally with himself. This coming
back [from estrangement] is his return to himself, and
thereby he is Spirit. The third moment, accordingly, is
that Christ has risen. Negation is thereby overcome,
and the negation of negation is thus a moment of the divine nature. This Son is raised up to the right hand of
God.

In this history the nature of God, namely Spirit, is
accomplished, interpreted, explicated for the community.

This is the principal matter: the meaning of this history is that it is the history of God. God is absolute
movement within itself, which is Spirit, and this movement is set forth in this individual. Several representations are here conjoined, and false connections in particular have been introduced. For example, the sacrificial death provides an occasion for representing God as a
tyrant who demands sacrifice; this is untrue. On the
contrary, the nature of God is Spirit, and thus negation
is an essential moment.^{a59}

[167] ^{w60} Now, however, a further determination comes
into play. *God has died, God is dead*: this is the most
frightful of all thoughts, that everything eternal and
true does not exist, that negation itself is found in God.
The deepest anguish, the feeling of something completely
irretrievable, the abandoning of everything that is elevated, are bound up with this thought.

However, the process does not come to a halt at this
point; rather, a reversal takes place: God, that is to
say, maintains himself in this process, and the latter is
only the death of death. God rises again to life, and
thus things are reversed.^{61}

The resurrection is something that in essence belongs
equally to faith. After his resurrection, Christ appeared only to his friends. This is not an external history suitable for unbelief; rather the appearances occur
only for faith. The resurrection is followed by the
glorification of Christ, and the triumph of his ascension
to the right hand of God concludes this history, which,
as understood by believing consciousness, is the explication of the divine nature itself. If in the first sphere
[the Kingdom of the Father] we comprehended God as he is
in pure thought, then in this second sphere [the Kingdom
of the Son] we start from the immediacy appropriate to
perception and sensible representation. The process is
now such that immediate individuality is sublated: just

as in the first sphere the seclusion of God came to an
end, and his original immediacy as abstract universality,
in accord with which he is the essence of essences, has
been sublated, so here the abstraction of humanity, the
immediacy of an existing individual, is sublated, and
this is brought about by death. But the death of Christ
is the death of this death itself, the negation of negation. We have had the same course and process of the
explication of God in the Kingdom of the Father, but here
it occurs in so far as it is an object of consciousness.
For here there existed the impulse *to perceive* the divine nature.

In connection with the death of Christ, we have
finally to emphasize the moment according to which it is
God who has put death to death, since he comes out of the
state of death. Thereby finitude, human nature, and
humiliation are posited as something alien to Christ, as
they are to him who is strictly God. It is shown that
finitude is alien to him and has been adopted from an
other; this other is the human beings who stand over
against the divine process. It is their finitude that
Christ has taken upon himself, this finitude in all its
forms, which at its furthest extreme is evil. This humanity, which is itself a [168] moment in the divine
life, is now characterized as something alien, not belonging to God. This finitude, however, in its being-
for-self against God, is evil, something alien to God.
But he has taken it upon himself in order to put it to
death by his death.^{w}

a^{62} This, therefore, is what this history involves.
The first sphere is the concept of this standpoint for
consciousness; the second is what is given with this
standpoint, what actually exists for the community; the
third is the transition into the community.

The appearance of God in the flesh occurs in a
specific time and in a particular individual. Because it

is an appearance, it passes by as something for itself
and becomes past history. This sensible mode must disappear and re-emerge in the sphere of representation. The
formation of the community consists in the transition of
the sensible form into a spiritual element. The manner
of this purification of immediate being is such as to
preserve the sensible element precisely in its passing
away. This is the negation as it is posited and appears
in sensible existence as such. This perception is given
only in an individual, and it is not capable of being
inherited or renewed. This cannot happen because a sensible appearance such as this is by its very nature momentary and must be spiritualized; it is essentially something that *has been*, and it will be raised up into the
domain of representation. For the Spirit that has need
of it, sensible presence can indeed be produced in pictures,[63] relics, holy places: there is no lack of such
mediations when they are needed. But for the spiritual
community, immediate presence, the now, has passed away.
Above all, then, sensible representation integrates the
past,[64] which for representation is a one-sided moment
since the present includes as moments within itself the
past and the future. Thus sensible representation includes [the image of] the *return* [of Christ], which essentially is an absolute turning back. But then the
transition from externality to internality receives--a
Comforter, who can come only when [169] sensible history
in its immediacy has passed by. This, accordingly, is
the point of formation of the community; it is the third
point, the Spirit.[65] [a]

[66] [b]This second consideration leads to the religious
sphere as such only where the divine itself is an essential moment. This anticipation, this imagining, this de-
siring of a new kingdom, a new heaven and a new earth, a
new world, was present among those friends and acquaint-
ances who were taught by Christ. This hope and certainty

penetrated into their hearts as an actuality and became
entrenched there. But the suffering and death of Christ
annulled his human relationships, and it is precisely at
his death that the transition occurs into the religious
sphere. It is a question of the meaning, of the way of
comprehending, this death. On the one hand, it is a
natural death, brought about by injustice, hatred, and
violence.[b]

$_w$67
Inasmuch as his teachings were revolutionary,
Christ was accused and executed, and thus he sealed the
truth of his teaching by his death. Even unbelief can
go this far in [the view it takes of] this story: it is
entirely similar to that of Socrates, only in a different
environment. Socrates, too, brought inwardness to consciousness: his δαιμόνιον is nothing other than this.
He also taught that man must not stop short with obedience to ordinary authority but must form convictions for
himself and act according to them. Here we have two
similar individualities with similar fates. The inwardness of Socrates was contrary to the religious beliefs of
his people as well as to their form of government, and
thus he was put to death: he, too, died for the truth.

Christ happened to live among another people, and
to this extent his teaching has a different color. But
the kingdom of heaven and the purity of heart contain,
nonetheless, an infinitely greater depth than the inwardness of Socrates. This is the outward history of Christ,
which is for unbelief just what the history of Socrates
is for us.

With the death of Christ, however, there begins the
reversal of [170] consciousness. The death of Christ is
the midpoint around which consciousness turns; and in the
conception formed of it lies the difference between external comprehension and that of faith, which entails
contemplation with the Spirit, from the Spirit of truth,
the Holy Spirit. According to the previously mentioned

mode of comparison, Christ is a man like Socrates, a
teacher who lived his life virtuously, and who brought
men to the awareness of what the truth really is and of
what must constitute the basis of human consciousness.
But according to the higher mode of contemplation, the
divine nature has been revealed in Christ. This consciousness is reflected in those often-quoted passages
which state that the Son knows the Father, etc.--sayings
which, in the first place, have a certain generality
about them and which exegesis can draw out into the arena
of universal views, but which faith comprehends in their
truth through an interpretation of the death of Christ.
For faith is essentially the consciousness of absolute
truth, of what God is in and for himself. But we have
already seen what God is in and for himself: he is this
life-process, the Trinity, in which the universal places
itself over against itself and therein remains identical
with itself. God, in this element of eternity, is the
self-conjoining of himself with himself, the completion
of himself with himself. Only faith comprehends and is
conscious of the fact that in Christ this truth, which
exists in and for itself, is perceived in its process,
and that through him this truth has been first revealed.[w]

[b]In the hearts and souls [of believers], however, it
is now certainly not a question of morality, nor in general of the thinking and willing of the subject within
itself or from itself; rather what is of interest is an
infinite relationship to God, to the present God, the
certainty of the kingdom of God--finding satisfaction
not in morality, ethics, or conscience, but rather in
that than which nothing is higher, the relationship to
God himself. All other modes of satisfaction include the
fact that they are still qualities of a subordinate kind,
and thus the relationship to God remains a relationship
to something above and beyond, which in no sense lies
present at hand.

The fundamental characteristic of this kingdom of God is the *presence of God*, which means that the members of this kingdom are expected to have not only a love for humanity but also the consciousness that God is love. This is precisely to say that God is present, [171] that his presence must exist as one's own feeling, as self-feeling. The kingdom of God, the presence of God, *is* this determination; to it belongs the certainty of this presence. Since, on the one hand, the kingdom is this determination in a state of need or feeling [on the part of the subject], the latter must, on the other hand, distinguish itself from it, must establish a distinction between this presence of God and itself, but in such a way that this presence remains certain to it, and this certainty can exist here only in the mode of sensible appearance. Since this is the case, we have here the religious side [of the subject], and here the formation of the community begins. The content is the same as what is called the outpouring of the Holy Spirit: it is the Spirit that has revealed this. The condition of the mere man is changed into a condition that is thoroughly altered and transfigured by the Spirit, so that the nature of God is disclosed therein, and such that this truth obtains immediate certainty in accord with the mode of appearance.

In this fashion, accordingly, Christ, who at first was regarded as a teacher, friend, and martyr to the truth, obtains a totally different position. Up to this point only the beginning has been posited, which is now carried forward by the Spirit to an end, a result, the truth. The death of Christ is, on the one hand, the death of a man, a friend, who has been killed by violent means; but, conceived spiritually, it is this very death that becomes the means of salvation, the focal point of reconciliation. The perception of the nature of Spirit and of the satisfaction of its needs in a sensible fashion is, accordingly, what was disclosed to the friends

of Christ only after his death. Prior to his death he
was a sensible individual [who appeared] before them externally. The authentic disclosure [of what he was] was
given to them by the Spirit, of whom Christ had said,
"He will guide you into all the truth" [Jn. 16:13]. By
this he means: the truth will only be that into which
the Spirit will guide you. Regarded in this aspect, this
death assumes the character of a death that constitutes
the transition to glory, to glorification, which is however only a restoration of the original glory. Death,
the negative, is the mediating element by which the
original majesty is assumed to be obtained. The history
of the resurrection and ascension of Christ to the right
hand of God begins at the point where this history obtains
a spiritual interpretation. Religious history is where
a spiritual interpretation of the history of Christ before his death prevails, as indeed the [172] Gospels were
written only after the outpouring of the Spirit. Thus it
happened that the church community obtained the certainty
that God has appeared as a man.

      This humanity in God, indeed the most abstract mode
of humanity, the most complete dependence, the ultimate
weakness, the final stage of fragility--all this is
[represented by] natural death. "God himself is dead,"
it says in a Lutheran hymn, expressing an awareness that
the human, the finite, the fragile, the weak, the negative are moments of the divine. It is in God himself
that finitude, negativity, and other-being do not exist
outside of God, and as other-being they do not hinder the
unity with God. Other-being, the negative, are known to
be moments of the divine nature. Here is contained the
highest Idea of Spirit. What is external and negative is
converted in this fashion into the internal. On the one
hand, the meaning attached to death is that thereby the
human element is stripped away and the divine glory again
comes into view: death is a stripping away of the human,
the negative. But at the same time death itself is this

negative--the furthest extreme to which humanity as natural existence is exposed: this is God himself.

The truth to which men have attained by means of
this history, that of which they have become conscious in
this entire history, is the following: that the Idea of
God has certainty for them, that man has attained the
certainty of unity with God, that the human is immediately present Spirit, indeed so that in this history, as
Spirit comprehends it, precisely the portrayal of the
process is what man, what Spirit is--namely, both God and
dead implicitly. This mediation whereby the human is
stripped away is, from another point of view, the means
by which being-in-itself returns to itself, first coming
to be Spirit thereby.*b*

*w*68
Suffering and death interpreted in this way are
opposed to the doctrine of moral imputation, according to
which each individual is accountable only for himself,
and each is the agent of his own actions. The fate of
Christ seems to contradict this imputation, but this is
the case only in the sphere of finitude, where the subject stands as a single person, not in the sphere of free
Spirit. It is characteristic of the region of finitude
that everyone remains what he is. If he has done evil,
[173] then he *is* evil: evil is in him as his quality.
But already in the sphere of morality, and still more in
that of religion, Spirit is known to be free, to be affirmative within itself, so that its limitation, which
extends to evil, is a nullity for the infinitude of
Spirit. Spirit can undo what has been done. The action
certainly remains in the memory, but Spirit strips it
away. Imputation, therefore, does not attain to this
sphere. For the true consciousness of Spirit, the finitude of man has been put to death in the death of Christ.
This death of the natural has in this fashion a universal
significance: finitude and evil in general are destroyed.
The world has thus been reconciled; by this death, it has

been implicitly delivered from its evil. In the true
comprehension of death, the relation of the subject as
such comes into view in this way. Here any mere [outward]
consideration of history ceases; the subject itself is
drawn into the process. The subject feels the anguish of
evil and its own estrangement, which Christ has taken upon himself by putting on humanity, while at the same time
destroying it by his death.[w]

[b]It is with the *consciousness* of the community--
which thus makes the transition from mere humanity to the
God-man, to the perception, consciousness, and certainty
of the unity and union of divine and human nature--that
the community begins; this consciousness constitutes the
truth upon which the community is founded. This is the
explication of the meaning of reconciliation: that God
is reconciled with the world, or rather that God has
shown himself to be reconciled with the world, that precisely the human is not something alien to him, but
rather that this other-being, this self-distinguishing,
finitude as it is expressed, is a moment in himself, although to be sure a disappearing moment. But in this moment he has shown himself to the community.

For the community, this is the history of the appearance of God. This history is a divine history, whereby
the community has obtained the consciousness of truth.
This forms the consciousness, which is known [by the com-
munity], that God is triune. The reconciliation believed
in as being in Christ has no meaning if God is not known
as the triune God, if it is not recognized that he exists,
but precisely as the other, as self-distinguishing, so
that this other is God himself, having implicitly the
[174] divine nature in it, and that the sublation of this
difference, this other-being, and the return of love, are
Spirit. This consciousness involves the fact that faith
is not a relationship to something subordinate but to God
himself.

These are the moments with which we are here concerned and which establish that man has become conscious
of the eternal history, the eternal movement, which God
himself is. Other forms, e.g., that of sacrificial death,
reduce themselves automatically to what has here been
said. Sacrifice means the sublation of naturalness and
other-being. It is said that Christ has died for all.
This is not an individual act but the eternal divine history: it is a moment in the nature of God himself; it has
taken place in God himself. It is also said that in
Christ all have died. In Christ this reconciliation has
been advanced for all, just as the Apostle [John] compares
faith in the Crucified with viewing the bronze serpent.[69]

This is the presentation of the second [moment of
the] Idea, the Idea in appearance, the eternal Idea as it
has become [available] for the immediate certainty of man,
i.e., as it has appeared. In order that it could become
a certainty for man, it had to be a sensible certainty,
which however at the same time passes over into spiritual
consciousness, and likewise is converted into the immediately sensible, but in such a way that one sees in it the
movement and history of God, the life that God himself
is.[b]

NOTES FOR CHAPTER IV

1. Lasson's title for this chapter is "The God-Man and Reconciliation." The change is made primarily to obtain a stylistic parallel
to the title for Chapter III. However, it is also the case that
Hegel rarely uses the theologoumenon "God-man," although he appropri-
ates its meaning philosophically. More typically, he speaks of the
"appearance" of God "in the flesh . . . in a single man," or of God
"becoming" man, or of "the unity [or identity] of the divine and the
human" in a "single individual"--conceptions for which the term "incarnation" is a suitable expression. In the Concept of Religion,
Hegel refers to "the infinite Idea of the incarnation of God" as the
"speculative middlepoint" of the Christian faith and of his own
philosophy (*Werke*, 11:146; ET 1:151).

2. Lasson entitles this section "The Actuality of Reconciliation." However it is more precise to say that Hegel here advances
an argument for the possibility, necessity, and actuality of the
incarnation (or "appearance") of God in a single individual, although he does not employ these terms systematically in order to

designate phases of the argument. (For an elaboration, see the Appendix.) For Hegel the concepts of incarnation and reconciliation are closely related and are sometimes used interchangeably. Incarnation is the means by which the Idea of reconciliation is *historically* mediated, while the *implicit* universality of the latter is the condition of possibility for the former.

3. MS. heading: "β)." This heading indicates that the "third sphere" of Concrete Representation in the 1821 MS., the concept in the history of redemption or reconciliation, enters upon a second, more determinate stage with the representation of the appearance of God in the figure of Christ. The preceding discussion of the natural man has served as a propaedeutic to this turning point.

4. +Absolute truth as object, objectivity with absolute form -- Absolute Spirit -- process within itself as subject -- infinite subjectivity, absolute form with infinite validity within itself -- infinite purpose within itself.+

5. From the concluding stanza of Friedrich Schiller's poem "Die Freundschaft" (*Sämtliche Werke* [Munich: Carl Hanser Verlag, 1965], 1:93):

> Freundlos war der grosse Weltenmeister,
> Fühlte *Mangel*--darum schuf er Geister,
>   Selge Spiegel *seiner* Seligkeit!--
> Fand das höchste Wesen schon kein gleiches,
> Aus dem Kelch des ganzen Seelenreiches
>   Schäumt *ihm*--die Unendlichkeit.

For *Seelenreiches* (realm of souls), Hegel substitutes *Geisterreiches* (realm of Spirits). This line is quoted by Hegel at the very end of *The Phenomenology of Spirit*, trans. J. B. Baillie (London: Allen & Unwin, 1949), p. 808. I have followed Baillie's translation of it, which seems justified by both Schiller's context and Hegel's.

6. J. W. von Goethe, *West-Östlicher Divan*, Buch des Timur, Poem 2, "An Suleika" (*Goethes Werke* [Hamburg: Christian Wegner Verlag, 1949], 2:61):

> Um ein Fläschchen zu besitzen,
> Das den Ruch auf ewig hält,
> Schlank wie deine Fingerspitzen,
> Da bedarf es einer Welt.
>
> Einer Welt von Lebenstrieben,
> Die in ihrer Fulle Drang
> Ahndeten schon Bulbuls Lieben,
> Seeleregenden Gesang.
>
> Sollte jene Qual uns quälen,
> Da sie unsre Lust vermehrt?
> Hat nicht Myriaden Seelen
> Timurs Herrschaft aufgezehrt?

In line 3, Hegel writes *diese* (these) instead of *deine* (thy); in line 5, *Liebestrieben* (love-impulses) instead of *Lebenstrieben* (life-impulses). *Bulbul* (line 7) is the Persian name for "nightingale." Hegel omits the first stanza of "An Suleika," which reads as follows:

Dir mit Wohlgeruch zu kosen,	To caress thee with a fragrant scent,
Deine Freuden zu erhöhn,	To heighten thy delights,
Knospend müssen tausend Rosen	Budding, a thousand roses
Erst in Gluten untergehn.	Must first be burned to ashes.

Goethe's *West-Östlicher Divan*, a collection of poems interweaving Oriental and Occidental themes, was published in 1819, two years prior to Hegel's lecture manuscript; the poem "An Suleika," the second of two poems comprising the "Book of Timur," was written in 1815. Timur or Tamburlaine (1336-1405) was an infamous Oriental conqueror who subjugated parts of Persia, Russia, India, and Syria. Suleika is the Persian name by which Goethe addresses one of his lovers, Marianne von Willemer. As is the case with many of Goethe's lovers, she is an embodiment of a divine or cosmic lover. Hence in a sense the poem is addressed to God, and the meaning appears to be that just as Timur destroyed myriads of human beings to gain a kingdom, so the perfume maker consumes thousands of roses to produce a tiny flask of fragrant scent; likewise an entire world is needed to offer up a love worthy of God. By juxtaposing this poem with the line from Schiller, and by highlighting the words "Timur," "millions of souls," and "roses," Hegel seems to be saying that from the anguish or suffering (the "chalice") of this whole human world there "foams forth to God" his own infinite love.

The *Werke*'s version (12:282 [ET 3:72]) of the 1821 MS. at this point varies considerably; probably it is based on Henning's notes of the 1821 lectures. Following the quotation from Schiller appear these words: "The anguish that the finite experiences in being thus sublated does not give pain, since it is by this means raised to the rank of a moment in the process of the divine." Then only one line of "An Suleika" is quoted:

> Ought such torment to afflict us,
> Since it enhances our desire?

7. The order of the manuscript at this point is uncertain. In the original text, Hegel appears to have made only a twofold distinction between the Idea existing (α) implicitly and universally, and (β) in the form of "this visible [individual]" (now paragraph γ below). Subsequently he converted this to a threefold division, adding a lengthy point (β) in the margin (comprising our next three paragraphs), and writing over the β in the main text to convert it to a γ. Lasson reverses the sequence of β and γ, omits the reference to β where it occurs, substitutes the opening words of β for γ, and associates the concluding paragraph ("[This is the] consummation of reality . . .") with β rather than γ.

8. Lasson has smoothed out and expanded these opening sentences of the 1824 transcript. Griesheim reads: "This is the nature of the exigency. The question is now: By what means can it be satisfied?"

9. ^wThe possibility of reconciliation rests only on the conscious recognition of the implicit unity of divine and human nature; this is the necessary basis. Thus man can know that he has been taken up into God in so far as God is not something alien to him, in so far as he is not related to him as an external accident; rather he is taken up into God in accord with his own essence, his own freedom and subjectivity. This, however, is possible only in so far as the subjectivity that belongs to human nature exists within God himself.

This being-in-itself must become aware of infinite sorrow as the implicit unity of the divine and human nature, but only in accord with being-in-itself or substantiality, so that this finitude or weakness, this other-being, in no way impairs the substantial unity of the two.

The unity of divine and human nature, humanity in its universality, is the thought of man and the Idea, existing in and for itself, of absolute Spirit.^w (12:281; ET 3:71-72.)

10. Lasson transposes a paragraph of the Griesheim transcript that appears in Chap. III to this point. We have relocated it in its original position (see above, p. 115, n. 15).

11. Lasson here inserts a paragraph from the *Werke* that ought to follow the next section of the 1827 transcript in order to maintain the *m, a, b, w* sequence. Hence we have relocated it on p. 182. The content of the *Werke* paragraph relates as much to the 1827 material as it does to the 1824.

12. 12:285-286 (ET 3:75-76). This passage has been transposed from Lasson's location of it (see n. 11).

13. In the *Werke* (12:285), this sentence precedes the sentence beginning, "Man has spiritual interests . . . ." Lasson has shifted it to a more logical position.

14. As was customary in the theology of his time, Hegel uses *Christus* (Christ) as a proper name, designating Jesus of Nazareth, while the title *der Christ* (the Christ) designates the Messiah, the Son of God. Clear evidence for this is furnished below, Chap. V, p. 240 (see n. 24).

15. ⁺Action of this individual -- [how the] Idea takes its course in him such that his temporal presence is able to be a presentation of the Idea -- teaching -- life, suffering and death -- and resurrection.⁺

16. Confirmation and miracles are discussed in Chap. V.2.

17. ⁺(a) Teaching: (α) The universal and divine brought [to expression] by him in thoughts, in mind, for it *is* thought. (β) The actual -- precisely what remains belongs to the emergence, to the actuality [of Christ], and is capable of being portrayed for [sense] perception. -- But the remaining action, the remaining reversal
. . .⁺

18. [+]Humanity [must] prepare this soil for itself inwardly.[+]

19. [+]Emphasize 3 pages on this teaching.[+]

20. 12:290 (ET 3:81).

21. I am indebted to H. S. Harris for help in deciphering this parenthesis. To make sense of it, Lasson's insertions have been altered at several points.

22. Reference to the radical republicans of the French Revolution.

23. Hegel here conflates Matt. 6:26, 28 into an inaccurate quotation, while citing Matt. 6:31, which actually is quoted in the next sentence.

24. [+]Matt. 10:34[-37]: "Do not think [I have come . . .]."[+]

25. The MS. adds: "A father [crossed out] set against his son, a son against his parents, a brother against his brother."

26. The biblical text reads: "obey."

27. The translation of this passage has been guided by the rather different version of it that appears in the *Werke*, 12:294 (ET 3:85), based on the Henning notes of the 1821 lectures: "Christ calls himself . . . the Son of Man . . . . The Arabs mutually describe themselves as the son of a certain race; Christ belongs to the human race; this is his race." The 1821 MS. uses the term *Abalda* instead of *Araber*. In the *Werke*, reference is also made to the title "Son of God," and the contents of the next paragraph of the 1821 MS. are specifically associated with this title.

28. In these two paragraphs Hegel recapitulates the threefold argument of Section 1 concerning the possibility, necessity, and actuality of the incarnation or appearance of God (see n. 2).

29. This section of the 1827 lecture notes is located by Lasson at a later point (see below, n. 35). We have transposed it to what Jaeschke has shown to be the original location. The content of this section, its location in the *Werke*, and the recently discovered anonymous 1827 transcript, support Jaeschke's analysis.

30. This sentence is located by Lasson in the conflated paragraph below (see n. 33). According to Jaeschke, the original location is here (confirmed by the recently discovered 1827 transcript).

31. 12:291 (ET 3:81-82).

32. In the next paragraph Lasson conflates segments from the 1824 and 1827 lecture transcripts. (A similar conflation occurs only one other time, at the very beginning of the work.) The segments from the two lecture series are given in their original order

and can be read separately if preferred. The specific indication of sources is provided by Jaeschke.

33. At this point Lasson locates the sentence from the 1827 transcript that we have given in its original position, n. 30.

34. Lasson omits the next five sentences from the Griesheim transcript because they parallel the 1821 MS. The text has been furnished by Jaeschke from a copy of the Griesheim transcript at the Hegel-Archiv.

35. The next five paragraphs of the 1827 transcripts in Lasson's text have been transposed to their original position (see above, p. 193, n. 29).

36. +(δ) Life and Death.+

37. Reading *es* with the MS. The referent is uncertain, and Lasson changes the pronoun to *sie*, presumably to make it refer to "the determination of subjectivity."

38. +Teaching as such.+

39. The MS. adds: "as what befits it" (*wie Angemessenheit*).

40. +Death (α) in the divine Idea -- expresses itself immediately as divestment of itself, i.e., [the Idea] still is this divestment.+

41. The MS. reads *seinem* instead of *Christi*.

42. From the second stanza of the passion hymn "O Traurigkeit, o Herzeleid," by Johannes Rist (1641):

O grosse Not!	O great woe!
Gott selbst liegt tot.	God himself lies dead.
Am Kreuz ist er gestorben;	On the cross he has died;
hat dadurch das Himmelreich	And thus he has gained for us
uns aus Lieb erworben.	By love the kingdom of heaven.

43. The marginal note ends, *Aber dieser Tod ist zugleich darin.* The main text reads, *Dieser Tod ist darum insofern,* with the first three words crossed out. Lasson's text omits the adverbs *darin* and *darum*.

44. +To consider more closely. The speculative [element] is that the Son [the MS. reads "death"] goes to death as the divine (presupposition); in this speculative turn, he is for himself the absolute love. However, this speculative meaning -- that it is the divine as such which undergoes death -- is to be considered in its universal meaning. It appears [to be] a specific meaning and further a meaning of just this death. [At the same time, it is] death in regard to Spirit in Spirit, as a moment of Spirit. -- Death (β) [is a] moment in regard to the more determinate concept of Spirit.+

45. [+]Death here appearing as natural death -- yes, but . . .[+]

46. [+](δ) Although a natural death, [this is the] death of God, and immediately the relation of the same to us, the assurance therein.[+]

47. [+]Significance in its relation to the dissemination of the Christian Religion.
Polemical significance of the manner of this death -- [its] character and significance for the external [world]. Natural will surrendered. All traits of personality, all interests and purposes toward which the natural will might direct itself, everything great and of worldly value, [are] as nothing; [all these things are] buried in the grave of Spirit. This, too, [is here brought] into view. -- Revolutionary element to the extent that it gives the world another form. Love in immediate other-being; other-being, finitude transfigured -- other-being is what is ignominious.[+]

48. The MS. adds: "(Death is natural; every man must die. But) [Hegel has crossed out the following:] his external existence is one of honor, not that of a criminal."

49. The MS. adds: "(precisely in regard to the external signs of honor)" [(*nach, eben in dem äusseren Zeichen der Ehre nach*)].

50. [+](ε) Resurrection -- Ascension.[+]

51. The remainder of the paragraph, starting at this point, is quoted as a footnote in the *Werke*, 12:300 (ET 3:91), with the notation: "From Hegel's own manuscript, 1821."

52. Cf. Acts 2:27 ("For thou wilt not abandon my soul to Hades, nor let thy Holy One see corruption") and Ps. 16:10 ("For thou dost not give me up to Sheol, or let thy godly one see the Pit").

53. The MS. reads *und* rather than *ist*.

54. The three spheres of "Concrete Representation" of the 1821 MS. (See above, n. 20, p. 102.)

55. The last two paragraphs represent a transition to Part C of the 1821 MS., "Community, Cultus." Hegel here seems to acknowledge that the distinction between the third sphere of "Concrete Representation" (namely, "the concept in the history of redemption or reconciliation") and "Community, Cultus" is not a clear-cut one. The history of redemption includes not only the single individual in whom the divine-human unity was first accomplished, but also the community of individuals, the community of Spirit, in which reconciliation is brought to completion and Christ is universally actualized.

56. The organization of the remainder of Section 3 of Chap. IV is as follows: the text of the 1824 lectures is given on pp. 209-214, interspersed with supplementary materials from the *Werke*; and the text of the 1827 lectures is given on pp. 214-221, likewise in-

terspersed with supplementary passages from the *Werke*. The abun-
dance of texts from the *Werke* in this section complicates its arrangement.

57. 12:297-298 (ET 3:88-90).

58. The Lasson edition omits: "of absolute finitude."

59. There follows at this point in the Griesheim transcript a
paragraph on the confirmation of Christ as the Son of God, which
Lasson has relocated in Chapter V, where the matter of confirmation
and miracles is taken up more fully (see below, p. 248, n. 33).

60. 12:300-301 (ET 3:91-93).

61. At this point the *Werke* footnotes a passage from the 1821
MS. which in this edition is included in the text of the manuscript
above, p. 207 (see n. 51).

62. It might appear that this last section of the 1824 lectures
to appear in Chapter IV should rather be located at the beginning of
Chapter V, preceding the material on p. 238 from the 1824 transcripts. The content of this section actually parallels material
from the 1821 MS. at the beginning of Chapter V. However, Lasson has
followed the explicit division marking of the Griesheim transcript.
Hegel takes up the matter of the transition from "sensible presence"
to "spiritual presence" at both the end of the second part and the
beginning of the third part of his lectures on the Revelatory Religion, and there is considerable overlap of materials in this
transitional phase of the discussion.

63. *ᵂ*And indeed not as works of art but rather as wonder-working
pictures, generally in their sensible mode of existence.*ᵂ* (12:311;
ET 3:103.)

64. *ᵂ*And thus it is not merely the corporeal form and the body
of Christ that are able to satisfy the sensible need, but rather
the sensible aspect of his bodily presence generally--the cross, the
places where he walked, etc. Relics and other means serve this
purpose.*ᵂ* (12:311; ET 3:103-104.)

65. *ᵂ*Or the Spirit is known not so much as objective, but
rather only in this subjective mode as he exists in the sensible
presence of the church and lives in the tradition. In this form of
actuality, the Spirit is, as it were, the Third Person.*ᵂ* (12:311;
ET 3:103.)

66. See n. 56.

67. 12:295-296 (ET 3:86-87).

68. 12:304-305 (ET 3:96-97).

69. Cf. Jn. 3:14-16: "And as Moses lifted up the serpent in the wilderness, so must the Son of man be lifted up, that whoever believes in him may have eternal life." The Johannine comparison is placed on the lips of Jesus in the discourse to Nicodemus, referring to Num. 21:9 (anyone bitten by a serpent would live by viewing the bronze serpent).

C. THE KINGDOM OF THE SPIRIT

CHAPTER V

THE SPIRIT AND THE COMMUNITY[1]

Section 1. Standpoint of the Community in General[2]

[175] [m][We] still [need] to speak briefly of this [community] in accord with its Idea.[3] [To consider it] in concrete form, as tied to a [specific] history and empirical existence, would lead us too far astray, tempting as this would otherwise be.

The determinate transition of the Idea to sensible presence[4] [has] been accomplished [in Christianity]. Precisely this [is] the distinctive feature of Christianity and the Religion of Spirit. All moments [are here] developed to their completion. [+]This contrast of sensible presence and divinity, this individuality that is divine, and this ordinary consciousness[+][5] can only occur in the Religion of Spirit, which is certain of itself, and indeed,[6] certain of itself as the absolute truth. Accordingly, [man needs] to be afraid of nothing, not even of sensible presence. To shun sensibility in a monkish fashion is to exhibit cowardice of thought. Spirit [is much rather] present to itself in the sensible, [having therein] the sensible appearance of the divine, the immediate object.

231

[There is a] revolting arrogance that is directed
against [the] moment of sensible presence generally [and
against] [176] its congeniality. [But this arrogance is
precisely] a spiritless condition, which is what abstract
thought wants to be. Only the poet [understands this
congeniality]; he honors the sensible form, just as
Oriental religious life [honors the sensible form] as
having Spirit within it.[7] But [the poet] does not just
[honor] *his own* sensibility, nor the feeling of his subjectivity. Rather to honor sensible presence [entails
the] death of feeling; sentimentality--its fixation and
limitation--[means] stark contempt for the sensible
presence [involved] in infinite love. For this reason,
[we had] previously designated this speculative [occur-
rence], love in death, [as] a transition. [It was a] relationship of an individual sensible presence to individuals (love of women, tender dispositions--easy for a loving soul [such as] John, [but] infinitely hard for the
independent concept, for the male). The freedom of the
subject rebels [against] this reconciliation and unification, [against] reverencing a single living individual
as God. Not so the Oriental--[but then] he is nothing,
he is implicitly cast aside, without however having cast
himself aside, i.e., without [having] the consciousness
of infinite freedom within himself. Yet this love [that
arises from infinite freedom], this recognition, [is] the
supreme miracle, the highest of the realm of Spirit.

Accordingly, this sphere +of infinite love+ is the
Kingdom of the Spirit. It [has] infinite worth within
itself by knowing absolute freedom within itself as this
individual, and by maintaining this infinite power in
absolute otherness. Love equalizes all things, [but not]
in the sense [that] people nowadays love totally and live
in love, [implying] that the other ought to give himself
up to the same commonality--[which is] the most spiritless [of conditions]. Death runs counter to this love,
even a sentimental death, +[as when two lovers are]

prepared to drown themselves together.⁺ Only Spirit itself, which has grasped and perceived the truth, absolute
objectivity, provides the supreme independence.

   The intuition of this religion demands the despising
of all that presently exists; [it is] wholly polemical
[in its] ideality; [it disdains] power, what has worth,
the grandeur of the world. [The] intensity of this dis-
dain [is unlimited], ⁺and yet [177] [this religion
teaches one] to recognize sensible presence, [but] only
in a single individual and as infinite.⁺ [This is in]
absolute antithesis to Oriental religion--[an antithesis]
that makes Orientalism to be an enemy, [although it has]
within itself, internally, an infinite value, a most
solid stability, and [at the same time] a surrendering of
this stability.

   ⁸In the Christian Religion the divine Idea occurs as
in [a] present, immediate individual. For individuals
all worldliness has been concentrated in this individual;
this is the sole sensible presence that has value, the
infinite abstraction of the present. (Being in love [is
like this] too; but in this divine love [faith lives] at
the same time in an infinite abstraction from all worldliness. Subjective happiness, [my] being in love, according to my luck, with some particular individual, [is
here] annulled. Particular feeling, strictly private
[affection, are] opposed to the universal, being exclusive with respect both to this object and to my subjectivity. It is [not] the divine Idea that I desire but
its opposite, my exclusive particularity objectified.)

   ⁹Furthermore, this single individual has been removed
from the senses and raised to the right hand of God. Just
to this extent, there is [now] an individual presence only
for figurative representation--a certainty without *immediate sensible* presence, unlike the Dalai Lama in the Ori-
ent, or [the sacred bull] Apis, who are immediate sensible
presences. ⁺In this concentration of presence into
death,⁺ in the shameful death [of the cross], and in this

removal [of Christ], resides the fact that mankind is
[now] directed only inward, that all worldly grandeur (as
well as the weakness of immediate friendship) has disappeared. The image [178] that has been given to individuals as the infinite truth, [as the] divine Idea, is
[that of] the absolute unity of the universal and the
singular, of divine and human nature, infinite love that
exists only as infinite anguish, as the death of everything worldly and immediate.

The retreat to inner self-consciousness contained in
this perception is not Stoic in nature. The value of the
latter consists in the fact that it thinks by the strength
of its own Spirit, and it seeks the reality of thought in
the world, nature, natural things, and their connections,
without [experiencing] infinite anguish, [and having] at
the same time a thoroughly positive relation to the world.
Rather [it takes the form of a self-consciousness that]
endlessly divests itself of its particularity and individuality and has its infinite value only in that love
which is contained in infinite anguish and comes out of
it. All immediacy in which humanity might find some
value is thrown away; it is in absolute mediation alone
that mankind finds value, but of an infinite kind. This
subjectivity is truly infinite in and for itself, but man
is infinite only through this mediation, not immediately.
Thus he is capable of having an infinite value, and this
capability or possibility is his positive, absolute characteristic.

This characteristic contains the reason why the *immortality* of the soul becomes a specific doctrine of the
Christian Religion: the soul or individual subjectivity
has an infinite, eternal vocation to be a citizen of the
kingdom of God. This is [a] vocation, a life, that is
removed from time and the past, [existing] for itself,
and since it [is] also opposed to the past, this eternal
vocation is defined as a future of immortality. The infinite demand to see God, i.e., to become conscious in

the Spirit of his truth as a present reality, is not possible in this temporal present for the consciousness that
perceives sensibly and representationally.

Subjectivity has given up all external distinctions
in this infinite value, distinctions of mastery, power,
position, even of sex and wealth. Before God all persons
are equal. For the first time here and now, this [is a
reality] in consciousness, in the speculative and negative [elements] of the infinite anguish of love; herein
[resides [179] the] possibility [and the] root of truly
universal justice and of the actualization of freedom.
The highly formal justice of Roman life proceeds from a
positive standpoint and from the understanding. It has
no principle within itself for the absolute verification
of the standpoint of justice, but is thoroughly worldly.

[The] sexual freedom of women[10] and monogamy--all
these characteristics are connected with it.

[11]This speculative [mode] of love that arises from
infinite anguish, this purity of subjectivity, exist
through an infinite mediation; and this infinite mediation has its objective shape [in the] life, suffering,
death, and exaltation of Christ. This subjectivity is
implicitly universal, not exclusive, and the relation of
the many, [of] individuals, to each other, is the unity
of faith in the representation of faith, in this third
[the community of Christ]: it is neither human love
(love of mankind, sexual love) nor friendship.

Surprise has often been expressed that so noble a
relationship as friendship does not find a place among
the duties enjoined by Christ. The relationship of the
disciples [to each other] is not one of friendship, for
friendship is a relationship burdened by subjective particularity.[12] Men are friends not so much directly as
objectively in a substantial bond, in a third [factor],
in fundamental principles, absolute purpose, studies,
science; in brief, the bond is an objective content, not
affection such as that of a man for a woman who is this

unique personality, [has this particular] beauty. [The
unity of the disciples] is rather [founded] in the perception of that speculative [element], of that infinite
love which comes from infinite anguish; i.e., [it is
based on] the worthlessness of particularity and [at the
same time on] the mediation of love by means of it. The
love of [a] man for a woman and friendship can certainly
exist, but they are essentially defined as subordinate,
not as something evil but as something imperfect, not as
something indifferent but essentially as [a state in
which we are] not to remain; [180] they themselves [are]
to be sacrificed because[13] they could do injury to that
absolute direction and unity.[14]

   This unity in the infinite love that arises from infinite anguish is, accordingly, in no way a sensible,
worldly connection, not a connection of the particularity
and naturalness that still remain left over and are valid,
but rather a unity absolutely in the Spirit. Love as infinite anguish is precisely the concept of Spirit itself.
It becomes objective in Christ as the focal point of
faith at an infinite distance and sublimity, but [at the
same time] in an infinite nearness, uniqueness, and relatedness to the individual subject   +(humanity, death, infinite limitation taken up into the divine Idea),+ while
not [being bound] to the subject. It is nothing particular but rather is in itself universal; it [appropriates]
individuals, and as thus active in their subjectivity it
is the Spirit, indeed *the Holy Spirit*. The Holy Spirit
is in them; they are, they constitute, the universal
Christian Church, the communion of saints. Spirit is infinite return into itself, infinite subjectivity, not
imagined but actual divinity, not the substantial but the
present in-itself of the Father. The Spirit is not the
Son, Christ, who is the truth in the form of objectivity,
but is rather subjective presence and actuality, which
itself [is] thus subjectively present only through this
mediation [in the community]--precisely as divestment

[functioned] in that objective perception of love and its infinite anguish. This [is] the Spirit of God, or God as present, actual Spirit, God dwelling in his community. Christ [says]: "Where two or three are gathered in my name, there am I in the midst of you" [cf. Matt. 18:20];[15] "I am with you always, to the close of the age" [Matt. 28: 20]. Christ [is] dead, but by [saying] "with you, in you," he is the Holy Spirit. This [is] the absolute significance of the Spirit, this the highest, pure consciousness of the absolute Idea and of absolute truth, this significance as the self-consciousness of the latter.

[181] Accordingly, in this profound sense the Christian Religion is the Religion of Spirit, though not in the manifold, trivial sense of being a spiritual religion[16] +(venerating abstraction, regarding it as substance, essence). On the contrary, unification of the infinite antithesis,+ the true and sole speculative [enjoyment] of the nature of God, [or] of Spirit--[this is what constitutes the Christian Religion]. This is its content and perception, and it exists for ordinary, uneducated consciousness. +[The] antithesis [is]: God and the world, I, this *homuncio* [manikin].+

All men are called to blessedness. This [is] the highest calling, and it is alone the highest. Therefore Christ says that all sins will be forgiven men except for sin against the Spirit.[17] +People have often racked their brains trying to determine what sin against the Spirit is, and they have trivialized this notion in a variety of ways in order to dispose of it entirely.+ Everything else can be consumed in the infinite anguish of love, but this consuming process itself is nothing other than inwardly present Spirit. What is devoid of Spirit is not sinful by comparison with a knowing and willing directed against the acknowledged Spirit--it knows Spirit not and thus is innocent. But this is the innocence that precisely in itself is judged and condemned. +Let it [innocence] be as vain as may be--*nos prona*

natamus.[18]   Not to have shared in the truth, not to have
had eternal life in oneself, [this is the meaning that]
always comes through in one way or another.[+]

This communal aspect [of life] is accordingly the
distinctive region of Spirit. The Holy Spirit has been
poured out on the disciples. From then on they existed as
a community--the Spirit being their immanent life--and
joyfully they went out into [the] world, in order to elevate it to the universal community and to spread abroad
the kingdom of God.

First we have considered the pure concept of God in
the Christian Religion, then (b) its concrete representation or manifestation. This entire manifestation--which
itself is portrayed in the three spheres of thinking,
[182] representation, and actuality--is an appearance or
manifestation for an other, the region of existence, of
objectification, [but in this case,] of subjective immanence, of becoming immanent. Hence this is, thirdly
(c), the Kingdom of the Spirit.[19] [The] kingdom of God
is the Spirit. Thus subjects are implicated in the process. The divine Idea, which exists for them as infinite
love in infinite anguish, is within these subjects precisely in this perception: they [are] the community of
Spirit.[20]   At first, individuality is exclusive; [but] in
the infinite love it [is] led back [into community].
Christ [is] in their midst [and] thus [is] the Spirit:
this process itself [is] the Spirit.

In accord with this general definition, [we take the]
next step.[m]

·[a]*The third element*[21] is therefore the transition from
externality, from appearance, to inwardness. It is concerned with the certainty felt by the subject of its own
infinite, non-sensible essentiality, the certainty with
which it knows itself to be infinite and immortal forever.
It is concerned, further, with the fact that the subject
is filled by the truth, that this truth consists in self-

consciousness *as* self-consciousness, that it consists not
in the external but in the implicit truth of thought, the
representation of inwardness generally. Subjectivity and
the knowledge of its essence is, in the first place,
knowledge of a sensibly present content. This is particularly disadvantageous, but essentially transitory; it is
the point of beginning, with which [the process] does not
remain, a form that is to be sublated, that is defined
not merely as past but as belonging eternally to the
spiritual nature of God. This is the turn into the inward mode; this is the soil of Spirit--it is the community, cultus, faith.[22]

We have considered the manifestation of God first as
revelation, second as appearance. The third is knowledge or faith, for faith is also knowledge, but in a distinctive form. We have now to consider this third form.

[183] It is, accordingly, as follows: the divine
content is posited as self-conscious knowledge of this
content in the element of self-consciousness, of inwardness, so that, on the one hand, the content is the truth,
and on the other hand, it is the truth (i.e., the knowledge) of finite Spirit generally. In this knowledge,
Spirit has its freedom and is itself the process of casting off its particular individuality and of liberating
itself through this content.

Three aspects are to be considered with reference to
this community and its worship: first, the *origin* of the
community and the development of faith; second, the *existence* of the community; third, the *realization* of faith,
which simultaneously is the transition of faith, its
transformation and *transfiguration*.[a]

Section 2. *Origin of the Community*[23]

[m]This [is] the first aspect in accord with which we
comprehend once again the standpoint of exclusive indi-

viduality: Christ as this man who was temporally present
among his friends. [The] beginning, the forming of the
community comes about when his friends are filled by the
Spirit. [The first step is the] temporal presence of an
ordinary man--a beginning, therefore, of the highest externality of appearance. [Hence the] question [arises]
as to how [his friends] came or could have been brought
to recognize the divine Idea in this individual, to
acknowledge him as the Son of God--[the] question, therefore, of the *confirmation* [+]of the divine mission of
Christ [*Christus*[24]].[+] [The] proof of the truth of the
Christian Religion appears [+]to be able to be[+] reduced
to this point in this form. [+]([Assuming that his mission
was in fact confirmed,] this first individual then handed
down the content to others, [etc.].)[+]

This question immediately divides itself into two
questions. (α) Is it true *in general* that God has a
Son, that he sends or has sent him into the world? (β)
Was *this Jesus of Nazareth* in Galilee, a carpenter's son,
the Christ [*der Christ*[24]]?

The two questions are connected in such fashion that
if Jesus were not the Son sent by God, and if this cannot be proved true of him, then there would be nothing
at all to his mission. Either we should have to wait for
another, [+]if indeed [184] one is to come, if there is a
promise to this effect, i.e., if it is necessary in and
for itself, conceptually and ideally;[+] or rather, since
the correctness of the Idea is made to be dependent on
the proof of that mission, there is in general nothing
more and nothing further to think about with reference
to it.

But we must first ask the essential question: Is
such an appearance true in and for itself? It is, since
we [have] seen that God as Spirit appears only as "triune": he is his manifestation, [his] self-objectification while remaining identical with [himself] in this objectification; [he is] eternal love. This objectifica-

tion, in its completed development up to the extremes of
the universality of God [versus] finitude or death, is
the return into self that annuls the harshness of opposition; [it is] love in infinite anguish, which likewise is
healed in the process--[this is what] truth [is] in
philosophy, in and for itself. Only recent philosophy
[has] attained this conceptual depth. Here we shall have
nothing to say of the unphilosophical shallowness [+]that
wants to philosophize (thinking, common sense, enlightenment);[+] its contradictions are without any value, utterly spiritless, innocent in their sin against the Spirit
(in the sense indicated above), [+]prideful and vulgar,
ready with concepts, self-satisfied.[+]

But this concept must not be [thought of] as ready
in philosophy. By contrast, the situation of philosophy
is *to grasp conceptually what is*. The latter must [+]not
only be implicitly true, but it must also[+] be *actual in
advance*, for itself, [+]in general empirical consciousness.[+] All that is true begins in its appearance, i.e.,
in its being in the form of immediacy. The concept must
therefore [be] present in the self-consciousness of humanity, in Spirit as such, in the World-Spirit; and the
latter must have thus comprehended itself.[25] This self-
comprehending, however, is the necessity [that occurs] as
the process of Spirit, a process that exhibits itself in
the previous stages of religion, notably in the Jewish
and the pagan,[26] and that [must] have as its result this
concept of the absolute unity of divine and human nature,
the actuality of God, which is God's objectification of
himself as his truth. Thus [185] world history is the
exhibition of this truth as [the] result [that occurs] in
the immediate consciousness of Spirit.

[+]In time [there is] a succession of stages.[+][27] "When
the time had fully come, God sent forth his Son" [Gal.
4:4]. "When the time had fully come"--this means: when
Spirit [had] entered so deeply into itself as to know its
infinitude and [to perceive] the substantial in [a] sub-

ject [possessing] immediate self-consciousness, which
means in a pure subjectivity [that is not only] infinitely negative but precisely thereby absolutely universal.

The confirmation that *this particular individual* is
the Christ is another matter and refers only to the determinate statement that this particular individual [is
the Christ] and not another individual; it does not concern the question as to whether in this case the Idea
does not exist at all. Christ said: Do not run hither
and thither, the Kingdom of God is within you [cf. Lk.
17:23, 21]. Many others among the Jews and heathens have
been venerated as divine [men]. John the Baptist preceded Christ; among the Greeks and Romans [there was]
Demetrios Poliorketes, for example, to whom, when he came
to Athens, statues were erected as to a god. Roman emperors
[were] venerated as gods. Apollonios of Tyana and many
others [were] believed to be miracle-workers; +it [would
be] even more miraculous if [what is reported by them]
were not true, [because] understanding, insight, depth of
thought, honesty, [are] greater miracles than those they
narrate.+ Earlier, among the Greeks, Hercules [was] the
only individual who as a man--chiefly because of his
deeds, which were merely deeds of obedience--entered the
circle of the gods, became a god, a prototype. +Among
the Indians, moreover, this great multitude of incarnations [is found], this elevation of the Brahmins to
Brahma, [this] becoming-God.+

However, the infinite Idea of humanity could attach
itself only to Christ and see itself realized only in him
--+for the time had fully come, the Idea was completely
mature in its depths.+28 The history of his teaching,
life, death, and resurrection [has] taken place; thus
this history exists for the community, and it is *absolutely adequate to the Idea*. This is what must be regarded as the crucial point; [186] this is the verification, the absolute proof of a single individual; this is
what is to be understood as the witness of the Spirit,

the Holy Spirit. It is the Spirit, the indwelling Idea,
that has attested Christ's mission, and this is the verification for those who believed and for us [who possess]
the developed concept.

   We now take up the subject of *miracles*, which are
supposedly what comprise immediate verification. In and
for itself, this is only a relative verification. Christ
says reproachfully, "Unless you see wonders you will not
believe" [cf. Jn. 4:48]. "Many will come in my name,
doing signs, casting out demons, making the blind see,
the deaf hear, the lame walk, etc. I will declare to
them, 'I have never known you, depart from me!'" [cf.
Matt. 7:22-23].[29] What sort of interest still attaches
to the working of miracles? How many miracles by oracles,
by men, especially for example [by] the Neopythagoreans,
are not narrated! Besides, the relative [verification]
is temporal: miracle is limited to helping in the formation of the community and to establishing faith in this
individual; it had an interest only for those who are outside, for the conversion, so to speak, of Jews and heathens. But the community that is formed no longer requires miracles; it has within itself the Spirit that
leads into all truth. It is the Spirit [that verifies],
the power [*Macht*] of the Spirit--by its truth as Spirit--
over Spirit. Miracle is merely a physical power or force
[*Gewalt*] over natural connections and hence only a force
exerted on the consciousness that is limited in the consciousness of these limited connections. How could the
eternal Idea itself come to consciousness by the representations of such force?

   But there always remains a certain curiosity or in-
quisitiveness: How are the miracles to be construed or
explained? This is to conceive them in such a way that
they were not miracles at all but rather in some sense
natural effects. Such curiosity presupposes doubt and
disbelief,[30] [187] and would like to find a plausible
basis by means of which the moral virtue and integrity of

the persons involved might be saved--one is so reasonable
and well-meaning that Christ and his friends are allowed
to remain honorable people. [+]Therefore, [one makes] the
assumption that [miracle] is [indeed] a delusion, [but
not] an intentional one, i.e., not a deception.[+] Otherwise, the briefest way of settling the matter would be to
throw out the miracles entirely. If someone does not believe in any miracles, finds them opposed to reason,
[even those] of Apollonios of Tyana and others [which are]
well confirmed, then it helps not at all to want to prove
them to him. They must rest on sensible perception, but
[there is] in man an insurmountable objection to allowing
what is attested merely in such fashion to count as
truth. On the ground of sensible perception, he can find
hundreds and thousands of possibilities as to how it
turned out [naturally]. For here such possibilities and
probabilities are what count, and the proofs are themselves nothing but probabilities of the same kind, the
subjectivity of finite grounds.

The main point [is] that such curiosity proceeds already from unbelief. Faith, however, rests on the witness of the Spirit, not on miracles but on the absolute
truth, on the eternal Idea and its content, and from this
standpoint the miracles have little interest. They can
be cited as subjective reasons of an incidental and edifying character, or be put aside. [But it is of] no interest [to faith] to investigate [+]what the wedding
guests at Cana really drank, and if it was wine, whose
wine.[+] [+]Miracles are supposed to confirm, and [yet] must
themselves [first] *be* confirmed. That which is supposed
to be confirmed by them is the Idea; [the latter, however,] has no need of them, and therefore no need to attest to them.[+]

But this remains to be said: miracles [are], in
general, effects produced by the power of Spirit on the
natural [188] nexus, a higher intervention in the natural
process, [in] "the eternal laws" of nature. Speaking

generally, Spirit is this absolute intervention. Already
life intervenes in these so-called eternal laws of nature.
Life digests, i.e., it annuls or suspends the eternal
laws of physics [*Mechanik*] and chemistry. [The] means of
nourishment actually [exist] materially in accord with
the eternal laws of physics, and chemically in accord
with those of chemistry; life destroys these. Even more
than this, [the] power and weakness of Spirit affect life.
[There is such a thing as] death caused by fright; [people
can become] sick from grief. Joy and trust also [have
an effect on life]. Hypnotism [*Magnetismus*] has disclosed for us such powers in more familiar form. In all
times, [one finds such] infinite faith, infinite trust,
Spirit in Spirit: cripples are healed, the blind see,
the deaf hear, right up to the present day. Unbelief in
such occurrences and effects is based on a superstitious
belief in the so-called powers of nature and their independence of Spirit.

This first confirmation is an external and contingent mode of faith. Genuine faith rests on the Spirit of
truth, while the former still involves a relation to
sensible, immediate presence. Genuine faith is spiritual
and exists in the Spirit. [It] has as its basis the
truth of the Idea, and since at the same time this Idea
exists for figurative representation in a temporal, finite fashion in this individual, it can actually appear or
enter into play *as realized in this individual* [only]
after his death and [his] removal from the temporal
sphere. For only then is the process of this perception
itself completed as a spiritual totality. In other words,
the process consists in believing in Jesus, even when
faith no longer has before it as such the sensible appearance ⁺whose sensible perception would otherwise constitute the confirmation [of faith].⁺³¹

[189] This is represented figuratively as the outpouring of the Holy Spirit upon [the] departure of Christ.
"I will send you a Comforter, the Spirit; the Spirit will

lead you into all truth" [cf. Jn. 16:7, 13]. And for
this Spirit sensible history exists in essence only as
accomplished--sublated[32] to the right hand of God; it exists essentially as past history--past in the sense that
[everything] sensible is for representation. All eternal
history [is viewed] $^+$as something past,$^+$ [like the]
creation of the world.^{m}

 ^{a}The *origin* of faith and the community is the production of the doctrine of the Spirit (or better, of the
content of this doctrine). Thus, more precisely, it is
the explication of what we have already generally indicated in the process of making the transition to the community. To begin with, let us compare the community with
what we have already seen: we first considered the eternal Idea in the element of thinking, second in the element of divestment in the exhibition of a sensible, external, immediate mode. We have considered this, and it
existed for us. But who are *we*? We are nothing other
than the community itself, subjective consciousness.
This is manifest to us, we know about it: hence *we* are
the presupposition for which this exists. Here, then, we
have proceeded to the realization of the Idea, so that
Spirit exists *for* Spirit, and this is what Spirit *is* for
Spirit as sensible consciousness. Hence there are two
relationships of "for another." We are the one side;
this is objective to us here, as in a drama the spectator
has himself objectively before himself in the form of the
chorus. Thus here is the standpoint that is the content
for Spirit, and we must consider this relationship carefully.

 Initially, this Spirit is sensible consciousness;
however, it should not exist *for us* on this one side as
it does for consciousness. Or, in so far as we have determined it to be sensible, to this extent this side must
raise itself to our standpoint--if it is the true stand-
point--for considering the truth.

This consideration in fact presupposes the community. The origin of the community is the production of the content for the community, for subjective self-consciousness. As mentioned above, we have considered first the Idea in the element of thinking, [190] second how it realizes itself outwardly, posits itself in distinction. For the community, this order is reversed: the community begins with the sensible appearance, then proceeds to the production of the doctrine containing this content. Initially, the community is one of immediate self-consciousness, and truth comes to it in a sensible fashion as a sensible determination; it first elevates itself into being a community in order to attain eternal truth from this sensible mode.

Initially, then, the content is that of immediate consciousness, and truth could appear for the latter in a variety of sensible ways. For the Idea is one in all, is universal necessity; actuality can only be a mirror of the Idea. For consciousness, therefore, the Idea can issue forth from everything; it is always the Idea that is in these infinitely numerous drops, which reflect back the Idea. The Idea is figuratively represented, foreshadowed, recognized in the seed, which is the fruit, the final definition of the plant; it first dies away in the earth, and only through this negation does the plant spring forth. Such a story, perception, portrayal, and appearance can also be elevated to universal significance by Spirit, and thus the story of the seed or of the sun becomes a symbol of the Idea--but only a symbol, because these are forms of it that, in terms of their peculiar content or specific quality, are not adequate to the Idea; what is consciously known through them lies outside of them; the meaning they suggest does not exist in them as meaning.

The object that exists in itself as the concept is spiritual subjectivity, i.e., man. Man is in himself meaningful; meaning does not lie outside of him; rather

he is all-interpreting, all-knowing. He is not a symbol;
his consciousness *is* essentially history itself. The history of the spiritual does not transpire in an existence
that is not adequate to the Idea. Thus it is necessary
that the thought, the Idea, should become objective in
mankind. At the beginning, however, the Idea exists in
an individual in sensible perception; the latter must be
stripped away and the significance, the eternal, true essence, be raised up. This, however, is the faith of the
emerging community. It begins with an individual, but
the individual man is transformed by the community. He
is known as God, and indeed is characterized as [191] the
Son of God who is involved in everything finite that belongs to subjectivity as such; but his form, which is
finite, disappears before his substantiality. It is a
question of the transformation of sensible appearance into the knowledge of God. Thus the community begins from
faith, but on the other hand faith is produced in it by
the Spirit. We have now to bring out the different sig-
nifications of faith and of *confirmation*.

[33]What is involved in the *confirmation* of this individual is essentially the witness of the Spirit, the indwelling Idea, the Spirit in itself. This is here
brought to perception; it is given as an immediate witness of Spirit to Spirit, which recognizes in its true
necessity only the conceiving Spirit. Outward confirma-
tions are of a subordinate character and do not belong
here. The Son is recognized essentially by the community
as the one who has been raised to the right hand of God.
This means that he is essentially determinative for the
nature of God itself, at which point sensible confirmation falls away. Miracles belong to sensible confirmation, since they occur for the empirical, external consciousness of faith. This is another field, another soil;
but one imagines that this individual must have confirmed
himself by the glittering phenomenon of miracles, by absolute power over nature. We have already spoken of the

fact that man customarily represents God as the power of
nature. But it is no longer a question of signs and
wonders; Christ has renounced them. Moreover, by its
very nature miracle is an external, spiritless mode of
confirmation. It is rightly said that God and his powers
exist in nature in eternal laws and according to them:
the true miracle is the Spirit. Already the animal is a
miracle vis-à-vis plant life, and still more Spirit vis-
à-vis life, vis-à-vis merely sentient creatures. However, another mode of confirmation is the true one,
namely, through power over minds; it must be affirmed
that this is the genuine mode. Power over minds is not
external power like that of the church against heretics;
rather it is a power in the spiritual mode, which leaves
Spirit's freedom intact. This power has been expressed
through the great community of the Christian church. One
can say [192] that this is merely an effect of an external sort, but not without falling into contradiction.
For proof of the power is demanded, and this is the effect; the proof of the concept requires no confirmation.

Since faith begins in a sensible mode, it has before
it a temporal history. What it holds to be true is an
outward, ordinary occurrence, and its confirmation is by
means of the historical [*historisch*], juridical method of
confirming a fact, [which gives] sensible certainty. The
representation of the foundation [of truth] has as its
basis the sensible certainty of other persons regarding
certain sensible facts, and it brings other facts into
line with these. The life-history of Christ is thus the
outward form of confirmation. But faith alters its significance. For it is not merely a question of faith
taken as belief in this external history, but rather of
faith that this man was the Son of God. Thereby the
sensible content becomes something quite different; it is
transformed into something else, and what is then demanded is that the latter should be confirmed. The object has been completely transformed from something that

exists sensibly-empirically into a divine content, into a
moment of God himself that in essence is the highest moment. This content is no longer something sensible; thus
if the demand is made to confirm it in the previous,
sensible way, this way at once proves to be inadequate
because the object is of an entirely different nature.

If one defines the content in such a way that the
miracles of Christ are themselves sensible appearances
that can be confirmed in historical fashion, and if one
likewise regards his resurrection and ascension as sensible appearances, then with respect to the sensible it
is a question not of the relation of historical confirmation to these appearances, but rather of the relation of
sensible confirmation and sensible occurrence, taken both
together, to Spirit, to the spiritual content. The confirmation of the sensible, whatever its content, remains
subject to an infinite number of objections because at
its basis lies sensible externality, which is opposed to
Spirit and to consciousness. Here consciousness and object are separated, and this fundamental separation brings
with it the possibility of error, deception, and lack of
the education necessary to form a correct conception of a
fact, so that one can have doubts. [193] Sensible contents are not certain in themselves because they do not
exist through Spirit as such and because they have other
grounds, which are not posited by Spirit. It may be supposed that we must get to the root of things by a comparison of all the evidences and the circumstances, or
that grounds for deciding among one or another of the
possibilities must be found. However, this entire method
of confirmation, as well as the sensible content as such,
must be led back to the requirement of Spirit. What has
truth for Spirit, what it ought to believe, must not be
a sensible belief; what is true for Spirit is something
for which sensible appearance is subordinated. Since
Spirit begins with the sensible and then arrives at its
own worth, its relation to the sensible is at the same
time a negative relation.

This is a major characteristic, the same that occurs
in regard to all cognition in so far as it is directed
toward something universal. As is well known, Kepler
discovered the laws of the heavens. They are valid for
us in a twofold fashion: they are the universal. A
start was made from single instances; certain movements
were referred back to laws; but these are only single instances. One could therefore think that there might be
millions more of such instances, that there are bodies
which do not move in this way, and that even with regard
to the heavenly bodies there is no universal law. To be
sure, this is all well known, but the interest of Spirit
is that such a law be true in and for itself. This means,
however, that reason finds its counterpart in the law,
for it recognizes it to be true in and for itself. By
contrast, sensible cognition retreats into the background;
it is indeed the starting point--a starting point that
should be gratefully acknowledged--but such a law now
holds good for itself. Thus its confirmation is of another sort: it is the concept, and its sensible existence is now demoted to a dream-like image, above which
exists a higher region with its own fixed content.

The same circumstance obtains in the proofs for the
existence of God, which begin with the finite. The de-
fect in them is that the finite is conceived only in an
affirmative fashion; but the transition from the finite
to the infinite is at the same time of such a character
that the soil of the finite is abandoned and reduced
[194] to a subordinate status, to a distant image, which
now exists only in the past--not in the Spirit, which itself is absolutely present, which has abandoned that
starting point and stands on a foundation of an entirely
different sort. Piety can take advantage of any occasion
to edify itself; such, then, is its starting point.

It has been demonstrated that several of Christ's
quotations from the Old Testament are incorrect, so that
what ensues from these quotations is not grounded in the

immediate sense of the words. On this view, the Word is
presumably something fixed; but the Spirit makes of it
something that is true. Thus sensible history is the
point of departure for Spirit, and these two characteristics must be distinguished. What we are concerned with
above all is the return of Spirit into itself and spiritual consciousness. The church has rightly combatted the
opposition to miracles, the resurrection, etc., because
such opposition brought with it the presupposition that
the basis for claiming that Christ is the Son of God is
just such occurrences. This claim, however, remains secure for itself, whether or not it really has such a
starting point.

The transition is *the outpouring of the Spirit*,
which can transpire only after Christ has been removed in
the flesh, only after his sensible, immediate presence
has ceased; then for the first time the Spirit appears.
What the Spirit alone produces is something different,
has another form.[34] [196] We have thus arrived at the
proceeding forth of the Spirit in the community. Two
things are to be considered in regard to this emerging
of the spiritual being of the community in this self-
conscious Spirit. The first question is: What does this
Spirit know? It is itself an object [for its own know-
ing] because it is Spirit. Now what is its content, what
is its doctrine? Its content is that this objective
Spirit likewise posits itself, realizes itself in the
community; it now posits itself subjectively, or is subjectively posited, just as it was first objectively
posited.[35]

The first moment is that of God, his essence. God
exists not merely in general; rather he now exists as a
living, active God, the God who accomplishes activity,
who produces himself, makes himself objective: he himself *is* his activity. This objectivity has initially the
characteristic of distinction, of finitude; this is the
Son of God. That God has a Son is the testimony [197]

and decree of the Spirit; the Spirit is not yet conceived
but rather takes this decree directly from its own nature.
This is the second moment; the third is that the Spirit
defines itself as the unity of the first two. History
first obtains in thought the form by which it has absolute interest for the Spirit. This third moment consists
in what has already taken place in one respect in the
Son, namely, that the Spirit objectifies itself as the
unity of the first and the second moments, so that the
second moment, that of other-being, is sublated in eternal love. But love primarily gives expression to a relationship of one to an other such that the two extremes
remain independent; it expresses an identity into which
the two extremes are not absorbed. On the other hand,
here it is love that is defined as the objective--this is
the Spirit.

It is possible religiously to remain primarily with
the representation of the Son, as in the Catholic Religion, where the Mother of God and the Saints are exalted.
But the Spirit is encountered, as it were, only in representation as something dwelling in the church, sustaining
in it what it decrees. Thus [in the Catholic Religion]
the second moment in its sensible form has placed greater
stress on sensible perception than on spiritualization,
and the Spirit essentially became an object.

The other side is the inverse [of the second moment],
as doctrine forms itself in the emerging community. This
means that the eternal truth also exists in the community
as something posited, through it and in it. Thus this
inverted moment [the third] is that the infinite Spirit
does not abide in itself in an objective way but rather
brings forth Spirit in itself because it begets itself
in self-consciousness. This elevation happens by means
of the content that we have seen: this is the mediator.
For it is onesided to view faith in the form of subjectivity in such a way that the community, the individual
self-consciousness, raises itself up and is the produc-

tive factor. All activity is mediated; what is to be
brought forth must already exist in and for itself. Activity imparts only the determination of being-for-self;
spiritual activity is possible only under the presupposition of being posited. "Is it possible?" means, "Is it
already in and for itself?"

We have seen finite subjectivity taken up into this
content; reconciliation is already accomplished in itself.
[198] This is the representation of the Spirit; only by
means of this representation can reconciliation be
brought forth. Thus the activity of the community is already determined by the fact that reconciliation is accomplished in itself, i.e., that God is Spirit. The community produces this content. It is evident that the
community in itself is what produces this doctrine, this
relationship. The latter is not something produced from
the word of Christ, so to speak, but through the community, the church. The empirical aspect of such production,
by means of church gatherings, councils, etc., does not
concern us here. For us the question is: What is the
content in and for itself? This content is to be justified by philosophy, not by history; what the Spirit does
is no history [*Historie*].[36] Spirit is concerned only
with what exists in and for itself, not with something
past, but with what is absolutely present.[*a*]

[194][*b*][37] *The third element* still remains [to be
treated]. The first [aspect concerns] the *origin* of the
community immediately [in] the outpouring of the Holy
Spirit. The Spirit that comprehends spiritually this
history advancing in [the order of] appearance recognizes
in it the Idea of God, his life, his movement--all this
we have already observed. The community is comprised of
the individual empirical subjects who exist in the Spirit
of God. But at the same time, this content, history, and
truth of the community are distinguished from them and
stand over against them. On the one hand, faith in this

history, in reconciliation, is an immediate knowledge, an act of faith; on the other hand, the nature of Spirit in itself is this process, which is to be viewed both in the universal Idea and in the Idea in the form of appearance, and this means that the subject itself becomes Spirit and thereby a citizen of the Kingdom of God, and that the subject in itself traverses this process. [195] It has been set forth above that the human subject--the man [Jesus], in whom is revealed what by means of Spirit is for humanity the certainty of reconciliation--was marked out as singular, exclusive, and distinct from others. Thus the presentation of the divine history for the other subjects is something that is objective for them, and they must now traverse this history, this process, in themselves. In order to do this, however, they must first presuppose that reconciliation is possible, or more precisely, that this reconciliation has happened in and for itself and that it is certain. The perishing of sin and the negation of immediacy are indicated by the bodily, sensible death [of Christ]. In and for itself, this is the universal Idea of God; but the other side of the presupposition is that this is certain for man, and that this truth does not exist for him by means of specu-lative thinking. This presupposition implies the cer-tainty that reconciliation has been accomplished, i.e., it must be represented as something historic, as some-thing that has been accomplished on earth, in the form of appearance. For there is no other way of representing what is called certainty. This is the presupposition that we must initially believe.[38]

To the origination of faith there belongs first a man, a sensible human appearance, and second, spiritual comprehension, consciousness of the spiritual. It is a matter of spiritual content, of the transformation of im-mediacy into what has spiritual character. Confirmation is spiritual, does not lie in the sensible, cannot be accomplished in an immediate, sensible fashion. Accord-

ingly, objections can always be raised against the sensible facts. The transformation of something immediate
into a spiritual content is a transition that we have
seen in the form of the proofs for the existence of God--
where we [196] also have a sensible world, but the truth
is the infinite, not the sensible, immediate world of
finitude.

    This conversion, which already begins with the resur-
rection[39] and ascension, is what we call the origin of
the community. As to the empirical mode [of confirma-
tion], and investigations concerning the conditions sur-
rounding the appearance of Christ after his death, the
church is right in so far as it refuses to acknowledge
such investigations; for the latter proceed from a point
of view implying that the real question concerns the sensible and historical elements in the appearance [of
Christ], as though the confirmation of Spirit resides in
historic fashion in such narratives of one subject to
historical representation. It is said that the Holy
Scriptures should be treated like the writings of profane
authors. One can do this with regard to what concerns
the merely historic, finite, external. But for the rest,
it is a matter of comprehension by the Spirit; the profane elements do not constitute the confirmation of
Spirit.[b]

Section 3. Existence of the Community[40]

    [198] [b]The second [aspect concerns] the *realization*
[or *existence*] of the community.[41] The community itself
is existing Spirit, Spirit in its existence, God existing
as community.

    The first moment is the Idea in its simple universal-
ity for itself, having not yet progressed to judgment,
other-being, not yet being disclosed--the Father. The
second moment is that of particularity, the Idea in ap-

pearance--the Son. In so far as the first moment is concrete, other-being is indeed already contained in it; the
Idea is eternal life, eternal bringing-forth. But the
second moment is the Idea in its externality, such that
the external appearance when inverted becomes the first
moment and is known as the divine Idea, the identity of
the divine and the human. The third moment, then, is
this consciousness of God as Spirit. This Spirit as *existing* and *realizing* itself is the community.

The community begins with the fact that the truth is
at hand; it is known, extant truth. And this truth is
what God is: he is the triune God; he is life, this process of himself within himself, the determining of himself within himself. The second aspect of this truth,
then, is that it has also appeared, has a relation to the
subject, exists for the subject; moreover, the subject
has essentially a relation to it and is meant to be a
citizen of [199] the Kingdom of God. That the subject
itself ought to be a child of God implies that reconciliation is accomplished in and for itself in the divine
Idea, and that secondly it also appears and therefore the
truth is certain for mankind. Precisely this certainty
is the appearance, the Idea, as it comes to consciousness
in the modality of appearance. The third aspect is the
relation of the subject to this truth, the fact that the
subject, to the extent that it is related to this truth,
arrives precisely at this conscious unity, values itself
in this known unity, brings this unity forth within itself, and is fulfilled by the divine Spirit.

This is the concept of the community in general, the
Idea, which to this extent is the process of the subject
within and in itself, the process of the subject that is
taken up into Spirit, is spiritual, so that the Spirit
of God dwells within it. This its pure self-consciousness is at the same time the consciousness of truth, and
the pure self-consciousness that knows and wills the
truth is precisely the divine Spirit within it.[b]

a. Faith, Doctrine, and Church

m42 It is now the community that is formed and in which the Holy Spirit dwells; and from this Spirit the community explicates its faith.

In the first place,[43] it has a *faith*. Faith [is an] ambiguous word. Here [it means] faith in the truth, i.e., certainty of absolute truth--of what God is, God [as] Spirit and [with this,] his actualization. [This is] faith neither in authority nor [as a consequence of] what [has been] seen and heard; rather it is the eternal, substantial nature of Spirit that has come to consciousness here, exists for consciousness, [so] that what is true in and for itself has certainty for me. This can happen [for philosophical consciousness] through the *concept*--but here it is not so; [it happens] for spiritual consciousness as a whole, and for that reason it is called faith, which does not have to rest on grounds, authority, etc. Grounds or reasons [exist] for what is limited, for what appears, for the finite, not for the eternal, [because] grounds are always contingent. That I should come to have faith in the eternal can also appear to have grounds, but these [are] contingent, [200] indifferent, external [occasions], subjective in character, just as an accidental incident [may have] stirred an individual's heart. But the faith of the community rests solely on reason itself, on the Spirit, i.e., [on] a mediation that annuls all mediations. Hence it is necessarily expressed as a faith of many, engendered by God. As Adam [said of his wife], "Flesh of my flesh, bone of my bones" [cf. Gen. 2:23], so the divine Idea that exists in itself is in man, [who is its] image; this image is God--"Spirit of my Spirit"--a testimony to God.

In the second place,[44] faith as a form of *objective truth*--earlier [we have shown that it is] not *feeling*-- [is] an *object* of consciousness, and this antecedent truth alone is the ground that determines feelings.

Spirit [is] higher than [what occurs] in the form of feeling. [The] animal [has] feeling too. [Man is] consciousness, through whose content [feelings] are determined.
If feeling were only intended to designate immanence,
then it would be $^+$a religious feeling$^+$ indifferent [to
the content]. But feeling [is the] form that locks particular subjectivity within itself, also the natural man
and his will; $^+$[it is a] coupling that grasps and keeps
all [aspects of humanity] in one mass,$^+$ essentially impure. Spirit, by contrast, is from the first this conversion that is self-appropriating; by appropriating what
is liberated from feeling, Spirit conquers feeling, puri-
fies and determines it.

In the third place,[45] [the] *doctrine* of the Christian Church [is] the principal thing [that serves] to
awaken feelings--but feelings that proceed from the
teaching of truth, from representations [and from] objectivity, [and that are] therefore true feelings for
the first time. Doctrine is formed, created, and explicated from itself. $^+$[It is a] necessity that doctrine be
withdrawn from arbitrariness and contingency of insight,
and that [it] be preserved as truth that exists in and
for itself, as something secure. Therefore [it is] deposited in symbols, bound to fixed expressions,$^+$
$^+$whether [they have been] formed on the basis of written
sources or of [oral] tradition. In the written sources,
further development appears as an interpretation of the
Bible; in the tradition, as a positing, articulating,
doctrinalizing of tradition. [201] [The latter] is also
doctrine, also something given. Nothing [is simply]
created from itself: it is the Spirit of the community
as a whole [that creates]. [The] doctrine of the church
[is] not produced in the church but is cultivated by
[the] present Spirit. Historically, whether [doctrinal
propositions are found] in the Bible or in tradition is
not the primary issue; the community[46] possesses the infinite power and authority [needed] for its development,

[for] the progressive determination of its doctrine.[+]

The developed community is a *church*, which as an existing entity undergoes expansion, is secure [+]in its actuality,[+] rests upon itself, and endures through time. Thus organization enters into play. The church is the Kingdom of God, the achieved presence, life, preservation, and enjoyment of Spirit.

[We wish] to point out only briefly that the initial, polemical tendency of renunciation [+]that was opposed to anything worldly existing outside itself[+] implicitly falls away and is no longer valid. [A saying such as], "I have not come [to bring] peace, but a sword" [Matt. 10:34], [the] disruption of family bonds, the renunciation of property--all these of themselves fall by the wayside [+]and could only apply in special situations within the community[47] itself. "Give all that you have to the poor" [Matt. 19:21] contains within itself the insulation of this command. If everyone gave all that he possessed to the poor, then soon there would be no more poor to whom to give anything, or no more persons who would still have something to give. Or more likely, the poor would now be rich, and those who had been rich would now be poor, to whom would be returned what previously was theirs.[+] Family, property, temporal concerns come into being on their own; and it therefore comes about that out of the womb, commandments, and authority of the church there is formed a free life, and out of its eternal principles [a] [+]civil and[+] political life--[a] rational, secular kingdom [+]in accord with the Idea of freedom [and the] absolute character of justice. Because what is legal, rational, and universal belongs to the world, there remains to the church the salvation of individual souls [and the arena of] particular subjectivity; the worldly universal is a matter for itself.[+] [m]

[202] [48] [a]The second [aspect] is the continuation, the *existence* of the community, its self-maintenance.[49]

Within itself the community is an eternal becoming that
presupposes itself. Spirit is a self-knowing in self-
consciousness, a self-separating into finite rays of finite consciousness, and a return to that which it actually
is, a return in which divine self-consciousness breaks
forth. It is more precise to say that, in the existence
of the community, *doctrine* is already complete, and that
the individual is only drawn into this completed doctrine.

It is evident that a doctrine is necessary. Content
must be rendered representationally, and this is a content in which what is to be brought forth in the individual as such is accomplished and displayed in and for itself. The sacrament of *baptism* first appears in this
connection, so that the individual may be born not into a
state of wretchedness but into the community of the
church, and may be confronted not by a hostile world but
by a world that is the church. [Baptism means that] the
individual has to be reared only in a community which already exists as his world-condition.

[204] Doctrine arises in the individual through the
authority of the church. The beginning of all knowledge
is authority. Even in the case of sensible knowledge we
begin with the authority of being: it is as it is, immediately, as such it is valid for us--this is the authority of the sensible. Representations with which we
are familiar are authorities that we receive. They are
given to us as true; [205] they are not our own insight.
The latter first arises with spontaneity, with the re-
working, assimilation, retraction, appropriation of this
material.

This second moment, that of assimilation, entails
rebirth by means of doctrine. Man must be born twice,
first naturally, then spiritually; this was already the
case with the Brahmins. Spirit is not immediate; it exists only as it engenders itself from itself. This rebirth is no longer the infinite melancholy arising from
the [first] birth-pang; but there still exists the op-

position arising from the pure particularity of man, his
further interests, passions, his self-seeking, etc. The
natural heart by which man is imprisoned is the enemy,
which is to be resisted but which is so determined in
the community as to be implicitly overcome.

[206] Thus we do not have here the representation of
a perennial struggle as in the Kantian philosophy, where
striving is unending and the resolution is postponed into
infinity, and where one takes one's stand upon the
"ought." Here by contrast the contradiction is resolved.
Therefore, the nature of Spirit is represented to the individual in such a way that evil is implicitly overcome
and does not have an absolute autonomy or persistence,
as is the case in the Parsee religion, where an eternal
struggle takes place between light and darkness, or in
the Kantian philosophy, where a mechanical, external relation obtains between the sensible and the rational,
both of which remain autonomous. Here the power belongs
to Spirit, which is what is known here, the awareness
that what has happened as such, what has been found to be
the case, the natural being of man, can be undone. Here
is the awareness that there is no [207] sin that cannot
be forgiven, just as the natural will can be given up--
except for sin against the Holy Spirit, denial of the
Spirit,[50] since the Spirit alone is precisely the power
that can annul everything. It is precisely Spirit that
has to do with itself in the element of the soul, freedom, and spirituality that does not stand or remain opposite natural being, action, or deed. Only Spirit is
free; its energy is not restricted. No power is comparable to it or can stand opposite it; here there is no
spiritless condition of mechanism.

Many difficulties emerge thereby from the concepts
of Spirit and freedom. On the one hand we find Spirit as
universal Spirit, and on the other hand the being-for-
self of man, of the single individual. It must be said
that it is the divine Spirit that effects rebirth; this

is free divine grace, for everything divine is free.   It
is not fate or destiny.   On the other hand, however, the
self-consciousness of the soul stands firm, and one now
seeks to ascertain how much is due to man because of his
cooperation with his salvation.   A *velleitas*, *a nisus* is
left to him, but a rigid insistence on [his own contribu-
tion to] the relation is itself just what is unspiritual.
The first [element of] being, or self-being, is the concept in itself, Spirit in itself; that which is to be annulled is the form of its immediacy, its individuated,
particular being-for-self.   This self-annulling and
coming-to-self on the part of the concept is universal in
nature, as in the element of thought Spirit that comes to
itself is free Spirit; but free Spirit is unlimited, universal Spirit.[a]

[202] [b]*Doctrine* is developed in the community itself
only as something already presupposed and complete.   The
Spirit that was shed abroad is the beginning, that which
makes the beginning, which raises up.   The community is
the consciousness of this Spirit, the expression of what
Spirit has discovered and by which it has been touched,
namely, that Christ is for Spirit.   Hence doctrine has
been essentially brought forth and developed in the
church.   First it exists as intuition, faith, feeling, as
the felt, flash-like witness of the Spirit; but it actually is already at hand and is to be presupposed, and
thus it must be developed from the concentration and interiority of feeling into the mode of representation.
Accordingly, the doctrine of faith has been essentially
constituted in the church first of all, and subsequently
it is thinking, developed consciousness, that also as-
serts its rights and what it has otherwise attained
through the cultivation of thought and philosophy.   For
these thoughts, on behalf of these thoughts, and on behalf of this otherwise known truth, thinking first develops a consciousness that is only intermixed with

other, impure thoughts. Thus doctrine is developed out
of other concrete contents that are intermixed with im-
purities. This doctrine exists and must then also be
preserved. This happens in the church. There, what doctrine is must also be taught. It *is*, it exists, it has
value, it is acknowledged and immediately presupposed.
But it does not exist in a sensible fashion, such that
the [203] comprehension of this doctrine should take
place through the senses--as, e.g., the world is indeed
presupposed as a sensible entity, to which we are related externally and sensibly. Rather, spiritual truth
exists only as *known*, and the fact that it also *appears*
includes the fact that the mode of its appearance is precisely this, that it is taught. The church is essentially the teaching church, an organization comprised of
a teaching office, which is given the commission to expound doctrine.

The fact that the single subject is now filled by
the divine Spirit is brought about by mediation in the
subject itself, and mediation means that the subject has
this faith. For faith is the truth, the presupposition,
that reconciliation is accomplished with certainty in and
for itself. Only by means of this faith that reconciliation is accomplished with certainty and in and for itself,
is the subject able and indeed in a condition to posit
itself in this unity. This mediation is absolutely necessary.

The difficulty residing directly in the fact that
the relationship of the community to this Idea is a relationship of the individual, particular subject is annulled
by the blessedness achieved by this comprehension. This
difficulty is removed in the truth itself. It consists
in the fact that the subject is different from the absolute Spirit. This difference is removed, and the reason
for its being removed is that God looks upon the heart of
man, his substantial will, the innermost, all-encompassing
subjectivity of man, his inner, true, earnest willing.

In addition to this inner will, and as distinguished from
this inner, substantial actuality, there is still in man
his external and deficient side: he commits errors; he
can exist in a way that is not appropriate to this inward, substantial essentiality, this substantial, essential inwardness. The difficulty is removed by the fact
that God looks upon the heart, the substantial, so that
externality, other-being, finitude and imperfection in
general and as they are further determined, do no damage
to the absolute unity; finitude is reduced to an inessential state and is known as inessential. For in the Idea,
the other-being of the Son is a transitory, disappearing
moment, not a true, essentially enduring, absolute moment.

The subject is already born into this doctrine; it
has its beginning [204] in the context of valid, already
existing truth, and in the consciousness of it. The relation of the individual to this presupposed truth that
exists in and for itself has yet a second aspect. Since
the individual is born into the church, he is forthwith
destined, although at this point still unconsciously, to
participate in this truth, to become a partaker of it;
his destination is for this truth. The church expresses
this in the sacrament of *baptism*: man, the individual,
exists in the fellowship of the church, in which evil has
been overcome in and for itself and God is reconciled in
and for himself. Initially, doctrine is related to this
individual as something external. The child is at first
only Spirit implicitly, is not yet realized Spirit, not
Spirit as actual. He has only the capacity, the poten-
tiality, to be Spirit, to become Spirit in actuality.
Thus the truth is something external for the child and
comes to him first as a presupposition, as something
recognized, something valid. This means that the truth
necessarily presents itself at first to men in the form
of *authority*.

All truth, even sensible truth--although such is not

authentic truth--initially comes to men in the mode of
authority; i.e., it is something at hand that possesses
validity and exists for itself. It presents itself to me
as such, as something different from me. The world likewise arises in our sensible perception as an authority
confronting us: it *is*, we find it so, we accept it as an
existent entity and relate ourselves to it as to an
entity. It exists in a certain way and is valid for us
in the form that it exists. Doctrine, which is spiritual,
does not exist as a sensible authority such as this; it
must be *taught*, and it is taught as valid truth. Custom
is something that is valid, an established conviction.
But because it is something spiritual, we do not say: it
is, but rather, it is valid. However, because it comes
to us as an entity, we also say: it is. And because it
presents itself to us as something valid, we call the
mode [in which it thus appears] authority.

[205] Just as man has to learn sensible content from
authority, and to be content with what exists because it
exists--the sun is there, and because it is there I must
be content with it--so also he has to learn doctrine,
truth. The latter, however, arises not through sensible
perception, through the activity of the senses on us, but
rather through doctrine as an entity, through authority.
What is learned in this way must be taken up by the individual into himself in order to assimilate it, to appropriate it. As already mentioned, the inner Spirit is the
absolute possibility of such knowledge; it corresponds to
this content. What exists in human inwardness, i.e., in
man's rational Spirit, is brought to consciousness for the
individual as something objective; or what is found within the individual is developed so that he knows it as the
truth in which he exists. This is education, practice,
formation. With such education and appropriation it is a
question merely of becoming acclimated to the good and the
rational. Thus far it is not a matter of overcoming evil
because evil has been overcome in and for itself. The

child, in so far as he is born into the church, has been
born in freedom and to freedom. For one who has been so
born, there is no longer an absolute other-being; this
other-being is posited as something overcome, something
surmounted. This formation is concerned only with pre-
venting evil from emerging, the possibility for which
lies in mankind generally. In so far, however, as evil
emerges in man when he does evil, at the same time it exists as intrinsically a nullity, over which Spirit [206]
has power: Spirit has the power to undo evil.

Repentance or *penitence* signifies, that, by the elevation of man to the truth, transgression is dissolved, and
that man thereby recognizes truth in contrast to his evil
and wills the good, which is to say that through his repentance evil is nullified. Thus evil is known as something that has been overcome in and for itself, having no
power of its own. The undoing of what has been done can
happen not in a sensible fashion but in a spiritual
fashion; inwardly, what has been done can be undone. It
is removed from the sinner; he is reckoned as one who has
been adopted among men by the Father. It is the business
of the church that this acclimating and educating of
Spirit become always more inward, that this truth become
ever more identical with the self, with the will of man,
that this truth become his volition, his object, his
Spirit. The battle is now past, and the consciousness
arises that there is no longer a struggle, as in the
Parsee religion or the Kantian philosophy, in which evil
is indeed always to be overcome, yet stands in and for
itself [permanently] over against the good, the highest,
and in which there is nothing but an unending progression.
Here, by contrast, in the Spirit evil is known to be overcome in and for itself, and because it is overcome in and
for itself, the subject has only to effect a good will.
Thus evil, the evil deed, has disappeared.

[207] The community, whose concept we have seen
above, also *realizes* itself. The real community is what

we generally call the *church*. This is no longer the
emerging but rather the existing community, which maintains itself. In the existing community the church is
the institutional arrangement whereby its subjects come
to the truth, appropriate the truth to themselves;
thereby the Holy Spirit becomes real, actual, and present
within them, has its abode within them. The church is
the means by which the truth is in them and they exist
in the enjoyment and [208] activity of the truth of
Spirit, the means whereby they as subjects are the active
expression of Spirit.

The primary thing that is present in the church is
its universality, which consists in the fact that the
truth is here presupposed, that it exists as truth ready
to hand--not, as in the case with the emerging church,
that the Holy Spirit is poured out and brought into existence for the first time. This means an altered relation to the [church's] origin for [its] subjects, for
subjects in their origination. This presupposed, existent truth is the doctrine of the church, its doctrine of
faith. We know the content of this doctrine: it is the
doctrine of reconciliation. It is no longer the case
that man is elevated to absolute significance by the outpouring and decree of the Spirit, but rather that this
significance is something that is known and acknowledged.
It is the absolute capability of the subject, both within
itself and objectively, to share in the truth, to come to
the truth, to exist in the truth, to attain to the consciousness of truth. This consciousness of doctrine is
here presupposed and present.[b]

b. *Cultus and Sacraments*

[m][51] The doctrine [of the cultus concerns] an awakening
of souls, a continuous working for their salvation, a continuous activity [+]that is creative of souls, forming and
bringing them forth. [The] preservation of the community

[is] like the creation and preservation of the world[+]
and [entails] an eternal repetition of the life, passion,
and resurrection of Christ [+]in the members of the
church.[52] [This] is eternally accomplished [and] is portrayed as more or less externally mediated. The natural
will dies away [in] confession, penitence, and sorrow;
[by] partaking of the sacrament, [the sinner receives]
glorification and majesty. In [the] mass, this [is] objectively [represented by the] sacrifice of the mass,
[where] Christ is daily offered up.[+]

[+][The principal matter is] the completion of this
movement in the Spirit. [First there is the] natural
will; [then is introduced] its reconstruction, [up to the
point where] it is adequate to the rational, universal
will.

This theoretical, speculative consciousness [is
what] exists in and for itself, and is therefore divine
history.

We have spoken earlier [about the] mediation through
disposition and activity: [209] [reconciliation is
found] not alone, in and for itself, as accomplished in
and within Christ, [and the] divine history [is found] not
as it exists in the pure Idea of God; [rather these are
found] under the particular representation and determination [of the cultus, in other words] as the laying hold
of the history of Christ and his merit--as though another
[had] accomplished [redemption], and satisfaction [had
already] occurred through him, and as though he [had] offered himself up and our conversion had an absolute value
only in him. Absolute value [is found only] through the
[existence] in and for itself [of the Idea]: this [is]
represented in him. [The] general consciousness of the
divinity of this action and of its result [is shown] especially in the sacraments. Individual subjectivity
finds in them the consciousness of the communion and
presence [of reconciliation].[+] [53]

The *sacraments*--they correspond precisely to the

inner certainty of the truth, the immediate certainty of
the kingdom, of being received into it, of being [its]
citizens. [The kingdom of God is a] *mystical union*, the
implicit unity of divine and human nature. Here [in this
life there is a] partaking [of this union, and this] is
the certainty of it. [The] Spirit fills its community;
[here] each person [becomes] aware of being a member of
the community, aware, i.e., that God is in him and that
he is in God. This [certainty is] not an eternal assurance, attestation, or corroboration, but rather is
only partaking or communion. This enormous sublimity and
exaltation of the individual [comes] to consciousness
[for him in this way].

[54]It is in their *cultus* that the Christian confessions are distinguished from one another.[55] +In doctrine
they are one, although of course the particular relationship of the subject to the cultus also constitutes a part
of doctrine itself. It should be said, with regard to
the content of doctrine in general, that deviations occur
in that part of the content which is concerned with the
cultus.+

+Thus in the cultus, and more specifically in the
sacrament, which[56] is given for the sake of immediate
communion and immediate certainty, the unity of the subject and its absolute object, the kingdom of God, [is
presented]. [This applies especially to] the chief sacrament; whether several [are necessary we prefer] not to
consider here.[57] The immediate sensible side, [the] communion, is [expressed in] the mode of eating and drinking,
and this is in fact the only possible form. For, unlike
breathing and the relation of skin to air [perspiring?],
eating and drinking are just this: taking possession of
oneself consciously, and indeed in the individualized
[body] [210] as this and only this sensible, singular subject, [which is] itself a mode [of relationship] of the
individualized [body] to the universal, neutral [environ-
ment]. Here [the communion] occurs in the mode of an ex-

ternal, sensible object such that the divine is eaten and
drunk; this is a symbol of the divine whose significance
is found not only in representation but rather in sensible
communion as such, in immediate certainty. Hence the
sensible as such must be validated, must be transformed
or transubstantiated into the divine substance itself;
the two become one.⁺

[We intend] to mention only the Western [churches;
there is found here an] important vantage point in general ⁺for understanding⁺ the truth. Spirit is [pres-
ent] in doctrine in an objective form, and [the] sacrament is communion with God by [the] subject. [The only
point of] difference [concerns] whether such an object
[of communion] is the divine in an explicitly external
form. [The] *Catholics* venerate the host as such, even
when [it is] not [being] partaken of. The same [thing is
true of] doctrine, [for which they demand] obedience⁵⁸
[rather than] insight. [Here,] severe objectivity [pre-
vails]. ⁺[As already mentioned,] this form of external
objectivity of what exists in and for itself is not
limited to this sacrament, but [also] occurs elsewhere in
accord with this principle. Fixed in this way for itself, the doctrine of the church is to be taken up into
the possession of the church by its members in a purely
receptive fashion, as its further development and as its
tradition. Equally if not more unconditioned is the demand for action, for works.⁺ Likewise [demanded is the]
doing of works. Laity [are] excluded from the self-
knowledge of doctrine⁵⁹ and [are to] conduct themselves
receptively. [211] The [preaching and] dispensation of
grace [and of the] sacraments [fall to a] particular office. [The] church [is] the external proprietor and dis-
penser of the means of grace, which for this reason [con-
stitute] a mass.

[The] *Lutheran, Evangelical* [confession, by contrast,
regards the] host [as valid] only in faith and in [the
actual] partaking. This [is] its consecration in the

faith and [the] spirit[uality] of each one himself.[60]
The minister does nothing in particular; he does not con-
secrate the host, and the others [are] only the recipi-
ents. Every father of a household [is] likewise a
teacher, a baptizer, a confessor--and [the] host set
apart as a thing is only a piece of bread, not God.

The *Reformed* view lacks this mystical element. [The
communion is valid only as] a memorial, an ordinary psy-
chological relation; everything speculative [has] disappeared, being annulled in the relations of the community.
+The Reformed Church [is] therefore the place where divinity and truth collapse in the prose of the Enlightenment and of mere understanding, and in the contingency of
subjective particularity. Luther [was] fully justified
in not yielding, even though so many were suspicious of
him. Generally speaking, [it was a question of the]
antinomy between freedom and the objectivity of God or
grace.+

There are three representational modes to be considered with regard to the path of the soul, and the distinction between them is instructive: moral representation, [the mode of] piety or religiousness in general,
and the mystical-churchly. The first, *the moral*,[61] posits
an absolute purpose; [it posits] the essence of Spirit in
a purpose that takes the form of volition, and indeed a
volition that is only my will, so that this subjective
side is the principal matter. Law, universality, rationality are in me as my rationality; and likewise the volition and actualization that make these things my own,
[212] make them into subjective purposes, are also mine.
+And in so far as the representation of something higher,
or the highest, [the representation] of God and the divine, enters into this view, [this] itself is a subjective postulate of my reason, something essentially posited by me. It *ought* to be something non-posited, an
absolutely independent power; but in its not-being-
posited, I do not forget myself, so that even this not-

being-posited is itself a being-posited by me--I, my subjectivity, which ought not to be absolutely self-united
as infinite form, but rather [should] remain [conditioned
by] these subjective antitheses. In love I am also preserved, but in a wholly different way, namely, by surrendering my opposition, my positing, [my] seeming creation [of things] and of their relativity. The result is
the same, whether in the form of the postulate or of one's
[saying] with reference to God and redemption: my feeling of dependence, my feeling of the need for redemption,
are what come first. In either case, the genuine objectivity of truth is annulled.[+]

Piety adds the insight, with regard to decision and
still more with regard to universality and law, that this
is the divine will, a content [which] is firmly determined, and [that] power, even the power of a good decision, is a divine power. Piety is content to abide in
this quite general connection.

The *mystical* and *churchly* [mode of representation]
defines more precisely this connection between God and
subjective volition and being, and brings it to consciousness in the specific form that we see, the speculative
form of the nature of the Idea.

The moral view is that of free will as subjective;
the view standing over against it is its opposite, even
though its content [is] also the truth. And if the content is also that of Spirit, it can be represented as the
grace of God or predestination that extends to the uttermost contingency, as in the Calvinistic view, where the
effects of grace are taken as something purely external.
One sees here a collision, an antinomy between the freedom of man and unfreedom or loss of will, a mere surrender. The various churches and churchly representations
are themselves attempts at a resolution of this antinomy,
[+]this implicit and explicit antithesis [213] between the
divine and the finite.[+] However, the earlier attempts to
grasp this solution in thought have mostly been preoc-

cupied with the antinomy. The Lutheran conception is undoubtedly the most ingenious, although not speculative.

The resolution provided by Christianity is to understand that precisely the moral history of the soul exists
[validly] in and for itself, that the mystical, churchly
[mode of representation] is precisely the speculative
content of this resolution, and that the cult is the resolution for each self-conscious individual. Only in this
way, [therefore,] has [the individual's] own doing been
accomplished, because [the matter exists] as such in and
for itself.^*m*

^*a*Here are based the communion in and the consciousness of divine grace, the consciousness of being citizens[62] of the kingdom of God, which is called mystical
union. Here, too, is based the sacrament of the Last
Supper, where the consciousness of reconciliation with
God is given to man in a sensible, perceptible fashion--
the indwelling and lodging of the Spirit within him.

We have seen that there are three sorts of figurative representation of the content of this sacrament.
Its content originates in the representation that proceeds from the sensible; however, the sublation of this
sensible element occurs in prayer as the assurance of
grace and of the divine Spirit. It is represented figuratively that in the sacrament Christ is eternally sacrificed, and that in the heart he is resurrected; this is
correct.[63] The eternal sacrifice is the process by
which the individual makes it his own and by which its
being-in-itself passes away. But since this individual
belongs to grace and is reconciled, the resurrection of
Christ also takes place within him. The differences
within the Christian Religion are essentially related to
this point.

The first representation is that Christ is present
in the host in a sensible, bodily, unspiritual way
through the consecration of the priest, and that in this

externality is to be found the divine. [214] This is the
representation of the Catholics: the divine is eaten by
man in empirical fashion.

The second representation is that God is present
only in Spirit, in the spiritual mode of faith: this is
the Lutheran confession. It, too, takes its start from
eating and drinking, as in the Eleusinian mysteries[64] of
the consumption of an objectively present god. The advance from this, however, is that the individual takes
it into himself, leading to its progressive spiritualization in the subject. The Father exists only in so far as
he surrenders himself, and he first exists as real Spirit
in self-consciousness. This is the important determination that transubstantiation takes place only in communion and faith, only in a spiritual way.[65]

The third representation is that Spirit is not present here but rather only in memory and in representation.
This is the Reformed view; it entails a spiritless,
merely vivid recollection of the past--not the divine
presence, no actual spirituality. [66]These are the major
moments in the existence of the community.[a]

[b]The existence of the community is completed, as was
said, by partaking in the appropriation of the presence
of God. It is a question of precisely the conscious
presence of God, of unity with God, the *unio mystica*, the
self-feeling of God, the feeling of his immediate presence in the subject. This self-feeling, however, since
it exists, is also a movement, presupposes a movement, a
sublation of difference, so that a negative unity issues
forth. This unity begins with the host, with regard to
which there now exist three sorts of representation. According to the first, the host--this external, sensible
thing--becomes by consecration the present God, God as a
thing in the mode of an empirical existence. The second
representation is the Lutheran one, according to which
the movement indeed begins with something external, which

is an ordinary, common thing, but the communion, the self-
feeling of the presence of God, comes about only [215]
in so far as the external thing is consumed not merely
physically but in Spirit and in faith. God is present
only in Spirit and in faith. There is here no transubstantiation, or at any rate only one by which externality
is annulled, so that the presence of God is absolutely a
spiritual presence--the consecration takes place in the
faith of the subject. The third representation is that
the present God exists only in representation, in memory,
and to this extent does not have an immediate, subjective
presence.

The subject is to appropriate doctrine and truth,
and hence this third [moment--the consciousness of God as
Spirit][67] is the partaking of the presence of God in the
self-preservation of the community.[b]

Section 4. Realization of the Community[68]

[a]The third [aspect][69] is the *realization of faith,*
or the *realization of the spirituality of the community*
in universal actuality; thus at the same time there also
appears *the transformation, recasting, and alteration of*
the community.

Religion, as we have seen it, is spiritual religion,
and the community exists primarily in what is inward, in
Spirit as such. This inwardness, this subjectivity that
is inwardly present to itself, nòt developed within itself, is feeling or sensation. But the community also
essentially has consciousness, representation in the form
of doctrine, etc., which, however, brings with it separation and differentiation. The divine objective Idea confronts consciousness as an other, which in part is given
by authority, and in part is to be appropriated by acts
of devotion. Furthermore, the moment of communion is
only a single moment; and the divine Idea, the divine

content, is not seen, only represented. In the mode of representation, the now of communion dissolves partly into a beyond, into a heaven beyond, partly into the past, and partly into the future. But Spirit is itself absolutely present and demands a fulfilled present; it demands more than merely dull representations. It demands that the content itself be present, or that feeling and sensation be developed and expanded.

Thus the community confronts an objective reality vis-à-vis the kingdom of God in the community. On the one hand, this objectivity as an external, immediate world is the *heart* [216] with its interests; another form of objectivity is that of *reflection*, of abstract thought, of understanding; while the third and true form of objectivity is that of the *concept*. We shall now consider how faith realizes itself in these three elements.

The realization of faith or of religion in general is simply the reconciliation of Spirit. Initially, this reconciliation still has something opposing it, and we must consider its relation to this opposition, the manner in which it is annulled, how the Idea shapes itself therein and thus appears to run the danger of losing itself.[a]

a. *The World in Its Immediacy and Externality:*
    The Heart, the Church, the Ethical Realm

[a]The first thing that opposes reconciliation is the natural *heart*. Religious reconciliation proceeds into the heart as that which is most inward and deep; but on the other hand the heart is also particularized, natural, has passions, inclinations, selfishness, egotism, is forsaken by the universal in its onesidedness, and is separated from faith. The proximate reconciliation of the community with this worldliness, a reconciliation that exists only immediately, consists in the fact that the community itself takes all these passions, inclinations,

etc., into itself. The *church*, which has its existence
in its subjects, lets them do as they like, takes them
into itself as they are immediately, and thereby receives
into itself all coarseness, passion, etc. On the one
hand, the church is this struggle with what is worldly;
on the other hand, surrounded by a crude world, it falls
into worldliness and corruption. This initial reconciliation has, therefore, the character of corruption.[a]

[b]The third [aspect] is still the *realization of the
spirituality of the community in universal actuality.*[70]
In religion the *heart* is reconciled. This reconciliation
thus exists in the heart; it is spiritual. It is the
pure heart that attains this communion of the presence
of God in it, and consequently reconciliation, the enjoyment of being reconciled. At the same time, however,
this reconciliation is abstract and is opposed in general
by the world. The self that exists in this reconciliation, in this religious communion, is the pure heart, the
heart in general, universal spirituality; but at the same
time the self of the subject represents that aspect of
spiritual presence according to which a worldly element
in developed form exists in the subject, and thus the
kingdom of God, the community, has a relation to the
worldly. In order that reconciliation should be real, it
is necessary that in this development, in this totality,
reconciliation should be known, [217] available, and
brought forth [into reality]. Principles based on the
spiritual apply to the worldly realm; the principle, the
truth, of the worldly *is* the spiritual.

The spiritual is the truth of the worldly realm in
the more proximate sense that the subject, as an object
of divine grace and as one who is reconciled with God,
already has infinite value in accord with its determinate
character, which is then further developed in the community. On the basis of this character, the subject is
recognized as Spirit's certainty of itself, as the

eternity of Spirit. The determination to infinitude of
the subject that is in itself infinite is its. *freedom*.
The substance of the subject is that it is a free person,
and as a free person it is related to the worldly and the
actual as one who is present to himself, reconciled within himself, an utterly secure and infinite subjectivity.
This its determination ought to be foundational as it relates itself to what is worldly. This freedom of the
subject is its rationality--the fact that as subject it
is liberated and has attained this liberation through religion, that in accord with its religious determination
it is essentially free. This freedom, which has the impulse and determinacy to realize itself, is rationality.
Thus it is a matter of concern that this reconciliation
should also be accomplished in the worldly realm.

The first form of reconciliation is the immediate
one, and just for this reason it is not the true mode of
reconciliation. It appears as follows: at first the
community contains within itself, in abstraction from the
world, the element of spirituality, of being reconciled
with God, so that spirituality renounces the worldly
realm, placing itself in a negative relation to the world
and also to itself. For the world is in the subject; it
is there as the impulse toward nature, toward social life,
toward art and science. What is concrete in the self,
its passions, etc., certainly cannot be justified just
because they are natural; but on the other hand, monkish
abstraction [from the world] means that the heart is not
concretely developed, that it exists as something undeveloped, or that spirituality, the state of being reconciled, and the life of reconciliation are and ought to
remain concentrated within themselves and undeveloped.
But the very nature of Spirit is to develop itself, to
differentiate itself until it attains the worldly realm.

The second characteristic of this reconciliation is
that worldliness and religiosity indeed remain external
to each other, yet [218] still should enter into relation.

But the relation in which they stand can itself only be
an external one, or more precisely, a relation in which
one dominates over the other, and thus there is no reconciliation at all. The religious, it is felt, should be
the dominant element; what is reconciled, the *church*,
ought to rule over what is unreconciled, the worldly
realm. Accordingly, this is a union with the worldly
realm, which remains unreconciled; in itself, the worldly
is raw and crude, and as such it ought only to be domi-
nated. But the dominating power takes this same worldliness up into itself; as a result of its dominion, there
emerges in the church itself a worldliness devoid of
Spirit because the worldly realm is not in itself reconciled. A dominion predicated on the lack of Spirit is
posited, in terms of which externality is the principle
and man in his relatedness exists at the same time outside himself--this is the relationship of *unfreedom* in
general. In everything that can be called human, in all
impulses, in all relationships that have reference to the
family and to activity in public life, estrangement enters into play. The ruling principle is that man is not
present to himself, is not at home with himself. In all
these forms, he exists in a general condition of servitude, and all these forms count for nothing, are unholy.
Because he exists in them, he is essentially a finite and
estranged being and thus has no value; what has value is
an other. This reconciliation with the worldly realm,
with man's own heart, comes about in such a way that it
is precisely the opposite of [genuine] reconciliation.
The further development of this condition of rupture
within reconciliation itself is what appears as the corruption of the church, the absolute contradiction of the
spiritual within itself.

    The third characteristic is that this contradiction
is resolved in the *ethical realm*, or that the principle
of freedom has penetrated into the worldly realm itself,
and that the worldly, in so far as it has been formed in

accordance with concept, reason, and eternal truth, is freedom that has become concrete and will that is rational.[71] The institutions of ethical life are divine institutions--not holy in the sense that celibacy is supposed to be holy by contrast with marriage or familial love, or that voluntary poverty is supposed to be holy by contrast with active self-acquisition or what is lawful and proper. Blind obedience is regarded as holy, while the ethical entails an obedience in freedom, a free and rational will, an obedience of the subject toward the ethical. Thus it is in [219] the ethical realm that the reconciliation of religion with worldliness and actuality comes about and is accomplished.[72]

Reconciliation thus has three real stages: the stage of immediacy, which is more an abstraction than it is reconciliation; the stage in which the church is dominant, a church that exists externally to itself; and the stage of ethical life.[b]

b. *Abstract Mediation of the Worldly and the Spiritual: Reflection*

[a]The second form to which the church is related is that of *reflection*.[73] Through the touching of the inward by the worldly, reflection and thinking are awakened, as is the mediation of the real, worldly side with that of the ideal. This proximate and initial reconciliation can only be abstract; it is a self-disclosure of the understanding, of the reflection of universality, which at first is the abstract universality of understanding. Since reflection thus makes itself into a standard, there emerges a hostile relation to the church. Since the understanding fancies itself to be the content of religion, there emerges the sharpest possible apparent conflict. The community has the peculiarity of containing within itself the infinite antithesis between absolute Spirit, existing in and for itself, and subjective, in-

dividual Spirit; the latter in its character as individual self-consciousness represents the extreme of formal
freedom. In general, this extreme is what we have earlier called the most inward realm. The natural man in
his entire particularity exists in contrast to this innermost realm, and thus the subject is an infinite contradiction. This antithesis is now reconciled in and for
itself, of which religion is the portrayal. The antithesis is also implicitly reconciled in the concept, and
this is the subjectivity, the infinitude of the ego within itself, which earlier was designated as the principle
of immortality. The realization of faith here consists
in the fact that this inwardness no longer remains as the
merely inward and profound heart, but rather develops
within itself. If we say that faith has its foundation
in what is most inward, then the natural man must be distinguished from this. Because inwardness is not developed
within itself, the truth for it is a sensible history, a
representation of God; [220] it is spiritual truth given
merely in objectified fashion. What is required is that
inwardness be developed within itself, that it exist for
itself as the Idea, albeit only as subjective Idea. This
is what is meant by saying that faith is realized in
reflection. Initially, what is awakened is thinking in
general, which is the demand for the unity of what is
most inward with worldly particularity. This demand is
universality, and at first abstract universality. What
abstract universality now produces or manifests from itself is that infinite being-within-self, or pure thinking
within itself, turns against authority and demands the
form of autonomy with regard to the whole of the content
that is considered by it to be true. Faith is indeed the
testimony of Spirit to the truth. The sentiment of devotion receives and has within itself the fulfillment
given by the Spirit. But in this case the individual himself does not exist for himself; the truth has the form
of authority, and the self finds lacking in it the char-

acter of its own being-for-self.

The second form, therefore, is the one in which
thinking produces secure definitions within itself and
from itself. It discovers within itself a content, namely, that it is natural man, but since it is still the
universal, and since its activity is that of universality,
it extracts from the content an affirmation and gives it
the form of universality, arriving thereby at secure definitions. For example, familial relations, family life
and love, justice in general, contractual agreements, the
relation of individuals to official authority, the relations pertaining to sovereigns and states--these are all
essential relations according to the testimony of Spirit.
These have become secure conditions for man: the family
vs. celibacy, justice vs. the poverty demanded by the
church, obedience to civil authority vs. the blind obedience of the church, which demands that one surrender one's
own will and know nothing of secure definitions within
and from oneself. Reflection thus arrives at a secure
content; the latter becomes secure by obtaining the form
of universality and the form of identity with itself.
Thereby thinking takes up a position of opposition to the
church: nothing is permitted to contradict it. Whatever
contradicts these secure definitions is invalid; preten-
sions and ordinances of the church that contradict them
count for nothing.

It is abstract thinking with its principle of identity that then attacks the inner content of the church
even more radically. [221] This content is concrete, entailing the unity of the universal and the particular,
the divine Trinity. This concrete content stands in contradiction with the law of identity. Likewise, the relation of God to man, grace, the unity of divine and human
nature, the mystical union--all of these represent an absolute coupling of antithetical qualities. Thus in thinking this content is annulled, and reflection has as its
final result the objectivity of identity itself, namely,

that God is nothing other than the highest essence, without determinate qualities, empty, for every determination makes [what is determined] concrete. God becomes something above and beyond for cognition because the latter is only a knowledge of concrete content. Reflection in its completed form is the antithesis of the Christian Church.

There are two forms of this antithesis. For the first,[74] what counts as true is empty unity; this emptiness is a negation of the subject, which knows itself as concrete. On this side of the empty essence stands a finitude that has become free for itself, that has an absolute value in itself, and is autonomous. Finitude operates as its own standard in various forms, e.g., as the personal uprightness of individuals. The further consequence is not only that the objectivity of God is removed into the beyond and negated, but also that all other objective qualities, all qualities that are valid in and for themselves and that are posited in the world as just and as ethical, disappear. Since the subject draws back to the pinnacle of its own infinitude, what is good, just, etc., is contained only within it; these constitute its subjective character, these are its own thoughts. The fulfillment of this good derives from natural caprice, from contingency and passion, etc. The subject is simply the consciousness that objectivity is enclosed within itself and therefore has no independent existence for it; only the principle of identity is valid. This subject is abstract; it can be filled with any sort of content. It has the capacity, which is thus rooted in every human heart, of subsuming every content. Subjectivity is thus caprice itself and the knowledge of its absolute power-- its power to produce objectivity, the good, and to be able to give it a content.

The second form of this antithesis is that the subject does not exist for itself with regard to the unity toward which it has extended itself, and therefore it does not confer upon itself an affirmative particularity; rather it has [222] the determination to submerge itself in the unity of God. Thus the subject has no particular purpose and no absolute purpose other than that of willing itself for the sake of the One, of existing only for the sake of the One, of making its purpose the glory of the one God. This form is religious; it contains an affirmative relation of the subject to its essence, which is this One, and to which the subject yields itself up. This religion has the same content as the Jewish Religion, but the relations in which men stand are broadened. No particularity remains within it; the Jewish sense of national value is lacking. Here there is no limitation; man relates himself to the One as a purely abstract self-consciousness. This is the characteristic of the *Muhammadan Religion*.[75] In it Christianity finds its antithesis because it occupies a sphere comparable to that of the Christian Religion. It is a spiritual religion like the Jewish; but its God exists for self-consciousness only within the absolute, knowing Spirit, and to this extent he stands with the Christian God on a level at which no particularity is retained. Whoever fears God is accepted by God, and man has value only in so far as he stakes his truth on the knowledge that this is the One, the essence. The distinction between subjects according to station in life or class is annulled, although there can be classes as well as slaves--but this is only accidental.

The antithesis consists in the fact that in Christ spirituality is *concretely* developed and is known as Trinity and as Spirit, and that the history of man, his relation to the One, is a *concrete* history. It begins with the natural will in its inauthentic state, which it surrenders, and by this negation it progresses toward its own essence. Muhammadanism hates and proscribes everything concrete: its God is the absolute One, in relation to whom man retains for himself no purpose, no particu-

larity, no distinctiveness. Man in his existence does
undoubtedly particularize himself by means of his inclinations and interests, and these are all the more savage
and unrestrained because here reflection is lacking. But
the complete opposite is also found here, namely, the
tendency to let everything take its own course, indifference with respect to every purpose, absolute fatalism,
indifference toward life; no practical purpose has any
essential value. But since men are in fact practical and
active, their purpose can [223] only be that of bringing
about the veneration of the One in the whole of humanity.
Thus the Muhammadan Religion is essentially fanatical.

The reflection that we have been considering occupies
the same stage as Muhammadanism in one respect, namely,
that God has no content, is not concrete. Christ's exaltation to be the Son of God, the transfiguration of
self-consciousness, etc., have no place here.[76] The distinction[77] consists in the fact that this independence of
Muhammadanism [from everything concrete] is not set forth;
here, on the other hand, subjective reflection retains
for itself the fulfillment of its contingency and caprice.
This is the religion of the *Enlightenment*, of abstract
thinking, where it is in fact indicated that the truth is
not recognized and cannot be known, and that the truth
does not exist for subjective self-consciousness but
rather only for its opinions, contingencies, and pleas-
ures.

In this last mentioned form, a reconciliation may
also be recognized; thus this final appearance is also a
realization of faith. Since in fact all content, all
truth perishes in this infinitely self-knowing particular
subjectivity, the principle of subjective freedom thus
comes to consciousness therein. What is known as inwardness in the [Christian] community is now developed within itself; it is not only inwardness and conscience but
subjectivity, which judges and distinguishes itself, is
concrete; it knows the universal within itself, knows

what it produces from itself, namely, subjectivity that
is for itself, that is determined from within itself, and
that is the completion of the subjective extreme until it
has attained the Idea in itself. [224] The deficiency
here is that this is only formal and lacks true objectivity; it represents the ultimate pinnacle of formal development without inner necessity. Objectivity must be
set free for the true consummation of the Idea--the totality of objectivity within itself.[a]

[225] [b][78] The second stage is that the ideal side
emerges for itself in religious consciousness. Inwardness knows itself to be present to itself precisely in
the reconciliation of Spirit with itself; and this knowledge of being present to self is precisely thinking.
Thinking means to be reconciled, to be present to self,
to be at peace with self (although in the form of a
wholly abstract, undeveloped peace). Thinking is the
universal activity of the universal, and stands in general contrast to the concrete, to the external. It is
the freedom of reason that has been acquired in religion
and now knows itself to be for itself in Spirit. This
freedom now turns itself against merely spiritless externality and servitude, for the latter is absolutely opposed to the concepts of reconciliation and liberation.
Thus thinking enters in, defying and destroying externality in whatever form it appears. This is the negative
and formal act, which in its concrete form has been called
the *Enlightenment*. The Enlightenment has turned thinking
against externality and has maintained the freedom of
Spirit that resides in reconciliation.

This thinking first emerges as abstract universality
in general and is directed against what is concrete in
general. For this reason, it is also directed against
the Idea of God, against the Idea that God as triune is
not a dead abstraction but rather relates himself to himself, is present to himself, and returns to himself. In

concreteness there are determinations [226] and distinctions. Since abstract thinking turns against externality
in general, it also is opposed to distinction as such
because in distinction an externally opposed entity is
indeed present--but in the Idea of God, in the truth,
this externality is likewise resolved. Therefore, this
thinking is concerned to annul everything that is concrete and determinate in God. Abstract identity prevails
as the rule for this abstract thinking, this understanding. When everything concrete in God has been thus eradi-
cated, this is expressed by saying that one cannot know
God. For to know God means to know him according to his
determinations or attributes; but [on this view] he is to
remain a pure abstraction. The principle of freedom, inwardness, and religion itself is grasped by this formula,
but to begin with only abstractly.

The other means by which determination enters into
universality, according to this abstraction, are the
characteristics that reside in the natural impulses and
tendencies of the subject. From this standpoint it is
said that man by nature is good. This pure subjectivity
indeed holds out for the category of the good, since the
latter coincides with this identity and pure freedom;
but the good itself must remain for it an abstraction.
Here the category of the good is nothing other than the
caprice and contingency of the subject. This represents
the extreme of this form of subjectivity and freedom,
which renounces the truth and its.development and moves
within itself, knowing that what it regards as valid are
only its own definitions, and that it is the master of
what is good and evil. This is an inward weaving within
itself, which can just as readily assume the form of hy-
pocrisy and extreme vanity as it can peaceful, noble,
pious aspirations. This is what is called the pious life
of feeling, to which *pietism* also restricts itself. Pietism acknowledges no objective truth and opposes itself to
dogmas and the content of religion, while still preserv-

ing an element of mediation, a relationship to Christ,
but this is a relationship that is supposed to remain one
of mere feeling and inner experience. Such piety, together with the vanity of subjectivity and feeling, are
then turned polemically against philosophy. The result
of this subjectivity is that everything fades away in the
subject, without objectivity, without firm determinacy,
without development of God.

[227] The mode first designated [i.e., the Enlight-
enment] represents the ultimate pinnacle of formal cultural development in our time. But the two extremes opposing each other in the development of the community are,
first, the unfreedom and servitude of Spirit in the absolute region of freedom, and second, abstract subjectivity,
subjectivity without content.*b*79

c. Realization of Faith in the Concept: Philosophy

[224] *a*The third relation of faith is to the *concept*,
to the *Idea*. Once reflection has invaded the sphere of
religion, thinking or reflection assumes a hostile attitude toward the role of representation in religion and
its concrete content. Thinking, however, once it has begun, does not stop: it carries through, empties heart
and heaven; the knowing Spirit and the religious content
take refuge in the concept. Here they must find their
justification; thinking must grasp itself as concrete and
free; it must not maintain the distinctions as merely
posited, but must release them freely and thereby recognize the content as objective.80

Philosophy has the task of establishing the relation
[of conceptual thinking] to the two preceding stages.
Religion, the need for religion, can take refuge in experience and feeling as well as in the concept; it can
limit itself to the former, thereby giving up the truth,
renouncing the prospect of knowing a content, with the
result that the holy church no longer has any community

and is atomized. For community is based on doctrine, but
each individual has his own feeling, his own experiences.
This form does not correspond to Spirit, which wants to
know. Thus philosophy stands opposed to two points of
view. On the one hand, it appears to be opposed to the
church: in common with the development of culture and
with reflection, it is unable, because it conceptualizes,
to remain with the form of representation; rather it conceives that content in the form of thought, while at the
same time recognizing the necessity of the form of representation. But the concept is the higher form because it
has its own content and also because it embraces the
various forms while granting to them their justification.
On the other hand, philosophy is opposed to the Enlight-
enment--opposed to its indifference toward the content,
to [225] its subjective opinion, to its despair that renounces the truth. The goal of philosophy is to know the
truth, to know God, for he is the absolute truth. Nothing
else is worth troubling about by contrast with God and
his explication. Philosophy knows God essentially as
concrete, spiritual, real universality, which is not
jealous but rather imparts itself. Light by its very nature imparts itself. Whoever says that God cannot be
known is saying that God is jealous, and makes no serious
effort to assert something about God when he speaks of
him. The Enlightenment--that vanity of understanding--is
the most vehement opponent of philosophy; it is displeased when the latter indicates the element of reason
in the Christian Religion, when it shows that the testimony of Spirit to the truth is deposited in religion.
Thus the task of philosophy is to show the rationality of
religion.

[231] [81]The purpose of these lectures has been to
reconcile reason with religion in its manifold forms, and
to recognize these as at least necessary. This religious
[232] knowledge attained through the concept is by its
nature not universal.[82] Moreover, it is only the knowl-

edge of a community [of philosophy]; and hence three
stages are constituted with reference to the Kingdom of
the Spirit: the first position is that of immediate,
ingenuous religion and of faith; the second is that of
the understanding of the cultured, so-called, of reflection and Enlightenment; and finally the third is that of
the community of philosophy.*a*

[227] *b*The third stage consists in the fact that
subjectivity develops the content out of itself, to be
sure, but in accord with necessity, that it knows and
acknowledges this content as necessary and as objective,
existing in and for itself. This is the standpoint of
philosophy, according to which the content takes refuge
in the concept and obtains its justification by thinking.
This thinking is not merely the process of abstraction
and definition according to the law of identity; rather
it is itself essentially concrete, and thus it is comprehension, meaning that the concept determines itself in
its totality and as Idea. It is free reason, which exists for itself, develops the content in accord with its
necessity, and justifies the content of truth. This is
the standpoint of a knowledge that recognizes and knows
the one truth. The purely subjective standpoint, the
evaporation of all content, and the Enlightenment of the
understanding recognize no content and hence no truth.
The concept indeed produces the truth--this is subjective
freedom--but it recognizes this truth as at the same time
not produced, as a truth that exists in and for itself.
This objective standpoint is alone capable of bearing
witness to and expressing the testimony of Spirit in a
cultured, thoughtful fashion.[83] Therefore, it is the
justification of religion, especially of the Christian
Religion, the true religion; it knows precisely the *content* [of religion] in accord with its necessity and reason. Likewise it knows the *forms* in the development of
this content. We have seen these forms: the modes of

the appearance of God, the representations of sensible
and spiritual consciousness that have arrived at universality and [228] thought, the complete development as it
exists for Spirit. The content is justified by the testimony of Spirit, in so far as it is thinking Spirit. The
testimony of Spirit is thought. Thought knows the form
and determinacy of the appearance, and hence also the
limits of the form. The Enlightenment knows only of negation, of limit, of determinacy as such, and therefore
does an absolute injustice to the content. Form and determinacy entail not only finitude and limit, but as the
totality of forms they are themselves the concept, and
these various forms are themselves necessary and essential. Sustained by philosophy, religion receives its
justification from thinking consciousness.[b]

[w]84 In faith the true *content* is certainly already
found, but it still lacks the *form* of thinking. As we
observed earlier, all forms--those of feeling, representation, etc.--can indeed have the content of truth, but
they themselves are not the true form, which makes the
true content necessary. Thinking is the absolute judge,
before which the content must verify and attest its
claims.

Philosophy has been criticized for placing itself
above religion. But as a matter of fact this is false
because [229] philosophy has only this and no other content, although it gives it in the form of thinking; it
places itself only above the *form* of faith, while the
content is the same in both cases.

The form of the subject as an individual who feels,
etc., concerns the subject as a single individual; but
feeling as such is not rejected by philosophy. The question is only whether the *content* of feeling is the truth
and can prove itself to be true in thought. Philosophy
thinks what the subject as such *feels*, and leaves it to
the latter to come to terms with its feeling. Feeling is

thus not rejected by philosophy but rather receives
through philosophy its true content.^{w}

[228] ^{b}Ingenuous piety has no need of [justifica-
tion]; it receives the truth as authority and experiences
satisfaction, reconciliation by means of this truth. But
in so far as thinking begins to posit an opposition to
the concrete, and to place itself in opposition to the
concrete, the process of thinking consists in carrying
through this opposition until it arrives at reconciliation.

This reconciliation is philosophy. Philosophy is to
this extent theology. It presents the reconciliation of
God with himself and with nature, showing that nature,
other-being, is implicitly divine, and that finite Spirit
in part raises itself to reconciliation (this being intrinsic to its essence), and in part arrives at this
reconciliation, or brings it forth, in world history.
This reconciliation is the peace of God, which is not
"higher than all reason,"^{85} but which rather is first
known and thought through reason and is recognized as
true and divine. This reconciliation by means of the
concept is the purpose of these lectures.

[232] ^{86}Opposed to philosophy is the vanity of understanding, which is displeased by the fact that philosophy
points to the truth in religion and demonstrates that
reason resides within it. This Enlightenment wants to
have nothing further to do with the content, and therefore is quite displeased that philosophy, as conscious,
methodical thinking, posits an end to the conceits, the
caprice, and the contingency of thinking. These lectures
have attempted to contribute a guide to this rational
knowledge of religion and to the general advancement of
religious faith [*Religiosität*].^{b}

Section 5. Passing Away of the Community[87]

[231] *m*[88] Formally speaking, [the following sequence
applies to historic phenomena]: *origin, preservation,*
and *perishing,* with the latter following upon the former.
But ought we to speak here of such [when] the Kingdom of
God [has been] established eternally? If so, then such
a *perishing* or *passing under*[89]--in fact a *passing over*
to the Kingdom of Heaven--would apply only to individual
subjects, not to the community. [The] Holy Spirit as
such lives eternally in its community. +Christ [says]:
"The gates of hell shall not prevail against my teaching."+[90]   To speak of a *passing away* would mean to end on
a discordant note.

[229] [91][We shall undertake an] empirical description of the so-called signs of the time [in which the
Christian Religion now finds itself. Let us] compare
[it] with the age of the Roman Empire.
[92](α) In how few textbooks, [230] one might ask,
[is] the content of the Christian faith still taken to be
true? The gods, and everything else regarded as true in
the Greek and Roman worlds, [had, in the age of the Emperors,] fallen into the hands of men and were created by
them, [with the result that] the gods and all else were
profaned.

[229] +(β) [It was an age] when rationality necessarily[93] took refuge solely in the form of private rights
and private goods because the universal unity based on
religion had disappeared, along with a universal political life. [The individual,] helpless and inactive, with
nothing to trust, left the universal [alone] and took
care for himself. [It was an age] when that which exists
in and for itself was abandoned even in the realm of
thought; just as Pilate asked, "What is truth?", so now
the mania for private goods and enjoyments [is] the order
of the day.[94]   [Only] moral opinions and personal deeds,
views, and convictions [remain], lacking in objective

veracity and truth. The opposite [of such truth is what
counts]: I acknowledge only what[95] I subjectively intend. [For a long time,] the teaching of philosophers
has corresponded [to such a view.] We know and recognize
nothing of God, [having] at best a dead and historical
mode of cognition.

When[96] the time is fulfilled and what is required is
justification by the concept, then the unity of the internal and the external no longer [lives] in immediate
consciousness, i.e., in actuality. [This unity is] no
longer justified by faith [but is rather only asserted
with] harshness and [by] objective commands and external
supports.[+]

[230] [In order to cultivate] faith in objective
truth, especially among the people, i.e., the lower
classes, the teaching of this truth was [entrusted to]
the clergy. [This is] the office that always [has] to
stimulate religion, in whose service it stands. [When
the clerical office falls into] argumentation (especially
that pertaining to past history), moralistic representations and inducements, moralistic or subjective feelings
and virtuosities, then [the latter] are put in place [of
religion]. When [one] treats [religious truth] as historic, that spells an end [to it]. The speculative
truth [is no longer heard], according to which the Gospel
is preached to the poor (for they [are the ones] closest
to infinite anguish), and according to which the teaching
of love in infinite anguish, [of] a substantial bond to
the world, is [proclaimed]. [Instead of this, what is
sought] by the natural means of moralistic representation,
with its claims for its "rights" and its [ever ready]
opinion, are enjoyment, love without anguish. The salt
[has] lost its savor.[97] [+]When everything has been thus
satisfied in its finitude, when all that is foundational
and secure has been tacitly removed, and [man is] inwardly empty of objective truth, of the content of objective truth and its method, then one thing [remains]

certain: finitude turned in upon itself, arrogant bar-
renness and lack of content, the extremity of self-satisfied enlightenment.[98] +

+What the connection of this decay with the mode of
religion itself [is], at the point where the doctrines
of religion [have become] representations, mere factual
data, [has been shown above]. It is thinking as a reflective activity, the need [of understanding], which
causes what is secure to waver, dissolves everything
dialectically, and leads it back to the subject, whether
it be an empty abstraction of the universal or [the empirical content] reduced to feeling, which it makes into
the foundation.

[The] people who [possess] not a concrete, ever-
insistent[99] reason, and who [231] know not how to help
themselves with regard to their interior impulses, [the]
classes for the sake of whose development the truth can
only exist in the form of representation, [and who] experience precisely infinite anguish and the exigency [for
reconciliation]--these people and classes are abandoned
by their teachers. The latter have helped themselves by
means of reflection, and have found their satisfaction in
finitude, subjectivity, and precisely thereby in vanity;
but the substantial kernel of the people cannot find its
satisfaction there.

[If,] instead [of allowing] reason and religion to
contradict themselves, [we] resolve this discord in the
manner [appropriate] to us, [then we have the] reconciliation in [the form of] philosophy. How the present day
is to solve its problems is to be left up to it. In
philosophy itself [the resolution is only] partial.
These lectures have attempted to offer guidance to this
end.+

[In fact] religion [must] take refuge in philosophy;
[from the point of view of] the world, a passing away
takes place in it, [but this concerns] only its form of
externality, of contingent occurrence. But philosophy,

[as we have said, is] partial: [it forms an] isolated
order of priests, [who hold sway in their] sanctuary,
[who] are untroubled by how it goes with the world, [who
must] not mix with it, [and whose work is to protect]
this possession of truth. How things turn out [in the
world] is not our concern.$_m$100

NOTES FOR CHAPTER V

1. Lasson reads: "The Spirit and the Church." However, the
term commonly used in this chapter is "Community" (*Gemeinde*), not
"Church" (*Kirche*). In the 1821 MS., this part is designated "C.
Community, Cultus," indicating the third and final main division of
the Revelatory Religion, subdivided into three sections: "(α)
Standpoint of the Community in General"; "(β) Existence of the Community, Cultus"; "(c) Passing Away of the Community." (Hegel himself mixed the Greek and Roman section letters.) In 1824 and 1827,
additional sections were added or substituted, producing the five
sections of our edition.

2. This is the heading used by the 1821 MS. in the margin.
Lasson's heading for this section, "Renewed Subjectivity and the
Community," is suggestive--but it would have been even more so had
it been possible to write "Intersubjectivity" in place of "Subjectivity." Although Hegel did not use the expression "intersubjectivity," it fits his intention perfectly. Human subjectivity, when
it is renewed, transfigured by the indwelling of the Spirit, becomes a *communal* subjectivity, giving up its old independence and
exclusivity. The "infinite love that arises from infinite anguish"
creates a unique and unsurpassable intersubjectivity, distinguishable from all other forms of human love and friendship. This section, one of the richest of the lectures, is much abbreviated in
1824 and disappears completely in 1827.

3. $^+$God -- spirituality -- existence of the same -- Idea in
sensible presence -- [in order] for others to have this Idea.$^+$

4. *Die sinnliche Gegenwart.* This expression, used frequently
in the following pages, refers to the "sensible presence" of God in
Christ, a presence that must be sublated in the spiritual community,
since Christ is no longer immediately present in a sensible mode,
although he is imaginatively or figuratively present, present in
the mode of representation for faith.

5. $^+$I, this [manikin] -- *ego homuncio* -- should not resist
evil like Jupiter; [the] *ego homuncio* should by contrast --
Modesty, making oneself humble, in order to be humble in
truth, in order to be allowed to be base.$^+$
See below, p. 237. The contrast appears to be between super-

human and manikin strength. Perhaps Hegel anticipates Nietzsche
here in his estimate of the "virtue" of Christian humility. In the
Religion of Spirit, because the contrast of sensible presence and
divinity, or the antithesis of divine and human Spirit, has been
overcome, human beings no longer need to be manikins.

6. The MS. repeats *und* instead of reading *und zwar*.

7. +Two aspects: (α) abstraction of thought, universality;
(β) subjective particularity, feeling.+

8. +Particular determination of subjective self-consciousness:
(β) How is self-consciousness defined on the subjective side? How
is it overcome for [self-consciousness] and in him [this individual]?
How is this severity, this overcoming, portrayed? This individual,
[this] sensible presence is, however, the overcoming epitomized --
only one, therefore universal -- himself ideal.+

9. +Because [he is] *universal* singularity, just for that reason [his] form [is]: singularity in universality. Thus (β) the
definition of the subject is (αα) to have disappeared [into the
grave], (ββ) the positive aspect of this subjectivity as an unending
surrender of its particularity and naturalness, [of everything that]
belongs to it in this world.+

10. [*Die*] *Geschlechtsfreiheit der Frauen*. This probably refers to the free sharing of sexual partners, which Hegel thinks may
have been practiced in the primitive Christian community and which
he mentions as a possibility implicit in Jesus' ideal of the community in "The Spirit of Christianity and Its Fate" (*Early Theological Writings*, trans. T. M. Knox [Chicago: University of Chicago
Press, 1948], p. 280). *Both* sexual freedom *and* monogamy are com-
patible with the infinite value of the human being, based on the
love that arises from infinite anguish. The expression might mean
"freedom from sex," but this seems unlikely in the context and in
light of Hegel's criticism of celibacy.

11. +(γ) Extension of the specific concept to the community.+

12. +That wherein they [are] obj[ectively one] must be a
third, [a] syllogistic conclusion [suitably expressed] for imagining
subjects who exist for themselves.+
The meaning seems to be that the "third"--the community of
Christ--must be represented in sensible form as the "body" of Christ
for imagining subjects.

13. The MS. reads *dass* instead of *weil*.

14. +(α) The third, [the] objectivity that mediates. (β) As
subjectivity, a self-conscious yet universal unity, a singularity
existing in and for itself.+

15. The text of Matt. 18:20 reads "them," not "you."

16. For the same reason Hegel would probably object to the

expression "Spiritual Community," frequently used by the English translation of the *Werke*, although not found in the original. The expressions he uses are *Religion des Geistes* and *Gemeinde des Geistes*, not *geistige Religion* or *geistige Gemeinde*.

17. +Matt. 12:31[-32]; Mk. 3:28[-29]: All sins will be forgiven men, even blasphemy, for they blaspheme against God; but whoever blasphemes against the Spirit will never be forgiven but is deserving of eternal judgment. This is a paraphrase and conflation of the two texts.

18. "We swim horizontally." In other words, one cannot swim in the ocean of the Spirit by attempting to stand upright on the bottom. To make sense of the next sentence it is necessary to alter Lasson's bracketed insertion.

19. Here is an explicit reference to one of the three "Kingdoms" in the 1821 manuscript (see also above, p. 232, and the occurrence in the 1824 lectures below, p. 291). This discussion indicates Hegel's awareness that the distinction between "Concrete Representation" and "Community, Cultus," employed in the 1821 MS. in conformity with the pattern adopted for "Determinate Religion," does not work well for the Christian Religion. The topics taken up under the latter category really must be included as an element within the former. The "concrete manifestation" of Christianity includes its appearance in the three modalities or elements of the divine Idea: God in and for himself apart from the world ("the Kingdom of the Father"), God's self-diremption in the creation and reconciliation of the world ("the Kingdom of the Son"), and God's self-redintegration through the completion of reconciliation in the community of the Spirit ("the Kingdom of the Spirit"). Having already employed the third of these expressions in the original lectures, Hegel would not have found it difficult to expand the terminology to designate the three main divisions of the lectures in 1831.

20. +Faith, laying hold of the merit [of Christ].+

21. The third main division of the 1824 lectures, picking up the argument where it breaks off on p. 214. The Griesheim transcript has a heading, *Das dritte Element*, at this point, marking the transition.

22. wOut of the ferment of finitude, as it rises into a foam, wafts forth Spirit.w (12:330; ET 3:124.)

23. Hegel added this heading to the 1821 MS. as a way of specifying the "next step." However in this MS. it is still a part of the first major section, "Standpoint of the Community in General."

24. These terms demonstrate that Hegel customarily used *Christus* ("Christ") as a proper name designating Jesus of Nazareth, indeed as synonymous with the latter, while the title *der Christ* ("the Christ") designates the Messiah, the Son of God. The distinction is not between the earthly and the risen Christ, since the name can refer to both, but between a *name* and a *title*, with the latter

designating the divine identity and role of the individual who bears
the name.

25. +Another mode of necessity.+

26. I.e., the Greek and the Roman.

27. *w*We have seen God as the God of free men, though still
first in the subjective, limited forms of Folk-Spirit and in the
contingent shape of fantasy; next we saw the anguish of the world
following upon the suppression of Folk-Spirit. This anguish was the
birthplace for the impulse of Spirit to know God as spiritual, in
universal form and stripped of finitude. This need was created by
the progress of history and the upbuilding of World-Spirit. This
immediate impulse, this longing, which wants and desires something
determinate--this instinct, as it were, of Spirit, which is im-
pelled to seek for this--demanded such an appearance, the manifestation of God as infinite Spirit in the form of an actual man.*w* (12:
319-320; ET 3:112.)
Lasson locates this passage from the *Werke* in relation to the
discussion of the exigency for reconciliation in Chap. III (p. 152,
n. 47). However, in the *Werke* itself it appears in the present context, which is more appropriate. It offers a characteristically
Hegelian recapitulation of the argument in the preceding paragraph
concerning the necessary progression toward the moment of incarnation through the previous stages of religion, notably Greek and
Jewish. It can be construed as an exposition of the marginal comment, "In time [there is] a succession of stages." Although it is
not found in the 1821 MS. itself, it may well be from the Henning
transcript of Hegel's oral presentation of these lectures.

28. +Another -- Hercules -- imperfect, e.g., his heroic deeds
by no means [accomplished] through the nature of Spirit.+
This marginal addition is included in the *Werke* in edited
form: "In the heroic deeds of Hercules, the nature of Spirit is
still imperfectly expressed" (12:320; ET 3:113). Lasson locates
this addition after the second sentence below, which surely is erroneous because the Hercules passage is a continuation of the marginal addition included by Lasson in the text, to which we have attached it (likewise the *Werke*). Also in the margin, just below the
Hercules passage, are the words "portrayed in his story" (possibly
"this story portrayed"), followed by another group of undecipherable
words.

29. Hegel's version of this saying differs considerably from
the actual text, which he appears to conflate with Matt. 11:5. A
marginal note makes a partial correction.

30. +[One might advise:] don't have doubts and then they are
resolved! -- But I *must* have them, I cannot lay them aside un-
answered; [they] press upon me and rightly should be answered. The
necessity of answering them rests on the necessity of having them.
The necessity of having them [is found] in reflection. [Reflection]
makes this claim, i.e., [it treats] the requirement as absolute.
These [are] finite grounds -- [but] it is precisely in piety that

finite grounds,[+]or human understanding so-called, have long since
been set aside.[+] (Cf. *Werke*, 12:325; ET 3:118-119.)

31. [+]It is said: "If only he were seen -- if only I had the
sensible before me -- if only I were to see this man in an ordinary
way and hear the words of his mouth!" [But] a sensible confirmation
cannot occur by means of such eye-witnessing. The [eye witness]
could err; he himself is supposed to have seen it, but he himself
[is] also only a witness; [his eye-witnessing] helps not at all.
His credibility [must] therefore [be tested, a] juridical interroga-
tion [must] take place; [but this too] does not help.[+]

In this paragraph as a whole, Hegel is saying that the Idea
precisely *as it appears in Jesus* can *now* be confirmed only spiritually, not immediately or sensibly. Moreover, the essential
reality of Jesus--the appearance of the Idea of divine-human unity--
can be properly apprehended only after his death, by spiritual
faith. Jesus was in historical, sensible fact the God-man, according to Hegel (a fact most concretely expressed by the *infinite love*
that arises from the infinite anguish of the cross), but he can be
properly (i.e., spiritually) perceived as such only by faith after
his death and departure. Finally, even a direct sensible perception
of Jesus could not provide a confirmation of the truth claimed for
him.

32. Note that Hegel here uses *aufgehoben* where one might have
expected *aufgestanden*, *erhoben* or *aufgegangen* ("raised," "ascend-
ed"). For Hegel the resurrection of Jesus from the dead indeed entails an *Aufhebung*--an annulling of his sensible presence, yet a
preservation of his real presence and its transfiguration into the
modality of Spirit.

33. Lasson has transposed this paragraph of the Griesheim
transcript from its original location near the end of Chap. IV (see
n. 59). However, as noted above, the last pages of the second part
of the 1824 lectures already parallel material in the third part of
the 1821 MS. This is the better context for the discussion of confirmation.

34. Lasson here inserts a section from the 1827 lectures that
we have relocated below (p. 254) in order to preserve the *m, a, b,
w* sequence.

35. [w]The activity involved in faith in implicit reconciliation
is, on the one hand, the activity of the subject, but on the other
hand, the activity of the divine Spirit; faith is itself the divine
Spirit that works in the subject. But the latter is not in this
case a passive receptacle; rather the Holy Spirit is equally the
Spirit of the subject because the latter has faith; in the exercise
of this faith it acts against its natural life, discards it, puts
it away.[w] (12:336-337; ET 3:130-131.)

36. Here Hegel's antihistorical impulse comes to the fore,
standing in some degree of tension with his equal emphasis on the
sensible, historical presence of God in Christ. Such tensions account for the conflict of interpretations in Hegel scholarship.

Hegel's use of the term *Historie* (rather than *Geschichte*) is significant here. He does not intend to deny that in the more fundamental sense Spirit is historic (*geschichtlich*) in its process of
self-distinguishing and self-redintegrating. In the preceding chapter he speaks of "the eternal history [*die ewige Geschichte*], the
eternal movement, which God himself is"; the death of Christ is "the
eternal divine history [*die ewige göttliche Geschichte*]" (above, pp.
220-221; cf. p. 212). But this historicity of God is not subject
to the external, empirical mode of investigation suitable for past,
factual data; in this sense it is no *Historie*. But the question
remains unresolved as to the relation between the empirical, sensible, outward aspects of the existence of Christ, which presumably
are subject to historiographical investigation, and the eternal divine history that is sensibly present in this individual. This relation is never clarified by Hegel. He seems to want to say that
what is *in fact* sensibly present in Christ can be recognized *as
such* only by faith, spiritually, not by historical investigation.

37. Here the 1827 lectures begin their treatment of the third
part of the Revelatory Religion. The point is not marked by a
heading but rather by the words of the first sentence, which are not
included in the text by Lasson but cited in his appendix (II/2:237).
Lasson also apparently rearranged the order of the first part of the
next sentence to make it fit more smoothly into the context to which
he assigns this section (see above, n. 34).

38. *w*It is a question here only of contingent subjectivity.
With the one characteristic of faith, that the subject is not what
it is meant to be, there is joined at the same time the absolute
possibility that it may fulfill its destiny of being received by
God in grace. This is the subject matter of faith. The individual
must grasp the truth of the implicit unity of divine and human nature, and this truth he grasps by faith in Christ. Thus for the
individual God is no longer something above and beyond, and the apprehension of this truth is in direct contrast to the first basic
characteristic, according to which the subject is not what it ought
to be.*w* (12:335; ET 3:128-129.)

39. Thus the resurrection belongs as much to the history of
the community as it does to the history of Christ (cf. Chap. IV.3).
The resurrection constitutes the point of transition from the Kingdom of the Son to the Kingdom of the Spirit. Demythologized, the
resurrection means for Hegel the spiritual presence of Christ in the
community, Christ's present *as* Spirit. However, he uses resurrection language with reference to this reality only infrequently.

40. In Lasson's edition, this is the third and final section
of Chapter 5, comprised of three subsections: (a) Faith, Doctrine,
and Cultus of the Community; (b) Transformation of the Community;
(c) Passing Away and Renewal of the Community. However, in the 1824
and 1827 lectures, the second subsection comprises an independent
concluding section; and in the 1821 manuscript the third subsection
(without the words "and Renewal") comprises an independent conclusion. It is misleading to subsume these latter two sections under
the "existence of the community." Accordingly we are restricting

the present section to Lasson's subsection (a). Even in this more constricted form, the organization of the section is clarified if it is subdivided into two parts: (a) Faith, Doctrine, and Church; (b) Cultus and Sacraments. We have added these subsectional headings. The opening paragraphs from the 1827 lectures provide a general introduction to the discussion of the existence of the community, thus justifying their location out of the usual order.

41. Lasson omits this sentence from the text but provides it in his appendix (II/2:237). The "first aspect" for both the 1827 and 1824 lectures concerns the origin of the community (above, pp. 254, 246).

42. The MS. adds: "β) Being of the Community, Cultus." This marks the beginning of the second subsection of Part C of the 1821 lectures.

43. The MS. reads: "αα)."

44. The MS. reads: "ββ)."

45. The MS. reads: "γγ)."

46. The MS. reads *sie* ("it") instead of *Gemeinde*.

47. The MS. reads *ihrer* ("it") instead of *Gemeinde*.

48. For the remainder of this subsection Lasson interweaves passages from the 1824 and 1827 lectures in a way that only makes the content more confusing. We have separated the materials, giving first the 1824 text, then the 1827 text.

49. Lasson omits this transitional sentence from the Griesheim transcript.

50. ^wThe violation of absolute truth, of the Idea of that unification of the infinite antithesis, is thereby declared to be the supreme transgression.^w (12:315; ET 3:108.)

51. The MS. adds: "γ) Cultus."

52. ^wIf the permanent preservation of the community, which is at the same time its unbroken creation, is the eternal repetition of the life, passion, and resurrection of Christ in the members of the church, then this repetition is expressly accomplished in the sacrament of the Last Supper. The eternal sacrifice here means that the absolute content, the unity of the subject and of the absolute object, is offered to the individual for immediate communion; and since the individual is reconciled, this completed reconciliation is the resurrection of Christ.^w (12:338; ET 3:132.)
This passage from the *Werke* parallels the 1821 MS. at this point and is possibly based on the Henning transcript of the 1821 lectures. Lasson, not noticing the parallel, footnotes this passage in relation to the 1824 lectures on p. 274 (n. 63).

53. [+]But in order for representation to render this contemporary and thus to create[+] a sensible object, that [the] unity of subject and object . . .

54. In Lasson's text this paragraph follows the next one, as the first part of the paragraph that begins, "[We intend] to mention . . . ." Although the contents may have appeared to make better sense to Lasson in his order, in the 1821 MS. itself the order is clearly the one we are following (Jaeschke supports our reconstruction).

55. [+]Council of Trent was accepted only by the priesthood in France. Hence a law for the faithful.[+]
The first sentence was cancelled by Hegel. Lasson erroneously attached the second sentence to n. 60, reading *Gese(t)z* as *Genuss*.

56. The MS. reads *wird* instead of *das*.

57. [+]Confession, also a Catholic sacrament.[+]

58. [+]Subjection.[+]

59. [+][From] further formation [and] discussion [of doctrine] [*Fortbildung, Mitsprechen*].[+]

60. [+]Evangelical doctrine.[+] (See n. 55.)

61. [+][It] finds its antithesis in the wholly external relation of self-consciousness--a relation which, taken by itself, might appear either as the fourth or as the first [representational mode], a despotic, oriental relation, a denial of one's own volition, thinking, etc.[+]
Lasson places this marginal addition in the text, but it really functions more as a footnote to the text.

62. The 1824 lecture transcript reads *für der* instead of *Bürger*.

63. See n. 52.

64. Religious mysteries at Eleusis, in ancient Attica, in worship of Demeter and Persephone.

65. [w]Sensible presence is nothing for itself, nor does consecration make the host into an object of veneration; rather the object exists in faith alone, and thus it is in the consuming and destroying of the sensible that we have union with God and the consciousness of this union of the subject with God. Here the great thought has arisen that, apart from communion and faith, the host is a common, sensible thing: the process truly takes place only in the Spirit of the subject.[w] (12:339; ET 3:133-134.)

66. Lasson omits this last sentence from the Griesheim transcript. See n. 69.

67. See above, p. 257.

68. As indicated in n. 40 above, Lasson makes this section into a subsection of the section entitled "Existence of the Community." However, in the 1824 and 1827 lectures, this section comprises an independent concluding section (it is not found in the 1821 MS. at all). In the 1824 lectures, it is called "Realization of Faith," and in the 1827 lectures, "Realization of the Spirituality of the Community in Universal Actuality" (the latter heading is adopted by the *Werke* in slightly revised form). The wording of both headings occurs in the first paragraph of the 1824 lectures, as does the term used by Lasson for his subsection heading, "Transformation of the Community." However, the term "realization" is more appropriate because in this section Hegel describes three ways in which faith (or the "spirituality of the community") is "realized" in objective reality (or "universal actuality"). To bring out these three modes of worldly realization, we have added subsectional headings at the appropriate points: (a) The World in Its Immediacy and Externality: The Heart, the Church, the Ethical Realm; (b) Abstract Mediation of the Worldly and the Spiritual: Reflection; (c) Realization of Faith in the Concept: Philosophy. We have also found it necessary to change the order of Lasson's text at points in order to preserve Hegel's original structure (see the relevant footnotes).

69. See above, p. 239. Lasson adds the words "in the existence of the community," which are not in the Griesheim transcript. The words actually belong at the end of the preceding "*a*" section (see n. 66). By this change, Lasson makes Hegel's structure conform to his own. What Hegel intends to take up in this section is not the third moment *in* the *existence* of the community, but rather the *realization* of the community *as* the third aspect of the third major element of the Revelatory Religion.

70. Lasson omits this first sentence from the text but provides it in his appendix (II/2:237). See nn. 37, 41.

71. This theme is explicitly developed by Hegel under the category of "objective Spirit" in the *Encyclopedia*, §§ 483 ff., and in the whole of the *Philosophy of Right*. The term used here is *Sittlichkeit* or *Sittliche* (ethics, ethical realm, ethical life, social ethics), not *Moralität*, which refers to the subjective morality of conscience.

72. [w]It is in the organization of the state that the divine passes into the sphere of actuality; the latter is penetrated by the former, and the worldly realm is now justified in and for itself, for its foundation is the divine will, the law of justice and freedom. The true reconciliation, whereby the divine realizes itself in the field of actuality, consists in the ethical and juridical life of the state: this is the true subjection of worldliness.[w] (12:343-344; ET 3:138.)
The source of this passage may be the 1831 lectures; in content it is quite similar to passages in the *Philosophy of Right*.

73. *Reflexion* is a mode of thought that is distinct from sense perception on the one side and conceptual or speculative thinking on the other. Just as a ray of light is thrown back from the surface

of a mirror, so "reflective" thinking seeks to know objects not in
their immediacy but as derivative, mediated, reflected. It attempts
to discover the universal attributes that govern particular entities;
but like understanding (*Verstand*), of which it is a form, it is unable to grasp the dialectical identity that underlies its diverse
universals. It thus remains a finite, "alienated" mode of thought,
oscillating between an abstract, empty unity on the one hand and a
capricious, arbitrary individualism on the other. (See *Enc.*, §§ 21-
22, 24, 81, 112, 174-175.) The decay and fragmentation of the
bourgeois world to which Hegel alludes in the concluding section of
the 1821 MS. below is attributable in part to the work of "reflection" in modern science, economics, and technology.

74. Hegel here describes the religion of Enlightenment rationalism, which is the ultimate expression of knowledge in the mode
of "reflection" or "understanding" (*Verstand*). See the third paragraph below.

75. This is the only significant discussion of Muhammadanism in
the *Philosophy of Religion* (there is a brief reference to it earlier
in this volume, above p. 189, and another in Part II where it is compared to Judaism [Lasson, II/1: 100]). It lacks a place in Hegel's
schema of determinate religions. The reason appears to be that, unlike the other religions, Islam does not represent an earlier phase
of religious consciousness that has been or can be sublated in the
Absolute Religion. Rather, it stands in antithesis to Christianity
as a contemporary rival. Thus the proper place for its treatment, in
Hegel's scheme, is in the context of various challenges to the Christian Religion in the modern world, which may bring about the transformation of the latter or even its dissolution. Hegel's discussion
of Muhammadanism at this point suggests that it represents the ob-
verse of rationalism, a negative form of rationalism.

76. [w] [For the Enlightenment,] Christianity is valid only as a
set of teachings and Christ only as a messenger sent by God, a
divine teacher, thus a teacher like Socrates, only more distinguished
than he, since he was without sin. This, however, is only to go
half way. Either Christ was only a man or he was the "Son of Man."
Nothing would be left of the divine history, and Christ would be
spoken of as he is in the Koran. The difference between this standpoint [the Enlightenment] and that of Muhammadanism consists only in
the fact that the latter, whose perception is bathed in the ether of
limitlessness, absolutely surrenders, as this infinite independence,
all particular interests, enjoyment, position, individual knowledge,
all vanity. On the other hand, the standpoint of rational Enlightenment gives man an abstract standing for himself, since for it God is
beyond this world and has no affirmative relationship to the subject,
so that man recognizes the affirmative universal only in so far as
it is in him. But he has it in him only abstractly, and therefore
its fulfillment occurs only by means of contingency and caprice. [w]
(12:349; ET 3:144.)

77. Between the "reflective" thinking of the Enlightenment and
Muhammadanism.

78. This section from 1827 is located by Lasson after the second paragraph below of the 1824 transcripts, which take up "the third relation of faith." However, it is clear that this "second stage" belongs to the second form of realization, that of reflection. Hence we have relocated this segment of the 1827 lectures.

79. ^wEach person thus has his own God, Christ, etc. The particularity in which each has his own individual religion, world view, etc., undoubtedly exists in man, but in religion it is absorbed by life in the community. For the truly pious man it no longer has any value and is laid aside.^w (12:346; ET 3:141.)

80. Lasson here footnotes a one-sentence passage from the *Werke*. It is unnecessary to do so because the passage is almost exactly paralleled by the 1827 text below, p. 292 ("The content is justified by the testimony of Spirit . . . and hence also the limits of the form").

81. This concluding paragraph of the 1824 transcripts is located by Lasson in his final section, "Passing Away of the Community and Its Renewal." However, there is no such section in the 1824 lectures, and this paragraph is clearly the conclusion in the 1824 lectures to the section on "Realization of the Community."

82. That is to say, it is not universally available to the whole of humanity in the way that religious knowledge attained by means of representation is. Cf. the discussion of the "partiality" of philosophy in the 1821 MS. below. Thus, although philosophy may be the "highest" stage, it is not as universal as religion, and the latter has a permanent "position" (*Stand*) in the Kingdom of Spirit.

83. _w^wAnd it is contained in the better dogmatic theology of our time.^w (12:351; ET 3:146.)

84. 12:353-354 (ET 3:148-149). This passage from the *Werke* is placed by Lasson in a footnote at the end of the second paragraph of text from the 1827 lecture transcript below. However, the passage clearly relates to the discussion of content and form in the paragraph just above, and thus its more logical location is here. Also, there seems little reason to doubt that this is authentic material from the 1831 lectures. For these reasons, and because this is a well-known and important passage in the *Werke*, we have placed it in the text rather than in a footnote, and at this point.

85. A reference to Luther's translation of Phil. 4:7.

86. This concluding paragraph of the 1827 transcripts is, like that of 1824, located by Lasson in his final section. However, this paragraph is clearly the conclusion in the 1827 lectures to the section on "Realization of the Community."

87. MS. heading: "c) Passing Away of the Community"
Lasson makes this section into the final subsection of the section entitled "Existence of the Community." However in the 1821 MS., it comprises an independent concluding section; it is not

found in the 1824 and 1827 lectures, and is replaced in them by the
preceding section, "Realization of the Community." Lasson adds to
the section title the words "and Its Renewal"--an unjustifiable
editorial interference (he does distinguish the original title from
his addition by means of quotation marks) because Hegel makes no
reference to a "renewal" of the community in this concluding section of the 1821 MS., although Lasson tries to provide for it by including the final paragraphs of the 1824 and 1827 lectures in this
section. Lasson has been accused by certain critics of an attempted
"Christianization" of Hegel at this point--the only evidence for
such a charge in his editorial work. It should be kept in mind,
however, that this negative or ambivalent conclusion is found only
in the earliest version of Hegel's lectures; it is lacking in the
1824, 1827, and 1831 series.

In addition to the matters of title and structure, Lasson's
procedure in this final section, one of the most difficult in the
manuscript from an editorial point of view, is especially problematic. He mislocates the first three paragraphs of the section,
he misreads several difficult words, and his editorial insertions
are sometimes off the mark. Our corrections are based on an analysis
of the microfilm of the manuscript and on information provided by
Jaeschke in correspondence with the editor. Jaeschke concurs with
our reorganization of the section.

88. Lasson locates this paragraph just before the concluding
paragraph of the MS., where it makes little sense. However, it
actually occurs immediately after the heading at the top of MS. p.
104a. (See n. 91.) Our relocation of the paragraph parallels the
order of the *Werke*.

89. Note the interplay in this paragraph between *Untergehen*
(perishing, passing under), *Übergang* (passing over), and *Vergehen*
(passing away).

90. Cf. Matt. 16:18. The reference in the biblical text is
not to the teaching of Christ but to the church.

91. A doublet to these two sentences occurs on the preceding
page of the MS., p. 103b, followed by an empty space: "Since [we
have spoken] of the origin and then of the existence and preservation of the Christian Religion, an empirical description of the condition [in which it presently finds itself needs to be undertaken.]
It might occur to us to compare it with the age of the Roman Empire."
Lasson begins his version of the section with this doublet. However, apparently Hegel decided, after a false start on MS. p. 103b,
to restart the final section on the top of p. 104a with a heading
and the preceding paragraph, followed by these two sentences.

92. Lasson locates this paragraph after the next two, forming
the first part of the paragraph beginning, "[In order to cultivate]
faith in objective truth . . . ." However, in the manuscript this
segment of the paragraph immediately follows the preceding two sentences. At the end of it occurs a sign (#) designating that the
next two paragraphs in the margin should be inserted at this point.
Moreover, Hegel added an α and a β to specify the order of the first

two points. Following Jaeschke, we read the text of the first sentence as follows: "In wie wenigen Lehrbüchern, könnte man fragen,
[wird] noch für wahr gehalten dieser Inhalt des christlichen
Glaubens?" instead of Lasson's reading: "In wie wenigen Lehrbüchern
[ist noch von der Lehre der Kirche die Rede?]. Was wird, könnte
man fragen, noch für wahr gehalten [von] diesem Inhalt des christlichen Glaubens?"

93. Reading *das Vernünftige notwendig* instead of Lasson's *das
vernünftig Notwendige.*

94. The punctuation of the preceding two sentences has been
revised.

95. The MS. reads *weil* instead of *was.*

96. *Wenn* appears in the MS. and should not be bracketed.

97. At approximately this point the paragraph passes into the
margin. One possible explanation is that the paragraph originally
ended with the words, "The salt [has] lost its savor," followed by
the concluding paragraph, "[In fact] religion [must] take refuge
in philosophy . . . ." When Hegel added to the manuscript, he
originally wrote into the right hand margin of MS. p. 104a, then,
by means of another sign (#), made a transition to empty space at
the bottom of p. 103b for the next three paragraphs, whereupon the
text returns to the concluding paragraph at the bottom of 104a.

98. Reading *Spitze der Ausklärung, befriedigt in sich*, instead of Lasson's *skeptische der Ausklärung, befriedigt in sich.* The
word play between *Aufklärung* (the standard German term for *the* Enlightenment, lit. "clearing up") and *Ausklärung* (lit. "clearing out")
cannot be expressed in English; later Engels made it famous.

99. What Hegel means by *gedrungenbleibende Vernunft* is not
clear. In the manuscript the word is difficult to decipher; perhaps
another term is intended, although the *Werke* offers the same reading.

100. MS. inscription: "Concluded 25 August 1821. Repeated
several times."
In the first edition of the *Werke* (1832), material from the
concluding section of the 1821 MS. was lacking entirely. One of
the notable changes of the second edition (1840) was its provision
of this extraordinary conclusion, but in a form significantly different from that found in the MS. itself. The most probable explanation is that Bruno Bauer (the editor of the second edition) in-
terwove passages from the now-lost Henning transcript of the 1821
lectures (see the Editor's Introduction). If this is correct, and
if Henning's transcription was accurate, then we may have in this
case certain modifications introduced by Hegel himself when he delivered the lecture. However, on disputed points it is safer to
follow the text of the manuscript, since we can be reasonably certain of what Hegel wrote down, less so of what he may actually have
said.

To illustrate the differences, and to provide as much data as possible on how Hegel may have ended his 1821 lectures, it seems advisable to reproduce in full the concluding section from the second edition of the *Werke* (this of course is not done by Lasson himself). The following should be noted in particular: (1) The *Werke* omits Hegel's statement in the MS. that the "perishing" (*Untergehen*) --which actually entails a passing over (*Übergang*) to the Kingdom of Heaven--applies only to individual subjects, not to the community; and also that the "passing away" (*Vergehen*) of the religious community pertains only to its external, contingent forms as perceived by the world, not its true substance. (2) Following the MS. statement, "To speak of a passing away would mean to end on a discordant note," the *Werke* adds: "Only, how can it be helped? This discordant note is present in actuality." (3) In the *Werke* the last sentence of the text concludes as follows: ". . . are not the *immediate* practical business and concern of philosophy"--as though to imply that in the long run the practical concerns of the world are indeed the concern of philosophy.

^wBut if now, after having considered the *origin* and *existence* of the community, we see that in attaining realization it falls into a state of inner discord in its spiritual actuality, then its realization appears to be at the same time its *passing away*. But ought we to speak here of a *perishing* when the Kingdom of God is founded eternally, when the Holy Spirit as such lives eternally in its community, and when the gates of hell are not to prevail against the church? To speak of a passing away would mean to end on a discordant note.

Only, how can it be helped? This discordant note is present in actuality. Just as in the age of the Roman Empire, because universal unity based on religion had disappeared and the divine was profaned, and because, further, universal political life was helpless and inactive, lacking in confidence, reason took refuge only in the form of private rights; or, because what exists in and for itself was abandoned, individual well-being was elevated to the rank of an end--so too is it now. Moral opinions, personal views and convictions without objective truth, have attained authority, and the mania for private rights and enjoyments is the order of the day. When the time is fulfilled and what is required is justification by the concept, then the actuality of the unity of the internal and the external no longer exists in immediate consciousness and is not justified by faith. The harshness of an objective command, an external support, and the power of the state can effect nothing here; the process of decay has gone too deep for that. When the Gospel is no longer preached to the poor, when the salt has lost its savor, and all the foundations have been tacitly removed, then the people, for whose ever-insistent reason the truth can exist only in the form of representation, no longer know how to help their interior impulses. They are nearest to the condition of infinite anguish, but since love has been perverted into a love and an enjoyment from which all anguish is absent, they seem to be abandoned by their teachers. The latter have, to be sure, helped themselves by means of reflection, and have found their satisfaction in finitude, in subjectivity and its virtuosity, and precisely thereby in vanity; but the substantial kernel of the people cannot find its satisfaction there.

For us, philosophical knowlege has resolved this discord, and
the purpose of these lectures was precisely to reconcile reason
with religion, to recognize the latter in its manifold forms as
necessary, and to rediscover in the Revelatory Religion the truth
and the Idea. But this reconciliation is only a partial one, lacking outward universality. Philosophy forms in this connection a
sanctuary apart, and those who serve in it constitute an isolated
order of priests, who must not mix with the world, and whose work
is to preserve the possession of truth. How the empirical present
day is to find its way out of its discord, and how things are to
turn out for it, are questions that must be left up to it and are
not the *immediate* practical business and concern of philosophy.[w]
(12:354-356; ET 3:149-151.)

COMMENTARY ON THE TEXT

This commentary does not purport to offer a detailed exegesis of every difficult passage or obscure reference in the text, nor does it provide a summary of the secondary literature as it bears on specific issues. To undertake an analysis in detail would require a separate volume of comparable length, similar to the growing number of commentaries on the *Phenomenology of Spirit*. Rather the purpose of the present undertaking is to offer, within brief compass, an interpretation of the major theological issues and an overview of Hegel's theses as they develop in each of the sections of the text. The section-by-section arrangement will facilitate the correlation of commentary and text without a complicated apparatus. Matters concerning the sources, structure, and arrangement of the sections are taken up in the footnotes, and the commentary avoids repetition of materials found in the notes.

Readers are referred also to my chapter on Hegel in Volume I of *Religious Thought in the Nineteenth Century*, ed. Ninian Smart et al. (Cambridge: Cambridge University Press, 1979). Although some duplication of material has been unavoidable, the chapter offers a general overview of Hegel's religious thought in its philosophical context and includes a bibliographical essay, while the Appendix provides a more detailed discussion of the present text. The duplicated material is used with the permission of Cambridge University Press.

I.1. The Concept of the Revelatory Religion

The Christian Religion is the Revelatory, Consummate, Absolute Religion because in it the *concept* of
religion has become an *object* to itself, is *posited*,
comes fully to *consciousness*--the very same concept that
had been struggling for articulation throughout the history of religion.

Hegel sets forth a detailed definition of the "concept of religion" in the first major division of his
Lectures on the Philosophy of Religion.[1] In the opening
section of the third part, he reiterates this definition
of religion, which is now shown to be identical with the
content of the Christian Religion. "Religion, in accord
with its general concept, is the consciousness of God,
consciousness of absolute essence" (p. 2). As such it
constitutes a *relationship* between finite Spirit and infinite or absolute Spirit (pp. 4 ff.). This relationship may be viewed from two sides: first, from the side
of the *rise* or *elevation* of finite consciousness to the
absolute (the "phenomenological" structure of religion);
second, as the *self*-consciousness of God who knows *himself*, comes to be for himself, in the human consciousness
of him (the "speculative" or "theo-logical" structure of
religion; see esp. pp. 9-10). Thus if religion is defined as "consciousness of God," the "of" is to be construed as both an objective and a subjective genitive.
Hegel criticizes in various ways all "abstract" views
that tend to dissolve the religious relationship into
either a bad, unrelated infinitude or an autonomous, self-
subsistent finitude. God *is* infinite and objective, and
we know him as such because he manifests himself openly
and absolutely. But he is not merely an object that
stands above and beyond us; rather he indwells our subjective religious consciousness as its inmost essence.
"The consciousness of God means that the finite consciousness has this God, who is its essence, as an ob-

ject. . . . The content and object of religion is this
whole--*consciousness relating itself to its essence*,
knowing itself as it knows its essence and knowing its
essence as its own" (p. 2). Or as Hegel remarks in another context, "Spirit . . . is the living process by
which the implicit unity of divine and human nature becomes explicit, is brought forth" (p. 46). This process
epitomizes religion and is the central content of the
Revelatory Religion, which is the Religion of Spirit par
excellence.

I.2. Characteristics of the Revelatory Religion

The "characteristics" (*Bestimmungen*) enumerated in
this section are four in number, the most fundamental of
which is *revelation* or *revealedness* (*Offenbarung, Offen-
baren*), from which this religion derives its name. "*What*
God is, and the fact that he is known *as* he is, not
merely in historical or some similar fashion as in the
other religions, is made manifest [*offenbar*] in it. Open
manifestation [*die offenbare Manifestation*] is its character and content, namely, the revelation, manifestation,
being of God for consciousness" (p. 11). Revealedness
constitutes the very essence of God, who discloses himself eternally in and as the process of self-diremption
and return-to-self. "A Spirit that is not open or manifest [*offenbar*] is no Spirit" (p. 13). Thus the revelatory character of the Christian Religion refers in the
first instance not to *something* that is revealed but
rather to the primary attribute of God. In the final
analysis there is nothing concealed or mysterious about
God; he makes himself utterly open and is rationally comprehensible. Hence the Revelatory Religion is also the
Absolute Religion in the sense that absolute knowledge of
the absolute is attained--but in the mode appropriate to
religious representation, not philosophical conceptuali-
zation.

Truth and *freedom* appear to be dialectically related
characteristics, both closely associated with revealedness. To know God in truth is to know him *as he is*, and
he is known as he is in and through his revealedness. To
know something as the truth is to know it in its objectivity, but without its being alien or strange to the
subjectivity of the knower. Jewish Religion achieved the
first aspect of this requirement but not the second, while
Greco-Roman Religion failed in the knowledge of truth,
since its finite gods (whether beautiful or expedient)
were ultimately illusory, and true reality--fate, neces-
sity--remained concealed and inscrutable. In regard to
freedom, however, Christianity approximates Greek Religion
rather than Jewish. In his discussion of the Greeks,
Hegel suggests that God must become "the God of *free* men"
--of men who stand in a free relation to God so that God
and man can say of each other, "That is Spirit of my
Spirit" (*Werke*, 12:93-95; ET 2:222-224). This freedom is
now fully actualized in Christianity as the religion of
freedom par excellence--a theme more explicitly developed
in the *Philosophy of Right* and the *Lectures on the Philosophy of History* than in the present text.

The concrete form in which truth and freedom appear
in Christianity is that of *reconciliation*, which is the
universal divine process by which the separation and
estrangement consequent upon the positing of nature and
finite Spirit as genuinely "other" than God is overcome.

*I.3. The Positivity and Spirituality of the Revelatory
      Religion*

In the 1827 lectures a discussion of the "positivity" (*Positivität*) of the Christian Religion replaces the
consideration of its other *Bestimmungen* in the 1821 and
1824 lectures. The *revelatory* (*offenbar*) religion is
also a *revealed* (*geoffenbart*) religion, which is to say

that it is a *positive* religion, given to consciousness in sensible, historical fashion. Hegel came to recognize that positivity is necessary because "*everything must come to us in external fashion*" (p. 17), and because external authority plays an essential role in human affairs, as positive law indicates as well as positive revelation (a corpus of normative, authoritative doctrines). Yet the essential, rational truth of the Revelatory Religion, while mediated positively, derives solely from its *spirituality* and can be verified only by the witness of the Spirit, not by historical proofs (see Chap. V.2). In contrast to the whole debate in late Enlightenment thought over reason vs. revelation, Hegel ingeniously claimed that the *revealed* religion is also one in which reason and truth are made open, manifest (*offenbar*). The term "revelatory" gathers up both the positivity and the spirituality of this religion.

For the significance of the last paragraph of this section (p. 25) concerning Hegel's understanding of the distinction between historical (*historisch*) and conceptual or speculative modes of interpretation, see n. 28.

I.4. *Transition to the Revelatory Religion*

In the 1827 lectures, as a means of describing the "transition" (*Übergang*) to the third and final division of his Philosophy of Religion, Hegel offers a "survey" (*Rückblick*) of the preceding two divisions. Our commentary at this point is based not on the particular survey provided by this section but on a study of the whole of the Philosophy of Religion and on an attempt to uncover its ingenious dialectical structure.[2] The most efficient way of proceeding is to offer a schema (p. 318) that illustrates this structure. The work as a whole is divided into three major parts: Concept of Religion, Determinate Religion, and Revelatory Religion. These in turn corres-

318

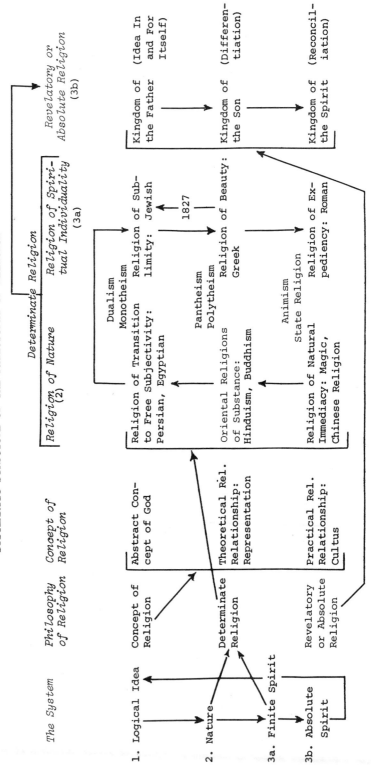

SYSTEMATIC STRUCTURE OF THE PHILOSOPHY OF RELIGION

pond to a modification of the threefold structure of
Hegel's speculative system: the Logical Idea, Nature-
Finite Spirit, and Absolute Spirit. The modification is
required because the second moment in the dialectic of
religion, that of differentiation, corresponds to both
Nature and Finite Spirit, which, in the system as a
whole,[3] are treated as separate moments, while the third
moment of religion, that of reconciliation, corresponds
to Absolute Spirit, which represents the telos that encompasses all of the preceding moments. Underlying this
modified triadic structure is of course Hegel's version
of the trinitarian process of the divine life: the Idea
of God in and for itself (the "Father"), God's existence
in self-differentiation or other-being (the "Son"), and
his self-reconciliation or return-to-self (the "Spirit").
Hence the culminating attainment of Hegel's Philosophy of
Religion--the philosophical transfiguration of the doctrine of the Trinity as set forth in the Christian Re-
ligion--also serves as its foundation.

Each of the major parts of the Philosophy of Religion is further divided in accordance with this triadic
structure. Constituting the Concept of Religion are,
first, the "abstract concept" of God (the religious "object" as infinite, absolute, universal substance), and
then two modalities of religious "relationship" in which
the religious subject comes into play. The first of
these, the "theoretical" aspect of the relationship, subsists in the several forms of religious consciousness, of
which "representation" (*Vorstellung*) is definitive, while
the second, the "practical" relationship, is manifest in
cultus or worship; these two correspond in turn to the
second and third moments of the divine life, differentiation-estrangement and reconciliation-return.

The organization of Determinate Religion is more complex but, within each of its two basic divisions, which
treat the religions of nature and of spiritual individuality, the same triadic structure obtains. Hegel begins

with an analysis of the primitive religions of "natural
immediacy" or magic (animism), which because of their belief in universal spiritual presences that pervade and
empower all things, correspond in a crude way to the
highest religion, that of Spirit and reconciliation.
Thence he progresses to the religions that posit the divine as substantial power that is other than human yet
also its universal ground (Hindu and Buddhist pantheism),
and finally to a dualism between the natural and the
spiritual in which the latter continues to be represented
by quasi-sensuous images such as "light" (Persian and
Egyptian religion).

The religions of spiritual individuality correspond
to this progression but in *reverse order*. Judaism, the
Religion of Sublimity, parallels the highest of the nature religions but moves beyond it to a genuine monotheism that understands God as "spiritual subjective
unity" in radical distinction from the created world.
The otherness of God and world is never really overcome
for Judaism, which remains fixated on the one, transcendent God and generates the religious condition of anguish
(*Schmerz*). In sharp contrast, the immanence of Greek religion celebrates the nobility and freedom of the human
Spirit and the beauty of its bodily form, of which the
gods are projections. Hegel regarded Jewish and Greek
religion as representing equally valid and necessary,
although complementary, religious principles, and in 1827
he reversed the customary order in which he treated them.
In the other lecture series (most clearly in 1824), he
moved from Jewish to Greek religion, depicting them as,
respectively, religions of transcendence and immanence,
monotheism and polytheism, paralleling the religions of
light and substance, anticipating the Kingdoms of the
Father and the Son. Finally, Roman religion represents
a reversion to the expedient or utilitarian function
first evident in the religion of magic. The end sought
by religion is happiness, and the collectivized content

of happiness is the state. The Romans divinized the
state, and the gods they invented or had plundered from
Greek and Egyptian temples were made functionaries of
state interests. However, such finite gods proved to be
intrinsically unsatisfying, and thus the religion whose
end was happiness issued in the absolute unhappiness
(*Unglück*) of Spirit.

The truth of the reconciliation of finite and infinite could arise not in the Greco-Roman world but only
among a people who possessed the pure Idea of the One,
yet were painfully separated from it. The confluence of
Jewish anguish (vis-à-vis the unattainable transcendent
God) and Greco-Roman unhappiness (vis-à-vis the unredemp-
tive character of finitude) marks the moment of transition to the Absolute or Revelatory Religion. The structure of the latter will be considered in the next section, but it is worth noting here that the Revelatory
Religion not only instantiates the final moment of
Hegel's religious system but also encompasses within itself all three of the moments, whereas each of the Determinate Religions embodies only one of these moments. The
formal parallel is between the Revelatory Religion and
the two main *divisions* of Determinate Religion, nature
and spiritual individuality, which finally are sublated
in the Absolute Religion.

I.b. Division of the Subject; and
II.2. The Development of the Idea of God

These two sections essentially parallel each other,
the first being found in the 1827 lectures and the second
in the 1821 and 1824 lectures. The development of Hegel's
structural schema for the Revelatory Religion is described in n. 20, p. 102. The mature division at which he
first arrived in 1824 sets forth the structure of Christianity in terms of three "spheres," "moments," or "elements" in the "development of the Idea of God." These
moments are not simply contingent occasions in the out-

ward manifestation of God but rather have their basis in
the immanent trinitarian life of God, i.e., in the "divine history" itself. This becomes even more explicit
in 1831, when the moments are referred to as three determinations of the divine "self-revelation," and they are
now given the specific trinitarian designation of the
three Kingdoms of Father, Son, and Spirit.

(a) The Idea of God In and For Itself. God subsists
in his *eternity* prior to the creation of the world and
outside the world--the *immanent* or *preworldly Trinity*,
which includes within itself the dialectic of differentiation and return-to-self of the universal, absolute
One: the Kingdom of the *Father*. In this first moment
God is known to us in the mode of *thought*. (Chap. II.3
of this edition.)

(b) Divine Self-Differentiation and Incarnation.
God creates a world of nature and finite Spirit, posits
an *other* than himself in an act of separation, differentiation, diremption, yet himself enters into and is *implicitly* identical with this otherness: the Kingdom of
the *Son*. This entails a passage from the preworldly to
the *worldly* or *economic Trinity*. Here God is known to us
in the mode of *representation* and sensible perception:
we may speak of the "appearance" or "incarnation" of God
in specific temporal-historical events of the *past*.
This second moment has two subordinate motifs: first,
the theme of differentiation, estrangement, and the
exigency for reconciliation (Chap. III of this edition);
second, that of the history of redemption and reconciliation (Chap. IV). The lecture series differ as to when
this second motif (the "reversal" and beginning of the
"return") is actually initiated. Is it with the creation of human being (1821) or with the sending of the
Son (1824, 1827)? In either case it anticipates the
third major moment but is distinguished from it as its
positive-historical foundation.

(c) Divine Self-Reconciliation and Spiritual Presence. God re-unites with himself what has been differentiated and estranged from him--the moment of redintegra-
tion, of return-to-self, of sublation of the difference:
the Kingdom of the *Spirit*. Here the reconciliation initiated in the second stage of the second moment is
brought to completion. Since the latter part of the
second moment and the whole of the third are concerned
with different phases of the process of reconciliation
(the first historical and initiatory, the second present
and fulfilling), Hegel has some difficulty in establishing a distinct boundary between them. God now is known
to us in the mode of *feeling, experience, subjectivity*,
i.e., in the life of the *cultus*. He is no longer simply
thought or represented but rather is known in the mode of
communion. The time is *now*, the *present*, the moment of
spiritual presence. And the place where God is found is
no longer outside the world or in the world in an objec-
tive-historical mode; rather it is the "inner place," the
intersubjectivity of the *community* of faith. (Chap. V of
this edition.)

Between these three moments Hegel establishes something like a triple mediation, analogous to the mediation
that obtains between the branches of philosophy (Logical
Idea, Nature, Spirit). First, the Father mediates between the Son and the Spirit: this means that neither
positivity nor spiritual presence may be collapsed into
each other; rather both are essential and irreducible
moments in the dialectic of the divine life. Second, the
Son mediates between the Father and the Spirit: this
means that the "primordial" and the "consequent" natures
of God are distinguished, mediated by the events of creation, fall, incarnation and redemption--events by which
the divine Idea is "existentialized," "spiritualized."
Finally, the Spirit mediates between the Father and the
Son: this means that the unity and difference of God,
the distinction between creator and creature, finite and

infinite, does not remain ultimate and unbridgeable; estrangement is not the final word but rather reconciliation. These mediations are often forgotten when Hegel is
accused of one or another reductionist interpretation of
the Christian Religion.

II.1.   The Abstract Concept of God

As indicated by n. 2, p. 99, this section fits only
awkwardly into the structure for the Revelatory Religion
at which Hegel finally arrived, and in 1827 and 1831 he
transposed it to the Concept of Religion where it was
incorporated into his defense of the proofs for the existence of God (ontological, cosmological, teleological).
As such it is not part of but is *presupposed* by the concrete representation of the three moments of the Idea of
God in the Christian Religion. We have retained it in
its present location--in fact *between* the Introduction
and the Development of the Idea of God--because it occurs
there in the 1821 and 1824 lectures. But it seems appropriate not to provide a commentary on it here since it is
not an *integral* part of the present text; and more im-
portantly, an adequate analysis of Hegel's innovative
approach to the question of the proofs for God's existence would require more space than can be alloted to
this Appendix.[4]

II.3.   The Idea of God In and For Itself: The Trinity

The doctrine of the Trinity, in Hegel's view, is the
"central point" and "absolute truth" of the whole of
philosophy (p. 79), the "fundamental determination" of
the Christian Religion (*Werke*, 11:40; ET 1:39). When he
uses the term "Trinity," he ordinarily means the immanent,
logical, or preworldly Trinity, i.e., the *actus purus* of
the inner divine life, the process of diremption and return contained *within* the eternal Idea.

The immanent character of this process is brought

out by the suggestion that what is involved is a "play" or "show" of distinction and sublation, "a play of love with itself in which no seriousness is attributed to other-being," (pp. 87, 117). Love is in fact the most intrinsic attribute of the triune divine life. Love entails both a distinguishing of two and a sublation of the distinction, so that the two are actually one. Love means to have one's self-consciousness not in oneself but in another, to find oneself in the *other* as one's *own*. It describes a *union mediated by relationship and hence difference*. This union is what constitutes personhood or personality. To be a person means to be reflected into self through distinction, to find one's self-consciousness in another, to give up one's abstract existence and to win it back as concrete and personal by being absorbed into the other.

This means, then, that God's being is intrinsically personal: he is the one true and perfect person. However, there are not three "persons" in God as represented by traditional church dogma, for this notion, when pursued literally, leads to three Gods and the loss of divine subjectivity and unity. The names "Father," "Son," and "Spirit" are figurative, childlike ways of expressing the three moments constitutive of the interior dialectic of the divine life--unity, differentiation, return; or universality, particularity, and individuality. In truth, all three are "Spirit," and Spirit represents the result or totality, the end of the divine life that is also the beginning. When the understanding (*Verstand*) encounters the trinitarian "persons" it attempts to count them and puzzles, "How can three equal one?" Comparable puzzlement appears in the prefigurations of the Trinity in the triads of Hindu and Greek religion, of Plato and the Pythagoreans, of Alexandrian Neoplatonism and Gnosticism, and finally of Böhme and Kant. Hegel makes a good deal of these prefigurations because they represent "fermentations" of the Idea of the Trinity as the true category. But they all

reflect the finite perspective of the understanding,
whereas the Trinity can be properly grasped only speculatively. The speculative Idea of God's self-differentia-
tion/sublation resolves the contradictions inherited from
tradition, both pagan and Christian, and grasps the true
μυστήριον of God's being.

     Implicit throughout Hegel's work, although rarely
discussed explicitly, is the correspondence between the
immanent and the economic Trinities. To become a concrete, spiritual, actual God, the logical or immanent
Trinity (the "primordial" nature of God in Whiteheadian
language) must be reenacted in the economic Trinity (the
creation of the world and finite Spirit as other-than-God
and the sublation of the difference). In this sense God
is dependent or "consequent" upon the world to become God
in the true and actual sense. God is God-in-process.
Yet this dependence is already posited as the immanent
intermediation of the logical Trinity; and the dependence
of God upon the world is therefore independence, the
necessity of creation is the purest freedom, the divine
self-othering is gratuitous love. An ultimate harmony
prevails between the primordial and consequent natures of
God--or, in more classical language, between the inward
"processions" and the outward "missions" of the Trinity
--without the two being collapsed into an undifferentiated identity. The otherness within the divine life is
the condition of possibility for otherness as it appears
in the form of the finite world and consciousness. Conversely, the economic Trinity (in truth the whole πλήρωμα
of God and world) gives actuality and life to the inner
distinctions, encompassing the immanent Trinity as the
first of its moments.[5]

     Represented schematically, the Hegelian double
Trinity looks something like the figure on the following
page.

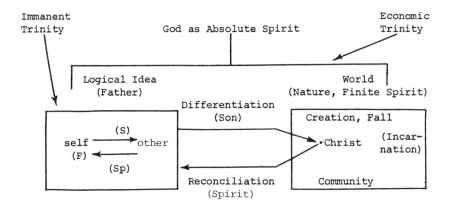

III.1. *Creation and Preservation of the World*

Hegel's transition to the economic Trinity actually occurs when he takes up the theme of the creation and preservation of a finite world that is genuinely "other" than God. To be sure, creation *corresponds* to the second moment of the interior dialectic of the divine life; but Hegel makes it clear many times that the created world is not simply *identical* with God in the moment of self-differentiation (the "eternal Son of the Father"). This would entail a crude pantheism, which Hegel consistently avoids.[6] "It is only the picture--floating in the indefinite blue--of the world as *one thing, the all*, that could ever be considered capable of combining with God: only on that assumption could philosophy be supposed to teach that God is the world: for if the world were taken as it is, as everything, as the endless lot of empirical existence, then it would hardly have been even held possible to suppose a pantheism which asserted of such stuff that it is God." (*Enc.*, § 573; cf. §§ 50, 151.)

Hegel's position may rather be described as that of *panentheism*: the world exists *in* God but is not identical *with* God. On the one hand, the divine Idea retains an ontological primacy vis-à-vis the world in the sense that the divine differentiation *ad intra* is the condition for the possibility of creating a world of nature and

finite Spirit *ad extra* whose destination is *also* to be
the otherness of God. On the other hand, the moment of
divine self-othering must take on "the determinacy of
other-*being*, of an existent entity," in order for there
to be *genuine* difference. Thus the absolute Idea "releases the other to exist as a free and independent
being" (p. 118). The element of genuine difference is
essential for both God and world. God becomes a concrete,
"spiritual" God only by actually appearing in the finite
world he has posited as distinct from himself. In *this*
sense God is dependent on the world: "Without the world
God is not God" (*Werke*, 11:194; ET 1:200). Conversely,
the world needs the difference if it is to retain its actual contingency and empirical existence, its continuous
dependence on divine creativity and preservation, and is
not to be absorbed acosmically into the Godhead. But the
element of explicit and present *difference* presupposes an
implicit and teleological *identity*, for the destination
of both God and world is to achieve actuality together,
to move towards union in an eschatological consummation.
The quality of the natural world, as a moment in this
process, is precisely to sublate itself, "to pass over,"
"to take itself back into the final Idea" (p. 112). As
a dialectical thinker, Hegel can never speak of identity
without difference, nor of difference without identity:
the truth lies in their mediation. In this respect he
shares with Augustine, Aquinas, and the medieval and
German mystics the great Neo-Platonic schema of *exitus et
reditus*, emanation and return. In such a schema, nature
and the created order may be understood to be *genuinely*
different from the creative ground of being but not *radically* or *wholly* different, because an underlying identity
is sustained by God as the beginning and the end of all
things.[7]

Hegel describes briefly the two constituent elements
of the world: nature and finite human Spirit. Nature may
be grasped as a "system," an "organization," in which the

divine Idea is reflected; hence nature can be a revelation of God, as the nature religions attest, and as Hegel
sought to demonstrate in his Philosophy of Nature (the
second part of the *Encyclopedia*). When life passes over
into Spirit, human being emerges. Finite human Spirit
begins from immediacy and is intrinsically a process of
raising itself up from the sensible to the infinite by
means of thinking. Two aspects of human being may be
distinguished: on the one hand, the *concept* or *possibility* of man as the *imago Dei*, as implicitly divine; and on
the other hand, his *actual existence* "according to nature," which does not correspond to the concept and is
ungodly. It is the second of these that is thematized
in the latter two sections of this chapter.

III.2. Man as Finite and as Natural Spirit

     Although man is indubitably a finite and natural
being, his distinctive quality vis-à-vis the whole of the
natural order is his spirituality, *according to which* he
is intended to exist. To exist the other way, "according
to nature," or as "natural man" (see n. 23, p. 164),
means to constitute one's existence, to establish the
criteria for one's life, according to the immediacy, particularity, and externality of physical nature; it means
to allow one's desires, appetites, physical needs, and
private self-seeking to dominate the will rather than
thought. Nature itself is not evil; but when it is allowed to serve as the criterion and telos of human being
it becomes the occasion for evil. Hegel is here clearly
attempting to translate the Pauline anthropology (κατὰ
πνεῦμα, κατὰ σάρκα) into his own idiom, as well as to
distinguish his position from that of the Enlightenment
and Kant. He devotes considerable attention to refuting
the Enlightenment notion that man is either good or evil
"by nature." There is a sense in which man is *both* good
and evil "by nature." If "by nature" one intends to refer to man's *implicit* being, his having been created in

the image of God, then he is good; but at the same time
this implicit being is evil in so far as it suggests the
state of natural immediacy, from which man as Spirit must
separate himself. Because of the ambiguity of the phrase,
it is misleading to claim that "by nature" man is either
good or evil. In fact, both good and evil presuppose a
stepping forth from the state of nature and the emergence
of consciousness, knowledge, responsibility, and freedom
of choice. (The discussion of this matter is clearest
in the 1827 lectures, pp. 137-142.)

Knowledge or cognition (*Erkenntnis*) is an act of
judgment (*Urteil*) that posits separation, negation, disunion in the process of arriving dialectically at reflective syntheses beyond the undifferentiated identity of
the precognitive natural state. It thus gives rise to
what Hegel calls "estrangement" (*Entfremdung*), which is
not strictly speaking in itself evil but rather is the
inherent condition of other-being at the stage of consciousness or knowledge. Estrangement seems to be Hegel's
way of describing the instability or fragility intrinsic
to the human condition as both finite (natural) and spiritual (free, conscious). Estrangement, however, is the
precondition or occasion of evil because in virtue of it
human beings knowingly choose to actualize the state of
separation, to exist in self-isolation and gratification
of natural desires, to exist "according to nature." At
the same time the estranged person *knows* the antithesis
within himself between good and evil; he recognizes that
he is the one who is evil. Hence the knowledge of estrangement both *occasions* evil and *recognizes* the fact of
evil when it occurs; without the recognition, there would
be no evil in the proper sense.

Estrangement gives rise not only to evil but also to
the exigency for reconciliation, as may be seen when estrangement is associated with the anguish of Jewish religion and the misery or unhappiness of Greco-Roman religion. Anguish arises from the awareness of the un-

bridgeable contradiction between good and evil, God and
man, whereas misery expresses the inability of humanity
ever to find happiness in finite and worldly ends. When
the awareness of estrangement and evil attained the infinite degree--or "when the time had fully come"--there
arose a recognition of the need for universal, divine,
absolute reconciliation.

The form of evil constantly emphasized by Hegel
represents, in terminology made familiar by Kierkegaard,
Barth, and Reinhold Niebuhr, the sin of finitude, despair, sloth, sensuality. Notably, Hegel fails to thema-
tize the dialectically opposite form of sin to which
these theologians have called attention, and which in the
post-Hegelian context has been perceived as the more radical form, namely, the sin of infinitude or pride, of
idolatrous self-projection into divinity. The reasons
become partially clear from the way in which Hegel reads
the story of the Fall.

III.3. *The Representation of the Fall*

Hegel is attracted to the story of the Fall because
of its profound attempt to understand the dialectical relationship of knowledge to both good and evil. However,
the imaginative, mythical form in which the story is cast
is unable to grasp the dialectic as such but rather represents it as a series of contradictions and ambiguities.
The story is unable to resolve these contradictions but
merely displays them, indeed in its own contradictory
form. Hegel's exegesis seems intended primarily to ex-
pose these contradictions and to replace them with his
own speculative version of the origin of evil. For example, with regard to *knowledge*: on the one hand it is
prohibited by God as the source of evil and death, yet on
the other hand it is seen to constitute the essence of
human Spirit, the very likeness of God in man (God himself confirms this dictum of the serpent, Gen. 3:22). On
the question of *mortality* and *immortality*: is man without

sin immortal (as implied by the notion that death is the
penalty for sin), or does he rather become so for the
first time only when he has eaten of the tree of life?
Hegel himself maintains that mortality is necessarily
connected with finitude and is not a punishment for sin
(see n. 58, p. 167). Despite his bodily mortality, man
attains true immortality through knowledge (just the opposite of the initial prohibition), and the mythical
tree of life is rendered superfluous (perhaps Hegel also
intends to suggest a conflict between the two trees of
the story). Or on the matter of the *expulsion* from the
Garden: is man expelled because he has *already* acquired
eternal knowledge (Gen. 3:17-18), or to *prevent* him from
living forever (3:22-23)? Related to this, is *labor* a
punishment for sin or a nurturing of consciousness?

By contradicting itself in these and other ways, the
story of the Fall points beyond itself to the speculative
truth: knowledge is the spiritual essence of man and intrinsically good, yet when conjoined with finitude it
yields negation, separation, estrangement, and thence
evil. Evil is now seen to be a dialectical necessity in
the rise of consciousness, not an inscrutable, absurd
force. Knowledge entails the "injury of separation,"
yet "heals the wound that it itself is" (pp. 133, 155,
157). Through such an interpretation, Hegel effectively
blunts the profounder insight of the Adamic myth into the
irrational, tragic dimension of evil, and especially
avoids the close association of knowledge and idolatry in
human sin, as well as the role played by temptation and
self-deception.

IV.1. *The Possibility, Necessity, and Actuality of Incarnation*

Despite the central importance of the doctrine of
the incarnation for his thought, Hegel never discusses it
in terms of the language and problematic of classical
Christology: two natures (divine and human), one person

(of the incarnate Logos), hypostatic union, *communicatio idiomatum*, etc. He does not need to because he is working with an anthropology of divine-human union that avoids the conventional aporia of incarnationist Christology. Rather he offers a speculative transfiguration of this doctrine in terms of an argument for the possibility, necessity, and actuality of the incarnation (or "appearance") of God in a single individual (see n. 2, p. 222, and n. 28, p. 225).

The *possibility* of such an incarnation is based on the general concept of "incarnation," meaning, in Hegel's view, the ideal unity or implicit identity of divine and human Spirit, the Idea of reconciliation, the "universal divine Idea." For Hegel, "Idea" is the instantiation of concept or thought by which it is objectified, achieves reality (cf. *Enc.*, § 213). As such, it is equivalent to the classical understanding of "Word" or "Logos" (the outward expression of inner thought), so long as the latter is not hypostatized. Thus when Hegel speaks of the "appearance of the divine Idea," he offers his own version of traditional theological language concerning the "incarnation of the divine Logos." Now this divine Idea--the Idea of divine-human unity--is realized *implicitly* in the *whole* of humanity. This is what Hegel intends by twice quoting the line of Schiller: "From the chalice of the entire realm of Spirits foams forth to God his own infinitude."[8] On the one hand, God is not abstract infinitude, cut off from the possibility of appearing, but is a concrete God, capable of entering into finitude, negation, and suffering, as connoted by Schiller's image of the chalice and Goethe's image of crushed roses in the poem "An Suleika": from the suffering of this *whole* human world there "foams forth to God" his *own* infinite love. On the other hand, humanity is capable of *receiving* this appearance, of being assumed into communion with God, recognizing the universal as *its* goal, as *its own essence* (see especially the passage from the

Werke, n. 9, p. 224).

The question of the *necessity* of the incarnation has two aspects. The first is grounded in the process of self-differentiation intrinsic to the divine life (cf. Chap. II.3). "God, considered in terms of his eternal Idea, *has* to generate the Son, *has* to distinguish himself from himself; he is this process of differentiating, namely, love and Spirit" (p. 191). It is intrinsic to the divine Idea that God should become a concrete, spiritual, *incarnate* God, that he should become absolute *Spirit* and not simply remain the absolute *Idea*. In this sense God "must" *send* the Son into the world; he "must" *appear* under the conditions of finitude and share in its negativity, anguish, and death. Yet this divine necessity, because it is already *internal* to the divine life, is at the same time divine freedom: the preworldly trinitarian "play of love with itself" is complete, apart from its worldly manifestation. Hence it would be appropriate to speak of a "gratuitous" or self-imposed divine necessity.

The second aspect of necessity adheres not to the divine condition but the human. Everything *first* comes to consciousness in an external, empirical fashion, according to Hegel; hence the consciousness of reconciliation first arises not in the form of philosophical speculation but rather in that of historical certainty. "Only what exists in an immediate way, in inner or outer perception, is *certain*. *In order for this divine-human unity to become certain for man, God had to appear in the world in the flesh*" (p. 181). Hegel stresses not only the sensible, positive way that consciousness of divine-human unity must be mediated, but also the fact that this consciousness must *come to* humanity. In view of the estrangement into which the human condition has fallen, the truth must *appear* in order for it to be *recollected*, and incarnation characteristically takes on the aspect of "appearance" (*Erscheinung*) for Hegel.[9]

With regard, finally, to the *actuality* of the incarnation, the Idea of divine-human unity appears in history
not in a multiplicity of incarnations but in *one particular individual*, who is not merely a divine teacher or a
teacher of morality but the "God-Man," the "Son of God,"
because in him the divine Idea is realized *explicitly* and
in its *consummate development*. Why should this be the
case? Because it is only in a single individual that we
find the *concrete* unity of universality and subjectivity,
of infinitude and finitude. The individual represents
the final pinnacle, the fullest actualization, of Spirit
in its subjectivity: "Once is always" (*Einmal ist alle-
mal*) (pp. 172-173).[10] This does not seem quite to
settle the matter, because it is conceivable that such a
concrete unity could be differently manifested in several
individuals. Perhaps principles of efficiency and suf-
ficiency are operative here in an unspoken way, together
with the assumption that ultimacy is in some sense exclusive or unitary. Moreover, if there were several God-
men, each equally consummate, they would have to be compared under an abstract category (such as God-manhood)
and the concreteness associated with the appearance of
the truth would be lost.

How are we to determine whether any particular individual is *this* individual, the one who stands over
against all the others as the ground of their certainty?
This determination, says Hegel, is a matter for history
to make, not philosophy (pp. 191, 242). But *how* is history to be read? How is the claim of the Christian community that Jesus of Nazareth is this individual, the
Christ, to be confirmed? At this point Hegel is not entirely consistent, although his dominant emphasis is
clear. The confirmation that Jesus was the one in whom
the divine Idea was concretely and consummately actualized
is a matter of the *witness of the Spirit* to the community
of faith; it is a proof of the Spirit, not a proof by
miracles or any other sort of merely historical evidence

(see Chap. V.2). Indeed, apart from the witness of the
Spirit, Jesus may be viewed only as an ordinary man in
accord with his external circumstances--a Socrates, a
martyr to the truth. But there is another, less dominant motif that surfaces when Hegel takes up the teaching
of Jesus and his passion and death. Here he purports to
give an account of how the Idea of divine-human unity
takes its course in the history of this individual such
that his temporal presence is able to be a *presentation*
(Darstellung) of the Idea--indeed a presentation that is
"absolutely adequate to the Idea" *(schlechthin der Idee*
gemäss) (n. 15, p. 224, and p. 242). "It is the divine
Idea that courses through this history"; moreover, the
words of Christ, his teachings, "confirm the truth of the
Idea of what he has been for his community" (pp. 200,
190).[11] Statements such as these reflect the utter
seriousness with which Hegel, at least during his Berlin
period, affirms the factual positivity of the incarnation
of the divine Idea in the historical Jesus. It would be
wrong to suggest that he equivocates on the question as
to whether Jesus was *in fact* or was only *believed* to be
the God-man. Rather, his position is that what Jesus was
in fact--his identity as the consummate appearance of the
divine Idea--can be *properly* perceived and affirmed not
in a merely historical but rather in a spiritual mode, by
faith, after his death and removal from the immediacy of
apprehension.

IV.2. The Teaching of Christ

Thus the actual life-history or "story" of Jesus is
a matter of central importance for Hegel. Although his
exegetical procedure is utterly uncritical, manifesting
an indifference or even hostility toward concrete historical questions and critical methods, his theological
insight is often striking. This is evident from his
treatment of the teaching of Jesus, which focuses on the
kingdom of God and love--themes inherited from his early

writings and presented with great religious power.

The *kingdom of God* is not an abstract symbol; rather it means that God passes out of universality into reality, the world, thereby actualizing himself. It is a way of representing the efficacious *presence* of God, who is not a transcendent Lord dwelling in the heavens. It symbolizes reconciliation as an actuality or state of affairs (*Zustand*), a new world-condition (*Weltzustand*), which is not, however, to be understood as an external political condition but as an inward spiritual one. Jesus' teaching abstracts from what in the world is regarded as great and powerful and elevates it to "the spiritual world," "the heaven within." It engenders a free human fellowship or communion with God, replacing the old lordship-bondage relationship among human beings and between God and humanity. Because this new condition finds its representation initially in the life of Jesus, there is a sense in which he *is* the kingdom of God among men. This is especially clear with respect to his teaching about *love*, which he himself exemplifies. Hegel distinguishes three elements in Jesus' proclamation of love: love for the neighbor in particular circumstances and relations; love among the apostles, a love that constitutes a unique form of community, the love of one another for the sake of the community; and a higher divine love, the ground of which is the Holy Spirit.

With respect to both the announcement of the presence of God's kingdom and the teaching of love, we find a *revolutionary* proclamation, a breaking away from everything established, a negation of what presently exists. Indeed, it was just this revolutionary proclamation, and his association with a suffering, oppressed people, that led to Jesus' fate on the cross, although the proclamation did not take on an overtly political character. In "The Spirit of Christianity and Its Fate" (1798-99), Hegel had been critical of the fact that Jesus "could only carry the Kingdom of God in his heart" and was unable to

actualize it in the world. Thus he advocated flight from
the world and "freedom only in the void," although he may
have perceived the revolutionary potentialities of the
kingdom.[12] In the Revelatory Religion this criticism has
disappeared, in light of Hegel's altered perception of
what constitutes religious revolution.

IV.3. The Passion and Resurrection of Christ

Death represents the ultimate pinnacle of the finitude, negation, and conditionedness of ordinary human
life. Thus to say that "God himself is dead" on the
cross of Christ (p. 202 et passim) is to refer to the extremity of divine self-divestment, the uttermost proof
that God took on human form. But death also represents
the "highest love" that arises out of "deepest anguish"
(p. 207 et passim). By the very intensification of finitude to the limit, the latter is sublated and the reality
of reconciliation is disclosed. The death of Christ is
a sacrificial, atoning, redemptive death for us not because God is actually satisfied by a price that has been
paid but rather because it is shown that reconciliation
is his eternal nature, the fundamental law of reality.[13]

Hegel notes that Jesus did not die a natural death
but rather the degrading death of a criminal on a cross.
In this fashion there occurs a transfiguration of civil
degradation: the lowest is made the highest; the cross
signifies a revolution against all that is established,
a challenge to the substantial foundation of the state.
The death of Jesus is of a piece with his life: "Inasmuch as his teachings were revolutionary, Christ was accused and executed, and thus he sealed the truth of his
teaching by his death" (p. 215).

The resurrection and ascension of Christ signify in
representative fashion the return of the divine Idea to
itself, the death of death, the negation of the negative,
the exaltation of human nature to heaven, the accomplished
identity of divine and human nature. They show that the

divine "process" does not come to a halt with the death
of God; rather God "maintains himself in this process,
and the latter is only the death of death. God rises
again to life, and thus things are reversed" (p. 212).
Of course, the sensible, representative forms in which
this doctrine is couched must be philosophically transfigured: the resurrection has nothing to do with empty
tombs and physical appearances. The reality of the resurrection is a reality for faith alone, not for external
history; even the appearance stories catch the significance of this by showing that Christ appeared only to his
friends.

The association of resurrection and faith suggests
that the resurrection-event constitutes a transition from
the sensible presence of God in a single individual to
the spiritual presence of God in the community of faith.
It can be treated under the figures of both "Son" and
"Spirit," and thus considerable overlap in content occurs
between the last section of Chapter IV and the first of
Chapter V. It is not possible to pinpoint a precise historical moment of transition from sensible to spiritual
presence, since the resurrection is not a past spatio-
temporal datum (e.g., the "raising" of Jesus' body on the
"third day") but rather is an ongoing historic process.
Hegel uses a revealing expression when he says that the
"sensible history" of Christ has been "sublated to the
right hand of God" (p. 246). The *Auferstehung* (resurrection) of Jesus entails an *Aufhebung* (sublation)--an annulling of his sensible presence, yet a preservation of
his real presence and its transfiguration into the modality of Spirit. The resurrection *means* the spiritual
presence of Christ in the community, Christ's presence *as*
Spirit, the universal actualization of the redemption accomplished definitively in him.

V.1. Standpoint of the Community in General

This rich section, found only in the 1821 lectures,
is concerned with the transition from sensible to spiritual presence, or from the Christ of history to the community of Spirit; the transition is treated in sparser
form by the other lecture series at the end of the preceding chapter. Hegel begins by reminding his hearers
that the Religion of Spirit does not shun the sensible
presence of God in "monkish fashion." Yet the particular
individual in whose life, teaching, suffering, and death
God is believed to have been definitively present has
now been removed from the senses and has been "raised" to
the right hand of God; he is no longer immediately present but rather imaginatively or representatively present
for faith in the community of Spirit. In consequence,
God himself is no longer present in the form of historical objectivity but rather in the mode of inwardness or
subjectivity, for which faith is the appropriate mode of
cognition. (Catholicism, in Hegel's view, has been unable to make this transition successfully and retains an
objectivizing, historicizing view of divine presence.)

However, this is a peculiar form of subjectivity.
It is a *renewed, transfigured, communal* subjectivity--in
essence a unique and unsurpassable *intersubjectivity,*
engendered by the "infinite love that arises from infinite anguish" (pp. 235-236), distinguishable from all
other forms of human love and friendship. Privatistic
and exclusivistic modes of existence are set aside, as
are all distinctions based on mastery, power, position,
sex, and wealth, and in their place is actualized a
truly universal justice and freedom.

The community in which God dwells is the community
of faith, the community of *Spirit.* The name "Holy Spirit"
refers to the unifying and liberating power of divine
love arising from infinite anguish--the same love that
was objectively represented on the cross of Christ but
that now works inwardly, subjectively, building up a new

human community. "This is the Spirit of God, or God as present, actual Spirit, God dwelling in his community" (p. 237). The community of Spirit is identical with the kingdom of God proclaimed by Jesus: "the kingdom of God *is* the Spirit," or more precisely, "the Kingdom of the Spirit" (p. 238), which is the name for the third sphere of the Revelatory Religion. Moreover, the risen Christ has been taken up into the Spirit and now exists "inter-subjectively" in and as the community of Spirit.

V.2. *Origin of the Community*

This section asks how it was that the Christian community came into existence after the death of Jesus. Its origin, suggests Hegel, is based on a "confirmation" (*Beglaubigung*) of the faith that "this Jesus of Nazareth in Galilee, a carpenter's son, [was] the Christ" (p. 240). (The *general* truth that God *has* a Son whom he has sent into the world was demonstrated in Chap. IV.1, and the argument is briefly recapitulated here.)

Such faith may be confirmed in two ways, one inauthentic and the other authentic. The inauthentic way is a sensible, immediate confirmation based on *miracles*, and Hegel launches an extended critique of miracles as a basis of certainty or faith. Although there may be a sense in which miracles happen because Spirit does in fact have an effect on nature and intervenes in natural processes constantly, miracles cannot be used as the basis of the confirmation of spiritual truth because they have an entirely external or sensible character and at best generate curiosity and a variety of probable explanations. Hegel concludes this discussion with a generalized critique of the "historical, juridical method of confirming a fact" (p. 249), which harks back to his discussion of the positivity of the Christian Religion in Chap. I.3. This leads to his famous statement that "spiritual content" "is to be justified by philosophy, not by history; what the Spirit does is no history [*Historie*]" (p. 254;

see the comment on this statement in n. 36).

The authentic mode of confirmation is by the "witness of the Spirit" or the "outpouring of the Spirit."
The divine Idea precisely "as realized in this individual" can be *properly* confirmed only *spiritually* "after
his death and removal from the temporal sphere" (p. 245).
Even a direct sensible apprehension of Jesus--an eye-
witness experience--could not confirm the truth that was
in fact sensibly present in him. Immediate contemporane-
ity offers no advantage at all; rather it obstructs spiritual knowledge. Ironically, Hegel's defense of the proof
of the Spirit is itself based on a supposed historical
proof, namely, Jesus' statement in the Gospel of John to
the effect that he must depart in order that the Spirit
may be sent, the Spirit that "will lead you into all
truth" (see p. 245, including n. 31).

V.3. *Existence of the Community*

Although it is essentially spiritual, the community
of faith necessarily takes on the form of a worldly organization, structure, or institution: it becomes *the
church*, which is the community as *realized* or *existent*
(*die bestehende Gemeinde*). Hegel notes how the original
renunciation of and opposition to the world, expressed
in the sayings of Jesus, falls away and is replaced by a
worldly institution, which enables the reconciling freedom proclaimed by the Gospel to be infused into the
structures of civil and political life (when this has
been accomplished, does the church itself become superfluous?). Hegel insists that such a church is essentially a teaching church, which promulgates *doctrines* having the character of positive authority, because the
truth it professes must be rendered representationally in
cognitive form and accepted as such, as well as believed
by the heart. These matters are taken up in the first
subdivision of the section, which we have titled "Faith,
Doctrine, and Church."

The second subdivision, "Cultus and Sacraments," is
the one in which Hegel discusses the central "practical"
activity of the church. He makes an un-Protestant move,
for the focus of Christian cultus or worship is found not
in preaching or prayer but rather in the sacrament of
Communion. This sacrament represents precisely the actualization and consummation of reconciliation, of divine-human union, which is the essence of the Christian
Religion. To describe this sacramental union, Hegel uses
the rather untheological term *Genuss*, which means "communion" in the sense of "enjoying," "partaking of." By
eating and drinking the body and blood of the Lord, the
communicant actually partakes of and enjoys the reconciling union of God and humanity; in this sense the communion entails an eternal repetition of the life, passion, and resurrection of Christ in the members of the
church. Or as Hegel expressed it in "The Spirit of
Christianity and Its Fate," the love made objective in
the life and death of Christ "becomes subjective again
in the eating."[14] The actual physical ingestion symbolizes the appropriation of religious truth. Hegel's
tendency to downplay the concrete historical development
of Christianity (as of other religions) is indicated by
his argument that the only significant difference among
the Christian confessions arises at the point of interpreting the sense in which Christ is present in the
eucharistic elements. Between the Catholic veneration of
the host as the prolonged sensible presence of Christ,
and the Reformed reduction of the sacrament to a mere
memorial, stands the authentic Lutheran view of the
spiritual presence of Christ, not in the elements as
such, but in the act of partaking, which is an act of
faith.

V.4. Realization of the Community

Hegel included under the cultic or "practical" aspect of religion its relation to secular life and the

realization of reconciliation not only in the community
of faith but also in the cultural and political forms of
the secular world. Despite earlier doubts, he believed
that such a realization had come about in Western Protestant bourgeois culture with the creation of what Fackenheim calls a "final secular-religious world," which
recognizes the immanence of the divine in three major
spheres of ethical activity: the family, economics, and
the state. The sanctity of these spheres is pointedly
affirmed vis-à-vis the monastic vows of chastity, poverty,
and obedience.[15]

Hegel has some such vision of "realization" in view
in the present section. He describes three ways in which
faith or the "spirituality of the community" is realized
in objective reality or "universal actuality" (see n. 68,
p. 305), although it is not clear why precisely these
three are selected, or whether they exhaust the possible
modes of realization, or what the connections between
them are (do they represent progressively more adequate
forms of realization, or are they simply not comparable
on such a scale?). The argument here is often obscure
and compressed, and one senses that Hegel is hastening
toward the conclusion of his lectures as time runs out.[16]

(a) The World in Its Immediacy and Externality: The
Heart, the Church, the Ethical Realm. The "immediacy" of
this world is represented by the human heart, where reconciliation is inwardly actualized. But this heart harbors
a worldly element within itself in the form of its passions, interests, and needs, which threaten to corrupt
reconciliation. Defense against this leads to the negative stance of asceticism vis-à-vis the world. A second
mode of worldly realization takes the form of an external
relation between the religious and secular spheres and an
attempted domination of the secular by the church (medieval Catholicism). Finally this secular-sacred contradiction is resolved and reconciliation is realized in the
ethical activity of bourgeois Protestant culture in the

form of rational freedom, as mentioned above (and described at great length in the *Philosophy of Right*).

(b) Abstract Mediation of the Worldly and the Spiritual: Reflection. "Reflection" (see n. 73, p. 305) is an undialectical mode of thought that oscillates between an abstract, empty unity, which it attributes to the absolute God, and a capricious, arbitrary individualism, which it predicates of individuals over against communal authority. Hegel finds reflection exhibited on the one side by Muhammadanism (the only serious external religious rival to Christianity) and on the other side by the religion of the Enlightenment (the most serious internal cultural threat). Both are forms of rationalism, operating on the principle of abstract identity, incapable of expressing the meaning of reconciliation.

(c) Realization of Faith in the Concept: Philosophy. The goal of these lectures, says Hegel, has been to reconcile reason with religion, to show the rationality and necessity of religion in its manifold forms, and thereby to advance the cause of religious faith. This reconciliation is based on the conviction that religion and philosophy, while assuming different *forms*, have the same *content*, which is the truth of the self-revealing God and of divine-human union. On the one hand, Christian faith has the true content but lacks the form of thinking, while on the other hand philosophy recognizes the necessity and temporal priority of the imaginative forms of religion while at the same time transcending them in the true form, which is the form of truth, the concept. The religious absolute (God) and the philosophical absolute (absolute Spirit) are finally identical, although known in different ways (pp. 289-293).[17]

Hegel intends to maintain a reciprocity in the relationship between religion and philosophy. He points out that religion can exist without philosophy, since its forms are adequate to the content and are available to all persons, but that philosophy cannot exist without

religion, since it has access to its content only through
religion, which it encompasses.[18] In an important book
review he once remarked that "a philosophy without heart
and a faith without understanding are abstractions from
the true life and existence of knowledge and faith. . . .
Thought and faith are to be seen as parts of a living
whole, each fragmentary by itself."[19] Thus a "reciprocal
relation" obtains between religion and philosophy, through
which each is fructified by the other.[20] If philosophy
is "higher" than religion, this is because the form of
the concept is higher than that of faith, but on the
other hand it is not universally available to the whole
of humanity in the way that the imaginative forms of
faith are (pp. 289-291, including n. 82).

However, Hegel finally is not as clear about the
reciprocity as he is about the hierarchical character of
the relationship, or, in his terms, about the *Aufhebung*
of religion in philosophy. In view of its proper subject
matter--"eternal truth in its objectivity, God and nothing
but God, and the explication of God" (a subject matter
abandoned by most theologians, in Hegel's view)--"philosophy is itself, in fact, worship."[21] "Philosophy is to
this extent theology," namely, that it presents the reconciliation of God with himself and with the finite world
and re-establishes the meaning and significance of the
classical theological dogmas (p. 293). Hegel's philosophy of religion offers something like a "philosophical
religion," which is not identical with any determinate
historical religion, including Christianity, but which
presents religious truth in speculatively "transfigured"
or "reenacted" form.[22]

V.5. *Passing Away of the Community*

When Hegel concluded his lectures in 1821 he ex-
perienced a rather frightful vision of contemporary
Christian decadence and of the collapse of the very secular-religious world into which he believed the community

of faith was in process of being "transformed" or "realized." As in the age of the Roman Empire, so now, he says, everything has been profaned and there is no true belief in God. A mania spreads abroad for private rights, goods, enjoyments; the religious basis of political life, of objective veracity and truth, has been lost. The clergy and teachers have abandoned their responsibilities, and the speculative truth of the Gospel is no longer heard, having been replaced by dead and merely historical modes of cognition. The salt has lost its savor; love *without* anguish is proclaimed. All that remains is "finitude turned in upon itself"--a prevailing scepticism, subjectivism, privatism. Apparently the vision did not recur because in subsequent years the ending of the lectures was completely different; but it is difficult for the reader at least to shake the vision off.

If we are in fact experiencing "the twilight of Christendom,"[23] does this not imply that the community of faith will "perish" or "pass away"? "To speak of a passing away would mean to end on a discordant note" (p. 294). Are we to conclude, then, that Christianity is no longer a living, vital religion, now merely to be "recollected," like Greek and Jewish religion? Or, more radically, that religion as such, like art, has now become "for us a thing of the past"?[24] But Hegel never says of religion what he says of art; for him religion remains an enduring, indestructible dimension of human Spirit. After his reference to "perishing," he introduces certain qualifications into his lecture manuscript (qualifications that are not fully preserved in the version provided by the *Werke*; see n. 100, p. 309). The Kingdom of God, he notes, has been "established eternally." The perishing or passing away ("in fact a passing over to the Kingdom of Heaven") applies "only to individual subjects, not to the community," in which the "Holy Spirit . . . lives eternally" and against which "the gates of hell shall not prevail"; and it concerns only the external, contingent forms of religion, not its true substance (pp. 294, 296).

These statements suggest that Hegel intended to distinguish between the decay of *Christendom* (which gives
rise to the present-day "discord") and the possibility of
the *community of Spirit* living on, especially in so far
as its faith and teaching have been transfigured by
philosophy, which would bring to light the purely revelatory, absolute essence of the Christian Religion, freed
from its cultural distortions and expressed in more adequate symbolic and imaginative forms. Indeed, the religious community *must* live on, in view of the "partial"
character of philosophy, which forms an "isolated order
of priests, . . . untroubled by how it goes with the
world" (p. 297), and whose conceptual forms are not available to the whole of humanity, so in need of redemption.
As a member of the philosophical priesthood, Hegel apparently believed that he could not be concerned (at
least not *immediately* concerned, n. 100) with the affairs
of the world. But as a member of the religious priesthood and of the community of Spirit, he could not avoid
being so. Otherwise, he could scarcely have condemned
those pastors and teachers who have abandoned the people
and failed to proclaim the Gospel of "love in infinite
anguish."

NOTES FOR APPENDIX

1. For a summary of it see the first section of my chapter on
Hegel in *Religious Thought in the Nineteenth Century*.

2. For a detailed discussion see the first two sections of my
Hegel chapter in *Religious Thought in the Nineteenth Century*. The
text of Part I, *Der Begriff der Religion*, is contained in *Werke*, 11:
85-252 (ET 1:89-258); and of Part II, *Die bestimmte Religion*, in
Werke, 11:253-12:188 (ET 1:259-2:323).

3. As set forth especially in the *Encyclopedia of the Philosophical Sciences*, trans. W. Wallace & A. V. Miller (2nd ed.; 3 vols.;
Oxford: Oxford University Press, 1970-1975). Abbreviated *Enc*. On
the triple mediation that obtains between the three branches of phi-
losophy--Logical Idea, Nature, Spirit--see *Enc*., §§ 187, 567-71, 575-

77; and Emil Fackenheim, *The Religious Dimension in Hegel's Thought* (Bloomington: Indiana University Press, 1967), pp. 84-112. On the modification required when this structure is applied to religion, see Malcolm Clark, *Logic and System: A Study of the Transition from "Vorstellung" to Thought in the Philosophy of Hegel* (The Hague: Martinus Nijhoff, 1971), p. 160.

4. For a good introduction to the issues, see Mark C. Taylor, "Itinerarium Mentis in Deum: Hegel's Proofs of God's Existence," *The Journal of Religion*, 57 (1977): 211-231; and Bernard M. G. Reardon, *Hegel's Philosophy of Religion* (London: Macmillan, 1977), pp. 88-99. James Yerkes is preparing a new translation of and commentary on Hegel's *Lectures on the Proofs of the Existence of God*, which considerably expand the treatment found in the Philosophy of Religion lectures. My own brief analysis of Hegel's ontological proof is found in the first section of my chapter on Hegel in *Religious Thought in the Nineteenth Century*.

5. On the dialectic of the two Trinities, see *Enc.*, §§ 381, 383, 384; and Fackenheim, *Religious Dimension*, pp. 149-154, 193-206 (esp. 205), 218-219.

6. See n. 7, p. 162; also Fackenheim, *Religious Dimension*, p. 130; and Emanuel Hirsch, *Geschichte der neuern evangelischen Theologie*, Vol. 5 (Gütersloh: C. Bertelmanns Verlag, 1954), pp. 238-239.

7. On the complex issues involved here, and for differing interpretations, see Stephen Crites, *The Problem of the "Positivity" of the Gospel in the Hegelian Dialectic of Alienation and Reconciliation* (Ph.D. Dissertation, Yale University, 1961), pp. 82-89, 91-94, 101-103; Reardon, *Hegel's Philosophy of Religion*, pp. 100-104; and Jörg Splett, *Die Trinitätslehre G.W.F. Hegels* (Freiburg/Munich: Verlag Karl Alber, 1965), pp. 141-142. Because of Hegel's Catholicizing tendency on this matter, I cannot agree with Splett's criticism of him for maintaining an all-too-Protestant priority of "accidental" grace over "substantial" nature.

8. *The Phenomenology of Mind*, trans. J. B. Baillie (rev. 2nd ed.; London: Allen & Unwin, 1949), p. 808; and p. 172 of this text.

9. In addition to passages in the present text, see *Werke*, 11: 160 (ET 1:165). Hirsch (*Geschichte*, 5:239., 255-256) believes that in this regard Hegel's position has evolved from that expressed in the *Phenomenology*. For further discussion of the issues involved here, see Crites, *Positivity*, pp. 236-237; and James Yerkes, *The Christology of Hegel* (AAR Dissertation Series 23; Missoula: Scholars Press, 1978), pp. 164-168, 171, 189-195.

10. See also *Philosophy of Right*, trans. T. M. Knox (London: Oxford University Press, 1952), § 348; Crites, *Positivity*, pp. 217-220; Yerkes, *Christology of Hegel*, pp. 169-170, 172-173.

11. An excellent discussion of the issues involved here is provided by Yerkes, *Christology of Hegel*, pp. 173-205. See also Crites, *Positivity*, pp. 213-216.

12. *Early Theological Writings*, trans. T. M. Knox (Chicago: University of Chicago Press, 1948), pp. 283-289, 301.

13. Cf. Hirsch, *Geschichte*, 5:258-259.

14. *Early Theological Writings*, pp. 250-251.

15. *Enc.*, § 517; *Philosophy of Right*, §§ 142-157, 257-270; Fackenheim, *Religious Dimension*, pp. 206-213, 232-233; Stephen Crites, *In the Twilight of Christendom: Hegel vs. Kierkegaard on Faith and History* (Chambersburg, PA: American Academy of Religion, 1972), pp. 35-40, 43, 51-54.

16. For the analysis that follows I have been helped by the articles by John E. Smith, "Hegel's Reinterpretation of the Doctrine of Spirit and the Religious Community," and Quentin Lauer, "Hegel on the Identity of Content in Religion and Philosophy," in *Hegel and the Philosophy of Religion*, ed. Darrel E. Christensen (The Hague: Martinus Nijhoff, 1970), pp. 157-177, 261-278.

17. See *Phenomenology*, pp. 797-798, 805-806; and *Werke*, 11:21-25, 150-151 (ET 1:19-22, 154-155).

18. *Enc.*, Preface to 2nd edition (ET 1:xx-xxi); Fackenheim, *Religious Dimension*, p. 116.

19. *Berliner Schriften*, ed. J. Hoffmeister (Hamburg: Felix Meiner, 1956), pp. 325, 328; Fackenheim, *Religious Dimension*, p. 192.

20. *Enc.*, § 573. Cf. Hirsch, *Geschichte*, 5:250; and Lauer in *Hegel and the Philosophy of Religion*, pp. 265-266.

21. *Werke*, 11:21, 38-41; ET 1:19-20, 37-40.

22. Lauer in *Hegel and the Philosophy of Religion*, pp. 273-275; Fackenheim, *Religious Dimension*, pp. 117-118, 185-192, 201 ff. For a critique of Hegel's understanding of the relation between religion and philosophy, see the last section of my chapter on Hegel in *Religious Thought in the Nineteenth Century*. Several other "limits" of Hegelian philosophy are discussed in this section.

23. The image used by Crites in the title of his book comparing Hegel and Kierkegaard on faith and history. The image, in turn, is based on Hegel's famous statement in the *Philosophy of Right* (p. 13) that "the owl of Minerva begins its flight only with the gathering twilight."

24. *Hegel's Aesthetics*, trans. T. M. Knox (Oxford: Oxford University Press, 1975), 1:11, 103.

INDEX

The Index does not include references to the Editor's Introduction and Appendix. Terms common to Hegel's philosophical vocabulary, such as "concept," "consciousness," "objectivity," "thinking," "Spirit," occur with great frequency in the text and are indexed only on a selective basis.

A

Absolute Spirit, *see* God, as absolute Spirit

Adam, 153, 155-156, 159

Alienation, *see* Estrangement

Anguish (Sorrow), 146-147, 148-152, 176, 177, 207, 212, 222n.6

Anselm, 48-50, 55-60, 101n.13

Antithesis (Opposition), 283-285, 293
see also Contradiction

Apollonios of Tyana, 242, 244

Appearance, 110, 112, 113-114, 121, 162n.13, 221
see also God, appearance of in a particular individual

Aristotle, 70, 81

Atonement (Satisfaction), 202-205, 209-210, 221

Authority, 261, 265-266

B

Baptism, 261, 265

Being, 22, 47, 52-54, 101n.13, 186, 256

Bible, interpretation of, 22-24

Böhme, J., 98, 115, 119

Brahma, 70, 105n.55

C

Catholic Church, 253, 271, 275

Certainty, 117, 171, 180-182, 217, 219, 221, 249, 255

Childhood, 126, 135

Christ (Jesus Christ),
his consciousness of relationship to God, 190, 225n.27
distinction between "Christ" and "the Christ," 299n.24
as incarnation of divine Idea, 171-173, 181-184, 190-191, 193, 198, 200, 210, 216, 224n.15, 233, 240, 242, 249-250, 301n.31
as new Adam, 156, 157
as ordinary man, 191-193, 198-199, 201, 215-217, 249-250, 306n.76
passion and death of, 199-221
see also Death
presence of as risen, 237-238, 269, 297n.4, 301n.32, 302n.39, 303n.52
teaching of, 184-199
its focus on love, 187-188
its representative character, 192
its revolutionary aspect, 188-189, 194-196, 215
its universality and inwardness, 184-186, 192, 194-195
see also Kingdom of God

351